The Chastity Plot

The Chastity Plot

LISABETH DURING

The University of Chicago Press CHICAGO AND LONDON

The University of Chicago Press, Chicago 60637
The University of Chicago Press, Ltd., London

Published 2021
Printed in the United States of America

30 29 28 27 26 25 24 23 22 21   1 2 3 4 5

ISBN-13: 978-0-226-74146-8 (cloth)
ISBN-13: 978-0-226-74163-5 (e-book)
DOI: https://doi.org/10.7208/chicago/9780226741635.001.0001

Library of Congress Cataloging-in-Publication Data

Names: During, Lisabeth, author.
Title: The chastity plot / Lisabeth During.
Description: Chicago ; London : The University of Chicago Press, 2021. | Includes bibliographical references and index.
Identifiers: LCCN 2020040403 | ISBN 9780226741468 (cloth) | ISBN 9780226741635 (ebook)
Subjects: LCSH: Chastity. | Chastity—History. | Sexual abstinence—Religious aspects—Christianity. | Chastity in literature.
Classification: LCC BJ1533.C4 D87 2021 | DDC 176/.4—dc23
LC record available at https://lccn.loc.gov/2020040403

♾ This paper meets the requirements of ANSI/NISO Z39.48-1992 (Permanence of Paper).

For Carol Cohn and Aly Sujo

Two paradises 'twere in one
To live in paradise alone.

ANDREW MARVELL, "The Garden"

For there are some eunuchs, which were so born from their mother's womb: and there are some eunuchs, which were made eunuchs of men: and there be eunuchs, which have made themselves eunuchs for the kingdom of heaven's sake. He that is able to receive it, let him receive it.

MATTHEW 19:12

Walking barefoot depresses the desire for coitus.

MAGNINO OF MILAN

Contents

Introduction

> That profoundly interesting subject, the value that men set upon women's chastity and its effect upon their education, here suggests itself for discussion, and might provide an interesting book if any student at Girton or Newnham cared to go into the matter.
>
> VIRGINIA WOOLF

Who cares about chastity? What has it meant and to whom? *The Chastity Plot* takes on Virginia Woolf's challenge. Almost one hundred years since Woolf wrote in her great feminist essay that "chastity may be a fetish invented by certain societies for unknown reasons," this profoundly interesting subject is not, in my view, exhausted.[1] Should we still wonder about the reasons chastity has played a role in moral thinking, why it complicates the career of eros in literature and in life? I argue that we should.

I write at a time when sexual harassment has finally managed to attract the attention of a wider public. Sex, we have discovered, has not made the world free and happy. In the workplace and in our attempts at intimacy and private affection, power is never far from vulnerability. What is new in the last few years is the readiness to use the language of abuse, and to consider seriously the poverty of our codes of sexual conduct. That the recognition is late in coming is hardly surprising. Respect and delicacy have never been high priorities in public life. For the left, other virtues have mattered more than chastity. Without generosity, honesty, and courage, a just polity is almost impossible. Sexual purity, by contrast, has no obvious role, unless that be a part in propping up the very systems of repression and stigmatization that the left commits itself to undo. The uneasy history of liberalism offers a counterpart. Liberals by and large discourage the state's intervention in the erotic lives of its subjects, as they earlier objected to similar interventions on the part of religion. For the liberal, as for the liberal's libertine predecessors, sexual morality is a matter of choice, and evaluating desire is a dangerous enterprise. But the laissez-faire approach to sexual behavior now looks unappetizing.

If traditional liberalism and radicalism have failed to provide much guidance, there is even less to expect from the guardians of conservative values. The religious right in the United States and other Western nations has in the last few years downplayed its worries about female modesty and sexual abstinence, not least because a number of conservative leaders would, on most measures, be considered sexual sinners, violators of the sanctity of marriage, or worse. Since the end of the Bush era, chastity has proved a difficult sell. Conservative groups such as Focus on the Family have amped up their campaigns against abortion and LGBTQ+ rights. Yet at the same time the rhetoric of evangelical abstinence campaigns now favors words such as *choice, empowerment,* and *autonomy,* stealing some of feminism's thunder by presenting a young woman's decision to defer sexual activity as her exercise of what nineteenth-century feminists called "personal rights."[2] What this implies for the reputation of chastity is interesting to consider.

Making Chastity "New"

"We live in a sex-crazed society," announces a book encouraging the young of both sexes to wait until marriage (*Gift-Wrapped by God,* 2004). Josh Harris's best-selling *I Kissed Dating Goodbye* (1997) is even more assertive in setting out the advantages of a principled resistance to the pressure the modern United States places on those who believe their faith counsels chastity.[3] The True Love Waits ministries, founded by Southern Baptists in 1993, praise the biblical marriages in which sex is part of God's providential design but counsel those looking for guidance that sex is a dangerous force, sinful and destructive if practiced "outside God's plan."[4]

Wendy Shalit, a young Jewish conservative, puts a comparable case for "healthy" sex avoidance in her *A Return to Modesty* (1999). Modesty, she argues there, is about "postponing sexual pleasure until the time is right." Returning to modesty will help the confused young women of today to find a more "secure sense of self" and the confidence "to set the boundaries between public and private." Looking into her own religious tradition, Shalit was impressed by the practice of *tzniut* (sexual modesty) observed by engaged couples whose pleasure in each other's company does not require them to touch or kiss. In the battle against misogyny, the decline of modesty's rule as the virtue responsible for defining female excellence has usually been taken as a small victory. A modest woman, a chaste bride, a blushing virgin: these were ideals easy to dismiss as patriarchy's bad conscience, its way of unloading worries about desire and legitimacy onto the bodies and souls of obedient women. Shalit wants to turn the tables. What if the old association of chastity with integrity were not the put-down feminist critics have led us to believe? Might not a culture that valued modesty, courtesy, honor, and sexual reticence go a long way toward discrediting the behavior to which she and her readers are accustomed, behavior that "debases women" and makes men "boorish"?[5]

In a series of conversations about Islamic piety and social agency recorded by the anthropologist Saba Mahmood in the years 1995–1997, Egyptian women from a variety of socioeconomic backgrounds insisted on the importance of female chastity and modesty. Participants in a flourishing women's mosque movement growing out of the Islamic Revival in Cairo, Mahmood's subjects explained to her that sexual modesty—including avoidance of contact with non–family members of the opposite sex, dress that conceals the body, and a demeanor designed not to provoke—is not a bitter pill that thoughtful women have to swallow if they are to flourish in a Muslim community. For them, the codes of female decorum were meaningful because they functioned as an ever-present reminder of piety: one observes the constraints without indignation because they are part of an honorable life and a valued tradition. Rather than prohibitive and insulting, the modesty code is, Mahmood concluded, a "positive ethics" in a specific sense. *Al-haya,* meaning the virtue of shyness, diffidence, or modesty, and *Ihtisham*—decency, sense of shame—belong to a "sequence of practices and actions" that, if sustained, allow piety to be the central organizing factor in the observant life. Did the cultivation of such seemingly passive characteristics, Mahmood wondered, seem to these women to enforce an inequality of the sexes they believed to be unjustified? No, she realized: the argument in favor of feminine chastity and modesty was understood as divinely ordained. While many points of religious interpretation could be—and were—challenged by these confident and articulate women, the centrality of the sexual ethic remained solid. It was not seen to hinder their pursuit of a satisfying life nor diminish their social status. Acknowledging the form of life in which her Cairo friends thrived meant understanding the religious meanings they gave to their sexual virtues.[6]

Unlike Mahmood's subjects, Wendy Shalit presents herself as on the defensive, an outlier in a world that doesn't understand. She, like the Christian conservatives who sponsor abstinence-only sex education and organize chastity rallies or purity clubs, feels herself to be speaking for a minority. They have a mission: to revive the buried treasure of chastity. And they believe that many contemporary problems—in the United

States at any rate—would be easier to solve if the population "returned" to a conventional, biblical, and heteronormative approach to moral life.[7] Why remain pure? the new apostles of Christian modesty ask. Why say no to casual sex and admit you want respect to accompany your moments of intimacy? Because purity is power, and taking a pledge of virginity means you can cross the threshold of marriage (surely everyone's objective) as a "whole person" with a "secure sense of self."[8] Because our hypersexualized public sphere objectifies the body and leaves those who succumb with a legacy of shame, their natural pride in their health and sensuality spoiled by a clinging sense of dirtiness. Sex enjoyed under the sanction of marriage, by contrast, does not degrade.

The "new chastity" comes in an antipuritanical package. It has learned from the American fascination with self-fulfillment and chooses to minimize such traditional elements of ascetic perfectionism as the zeal for sacrifice, abnegation, and self-denial. What it has not abandoned is the sexual double standard and the hypothesis of feminine passionlessness dear to nineteenth-century moral reformers and medical educators. The values implicit in this sexual double standard are not hard to tease out. Purity is a vocation for women, one for which men have little talent. This is less a matter of ideology than of biology, according to the advisers most prominent in the evangelical abstinence movement. If virtue is to triumph and the ideal of a monogamous, continent marriage to survive the ordeal of modern permissiveness, the credit will go to women. Sexual ethics are too important to leave to men. Their appetites are urgent; their capacity for restraint or discrimination is limited. It is women, always on the front line in modern morality wars, who must bear the overwhelming responsibility for curbing male lust and making abstinence appealing. Through a kind concession of nature, women are assumed to be innately inclined to modesty and resistance. Discipline, so difficult for those saddled with the male sexual equipment, is hardly as much an achievement for the female, since neither their urges nor their tastes for assertion are as strong.[9] Temptation is less of a threat to them, monogamy easier to tolerate, and the benefits of a conventional, stable family are supposed—in the case of women—to be more obvious.

Women's advantage in the battle for sexual virtue offers, however, little to celebrate, despite the compliments paid by the abstinence movement to female fastidiousness. Indeed, it creates a new rivalry between the slut and the good girl: blogs such as *Jezebel* may be tired of the term "slut-shaming," but those involved in cases of sexual harassment are familiar with its dangers.[10] Both in the contested cultural spaces of the global North and in the evangelical churches of the global South, women are continually cast as both the victim and the tempter. If the permissive society is to blame for eroding authority and standards, it is—to quote a Church of Scotland report discussed by Charles Taylor—"the promiscuous girl who is the real problem."[11] Sexual liberation comes with a price, and that price is paid by women, even if they escape the risks of unplanned pregnancies. Defenders of the new chastity point to the ways that gender continues to carve up the map of prestige inequitably: the liberated man is a player; the adventurous woman is a slut. Despite the unwillingness of modern societies to pin a scarlet *A* on the fallen woman, not only are her sexual experiments open to public scrutiny and scorn on any number of social media sites but, if Shalit and her conservative colleagues are right, remnants of her "wild times" will continue to linger psychologically in the form of depression and self-disgust.[12]

Why not, then, "be good"? It seems a small sacrifice, one that does not even jeopardize anyone's standing in the competition for sexual attention. Uncannily echoing the advice of Jean-Jacques Rousseau to Sophie (the perfectly modest and perfectly coy creation of Rousseau's fantasies), the leaders of contemporary purity movements tell young women that "chastity will make you sexy" (to quote Christine Gardner's recent study of the phenomenon).[13] Your abstinence now will be rewarded later by the delicious pleasures waiting for you when your patient prince comes to receive the gift of your maidenhead, your mutual excitement undiluted by too early indulgence and cynical familiarity. The new chastity's rhetoric, argues Gardner, is pro-sex and pro-empowerment. It is also, curiously, presented in secular packaging, despite its obvious affiliation with religious belief and practice.[14] What is true of the modern *secular age* (according to an influential and ambitious book by Charles Taylor) is not so much that it excludes religious experience, faith, and identity, or bans institutional religion. What makes an age or a culture "secular" is the coexistence as options of a number of distinct social practices and allegiances, with no sovereign background of belief holding them all together.[15] The crumbling of a unified Christendom has not abolished the believer nor rendered spiritual aspirations meaningless. But it has required them to justify themselves as special spheres and thereby encouraged the sense of exceptionalism so salient among recent apologists for religious—or at least Christian—sexual morality. Why the fervor, why the energy and money lavished on promotion, on political intervention, on public education and media blitzes? Because the new chastity is a fragile, embattled, and persecuted creature, recognized and protected by a special minority who resist the generalized moral laziness of the dominant culture, a culture corrupted by the sexual revolution. What the new chastity offers is a social role for the contemporary Christian who has no vocation for the cloister or for the intense interiority of the ascetic life. If the stakes are lower, so are the risks.

Looking back at more than forty years of ideological warfare against gender and sexual freedoms, even the most committed critic has to acknowledge the peculiar genius of the evangelical purity cult. Is purity old-fashioned? Not according to its American promoters, seeking to add the aura of nonconformity to a social message otherwise easily written off as uncool. Chastity has been rebranded: if you join the minority of the sexually pure, you will stand out—but stand out *in the world*. You will be visible as a member of an elite group whose confidence and moral clarity should have the potential to influence a wider public. The goal of the new chastity is no longer to flee the profane world, as sexual renunciants in an age of faith had understood. It is to win the world back, to convert it to a moral doctrine based on family values and heteronormativity rather than on Christian abnegation and transcendence. It seems that spiritual discipline—the aim traditionally associated with the practice of sexual renunciation—is no longer the prime mover. There is little talk about the older ideals, whether these be imitating the sacrificial heroism of the saints or aspiring to the quiet and uncomplaining docility of the virginal Mother of God. The new chastity, it would appear, relies on the triumph of secularism as it relies on the power of an aggressive marketing campaign and a tireless pursuit of political influence.

Confessing an admiration for the "rhetorical genius" of the sexy chastity message in the evangelical community, Christine Gardner wonders how it has managed to make feminism, not patriarchy, the true oppressor. Liberalism, by its lights, is the sinister and repressive regime that denies agency to a confused population, who are obliged to emulate the preferences of an out-of-touch elite.[16] Liberalism, together with the moral relativism it introduced into the mainstream, emerges from recent Christian conservatism as the enemy of civilized life, a menace to patriotism and to the family. The politics of evangelical antifeminism borrows lavishly from an anti-intellectualism long prevalent in American culture. Without denying the justice of women's desire for equality and representation, skeptical conservatives have denounced the feminist movement as the tool of a self-important academic cadre. Women should be valued, conservatives agree. But it would be a disaster if the fate of the female sex were to depend on the modern feminist movement, yet another conspiracy of the privileged against the real people.

The backlash against the sexual revolution of the twentieth century was real. Since the 1960s it has taken many forms. In the United States a moral crusade was generously funded and fueled by the fear that the liberals and progressives were taking over the soul of the nation. It created what Breanne Fahs calls a "sex-obsessed culture of chastity" and a highly mobilized subculture represented by chastity clubs, mass meetings led by charismatic speakers and celebrities, and an expansive media and social media presence. Fashioning an alternative "social space" where those who believed their piety estranged them from a dominant permissive culture could gather, this movement "constructed an identity based on enforced repression of sexual desire and expression" and encouraged "women to adopt the worldview that women are distinctly and essentially different from men and that sexuality is itself dangerous."[17] Laura Carpenter's précis of this crusade's history is worth quoting:

> By the mid-1980s, another series of developments had begun to work a dramatic transformation of sexual life in the United States. Starting in the mid-1970s, conservative Christians mounted a moral crusade intended to restore pre-1960s sexual norms, especially among adolescents. They won a key victory with the 1981 passage of the Adolescent Family Life Act (AFLA), which mandated the inclusion of pro-abstinence instruction in federally funded sex education programs and bankrolled curriculum-development efforts. Then, in 1982, the HIV/AID epidemic began. Viewed at first as a disease primarily affecting gay men, by the late 1980s HIV was recognized as a threat to heterosexual adults and teens as well. Quick to capitalize on public concern about HIV, as well as their growing political clout, moral conservatives redoubled their efforts to promote abstinence-focused education.[18]

Campaigns (such as True Love Waits and Silver Ring Thing) tried to lure unmarried Christians with the promise of a fairy-tale ending for those who could resist the pressures of a hypersexualized environment. Purity balls and solemn contracts between fathers and daughters encouraged identification with a supposedly endangered subculture, a special world reserved for those who committed to traditional gender roles. Survivors of the 1990s evangelical Christian culture who took to heart its scolding message to young white women now speak about the difficulty of escaping from the shame their upbringing engendered. Apparently purity doesn't always make sex better.[19] Abstinence-only education enjoyed federal funding for many years and all through the 1990s was the bright hope of evangelical cultural politics in the United States.[20] Yet the campaigns delivered disappointing results, having little impact on rates of adolescent pregnancy or sexually transmitted diseases.[21] Those who signed on for abstinence did indeed keep sexual temptation at bay . . . for eighteen months, on average.

The Virgin and (Our) State

> In an extraordinarily wide range of societies in the world one finds a peculiar "complex": ideologically it is held that the purity of the women reflects on the honor and status of their families, and the ideology is enforced by systematic and often quite severe control of women's social and especially sexual behavior.
>
> SHERRY B. ORTNER, "The Virgin and the State"[22]

Neither sexual freedom nor sexual unfreedom has brought paradise back. What stands out in our present difficulty is that we don't have a satisfactory way to put ethics and sex in the same company. It may be precisely the right moment to think again about sexual ethics, now with the advantage of several generations of conversation, tension, and mobilization around the issues of sexuality. But the jump from "sexual ethics" to "chastity" is not an obvious one. I am well aware that the historical demand for women to be chaste, modest, and obedient has done much to confirm female social subordination. And the vestiges of this demand linger, even as women move into conspicuous positions in politics, business, and the media. Sherry Ortner makes this clear in her important essay "The Virgin and the State" (1976). Women's purity has always played an economic as well as a prophylactic role, since the symbolic or even spiritual value of female virginity—"a symbol of exclusiveness and inaccessibility, nonaccessibility to the general masses"—helped consolidate the status of a group or family aspiring to be elite.[23] Yet the "purity-pollution idiom" binds women now as it has always done, in that "nothing much has changed in male attitudes toward and distrust of women. It is clear in contemporary cultures with female purity ideologies that women are still feared as ambiguous and dangerous creatures."[24]

If women in history have been excluded from public life, from the workplace, from education, from most forms of effective power, much of that campaign of belittlement and social containment has been carried on in the name of sexual purity. As guardians of the family and secure vessels of inheritance, women needed to be beyond reproach. The emphasis on chastity did not target only women: it has been used to discredit sexual minorities, to support the criminalization of homosexuality and prostitution, to justify the surveillance of children, and to uphold the censorship of experimental art and thought. Social order needed control of the body, and it was the bodies of the less powerful who were the obvious targets of such control. If chastity was necessary, as so many moralists, religious purists, and defenders of patriarchal social norms assumed, this was bad news for the female sex. In many ways it still is.

There are, nonetheless, reasons to put this virtue into a different frame, to listen to those inspired by the notion of chastity as well as to those repelled by it. In company with many other cultural and philosophical ideals, chastity is contradictory and heterogenous. It has many roles. It can be passive, defensive, the enemy of passion and assertion. And it can be violent, defiant, and challenging.[25] Chastity can stand for unalloyed conformity. But it can also stand for a relentless impulse toward sacrifice and self-dissolution, hard to reconcile with any social stability we can think of. The early Christian cult of perfect continence granted chastity heroic status and insisted that it mattered for both men and women. "Eunuchs for the kingdom of heaven" believed they could transcend the limits of nature, that the body and its needs would not hold them back. They dreamt of a transformation more metaphysical than moral. And that transformation could take them beyond the distinction of sex.

In the Kingdom of Heaven, Jesus said, there will be neither marrying nor giving in marriage. (Matt. 22:30; Mark 12:25; Luke 20:35).[26] Male and female, the "natural" markers of life in the flesh, will be no more. Everyone will be what angels are now. Chastity, understood as perfect continence renouncing sexual life and desire, is the practice here and now that can usher in those "Last Days." An apocalyptic eschatology promised, to those suffering under the chains of "this world," a condition where all things would be "made new" (Rev. 12 and 19). Millenarian dreams went along with a "fiercely ascetic" spirit.[27] Such dreams of renunciation as power were not unique to Christianity: in a number of myths and cults, the inviolate were endowed with extraordinary qualities. Greece and Asia Minor worshipped virgin goddesses, proud exceptions to all norms divine and human. The chastity plot enjoys the patronage of Artemis-Diana, who represents chastity in its most assertive mood. The cult of this goddess, once powerful across the eastern Mediterranean, shuns the conformity of the household and the bedroom, so too the legendary Amazons. Rebels against sex and marriage who take their cue from Artemis find their comfort zone in the woods, where the wild things are. Their virtue is raw and at times violent; their gender identity often androgynous. Medieval quest romance adopted some of the same symbolic ingredients, but it passed them through a moralizing imagination. Pastoral moved to tamer spaces and Diana's rough nymphs slid into allegory. Yet Christian stories still acknowledged the power of the innocent outlier. With chastity as their shield, warriors against vice could emerge from life's wilderness unscathed. The mighty fighter Lady Britomart, Spenser's Knight of Chastity, never knew the pain of defeat; the virginal Maid of Orleans had divine sanction to lead armies and defy the norms of gender. And the cult of the Virgin Mother offered Eve's descendants a glimpse of the glory that could be theirs if they chose the heavenly spouse that the Song of Songs promises to virgins.[28] Even in realms untouched by Christianity, the idea of a chaste warrior elite remained compelling, as fans of *Game of Thrones* will know. Just as the stellar knights of Arthur's Round Table could only join in the ultimate quest, the search for the Holy Grail, if their vows of chastity remained unbroken, so in George R. R. Martin's Westeros the members of the Night's Watch and the Kingsguard commit themselves to celibacy:

> Night gathers, and now my watch begins. It shall not end until my death. I shall take no wife, hold no lands, father no children. I shall wear no crowns and win no glory. I shall live and die at my post. I am the sword in the darkness. I am the watcher on the walls. I am the fire that burns against the cold, the light that brings the dawn, the horn that wakes the sleepers, the shield that guards the realms of men. I pledge my life and honor to the Night's Watch, for this night and all the nights to come.[29]

Westeros's female warrior, the armored and virginal Lady Brienne of Tarth, is, like Britomart, a pure and powerful shield against evil and corruption. The *miles Christi* flees the contamination of sexuality; so do his fictional counterparts. Ascetic self-control pays off. A certain association between truthfulness and sexual purity is confirmed again and again in literature and legend: once you know sexual feelings, it seems that your chances for a candor of spirit and intention diminish. Yet viewers and readers of Martin's wildly popular epic were not disappointed when both Jon Snow and Brienne succumbed to sexual desire. Chaste men and women in our day can seem naïve rather than heroic. We are out of the habit of looking at virgins with awe, unaccustomed to admiring them for saving themselves and others from the contagion of earthly slime. Enlightenment tolerance did not include tolerance for the mystique of mortification. The philosopher Immanuel Kant, otherwise well known for the carefulness of his domestic and professional life, made no secret of his scorn for the "fanatical" flavor of monkish chastity: "Castigation, vows, and other such monkish virtues are grotesqueries," he wrote in his 1764 *Observations on the Feeling of the Beautiful and the Sublime*.[30] It was the late eighteenth century and Kant did not expect to be contradicted. But once there was a time when his certainty would have seemed misplaced.

During Christianity's early years, the "arts of virginity" (as Michel Foucault called them in the fourth volume of his *History of Sexuality*) were the subject of an extensive patristic and didactic literature. This literature recruited elite and aspiring Christians in the second to the fourth centuries and sought to convert them to the practice of "holy continence," a mystically charged way of life.[31] Virginity is an ascent, its champions declared, a ladder to the beyond. Its practitioners can wean themselves from the flesh and live as if the kingdom of heaven had already arrived. The rise of chastity as a Christian ideal coincided with millennial expectations. Renouncing marriage and reproduction, rejecting earthly families in favor of the siblinghood of all believers, was a way of speeding up one's induction into the eschatological community. Absolute continence—sexlessness—was the preferred option of the strong, Paul explains to his community at Corinth. Marriage is only a necessary evil, an accommodation for those too weak to live without desire. The tradition of clerical celibacy, whose history is by no means a unified one, was a later way of sustaining this dream under very different conditions, when the millennial promise had faded and believers had to fashion institutional roles for themselves and their leaders. Monastic chastity, for instance, was a way for monks and nuns—and indeed for anchorites all through the medieval period—to demonstrate their "apartness," perhaps even their moral superiority "over the other orders of society."[32] That boundary—here are the sheep, there are the goats—was not always so important. In the first three centuries of Christian preaching, communities in Palestine, Syria, Turkey, Egypt, and throughout western Asia Minor and the Greek-speaking world were willing to experiment with a life unbound by social hierarchies. Some continued the Jewish and Roman practices of marriage; others imagined changes in family structures, even including their disappearance. Luke's Gospel called on disciples to leave their homes, their wives and brothers and parents and children, "for the sake of the kingdom of God" (Luke 18:29).[33] But the early church did not recognize absolute continence as an obligation for deacons, priests, or bishops; missionaries like Peter traveled with their wives.[34] Efforts to establish celibacy as a norm for the clergy began seriously in the fourth and fifth centuries, notably in Councils at Elmira and Rome. Chastity is not for everyone. Paul is definite about that. But later authorities took advantage of the special grace the Pauline preaching attributed to the strong and decided that those aspiring to preach and minister should be expected to adopt the celibate life.

Chastity as imagined by early and zealous Christians was less a moral value than an ontological miracle. The history of corruption and decay can end, now. It is true that continence of this radical type will isolate the initiate from most social and psychological norms. But that is a small price to pay for victory over degradation and admission into the life of the angels. Freed from the encumbrances of children and marriage, the celibate was enviable. The celibate's soul, carefully nurtured by denial, could be as unalloyed and untroubled as the world in the first hour of Creation. Corruption's days would be numbered if the battle of chastity could be won. In the history of the chastity plot, this discovery was a remarkable turn of events.

The story I tell about chastity is anchored in the Christian experience. Aroused by the stories of fall and redemption, Christians took an uncontroversial preference for sexual moderation and infused it with dread, beauty, and severity. The struggle against the flesh produced some saintly heroines (such as Thecla, sure of her vocation) and some tortured intellectuals (such as Augustine, convinced that lust would destroy him if he didn't destroy it). Yet it also produced, after a very long and very mixed history, an unsaintly and unheroic figure: the modern sexual subject in the West. Without Christianity's surrender to the virgin's spell, sexual morality would have taken a very different shape. It would still be recognizable, as even a cursory look at the Greco-Roman world would show. The prudent are careful with the passions Aphrodite sends; modesty and fidelity are widely prescribed, even without the blessing of the angels. Ascetic self-improvement was admired by thoughtful pagans. The struggle against erotic disorder was a popular subject for politicians, comic playwrights, and moralists. But Jesus's remarks about the eunuch still had the power to astonish ancient Greeks and Romans. Could the battle against sexual desire undo the slavery of the soul and lead a new kind of being out of the ruins of the old? This was a different type of expectation. The mystery of chastity is a Christian invention.

Before Christianity, the chastity plot knew only one model of sublimity comparable to the eunuch, a divine one. In Greco-Roman myth and cultic practice, Artemis enjoys an exceptional freedom from male rule and influence. Her power is related to her chastity, just as the special favor she extends to her devotees is dependent on their unwavering adherence to her code of purity. At some important level, the committed virgin is a defector from the order of gender. She is pure, but she is also rebellious, especially by the standards of sexual normalcy most societies take for granted. It takes nerve to resist marriage, to denounce the compromises and injuries of this popular institution. Histories and sociologies of sexual conduct have sometimes failed to recognize how central the antimatrimonial argument is to the case for chastity. It is easy to see that the libertine and the whore represent alternatives which the defenders of legitimate marriage must contest. It is less obvious that those who opt for a life of radical abstinence are also registering a protest against marriage. The code of Artemis the pure is not a domestic code. It promises freedom, but it says nothing about security. There are social as well as personal risks for those who, for various reasons and at various times, have repudiated the conjugal and procreative imperative. Artemis had permission from Zeus, her divine parent. Others are not so lucky.

If classical myth took heed of the virgin's defiance and made sure it remained an exception, the same ambivalence about chastity's antisocial power influenced the church's shifting views about its own war against carnality. How far did Christianity want to go in abandoning the world? The sanctified celibates who wanted to refuse their fleshiness and live as if the law of generation did not apply were extraordinary. But if they prevail, humanity does not. Chastity, as I understand it, exists in this contradiction. When it makes its peace with marriage, it loses. Violence or martyrdom appear again and again in the stories of unpacified virgins, rebels against marriage. Society will defend itself. And the poor reputation of chastity proves not so much society's admiration for the discreet regulation of sex as society's distrust of the exceptional and the anomalous. In the judgment of history, it is the marriage plot that has won. But that does not mean that the chastity plot should be ignored.

The literature of chastity confronts not only sexual politics but "real" politics—the strategies of power and oppression, the forging of dynastic alliances, the conflicts of values, the war between classes or gods. In the parade of chastity's defenders and victims, the characters we meet are as morally ambiguous as they are magnetic. There is Euripides's tragic boy virgin Hippolytus; St. Paul's disciple Thecla; the cold Chinese princess of Puccini's *Turandot*; the forty-nine murdering daughters of the Greek king Danaus; Edmund Spenser's chaste wanderers Belphoebe and Britomart; Elizabeth the Virgin Queen of England; Shakespeare's Isabella; and Samuel Richardson's Clarissa. They belong to a pantheon of the ambitious, the self-willed, and the socially dissonant. Overachievers in the campaign for perfection, the heroes and heroines of chastity pursue their own perfection and often leave confusion in their wake. To their fans, they are inspiring. To their detractors, they freeze the life out of the world.

At the heart of this book is the battle for chastity, its aspirations, its background, and its costs. My subjects include those who feared the power of sex, and I am interested in their motivations. Those who found aesthetic or spiritual profit in sexual abstinence are even more important. As Foucault argued, ascetic "technologies of the self" promise self-revelation at the very moment of self-dissolution. The sacrifice of sexual desires makes a rupture between the self and its past identity, as Augustine of Hippo saw clearly; but in the process the self is revealed in its nakedness and truth.[35] Naked truth, however, is difficult. A life concentrated on self-examination and purification could never be mainstream. Alongside the supreme technique of perfectionism, which demanded the libido's total renunciation, Christian practice offered other, more easygoing options. Moderates allowed that chastity could also be defined as modesty and monogamous fidelity. The idea of a "chaste marriage" was first prescribed to the lay believer in the early days of the Roman Empire's Christianization and then mandated to all after the Reformation, when the monkish ideal of consecrated virginity was denounced with considerable bitterness, and marriage was instituted in the Protestant world as the highest vocation for the faithful.

What I offer here is not an apology for chastity, nor a lament for its decline. My argument is that the chastity ideal has profoundly influenced a number of the West's social and personal aspirations, modifying the ways individuality, subjectivity, and psychological norms have been imagined in the modern world. Its presence can be detected in the desires that shape culture, art, and intellectual life. My strategy is to identify a "chastity plot," though one with a number of distinct variations. There is a major version, and that is the one I title the "eunuch's plot." And there is a minor version, the "maiden's plot." The maiden's plot exists comfortably in many moral or domestic traditions, in virtue of which the married are expected to conduct their lives with propriety and the unmarried, especially the female unmarried, are expected to abstain. In the maiden's plot, the concern about chastity usually demands the exclusive dedication of one woman to one man. A woman's premarital virginity, her modesty, her purity and readiness to blush are considered *the* criteria for her marriageability, an advance assurance that the children she produces will be legitimate and the marriage bed will not be polluted. Who doesn't know this one, the maiden's plot? It has far outstripped the eunuch's plot. It slides into that mainstay of novel and film, the marriage plot. But it is, as I claim, the weaker form: its success in history belies the fragile nature of the moral code it assumes and the anodyne character of the sexual ideal it celebrates. Maidens are undeniably more popular than eunuchs, just as love stories are more popular than the stories of saints. If the emphasis of this book reverses the trend, that is intentional. The eunuch's plot, although not a reliable source of entertainment, deserves a closer look.

I treat the chastity plot, or plots, with some respect. Blood has been spilled, and reputations destroyed; ideals have been fashioned, denounced, and refashioned, all in the name of chastity. It is time for theorists to take it seriously. Preceding me are adventurous critics—Friedrich Nietzsche, Sigmund Freud, and Max Weber, Michel Foucault and Peter Brown: all have acknowledged the power (and problems) of asceticism and the chastity plot. In many respects, I depend on the insights of those writers (Marina Warner, Stanley Cavell, Northrop Frye, and many others) for whom works of the imagination belong to the history of ideas, and images to the work of thought. I have learned most of what I know about how to approach my research questions from recent feminist and anthropologically inspired students of antiquity, early Christianity, and the Middle Ages. Sex and its history include this one.[36] While not a history of practices and habits, *The Chastity Plot* does intend to give a selective picture of various past sexual ideals and attitudes, especially those entertained by certain high-profile minds, some religious, some secular. There were some in whom the fervor for chastity was hot; others who found it disruptive, wrongheaded, hypocritical or impossible. Some believed the mystique of chastity was an insult to the married state; others that the cloister or the desert were the only places where the spirit could be free.

In any attempt at regulating sexual and reproductive behavior, we have learned to expect a political agenda. Such an awareness is one of modern feminism's undoubted achievements, now so commonplace that we can forget to do it justice. Sexual difference as a source of social anxiety and psychological contradiction is never far away from the main narrative line of the book. Chastity as a religious and moral ideal bridges the realms of myth and social practice, and not in a benign fashion. No one should deny that it is one of the reasons women in history have existed at the margins. Yet the politics at play in thinking about chastity need to be approached with care. Gender, power, and transcendence make a volatile mix, and one that offers many opportunities for confusion. A virtue that rewards restraint and submission at one moment provokes resistance and revolt at another. Militant chastity frustrates and allures; it is the making of martyrs, the sign of sovereignty, and the fast track to pathology. That is why it is interesting.

Chastity is a term that points in a number of directions. I limit the field with the help of a few recurring notions. One is asceticism, including the ascetic impulse as a cultural principle and a personal ideal. Another is the notion of plot itself, in its various connotations. Chapter 1 considers the claim of my title and asks: is there a "chastity *plot*," and what makes it a *plot*? There are plots that cluster around the figure of the eunuch, others that feature maidens, their problems, and their powers. Marriage plots are celebrated and at times subject to condescension. Chastity plots complicate the relationship of passion and action, pleasure and pain. Here I look further at the most significant critics of ascetic ideals, the demystifiers Freud and Nietzsche, and elaborate in some detail the relations of desire and repression.

Chapter 2 introduces a rare masculine hero of chastity: Hippolytus, the devotee of the virgin goddess Artemis. His fate demonstrates that virginity is a violent code and its service is at odds with the aims of society. Hippolytus is crushed because of his hostility toward sexual love. Aphrodite, goddess of sex, is a ruler who will not be insulted. My interpretation of Euripides's tragedy *Hippolytus* sets up a contrast: sophrosyne, the temperate self-control expected of Greek male and female citizens and honored by the doomed Phaedra, opposes ascetic extremism, the arrogant purity of the virgin, wild and untamed. This is a confrontation that does not end well.

Chapter 3 asks the question: does a woman have to marry? Literature has known rebellious virgins who despise the marital yoke. I have three examples: Turandot, the haughty Chinese princess who identifies with the moon; the forty-nine daughters of Danaus as remembered in a play by Aeschylus, who murder their husbands in their beds; and Tracy Lord, a clever modern woman who is unsure how to marry without losing something of value in herself. Generally speaking, virginal revolt is crushed in secular societies; marital eros demands its rights. Even the Danaids, who escape family life, are condemned to carry water in a sieve for ever and ever. Religion is the only place where a female celibacy plot can be entertained, but its accommodations are specific.

Chapters 4 and 5 detail the formation and elaboration of the Christian war against the flesh as it moves from Paul to Augustine, from Rome and Jerusalem to Alexandria and Carthage. Dominating the theological minds involved in this campaign was an image: the angelic vocation. Heaven is mirrored on earth in the lives of the consecrated virgins. Eden returns, and the kingdom of the blessed is foreshadowed in the renunciation of the marriage bed and all its works. The eschaton is at hand, and the time is short. In much of the patristic celebration of holy virginity we can hear a longing for pastoral innocence, for a world without guilt and even without knowledge; that pastoralism survives even as the chastity ideal goes through a number of revisions, symbolic as well as theological. Fleeing the world became for Christians not an indicator of weakness or cowardice but an embrace of the desert within. Despite much continuity in the content of pagan and Christian sexual ethics, despite tempting overlaps in the philosophical concepts employed, the event of Christianity was a watershed in the history of chastity. Almost everything chastity has accomplished, negatively and positively, can be credited to the Christians and their obsessions. These two chapters are the intellectual core of the book, and they engage in detail with the critical literature of recent years, a period in which pagan and Christian sexuality has become a flash point for scholars. Like many workers in this field, I use an interdisciplinary approach, incorporating a literary-critical perspective and treating philosophical, mythological, and theological material as elements in a narrative. Stories also make arguments, and in my practice the aesthetic and the conceptual are intentionally entangled.

That literary orientation becomes more dominant in chapter 6, which studies the significance of virginity in the sixteenth-century poetry, prose, and drama devoted to the problem of Elizabeth. The Elizabethan anomaly was political: how can the masculine symbol that is kingship be contained in the body of a woman? And it was religious: how can the Protestant conviction that marriage is the ideal state for the pious be reconciled with the refusal of marriage by a sovereign who claims most of the paraphernalia of a pagan goddess and a holy icon? The Virgin of the State replaces the Virgin of the Church. But Elizabeth's victory is unique and unrepeatable. Only a reigning prince is allowed the freedom from gendered determination. Other virgins are not.

Chapter 7 finds chastity in a deflationary mood. Saints and martyrs had taken the ideal of chastity into a special but airless realm. They were spectacular. Domestic females are not. As we have learned from a century or more of feminist criticism, the modern marriage plot defines the possibilities women can consider. It constrains their imaginations as well as their social action. Middle-class morality inherited a secular version of the chastity plot, and the strains still show. Two of Elizabeth's most important poets, Spenser and Shakespeare, mark the transition from classical and Renaissance models to modern uncertainties. Like their queen, they were fascinated by the politics and poetics of sex. Spenser sought to reconcile Diana and Venus, the chastity and the marriage plots, by dividing and multiplying chastity into an array of figures and vocations, including that of romantic marriage. Shakespeare responded by abandoning all respect for the eunuch's plot and the sexual absolutism it represents. Britomart, the Spenserian Knight of Chastity, is destined to marry and raise a family. Shakespeare's Isabella and Angelo, cold and virginal idealists, are tossed out of the cloister and forced into uncomfortable positions, without authorial approval or public sympathy. In the eighteenth century, sexual virtue for bourgeois females was articulated against a feared aristocratic model of license and display: the modest woman must be silent, chaste, and humble. A Puritan recasting of the religious domain claims to place women finally on a moral par with men, but the results are unfavorable for the spiritual virtuosi. The life of the novel's most outstanding virgin, Clarissa Harlowe, ends not in triumph but in tragedy.

The argument of chapter 7 revisits the themes of earlier chapters, but in a contrary direction. Shakespeare's realism about sex and the flesh eclipses Spenser's fantasy. This is a historical point. Bourgeois society had no place for the exceptional ontological status of the virgin, that asexual and angelic being liberated from social conditions and corruption. Saints did not fit into the agenda of the eighteenth-century novel, a literary form adapted to an age of disenchantment. Prophecy and charisma, magic and enchantment, these require other formal modes and probably other social contexts. It is marriage, rather than transcendence, that occupies the central moral position (and, indeed, the deeper psychological puzzles) for the men and women who read Jane Austen, Charlotte Brontë, Elizabeth Gaskell, Edith Wharton, Henry James, and George Eliot. The popularity of the "heroine's text," with its seemingly endless variations on the marriage plot, has left little space for rebels like Turandot or Thecla or the Danaids, for whom marriage represented alienation and subjection. The Protestant heroines of middle-class society are not permitted such a radical critique. Virginity is for them a marketable asset, helping to smooth the route to marriage. In Clarissa's case, as in that of all the pure women in whose honor the heroine's text was designed, the promised end is marriage. Marriage is the true summit in the career of the delicate woman. But in Richardson's novel marriage is fatally compromised.

This is the theme I take further in chapter 8, where I argue that, after the rape and death of Clarissa, the chastity plot has been lost. The injustices of heterosexual relations, and of what we have come to recognize as the sex-gender system, cast a shadow over the virtue this heroine went to such lengths to cultivate. From such a defeat, it is hard to imagine a recovery for chastity. In the last two hundred years, neither religious nor secular culture has presented us with good reasons to restore what Nietzsche called asceticism's saintly debauch, to aspire to the overstimulated condition of the virtuoso who makes a career of self-denial.[37] Bad reasons, on the other hand, are common enough. In the nineteenth, the twentieth, and even the twenty-first centuries, there are echoes of the chastity plot as well as attempts to reconcile it with the marriage plot, in ways I argue are untenable. The cult of pure womanhood is the most notorious and the one that contributed the most to a gender ideology based on rigid sexual roles, one in which femininity became associated with passionlessness, making chastity a natural condition rather than an achievement. Female virtue became less an ornament than a career.

Clarissa's problem was noted by feminists, who didn't relish repeating her experience. Whatever else women could accomplish, they had first to dispense with the ideal of the moral paragon, the disincarnate miracle. The reward of feminine virtue was convenient to the career of Pamela, Richardson's less tragic heroine. But to most observers, Pamela's solution is a sham and an insult, a cover-up of abuses that penetrate into the heart of family life and reveal its intimate promises as hollow. In the demystification of female chastity, the novel played a role. After *Clarissa*, the novel expanded its readership across Europe and its spheres of influence, its moral authority beginning to compete with that of religion. A cultural form denounced for its triviality was able, almost against its own intentions, to bring hard truths into the light. Among the most significant of these hard truths was the plight of the modern woman, lacking access to any of the resources needed for her freedom, power, and flourishing. In secular and bourgeois culture, the virtue that defines a woman's being is not in her own possession. Fathers, husbands, rapists, and carping critics deny her access to the inner integrity she thought her own. Chastity is finally an epistemological problem as well as a moral, social, and aesthetic one. It will not be solved until the injustices of gender are solved. It is time for some new plots.

1

Is There a Chastity Plot?

Every sentiment, particularly the noblest and
most disinterested, has a history.

MICHEL FOUCAULT

List, lady, be not coy, and be not cozened
With that same vaunted name Virginity.
Beauty is Nature's coin, must not be hoarded
But must be current, and the good thereof
Consists in mutual and partaken bliss,
Unsavory in th'enjoyment of itself.

Comus, in JOHN MILTON's *A Masque Presented at Ludlow Castle*

Two Virgins, Thecla and Pamela

I begin with two stories about virgins and gender roles. One dates from the early days of Christian hagiography and is set in Turkey, the other comes from England in the middle of the eighteenth century. Both are legends, loved in their own day and widely read for many years, testimonies to the power of belief over the power of fact. They share an intention: to explain how chastity is fought for and what the battle for chastity can do for the glory of those who prevail. Thecla was a young and noble virgin from the city of Iconium in present-day Anatolia. Engaged to a suitable young man named Thamyris, Thecla was everything a modest young lady should be. Then she looked out of her window and saw a crowd going into the house of her neighbor Onesiphorus, where people were seen clustering eagerly around a small man, "bald-headed, bandy-legged, of noble mien, with eyebrows meeting, rather hook-nosed, and full of grace."[1] He seemed a bit like a man and a bit like an angel. But it was his words that captivated Thecla.

For three days and nights she did not move from her window. She would not eat or drink. All she wanted to do was to hear about virginity, and to soak up the words of Saint Paul.

Paul's eloquence about chastity drove Thecla away from the marriage everyone wanted for her. She chased after the apostle, following him into prison.[2] Condemned, tied to a stake and set alight, Thecla was saved by a divinely sent rainstorm. She traveled on to Antioch, where she was threatened with rape, thrown to the wild beasts, and saved again. Finally the authorities let her go, acknowledging that Thecla was simply too much for them. Dressed in male clothing, Thecla followed Paul, and after his execution she lived on for seventy-two years, most of it in a cave. Thecla was a marvel to her contemporaries, an inspiration to aspiring female ascetics for the next 1,500 years. Other defiant virgins met a martyr's end. Protected by the Christian God, Thecla stands out as one of chastity's irrepressible warriors.

Pamela Andrews was the modest and pure heroine of the most popular novel of its time, Samuel Richardson's *Pamela, or Virtue Rewarded* (1740). She was a well-behaved servant girl of fifteen who had studied carefully in the eighteenth-century school of virtue. Assaulted by her aristocratic master, subjected again and again to harassment, confinement, and a number of attempted rapes, Pamela saved herself by the force of her integrity, her cunning, and her ability to faint at the right moment. Humble in her birth, Pamela would have been expected to minister to the pleasure of her "betters." All it took was one small slip to make her spoiled goods, easy prey for her master and his fellow rakes. An everyday occurrence, the fall of a lower-class woman hardly registered on the social map. Her ability to remain "upright" should have occasioned even less attention. But Pamela was different. Her struggle against any violation of her physical person is a marvel of heroic prudery and an early triumph for the middle-class sexual morality Richardson advocated. Victorious at last, Pamela abashes all detractors and convinces a skeptical upper-class society that her modesty is the model all women should follow, especially if they want to end up as she does: married to her tormentor, her "Virtue Rewarded" by her social elevation and the readers of her story "gratified by the combined attractions of a sermon and a striptease."[3]

Thecla and Pamela are both paragons of virtue, but in different registers. Their stories instantiate two versions of the chastity plot. They stand at opposite ends of a history, from the first century of Christian agitation to the England of the mid-eighteenth century. If we are to appreciate these two virgins, we must understand the value of what they represent. If chastity does not matter, then neither do they. What price a maidenhead?

Since Thecla and Pamela are heroic, their stories exemplary, there is more here than meets the eye. Wild and hungry beasts step back, flames do not consume the virgin who values her integrity more than her life; lower-class girls with no name and no property turn the powerful into penitent believers, enthralled by the mystery of a virgin who says no. Chastity is magic. It can be a sacrifice that elevates our fallen flesh to the condition of the angels, as such church fathers as Methodius, Ambrose, and Gregory of Nyssa believed. Or it is trivial, the affectation of a prude and a calculating fortune-hunter. Chastity is "much ado about nothing," as the title of Shakespeare's comedy has it. Can it be both? Is there something here we need to know?

One of the most sophisticated of chastity's critics, Virginia Woolf, has this to say in her 1929 feminist classic, *A Room of One's Own*: "That profoundly interesting subject, the value that men set upon women's chastity and its effect upon their education, here suggests itself for discussion, and might provide an interesting book if any student at Girton or Newnham cared to go into the matter."[4] What is the value of chastity? "Chastity may be a fetish invented by certain societies for unknown reasons," she remarks in discussing the broken-off life of Shakespeare's imaginary sister, pregnant, abandoned, and dead rather than triumphing in a theatrical career. How much of that can be blamed on chastity? "Chastity had then, it has even now, a religious importance in a woman's life, and has so wrapped itself round with nerves and instincts that to cut it free and bring it to the light of day requires courage of the rarest."[5] Women need such a courage, or else they will remain secluded and unknown. "The question of chastity, both of mind and body, is of the greatest interest and complexity," Woolf writes in the notes to her book-length 1938 essay *Three Guineas*. "Real or imposed," chastity was "an immense power," the social stigma "exerted on its behalf" strong in the past and hardly unknown in recent times, the grip of "its white if skeleton fingers can be found upon whatever page of history we open." This, she concluded, is "impossible to doubt." Whether chastity's power was good or bad for the chaste, Woolf leaves to us to judge. Prominent among the champions of female chastity was Saint Paul (a man sure of his own immunity to lust, but doubtful about that of others). Paul placed the chastity of women in the company of other feminine behaviors he believed desirable: women, he thought, should remain silent in church, avoid shame, and keep their hair covered. Yet the reasons for his preference seem confused. As Woolf observes in *Three Guineas*, "Chastity then as defined by St Paul is seen to be a complex conception, based on the love of long hair; the love of subjection; the love of an audience; the love of laying down the law, and, subconsciously, upon a very strong and natural desire that the woman's mind and body shall be reserved for the use of one man and one only."[6]

Men's interest in the sexual virtue of women is a puzzle for the skeptical reader, even for one familiar with the words of Saint Paul. The consequences of that interest are, however, less ambiguous. Woolf's irony does not disguise her distaste for the scenario she sketches. Society has accepted the prejudices of the apostle. Women must be constrained, and that need for subjection is in some unspecified way connected to the risks they run any time their chastity offers an occasion for doubt. Male sexual morality seems to be a simpler matter: men's ability to escape the compulsions of the flesh (for Paul does believe they are compelling) depends on women, thus it is women whose virtue is demanded. *Pamela*'s enthusiastic readers understood this very well: no one believes that good society in Bedfordshire is threatened by the rakish behavior of Mr. B. Indeed, the gentry's enjoyment of Mr. B's conversion to middle-class morality cannot conceal a certain amazement: can a man still be a man once he has worshipped at the shrine of chastity? Will not his ability to "lay down the law" be compromised? In the novel, Mr. B displays to his curious neighbors the traditional complacency of the man who has full reason to believe that his "woman's mind and body" are reserved for the use of himself and no one else. Pamela's perfect prudery has no equivalent among the aristocracy and ladies of breeding: her husband need lose no sleep worrying about whether his children are his own (Pamela is perfect enough to adopt Mr. B's natural daughter whose mother, less staunch than Pamela, has, after her "ruin," conveniently died). Female purity safeguards male honor. It is women's fall from virtue which society cannot bear, but loves to hear about.

Pamela Andrews profited from the code of pure womanhood. Propriety, respectability, self-respect and modesty are united in her good-looking fifteen-year-old person with a thorough knowledge of the Bible, a quick wit, and an inexhaustible flair for domestic organization. Other women were less impressed. The formidable Mary Wollstonecraft was convinced (in 1790) that the double standard of sexual morality damages both men and women. Truth and virtue must be common to all, and it is no compliment to women to maintain that their sensibilities are too "delicate," their understanding too easily strained, to allow them access to the hard work of moral judgment. When women are cherished for their purity and innocence, they turn into household pets, children in grown-up bodies, tempted to "play off those contemptible infantine airs that undermine esteem even whilst they excite desire," Wollstonecraft asserts, observing that "women are everywhere in this deplorable state; for in order to preserve their innocence, as ignorance is courteously termed, truth is hidden from them."[7]

This false innocence, Wollstonecraft continues, is not merely demeaning, imposed on women to ensure their dependence on men and their exclusion from the benefits of maturity: its real function is even worse. It is what encourages depravity and coquetry among women and, with the indolence women's education (or lack of that) creates in them, it is what prevents them from acquiring that rational virtue which Wollstonecraft treats with unmixed respect: "I have contended, that to render the human body and mind more perfect, chastity must more universally prevail, and that chastity will never be respected in the male world till the person of a woman is not, as it were, idolized."[8]

Chastity in women is supremely valuable, thinks Wollstonecraft. Is there any reason it should not be equally valuable in men? Wollstonecraft defends a conception of mutuality in love that has much to recommend it. As she puts it, a man who prefers a simpering, adoring, seemingly passionless creature has chosen to live with an insincere doll, a companion "without a mind."[9] Why should not both be capable of moderating their passions? Why shouldn't men as well as women learn to cultivate a dignified friendship in place of a libidinous game? Appetites are only "brutal" when "unchecked by reason," and the obligation to master them is not a sexual duty but "the duty of mankind."[10] In a relationship characterized by this shared chastity and modesty, adult affection can be kept alive when infatuation has cooled, as it must. But women who invest all their moral efforts into one single task—preserving their "honor," their chaste reputation—have degraded themselves and their shared humanity.

I put Pamela at the center of my investigation, together with Thecla, her more imperious forebear, because Pamela's defense of virginity is both typical and exemplary. Pamela's creator knew what he was doing. This earnest young woman with a taste for Puritan literature, to repeat Christine Gardner's phrase, "made chastity sexy." Few heroines have been as popular as Pamela; few have provoked as much skepticism. Was she calculating? Was her modesty real or feigned? What message can be extracted from a narrative in which a would-be rapist, exploiting the power of his situation and rank, is "rewarded" by the love and devotion of his all-forgiving wife? In falling for Pamela, English society found its model and its weak point. This was a society struggling to develop a moral code applicable to all classes and backgrounds, a society on the verge of economic upheaval and capitalist makeover, a society soon to be shaken by revolutionary and radical currents. Losing its traditional faith in sacred and aristocratic hierarchies, Britain in the eighteenth century chose to identify moral discrimination with a strangely passive and gendered image of sexual character. Morality was too important to be entrusted to men. And it was too important to be entrusted to anyone but a young, naïve woman infatuated with her own moral absolutes and committed to her chastity but happy to trade her sexual inexperience for the prize of marriage. This was where the future could rest. Without chastity, middle-class domestic ideology falls into incoherence; without the sexual double standard, the sanctity of the home is unprotected, the status of children uncertain, the transmission of inheritance unsecured. The middle class's values proved persuasive. Even without the Roman Catholic Church's preference for celibacy, moralists felt justified in recommending sexual restraint. As long as heterosexual marriage is the norm, anxiety about sexual purity is something to be encouraged, shared (if possible) by men and women, resisted in vain by the enemies of chastity. Women's part is more obvious than that of men. Their role is to be modest and respectable.[11] Sexually uninformed, punished if they stumble into experimentation or prove vulnerable to rape and seduction, "pure women" in the middle-class world Woolf observes with irony are grown-ups who aspire to the condition of little children, not so much people as "angels in the house." Welcome to the chastity plot.

"Reserving" a woman's mind and body, Woolf suggested, is more than the fantasy of an insecure male lover, prone to the "strong and natural desire" that she be his alone. It has been made into the dominant principle of female education. In order that women function as moral guardians, reliable vessels of a family or community's worth, they must care more than men do about sexual purity and innocence. All too often, that innocence is identified with ignorance; this was something that (before Woolf) Mary Wollstonecraft saw very clearly in her objections to Rousseau.[12] Must a virtuous woman be a stupid woman? It doesn't seem obvious. Yet many of the anxious supervisors of female upbringing in the seventeenth, eighteenth, and nineteenth centuries took great pains to ensure that English women, at least, would grow up with the blessings of ignorance. Better a docile child than an adult whose active intellect might venture too far from the safe and the prescribed.

What women know, and what they are discouraged from knowing, has something to do with the solicitude their sexuality inspires. What they may get up to, if that sexuality fails to be bridled and regulated with care, presents far too many challenges to the security of the family (with its investment in the integrity of succession or the legitimate inheritance of property). This is a subject on which that eighteenth-century sage Samuel Johnson believes he can speak with authority. In his journal entry for September 14, 1773, he reflects, "Consider, of what importance to society, the chastity of women is. Upon that all property in the world depends. We hang a thief for stealing a sheep, but the unchastity of a woman transfers sheep, and farm and all, from the right owner."[13] Those who imperil the chastity of women threaten society as we know it. Unchaste women are worse: embarrassing their husbands, provoking doubt and jealousy in their lovers. But why is Johnson so sure of the difference? If chastity is good, it should be good for everyone, "as desirable and becoming in one part of the human species as the other," as Henry Fielding put it in 1742.[14] The frivolous sophistry of the sexual double standard was acknowledged earlier by Christians at the time of Augustine. Asterius of Asmasea chides his male parishioners who envy Jews their freedom to discard unwanted wives. As he writes, "the law of self-control is not ordained by God for women alone but for men also." Those who blame adultery in women point out that female infidelity introduces "alien heirs" into houses and families, while men, even if they "approach many women, do their own hearth no harm."[15] But this is merely an excuse for licentiousness. Sexually erring men need watching. Incontinent and libidinous, they fail in the competition for self-mastery, even if they succeed on other terms. The masculine exemption casts a shadow over the modern, secular history of chastity. Men, in fact, have little to gain from their own sexual restraint and much to gain from its failures. Their conquests testify to their virility: their desires are effective and their powers acknowledged. Fornication, which should shame them, is secretly admired. It is an association a woman could not afford. Unchaste women are identified with weakness rather than strength, with what the Greeks called *porneia*, whorish sexuality. They are transgression in the flesh. And everyone is harmed by their behavior, as Johnson observes. Through the unreliable body of the unchaste woman, discord and pollution enter society. Nothing is safe. No attachments can be trusted, no meanings remain stable, no contracts are binding: If Cressida is false, cries Troilus, I am not me. If Desdemona is a whore, rages Othello, then life is not worth living, honor is a bubble and love is a sham. Emma the adulterer, Anna the adulterer, they leave death in their wake, children abandoned, affections spoiled.

Eunuchs and Maidens

There are two crucial versions of the chastity plot worth distinguishing. One is Pamela's. The other is Thecla's. From religion and the heritage of Western asceticism comes what I want to call the *eunuch's plot*, metaphysical and (often) masculine. To aspire to the condition of a disincarnate angel is to imagine oneself more than human, as "too good" for the world.

Philosophers are especially guilty of this hubris. Hiding their irritation with sensuality and human needs under the mask of a Platonic purity, philosophers looked favorably at the legend of angelism. Even the champions of modern scientific objectivity, who scorn talk of transcendence and angelism, prefer solitude and austerity as their most productive condition. When the cloisters empty out, the ascetics remain.

Few critics of the eunuch's plot have seen it as clearly as Friedrich Nietzsche, and any good genealogy of chastity exists in the shadow of his genealogy of "Ascetic ideals." Those who long to be "eunuchs for the kingdom of God," who say yes to the desert and celibacy, think they are listening "to a telephone from the beyond." Yet what is this distinctive "priestly faith" but a "pretext for hibernation," a "license for power" and a "saintly form of debauch"?[16] Liberation from sex, renunciation of that inexorable hunger and drive, appeared to Arthur Schopenhauer and to the early Christians as if finally there could be a release from the circuits of suffering, from the servitude of desire and the flesh. Nietzsche rushes to disabuse them. The ascetic ideal is perverse. In the context of apocalyptic expectations and an urgent desire to bring the realm of the living to an end, the eunuch's plot had a certain grandeur. But in a civilization interested in its own perpetuation, the doctrine of sexual renunciation collapses into incoherence. Can it be good to encourage the extinction of desire? However exotic the cult of the eunuch was, it did not find the ground it needed to survive.

Given the limitations of the ascetic "license for power," the war on sensuality needed other channels, other modes of operation. Much more popular was the one I am baptizing the *maiden's plot*. It is less a rival chastity plot than another form of valuation entirely, and it is the one that has survived. The maiden's plot cannot promise sainthood and otherworldly autonomy. Instead it offers more domestic rewards: modesty, obedience, and self-suppression. While the eunuch fled marriage, the chaste maiden fights to make herself worthy of it. While the eunuch rejects the social obligation of reproduction in a spirit Saint Jerome called "holy arrogance," the chaste maiden offers her virtue as a guarantee of the legitimacy of social reproduction, a sacrifice on the altar of family, patriarchy, race, name, class, and property. If the dream of the eunuch aspired to flee the body, the maiden's dream plants her ever more inexorably on the ground of the sexed and problematic body.

The eunuch's plot, at some level, denies the relevance of gender, even imagining a human condition unmarked by gender. The eunuch can afford indifference to the respectable values—those same sacred cows of family, name, position, class, and property. Like the Cynic whose austerity was a provocation to rival philosophical schools in the Hellenistic world, the eunuch troubles society by showing how little he needs it, disdaining much that more conventional people consider "natural" and "normal." The male *spadones voluntarii*, or voluntary eunuchs of whom Tertullian speaks in 213 CE, are the creation of grace rather than nature.[17] Rigorous abstention changes the body and clarifies the soul, turning the thoughts to the spirit rather than the flesh, and the crude marking of bodies for their sexual purposes becomes something the eunuch can forget. Such is not the case for the maiden. The maiden's plot insists on gender's law, legitimating the violence of gender inequality and proposing a strange set of criteria as the signatures of approved female sexuality: fear, resistance, and submission. If male heterosexual desire depends on the maiden's plot (and some scholars have worried that it does), then the prospects for relations between the sexes look grim. If Western morality depends on the perverse heroism of the eunuch's plot, then both religion and philosophy have a case to answer.

Put in these terms, it is hard to see why thinking seriously about chastity and its history would be anything but a waste of time. How can there be vitality and opportunity in such unpromising materials? In response, we can recall the two intrepid women, Thecla and Pamela, the follower of Paul who fled marriage and the virtuous serving maid who saves her virginity for her master. "Thecla's young body," writes the great historian Peter Brown, "stood stunningly alone. To preserve her virginity meant to preserve an individual identity rooted in her physical body, because expressed in the state of physical intactness that she had carried with her from her birth. Thecla was not a role model that only Christian women were expected to follow. Her intact body spoke to both men and women. It was a condensed image of the individual, always threatened with annihilation, poised from birth above the menacing pressures of the world."[18] Pamela also stood alone and menaced, determined to secure an integrity no one of her class was expected to possess. Claiming her sovereignty over her own physical body, she is an affront to the worldly who believe a servant's "innocence" is a presumption and a lie. Yet her willingness to die for her chaste truth, as her upper-class sister Clarissa will do a few years later, is a sign that the maiden's plot has larger ambitions, ambitions that can make a modern readership uncomfortable. Pamela is no martyr. Her "chastity" easily converts from Thecla-esque defiance to conjugal docility; marriage is no violation of her "intactness," as it seemed so clearly to be for Thecla and all the recruits to Christianity's eunuch plot. Yet Pamela understands what is at stake, and the eunuch's sublimity echoes in her resolution: "May I never survive one moment that fatal one in which I shall forfeit my innocence."[19]

Chastity plots, in their pure or radical form, stage a struggle against the social insistence on marriage and reproduction. "The world must be peopled," said Benedick in Shakespeare's *Much Ado about Nothing*. The chastity plot says: Why? What if I opt for a world that is not this world, for a suspension of ordinary and erotic ambitions in order to feel more intensely the pleasures of abstinence, the freedom of the angel, the magic of the perpetual maiden? Rather than pacifying the energies of eros, they demand eros's banishment. If the key is forcing a change, then there may be an opening. Resistance and denial, I want to suggest, are also constituents of narrative action, provocative in their own way. As themes, resistance and denial are the negative elements of myth, philosophy, and morality. As structures, they offer that essential block without which desire threatens to fade and depart. Both desire and antidesire shape lives as well as cultures; both desire and antidesire have plots of their own.

Both main types of chastity plot are relevant to my case. They are relevant, however, in differing degrees. In the eunuch's plot, a wish for something better interferes with the ordinary human acceptance of what cannot be changed. On fire with sublimity, the eunuch rejects the mortal condition (our condition, the local and cosmic situation of those born of human couplings and destined to return to the dirt, the condition of beings half rational and half irrational, part spirit and part mud). Sexual purity is interpreted as a way of changing what it is to be human. Fantasies of incorporeality belong to the eunuch's plot; visions of defeating nature and time belong here too. In the maiden's plot virginal scruples are mobilized against sexual violence or social conformity. The maiden's plot does not explicitly concern itself with ambitious metaphysical aims. The maiden wants to escape a predator or resist patriarchal pressure. If there is a drive toward freedom, it is not the freedom from the body or mortality as such but freedom from the encroachment of another upon my will, freedom to dispose of myself without coercion and brutality. But as Northrop Frye observed about the virgin, there are visions of exceptionality in the background of the maiden's plot. Symbolized in the romance convention of the virgin assailed, or the virgin whose purity heals and performs magic, is something more than the value of an intact piece of property. If the maiden's intact body matters, it is because her (and our) uncompromisable integrity matters. If virginity is more than "much ado about nothing," it is because it seems to shelter a certain secret, something private and unshared, a difficult (and perhaps indefensible) notion Frye called the virgin's "secret of invulnerability."[20]

The eunuch's plot is the business of religion, generally speaking. More narrowly, as Max Weber's sociology of religion argues, it is the business of salvation religions, ones that promise redemption from the world and the opportunity for mortal trash to become saintly, ones that try to work out ways that our condition could be exchanged for an enlightened and even an angelic one. The eunuch's plot thrives in the desert and in the cloister: even before the cloister became an institution, the anchorite or hermit was adept at finding times and places friendly to what Weber calls "abnegation of the world." Fleeing from the world: the Christian eunuch or consecrated virgin wants desperately to hasten this world's delayed end, to usher in the times of the Parousia, to bring time to a stop. The eunuch's renunciation and principled abstinence is called by Weber a type of "magical behavior." Ties of kinship and matrimony, themselves sources of power, are abjured in order to embrace inward, sacred values. Sexual renunciation, the eunuch's speciality, is a means of converting profane into religious states. Denying eros its service enables the virtuoso to practice "heroic" and "magical" form of asceticism. (There are also nonmagical and even worldly asceticisms, as Weber's famous theory of Protestant modernity explains.) Through sacrifice comes deliverance; through exemption from the natural and social order, it is possible to expect transcendence, purity, freedom, and power.[21] These are the beliefs mobilized in the eunuch's plot.

The maiden's plot places the markers for perfection closer to home. A virtuous young woman (it is only in rare circumstances a young man) struggles to define and defend the integrity of her selfhood, which, crudely interpreted, can be identified with her virginity, her sexual inexperience. In many cases virgins were not the movers and subjects of their own plots, and their integrity or selfhood is hardly of much relevance. It would be foolish to deny this. Women's autonomy, most traditional stories assume, is unacceptable, even unthinkable. The maiden who is neither a child protected in her father's house nor a wife enclosed by her husband's is basically "nobody"—that is, she is in a state of transition, "disturbingly ambiguous." The cultural theorist and critic Mieke Bal notes an "alienating anonymity" in the narratives of virginity readers can find in the Old Testament book of Judges: "the negative formulation" virginity receives in these stories, she writes, "is due to the temporally impossible suspension it [virginity] entails.... Existing between the positions of daughter and wife, the young, nubile woman belongs to nobody."[22]

Good virgins in the Bible are obedient and submissive ones. But they are also nameless beings, almost ciphers, unknown and barely described in a number of significant instances, of which the sacrifice of Jephthah's unnamed daughter is one (Judg. 11:30–40). "My only child," Jephthah grieves: he promised to give away whatever or whoever was the first to greet him when he returned home from battle, the first to come out of his house will be delivered to Yahweh. Good virgins exist in order to be given away, offered as gifts to forge the links of acknowledgment and dependence, loyalty and respect, that must seal relations between men and men, fathers and husbands, family and family, or, as in the case of Jephthah, man and God. The virgin child of Jephthah's house will be given away in fulfillment of a vow, not as a bride but as a burnt offering, killed as a sacrifice to God (and the only completed human sacrifice in the Old Testament).[23] She has no name, is given no description except she who has "known no man" (Judg. 11:40). The pure maiden is a precious offering promised, something of value that can be received and then, presumably, used. (In this case the virginity that guaranteed the maiden's value exists no longer.) How else do tribes and families account their interchanges, their mutual needs, rivalries, and confrontations except through the "network of virgins that constitutes a line of coherence"?[24]

There is much that is curious about the maiden's plot, especially in the version that is probably the most familiar. Here I am referring to the way female virginity is idealized in societies that are fixated on the normalcy of heterosexual relations: societies it is convenient to call patriarchal (and these are certainly in the majority); societies whose moral codes may bear the traces of religious prohibition and aspiration but where secular concerns (about marrying, about reproduction, about control of the young) dominate. In such societies virginity (we could call it "biological" or "anatomical") is a temporary or transitional phase in the life of a woman. It is something that signifies not through its value for the virgin but because of what it is meant to render "legitimate." Temperance and moderation are, on many accounts, things of value in and of themselves—for males, that is. Female sexual restraint, which will include modesty, premarital virginity, wedded chastity, and the avoidance of promiscuity, is important for other reasons, as an assurance of social legitimacy. The greater the sexual discretion of women, the more credit is transferred to the authority of men, and the more the transactions between men can proceed smoothly, without hiccup or mutual suspicion. This, roughly speaking, is the argument associated with the traditional maiden's plot, what we might call the patriarchal maiden's plot. Masculine honor depends on feminine honor, but only in very confined or codified terms. Women will not prove their honor by fighting, by showing loyalty under duress, or by telling the truth. Instead, they will prove their honor by devoting themselves to marriage and the preparation for marriage. It is legitimate for fathers to distribute their daughters and for husbands to expect a clean bill of goods.

Sexual purity, in such contexts, is the mark identifying something that can safely be exchanged between men or (in the exceptional cases of

Jephthah offering his daughter or Agamemnon sacrificing Iphigenia) between men and God. What happens on the completion of the ritual exchange (the marital act, the confirmation, the god's acceptance of the virgin sacrifice) is best left undescribed. The good girl will deliver her mysterious property as a way of assuring that the man who "receives" her has monopoly: first and final use, exclusive possession. Is virginity a property that is both alienable (for the virgin) and fixed in its singularity, as only one lover can "have" someone's virginity? Under a skeptical gaze, the value that is virginity is attenuated by the problem of proof and the difficulty of public access. What is demonstrable, what assumed? Once the maiden is deflowered, what has happened to the value of virginity? What kind of a gift is this anyway, this gift that cannot be "regifted"? A virgin is a virgin, the book of Judges establishes, if she has not "known a man." But how does anyone know what someone else doesn't know? What kind of mark of quality is this elusive "nothing," this condition of nonknowledge? The nameless daughter of Jephthah will never, she laments, "know a man," so she asks her father for two month's grace to "wander upon the mountains and bewail my virginity" (Judg. 11:37).[25] But just what is she bewailing?

In the literary and the legal stagings of the inquiry into a woman's virtue, it is precisely the epistemological problem presented by virginity that fascinates, frustrates, and bedevils.[26] When we look for something tangible in this virtue, the problems multiply. Female virginity acts like a fetish for those who are desperate to believe in it or horrified to imagine its absence. In an old and crude expression, a maidenhead is the "jewel" a maiden can hoard, and if hoarded, she can then give it away. But that "giving" is very difficult to represent. In a few cases, the fact of sexual experience does lend itself to signification: a pregnant woman is generally speaking not a virgin. Otherwise, those interested in finding the truth are doomed to disappointment, or worse. In a rage to know whether his wife is a whore, Othello wants something he should not need to have. Distraught by jealousy, he demands the "ocular proof," and presumably if he saw Desdemona in bed with Cassio, his doubts about her chastity would be confirmed, as Iago insinuates. Bodily evidence of virginity, however, is elusive, as is the positive confirmation of a woman's chastity. The history of chastity trials and chastity tests is an unhappy one, and not just for those who failed. Doctors and midwives were consulted; the law proved no more sagacious than the magicians. Superstition played a larger role than science. The fantasy of a membrane whose physical status would reveal the truth to the curious and intrusive investigator proved unreliable. So how does anyone know? If the maiden's claim is to be made good, what must she do? Die a martyr, as Christian virgins sometimes decided? Display herself in visible combat with those who threaten her integrity? Must we look for words and gestures, blushes and evasions? How can virtue—an inward condition—be established or confirmed?

While the eunuch stakes almost everything on the chance for otherworldly transformation, the maiden seeks to have her significance recognized in the world. She needs to test her virtue and see if it can command belief. And here—in the need for a belief that is always being withheld—the maiden's trials begin. Her modesty is challenged by a demand for something more spectacular. In this sense, the maiden's plot is paradoxical. She must make herself available to a scrutiny that is as performative as it is ideologically loaded, displaying herself as a piece of evidence in a battle between sexual innocence and sexual cynicism, between dignity and moral corruption, a battle she does not direct. Pamela Andrews did take control of the plot that would have seen her disgraced. Preserving her honor was life and death to her. Unusually, she manages to make the bridge between the inner testimony (the truth written in her heart) and public demonstration (the chatter and judgments of a skeptical community unimpressed by the protestations of a common serving maid). Pamela succeeds through the solicitude of her creator, who makes sure that Mr. B and the world are able to read the private diaries and letters that certify her innocence. Yet Pamela is in no position to maintain indefinitely the sexual purity she has fought tooth and nail to preserve. Marriage is the reward of the maiden, and marriage means bed, to put it crudely. Very few of the maiden's friends would go so far as to question the value of that reward, to ask whether it is also the state that best reflects the virtue for which she is famous. For only the eunuch has the power to resist the institution of marriage, and Thecla of Iconium, a maiden who claims the eunuch's privilege here, is both famous and unusual.

In this profane world, the maiden is normally destined to marry and deliver her purity as a gift, a sacrifice on the altar of social normality. Her exceptionality may be short-lived; her career as the wild young follower of Diana has been tolerated only because it is transient. Yet what the maiden represents, in the mythological and literary traditions, is a challenge to the cynical expectations of our world. If she can triumph in the demonstration of her innocence, her honesty, her sincerity, then the world's values will be exposed as inadequate and cheap. The maiden ennobles. She is also a kind of magic, although a secular and profane one. She brings nature into contact with spirit, and the process of generation, birth, and increase into contact with something more pure and alien, set apart and untouched. Often described as a lily, a rosebud unopened, an enclosed garden, or a fortress, the maiden is image rather than action, icon rather than narrative. In some contexts, the maiden's plot is a romance. It is pastoral and courtly. In others, it is the bourgeois form of female life, by which I mean that the maiden is used and exchanged as a commodity in the marriage market, her moral scrupulousness (her "virtue") necessitated by the anxiety of families about the legitimacy of their lines of descent. In these cases, perhaps the most common ones, the maiden is no rosebud or pearl to be protected and honored. She is a kind of prophylactic, a vessel for breeding that needs to be separated out from erotic traffic, secluded from the public sphere, so that her purity and inviolability can prove the honor of those associated with her. It is this understanding of the purpose of chastity which most postreligious accounts of the virtue assume. What else, they ask, could chastity be for? Why else, except to control women and legislate licit sexuality, would anyone have invented such a thing?

One might object that negation is not a promising start for a plot, since plots require motion, change of status, alteration of time and place, action and counteraction. But negation, as we shall see, is a powerful incentive. Here the chastity plot uncovers a secret that yielded considerable results. Denial is productive. The abnegation of power is a tool of power. If desire is violent, the refusal of desire can also lead to violence. This is true for both versions of the chastity plot, the ascetic's vow of abstinence and the forbearance intrinsic to the love-courtship-and-marriage plot. Violence can be exerted against the self, as in the ascetic's battle with self. Or it can be wielded against another, as in those traditional plots that describe the battle between temptation and resistance, between seduction and honor. Negation is creative: barriers arise to be assaulted; taboos exist to stimulate the inventive into defense or resistance; corruption is necessary so that innocence can triumph (or the other way around).

The mechanics of the chastity plot are predictable, and they survive under many generic conditions, from fairy tale and epic to the vampire cycles of young adult fiction. Literature would be unrecognizable without them. If there were no such thing as maidens fighting for their virtue or lovers lingering in a state of suspension, delaying the consummation of desire, the landscape of romance would be a barren place. Such dynamics of temptation and resistance come hither and go away, are essential to the traditional plot, creaky as it is. Northrop Frye names the "mythos of summer" the imaginative territory of romance, in particular quest romance.[27] The quest romance takes place in a magical world where ordinary natural laws are suspended and where the presence of a golden age, a protected garden, a childhood playground of green wood or watery glade recalls the fantasy of erotic innocence—an innocence not yet darkened by fear or constrained by prohibition.[28] The chastity plot is often a romance, in this sense: a pastoral fantasy of an exceptional state, where childhood or passivity can be prolonged indefinitely, where struggle and action and consequences just don't happen.[29]

The theological versions of the chastity plot—ones that will be less familiar to literary fans of narrative structure and narrative pleasures—offer an interesting alternative. The core story they build on is the story of the human race rather than any individual hero or heroine. Beginning in the primal state of innocence, that human race (call it Adam and Eve for short) lost its simplicity and was exiled to a world of sex, death, and reproduction. The soul, still recalling that original condition, accepts its yoking to a cycle of exhausting labor and inconsistent reward but registers its alienation in feelings of pain and guilt. Secured in its bondage to this world by the contracts of marriage and mortality, the soul dreams of its freedom. In the renunciation of sex, the refusal of marriage and reproduction, the soul reclaims its innocence. Life without sexual desire is the life of the angels. It is a foretaste of eternity, in the imagination of many Christian thinkers of the second to fifth centuries. Less radically, a swerve against sex can still be relevant to the hope of innocence recaptured if faithful and modest marriage is practiced.

Clearly the symbolism of chastity is distinct from the symbolism of eros and marriage. Their stories have, at various times in history, been sharply divided: that was when the eunuch ruled the field of chastity. At other times their stories have tended to blur and get confused: that is when the maiden rules. It is easier to find representations of chastity than explanations of it. We think we know about some of the purposes of marriage. "Marriage is a social invention, unique to humans," writes Stephanie Coontz in her witty book *Marriage, a History: From Obedience to Intimacy, or How Love Conquered Marriage*.[30] One "story," that marriage was invented for the protection of women, "is still the most widespread myth about the origins of marriage"; the other motivation, that its purpose was to oppress and confine women, is almost as popular a myth. Some anthropologists conclude that the procreative family was a way to monopolize females for mating purposes, or to stabilize the division of labor, increasing the chances for survival; it could also, importantly, be a tool in the creation of networks of cooperation beyond the immediate, face-to-face group: marriage exchanged women, opening up relations of support between groups now connected as kin, enabling accumulation, expanding the reach of private property, extending interests and providing the social resources on which communities and—later—states could draw.[31] What are the purposes of chastity? The question, to my mind, has never been taken on with the seriousness it deserves. Chastity in the abstract is a thin quarry, a "monkish virtue," in David Hume's opinion, twisted in meaning and overinflated by papal hypocrisy in Luther's view.[32] But embedded in its plots, chastity is neither innocuous nor dull. Where the plots of literature deliver the pleasures of aesthetic form, the ascetic plots I study propose to bring meaning and form to the messy domain of the sexual, to make something clear and ethically articulated, and even philosophically suggestive, out of the randomness and uncertainty of sexual desire. That the chastity plot is in many respects socially coercive and psychologically unhealthy, I do not want to deny. Shame and anxiety grow on the ground of the chastity plot. But they grow, too, on the ground of the marriage plot, the romance plot, and the free love plot. Sex without hesitation is not human sex, nor is desire without a shape and an investment in meaning: Sigmund Freud was neither the first nor the last to notice this. To be repelled by chastity's war against human messiness is simply to reverse the repulsion ascribed by erotic liberationists to those imagined as history's gatekeepers of sexuality. Our quarrel should be with the unimaginative and intolerant exercises of the "will to shape desire"; living in a shapeless desire is no place to be. "Love is the spiritualization of sensuality," Nietzsche wrote in *Twilight of the Idols* (1888). "It represents a great triumph over Christianity."[33] The idea of chastity did not tame lust. It did little to mitigate the insolence of sexual tormenters, or to protect the vulnerable, or to defend the victim of sexual aggression. If there is to be effective resistance to sexual injustice, it will not come from waving the flag of chastity. But Nietzsche's sly praise of love "spiritualized" gives us a hint of the resources to be gained by appreciating chastity as something more of the spirit than the body, something with the potential to interrupt and question our dominant social meanings.

The other struggle, against the dominant narrative of the "marriage plot," is also part of the work I assign chastity, and in this connection my plots do have a more attractive or at least more feminist political message. Is there sanctuary in the forest or the desert for those who want to say no to sex and marriage? Can we increase our respect for the "celibacy plots" Benjamin Kahan traces in the lives of exemplary American modernists and literary rebels: Marianne Moore, Andy Warhol, Henry James's Olive Chancellor?[34] Might there be an alternative, a "space" between the marriage plot and the "queer plot," between heteronormativity and homosexual identity? Some of the most interesting of contemporary queer theorists and scholars have drawn attention to the power of "nongenital sexualities" (Kahan) or practices of intimacy, enjoyment, friendship, companionship, and kinship that aim to secure spaces and acknowledgments outside traditionally defined gender identities and sexual orientations. Valerie Traub makes an eloquent case for the presence in the European Renaissance of a same-sex eroticism that, in her words, "mingled" chastity, friendship, and tribadism.[35] The goddess of chastity protects a disparate group of rebels against conventional matrimony, some who have no intention of closing their eyes to bodies and their pleasures, some who celebrate passion in the cloister or monastery, and some who find self-affirmation in the clothes of the opposite sex, like the Maid of Orleans.

Should Diana win in her battle against Venus? Most of our instincts speak against her. But the goddess with her implacable purity and her fierce bow and arrows did represent a place apart, an exception to the ideological confines of the family, home, and marriage, a way to live outside and unsocialized. Innocence and its counterpart, purity, are fraudulent ideals, if we are Nietzscheans or even Hegelians: they are fantasies of the timid, symptoms of hostility to life and intolerance of difference and mixture. To such tougher, more dialectical thinkers, admiring purity betrays a weakness for things brittle and inflexible; to yearn for innocence when you could be experienced is just stupid. But innocence can also represent a vision of things as they are, without our interference, untampered with, raw and alone. There is something to be said for that ideal. The eccentric battlers in the fight for chastity, a fight I depict in this book mainly through its theological supporters, were also pursuing an aesthetic I find intriguing, an aesthetic of abstraction and impersonality, a curious and unusual ideal of human identity. We should not be too quick to patronize them.

Getting to the Plot: Asceticism, Repression, and Pleasure

Among his many discoveries, Sigmund Freud, the founder of psychoanalysis, found a relationship between civilization and sexual renunciation. That relationship was neither casual nor benign: "The misunderstanding of sexuality is no intellectual error, nor an accidental ignorance, but one way in which culture conspires to 'obtain the mental energy it needs by subtracting it from sexuality.'"[36] *Civilization and its Discontents,* the book Freud published in 1930, reports on the injuries society has inflicted on the human "constitution."[37] Human sexuality is violent; human aggression also. Left alone, life under their domination would be neither quiet nor safe. Renunciation is the price the human race has been asked to pay for the benefits of civilization. The debt is far from being discharged. Some compensation has been offered for the drain on eros. Sublimation, idealism, and the curious pleasures of asceticism promise more circuitous rewards.

But the effects on human flourishing are real. Sexual denial causes pain and confusion. Repression is more than a hypothesis. It is part of a plot.[38]

When civilization exacts its sacrifice from the sexual instinct, the plot is in play. The *chastity plot* is my catchall term for all the ruses civilization has summoned to its aid in the war against the libido. The campaign of civilization against eros was merciless. It was also devious. Sigmund Freud and Friedrich Nietzsche are the messengers who brought the unpleasant news to the nineteenth- and twentieth-century heirs of the Enlightenment. Humankind has agreed to make itself unhappy. To become civilized, to accept the protection of society, is to become disciplined, and that is not a condition favorable to sensual enjoyment. With some concern and some malice, my precursors described the effects of the "ascetic ideal" (Nietzsche) or "civilized sexual morality" (Freud) on the human psyche. We get sick through repression. "Physiological well-being" is barely a memory to those infected by the ascetic disease, Nietzsche grumbles. At best, philosophers (to name just one of the ascetic species) choose chastity because they prefer not to be disturbed:

> We have seen how a certain asceticism, a severe and cheerful continence with the best will, belongs to the most favourable conditions of supreme spirituality, and is also among its most natural consequences: hence it need be no matter for surprise that philosophers have always discussed the ascetic ideal with a certain fondness.[39]

Fifty years or so before Freud's mature work on the diseases of civility, Nietzsche laid out the remnants of ascetic idealism for examination. He called his book *The Genealogy of Morals*, and its tone was pitiless. The philosophers are not wrong, at least about what is good for them. The "philosopher's pose *par excellence*" is this "peculiar, withdrawn attitude," world-denying, hostile to life, and suspicious of the senses. For philosophers, who need to be alone and to "creep about" in their gloomy "ascetic wraps and cloaks," the chastity instinct makes sense. A stimulation of sorts is what asceticism offers life in general and the life of the mind in particular. For the philosopher, that "timid little toddler," unsure on his feet, asceticism was a prosthetic support, gratefully accepted. For a long time, Nietzsche continues, the philosopher had to use "the mask and cocoon" of the ascetic ideal. Its "repulsive and gloomy caterpillar form" was the disguise of the contemplative type, a disguise meant to divert the general hostility such an "inactive, brooding, warlike" element would otherwise face (*GM*, III, §10). But for those of us who are not "sportsmen of sanctity," the popularity of ascetic values is a puzzle, and perhaps not a very stimulating one: "The ascetic treats life as a wrong road on which one must finally walk back to the point where it begins" (*GM*, III, §11). Turning "life against life" (*GM*, III, §13) is, paradoxically, a device "for the preservation of life." Its pain is invigorating—at least for those lives already at risk of degenerating. Sacrifices and mutilations act like a "spur in the flesh." Homeopathically, the ascetic ideal works for those whose disgust with existence has made them susceptible to the charms of self-torture. They have become sensitive to the pleasures of mortification and fatigue, connoisseurs of world-weariness. But they are ill, even in their own eyes. The chastity plot has turned the world into a madhouse:

> Read from a distant star, the majuscule script of our earthly existence would perhaps lead to the conclusion that the earth was the distinctively *ascetic planet*, a nook of disgruntled, arrogant, and offensive creatures filled with a profound disgust at themselves, at the earth, at all life, who inflict as much pain on themselves as they possibly can out of pleasure in inflicting pain—which is probably their only pleasure. (*GM*, III, §11)

Perverse? Beyond a doubt. Yet there is something triumphant here as well. In the madness of asceticism, Nietzsche finds a new and strange creativity. The effects of dulling the senses, starving the drives, saying no to sex, have made us skilled in the management of suffering and stimulus. We take our inhibited condition for granted. That is bad and probably irreparable, despite the hard work of psychoanalysts. On the other hand, we grow subtle through repression, at least according to Nietzsche. We have become "interesting animals," learning to idealize our weaknesses, to spiritualize our wounds. Much of that idealization borrows its strategies from religion, as I shall argue. A considerable part is also accomplished through art and specifically through literature, given that both poetry and narrative are powerful compensations for a disappointing reality.[40] "In a large sense," Geoffrey Galt Harpham wrote in his seminal book *The Ascetic Imperative in Culture and Criticism*, "asceticism is the 'cultural' element in culture . . . all cultures impose on their members the essential ascetic discipline of 'self-denial.'" Without the ascetic imperative, no self-criticism, no "hyperarticulated ambivalence," perhaps nothing we would recognize as aesthetic "form." Harpham, like William James before him, has a soft spot for the creative energy of self-denial, even while he acknowledges its fanaticism. There is always a double-motive in the ascetic—resistance to mastery and resistance to nonmastery. Harpham believes both art and science depend on this doubleness, and he sees even Nietzsche as accepting the contradictory outcome of his own anti-ascetic critique: "All honor to the ascetic ideal *insofar as it is honest!*" (*GM*, III §26).[41] Is there anything of value that is not part of a chastity plot?

Idealism as compensation for the failures of reality; ascetic "disgust" as a force responsible for so much we value in the name of the "civilized life": these are the ingredients of a Nietzschean genealogy of morals. It is one that feeds the analysis I want to make of chastity and chastity's complicated histories. Mine is also a genealogy. It is not a search for the causes or the consequences, the losers or the winners in the "battle for chastity," as Michel Foucault called it. It is not a story of "how this came to be," not a story of how sexual renunciation developed from philosophical preference into metaphysical drama and then shrank back into bourgeois priggishness. Such a narrative could be put together, and the central chapters of this book do show part of that drama of decline as it played out in the first two millennia of Christendom: how something that was a recommendation for the spiritual elite became an injunction for the masses, a command for the clergy, and ultimately a byword for repression and abuse. But such a history, despite its usefulness to the student of ascetic inheritances, would do justice neither to the slipperiness of my theme nor its radical capacities. We do not find, hidden in the neglected and at times implausible episodes of chastity's history, "a forgotten identity, eager to be reborn, but a complex system of distinct and multiple elements, unable to be mastered by the powers of synthesis," to borrow Foucault's description of the Nietzschean critical genealogy. History tries to remember. But its reminiscences are full of counterhistories, narratives that lead nowhere, associations that dissociate, memory traces that do not add up.[42]

"The history of a concept," Michel Foucault wrote in the introduction to *The Archaeology of Knowledge*, "is not wholly and entirely that of its progressive refinement, its continuously increasing rationality, its abstract gradient, but that of its various fields of constitution and validity, that of its successive rules of use, that of the many theoretical contexts in which it developed and matured."[43] Looking for the motives of the chastity ideal, as it "emerges" and as it changes shape, provides a lesson in toleration for silliness as well as nobility, for the surfaces as well as the depths, for what Nietzsche and Foucault recognize as the "petty malice" of the details and accidents that "accompany every beginning."[44] As Foucault puts it, "What is found at the historical beginning of things is not the inviolable identity of their origin; it is the dissension of other things. It is disparity."[45]

History, done with a patient attention to details and disparities, doesn't lead us to an epiphany, a clearing of the ground, or a welcome banishment of obscurity. In this, doing history never affords the satisfactions philosophy has encouraged its practitioners to want. It is the same with the historical genealogy of chastity. Are we the privileged heirs of an enlightened tradition who have overcome our ascetic illusions? Are we better than our ancestors? Are our sexual beliefs, customs, and ideals more rational, more civilized, more tolerant than those of the past? Flushed with the pride of erotic freedom and the conviction that liberalism as we know it requires an exemption from the rules of abstinence, we may feel we have outgrown chastity, or it has deteriorated beyond all possible usefulness. Yet the ascetic habit, as Max Weber famously argued, did not die. It merely changed shape, shifted its "fields of validity," its "rules of use," and its theoretical contexts. If its role under the dispensation of an otherworldly Christian faith was to prepare adherents to reject the world entirely, its function under the more practical dispensation of early modern Puritanism was (to quote *The Protestant Ethic and the Spirit of Capitalism*) "to subject man to the supremacy of a purposeful will, to bring his actions under constant self-control with a careful consideration of their ethical consequences.... This active self-control was also the most important ethical idea of Puritanism."[46] The abnegation of the ascetic in his desert splendor is an indulgence, a playground of self-involvement, compared with the productive discipline of the professional, the ethically restrained modern individual who devotes considerable powers of emotional steadiness to the work of self-monitoring, whatever the challenges in married life and courtship, in commerce and public life, in religious activities and personal friendships. The modern "inner-worldly ascetic," Weber argues, understands the life of perfection in the here and now. And that is peculiarly advantageous to the discipline of capitalist endeavor, to "rational" economic and political action governed by a "methodical way of life" rather than by abnegation, mortification, and erotic denial. What was "prophetic" inspiration and "charismatic" authority is now something much more mundane. The successful modern ascetic is no monk organizing time according to the sound of bells and the duties of prayer and penitence. Rather he (or she) rationally distributes time and energy in the service of profit, just as the scholar (another ascetic without a cowl) rationally distributes intellect in the service of science and knowledge.

Did the ascetic ideal develop when it was transformed, when it was displaced from a cave or convent to an office or study? As we shall see, Christians laid their hope for a return to a condition of prelapsarian innocence on the self-denial of the sexually continent. This was the glorious cult of virginity, and it promised redemption from sin and restoration of a corrupt carnality to a divinely sanctioned purity. Contemporary notions of creaturely excellence demand that individuals subject themselves to disciplines of physical self-scrutiny (am I thin enough, strong enough, toned enough?) and personal achievement (am I successful enough? hardworking enough? do I manage my time effectively?) Each time, the ideal or form encounters the pressure of reality, the diverse claims of competing meaning systems, of groups and institutions and concentrations of power. That is what it is for a thing to have a genealogy. And chastity also has a genealogy. The meaning of consecrated virginity remains active, even if obscured, in all the various variations on the theme of erotic self-denial, all the enactments of pleasure and pain, provocation and resistance. And the hubris of the ascetic virtuoso still inflects the West's sense of cultural superiority, according to which power over time and the market is more important than power over the body and its appetites. Which is "refinement," which "increasing rationality"?

In the sense Nietzsche gave the term, a *genealogy* of "x" is not the history of "x" nor a simple reconstruction of origins.[47] Competing uses, disparate meanings, and discordant judgments are entwined into the "descent" and "emergence" (*Herkunft, Entstehung*) of a thing or concept or idea:

> The whole history of a "thing," an organ, a tradition can to this extent be a continuous chain of signs, continually revealing new interpretations and adaptations, the causes of which need not be connected even among themselves, but rather just follow and replace one another at random. The "development" of a thing, a tradition, an organ is therefore certainly not its *progressus* towards a goal, still less is it a logical *progressus*, taking the shortest route with least expenditure of energy and cost,—instead it is a succession of more or less profound, more or less mutually independent practices of subjugation exacted on the thing, added to this the resistances encountered every time, the attempted transformations for the purpose of defence and reaction, and the result, too, of successful countermeasures. The form is fluid, the "meaning" (*Sinn*) even more so. (*GM*, II, §12)

The "forms" that figure in Nietzsche's text are moral ideas: guilt and shame, good and bad, noble and base, purity and punishment. They have no essence, no single and definitive way of laying claim to human souls or to the great events of history. Yet they are the ones with force, the ones that determine happiness and unhappiness. They demand and transform, dominate and insinuate. These are the notions that shape mental and cultural spaces, that imprint tone and value on particular social practices, functions, and transactions. Sexual renunciation is one of these notions. It has no one form, no single meaning, no characteristic use. When we look for its history, its evolution, we find instead a chain of signs, a succession of practices, fantasies, measures, and countermeasures. Not only does chastity prescribe resistance—resistance to the sexual urges, defenses against those gratifications Freud identified with pleasure and well-being. It has also been resisted, and the resistance against chastity has been a source both of pleasure and pain.

There are as many motives for the hatching of the chastity plot as there are interpretations of its meaning and purpose. Like many of culture's most significant products, chastity is overdetermined and contradictory. It rewards and punishes, inflates and diminishes. It promotes power and freedom, but at the cost of impotence and abjection. It elevates the spiritual by encouraging preoccupation with the carnal. It invents painful ways to deviate from nature while celebrating the simplicity of pastoral; it substitutes artifice for spontaneity, ambivalence for impulse, and the tangled for the straight. Indeed, all the values, the traditions, the organs Nietzsche subjects to genealogical critique are like this. When I follow Nietzsche's lead and offer a partial genealogy of the chastity plot, I will be leaving out as much as I will be putting in. I have not tried to construct a narrative tracing the genesis of sexual regulations and the many ways sexual practices have become taboo, unclean, forbidden, or consecrated. That could be done. If there were to be a history of European sexual ethics, it would cover the eras of faith and the eras of doubt, the passages from prudery to relaxation or from relaxation to prudery. Such a history would be interesting. But it is not my task. I want instead to catch chastity in its telltale moments of confidence, the points at which the plot became a drama alluring to the imagination and influential on the emotions. It did not attract all imaginations or influence all emotions. But it made a difference.

The chastity plot succeeded, not because it satisfied the interests of a powerful social lobby or represented an intellectual victory over its rivals but because it was as much a thing of fantasy as a social program. It created routes for psychic identification. It provided possibilities for subjects to form themselves into idealized versions of themselves. The reasons people want to subject themselves to moral prescriptions, to subordinate themselves to regulation and repression, may be mysterious. To think fruitfully about these mysteries, students of repression and sexual virtue need to be flexible, need to draw their theoretical tools from a number of places. We benefit from the searching analyses of Nietzsche, Freud, and recently Foucault and Judith Butler. Like these canny thinkers, anyone interested in the fate of sexual renunciation must rehearse the scenes of what Butler calls "passionate attachment" in the hope that understanding the entwinement of desire and denial will give us greater insight into our own ambivalence.[48]

By Nietzsche's lights, the ascetic plot is a cultural plot, a conspiracy to limit sensual and sexual life and to make denial look like power and achievement. A chastity plot is also a literary form, something we read about, something brought into being through a specialized use of the literary imagination. Before anything else, a plot is a mode of meaning-making, a machine of narrative production, allowing human desire to turn incidents into opportunities and accident into something meaningful. Since Aristotle first defined it in the *Poetics*, plot has meant something like "the minimal intentional structure of action."[49] If, as Paul Ricoeur nicely remarks, a "plot *makes* events into a story," desire is what makes us want to turn our lives into the form of story, to draw significance out of the random and transform the negligible into the essential.[50] Yet the ascetic plot is also what has the power to stimulate desire, to stage desire in a different way, on different stages. The variety of these plots—desiring, antidesiring, diverting, and displacing—will be surveyed in this book. Some plots squander much of life in the search for a purity that would repair life's insufficiencies, that would magically convert negligible and ephemeral meanings into the absolute discourse that angels had said to speak; some invest chastity in a market of sexual exchanges, or political advantages.

Caught in the Plot: Chastity, Desire, and Marriage

> From the point of view of plot, heroic chastity is subject to exactly the same literary defects as inveterate promiscuity: both are poor in the qualities of development and surprise.
>
> IAN WATT, *The Rise of the Novel*[51]

I believe there is a close connection between the pleasures of plot and the cultural prestige of sexual renunciation, but that connection needs to be justified. We can start by looking at theology and literature, where the basic elements of the chastity plot appear in their starkest forms. A few of those elements are questions: Why are we not innocent? How can we separate the pure from the impure? How can love both embrace carnality and transcend it? Some are solutions or rationalizations: Before we became so warped and sensually driven, we fell from grace, and the division between body and soul betrays that primordial disaster. To repair the damage, the appetites of the body need curbing and correcting; the objects of desire must be immaterial and disembodied, or at the very least hard to win.

There are many ways to tell the story about sex and repression, and we can quickly recognize the confrontation that gives these stories their edge. Perfectionists despise realists; true virtue has no time for compromise; the inviolate virgin wishes neither rape nor marriage; the saint struggles to silence the demands of his body. Hippolytus, the stubborn and idealistic adolescent of Euripides's tragedy, subject of my chapter 2, wants to be pure but fails to recognize the trouble purity causes in an impure world. A repentant saint like Augustine regrets his incontinence and makes all future Christians repay his debt by learning to fear their own concupiscence. Christian perfectionism transfers the battle against lust and temptation to the inner arena, forging the soul's heroic myth of triumph and redemption. Legend and literature lend to the aggressor a visible shape and agenda. In the Apocryphal Acts, Thecla of Iconium refuses the marriage her family requires of her. She is duly attacked by violent, enraged Roman noblemen, then confronted by lions and flames. Her virginity survives, as she miraculously fights off the rapists and rises above the pyre, while turning the beasts into pliant cats who lick her feet. In Richardson's *Pamela, Or Virtue Rewarded,* a virginal serving maid fights off the demands of her libertine master, crying, "May I never survive one moment that fatal one in which I shall forfeit my innocence."[52]

These are all chastity plots. But so is the dark contract that Freud believes moderns have forgotten: to be civilized, you have to deny yourself pleasure. As he is sorry to say, it is the route to power if also the breeding ground of neurosis. Nietzsche's chastity plotters agree. Asceticism may be perverse: what successful animal would choose to cause itself pain? But this perversion makes the ascetic special, and it casts a shadow over the cheaper satisfactions of the sensualists. Thwarting sexual desire is counterintuitive, if you want happiness and if you want to create stories other people want to read. Yet stories about thwarting turn out to be exciting themselves. The plot continues.

Civilization, in the classic opposition identified by Freud, achieves its ends by creating detours between arousal and fulfillment, inventing surrogate rewards for sensual renunciations, confronting desire with law. But the mix of pain and pleasure is not always easy to manage; therefore plots have to be constructed again and again. Plot itself, to push the analogy further along, mediates between desire and resistance by turning frustration into narrative enjoyment. *Enjoyment* here is a qualified term. When the opposition to desire is too strong either in art or in life, discomfort enters, even to the point of pain. Sadism is one way of interpreting the yields of that "enjoyable frustration"; masochism another. In her classic article on visual pleasure and narrative, Laura Mulvey points to the erotoperverse generation of the narrative machine: "Sadism demands a story, depends on making something happen, forcing a change in another person, a battle of will and strength, victory/defeat, all occurring in a linear time with a beginning and an end."[53] When desire is permitted but constrained, we have maiden plots.[54] When even marriage is too permissive, we have chastity plots. It is the chastity plot as a compromise formation between pain and pleasure, sadism and transcendence, masochism and metamorphosis, that interests me. Radical chastity opposes both marriage and sexual license. In a struggle of will against the ease and comfort of the organism, the cult of sexual renunciation proposes an exalted notion of independence. As a model for human perfection, it has more enemies than friends. Like all cultural configurations of sexual desire, accommodating or inhibiting, chastity depends on its contradictions. Those contradictions are what I want to describe within the framework of this odd notion, a "chastity plot."

Both eunuch and maiden plots diverge from marriage plots. In most societies, the marriage plot is, if not the most popular, the dominant tradition. Greek and Roman moralists, from the time of Plato to the waning days of the empire, assumed the value of heterosexual marriage to society, even while they vacillated about its private and philosophical rewards. I cannot claim the same social benevolence for my plots, especially the theological ones I will be studying in detail in chapters 4 and 5. A career dedicated to abstention and renunciation, to the refusal of marriage and reproduction, is generally at odds with the norm, difficult to fit into the institutions that occupy the center of the social stage. But that anomaly doesn't make it illegible, as I hope to show. An aspiration to sexual purity and avoidance can represent a countertradition. It can be expressed through exceptional or deviant patterns. Ascetic plots are forms through which lives are designed and justified. This is a point that the late work of Michel Foucault helps make perspicuous.[55] In the writings of a number of third- and fourth-century church fathers, as in the careful specifications of John Cassian addressed to monks in fourth-century France, Foucault observes the shaping of the "arts of virginity," the Christian ascetic's development of a project he describes as a spiritual and practical "work on the self." Foucault's categories happily mirror mine. What I call eunuch plots are experiential models, patterns to imitate and reflect on, symbolic designs that present the values and parameters of a life imagined as alternative to the "worldly" patterns to which most of us, early Christians or modern individuals, conform: map of courtship and the pursuit of love, maps of apprenticeship and achievement, education and mastery. Those who choose chastity as a career and a calling are separating themselves from the norms most of us accept. The narratives that make sense of their lives—the plots of a Thecla or a Eustochium, a Hippolytus or an Elizabeth Tudor or a Clarissa—escape some normalizing pressures but often at the price of provoking suspicion or disbelief. Can it really be true that some people prefer sexual renunciation to sexual happiness? The desert to the home or the palace? What do they think is gained by their sacrifice and their peculiar passion?

If chastity is, in some sense, antisocial (it is at odds with the power of the family and in some of my instances sharply critical of patriarchy), it does not exist in isolation from the social. Few chastity plots flourish in the absence of some communal support, institutional formation or public recognition. The advocacy of religion has been crucial, hedging the provocation that the chaste represent, translating it into terms the mainstream can tolerate. Institutions such as convents, cloisters, and monasteries regularize the choice of celibacy, providing a context for the deviance of the ascetic, if one that is vulnerable to outbursts of intolerance, some which have been as prolonged as the anticlerical campaigns of the "Reformers" in early modern Europe. Hostility to sacerdotal celibacy became a way Protestant reaction could define itself, an important rallying point in an era when shared doctrines were scarce among the breakaway sects and new religious practices still unformed. God and the saints were not easy for the Reformers to attack. Monks and nuns were another story. Sexual purity, repudiation of marriage and childbearing, these were oddities that Christians had been expected to admire as mysteries, elements in the special vocation of the religious. These "oddities" were the secrets of the Roman church's inner life, marking the wall between the spiritual and the profane, the gifted and the ordinary.[56] But what if they were rather signs of hypocrisy, blatant distortions of an original conception of Christian excellence, abuses that corrupt ecclesiastics imposed on a gullible population? Such were the objections early modern critics began to raise against the Christian chastity plot, as "holy matrimony" acquired a new respectability in the advocacy of Martin Luther and John Calvin. But the transition from the awe inspired by the celibate to the honor dedicated to the monogamously and decorously married was not a smooth transition.

The history of the Reformation is just one instance of a phenomenon I want to emphasize. Asceticism attracts violence. It is also a type of violence. Asceticism is violence contained, made self-directed, subtle, and reactive, as Nietzsche complained. Eros converted into denial is still eros and still imperious. Like the eros that aims at release, like the libidinal energy that pursues everywhere it can the means for its expenditure, the eros of the ascetic is multiple and circuitous. We observe such circuitousness in the careers of the ascetic virtuosi celebrated by the Christians of the second to sixth centuries, the heroes of the desert, the warriors against the flesh who fled the cities and their temptations, who competed to trim their appetites and needs down to nothing. On one reading, the Christian chastity plot was conceived as a battle plan against the rule of the demons. Sex and marriage had certainly been approved by the Creator. But with virginity and renunciation as practices cultivated in some of the communities of the Eastern Mediterranean (Syria, Egypt, Asia Minor being leaders in the movement), Christians recognized that a merciful Lord was offering a new option. Touched by the misery of creatures consigned to degradation by the tyranny of lust, God was willing to compromise on the command "Be fruitful and multiply." Some Christians wondered whether sexual desire itself had been God's punishment for our disobedience rather than the cause of that Fall. We had been designed as equals to the angels. But after Eden, we reproduce like beasts, stigmatized and mortified by our carnal imperatives. Enslaved by our appetites, how can we be free? Pagan philosophers had wondered as much. Christian ascetics took the battle further, arguing that extirpation of the passions—undoing the concupiscent self—could remake the history of the world, reopening the gates to paradisal innocence. That too, I will argue, was a violent plot.

The ascetic's program for self-improvement was a distinctive way of imagining excellence. It was also a means to acquire authority. It deviated from conventional moral and social norms because it made a virtue out of the attempt to escape the body, to put sensuality, domesticity, and social reproduction at a distance. Sometimes it did so by cultivating extreme states of pain and isolation, legitimated as "holiness." As one would expect from a countertradition, the values of ascetic virtuosity were and are difficult to communicate. They defy easy intelligibility. Such is not the case for the marriage-and-love tradition. It is easy to like, or at least easy to read about. Marriage plots, some of the most popular and prestigious forms of modern storytelling we know, rely on the promise of satisfaction as alternately promised and withheld, until it is finally (institutionally, publicly) sanctified. If lovers reach their goal too quickly, there is no plot. If satisfaction never arrives, there is no marriage. Marriage is a plot in other senses as well. Marriage tames the anarchy of the sexual instincts. If it does so through prohibitions not obviously conducive to the sensual happiness of its practitioners ("wedlock as deadlock"), it succeeds by making social stability seem an acceptable compensation for the sacrifice it requires. That is the ideological task of marriage. The marriage plot in fiction performs an invaluable service in promoting this task, giving shape and glamour to the dominant social tradition. But the marriage plot can also stimulate countertraditions, as one astute critic points out, arguing that "the very act of deciphering the many plots by which social ideologies of love and sexuality have given shape to another novelistic marriage tradition uncovers a simultaneous counter-narrative: the persistent 'undoing' of the dominant tradition by the contradictions concealed within the specific forms that its representations of 'life' and 'love' have assumed."[57]

Given that the confinement of sexual activity within marriage represents a renunciation that might be unwelcome, that restriction needs to be made more palatable. Hence the significance of romantic love. The greater the value of the sexual object, the more renunciation loses its painful aspect. For marriage to become the subject of narrative enthusiasm as it did in European literature since the early 1800s, the love object needed considerable propping up. The literature of "true love" obliged. Romantic love, an erotic and spiritual rapture that for a very long time few people had ever seen or heard of, acquired a good many of the myths and conventions we associate with the love-and-marriage tradition from an essentially adulterous ideal, that of courtly love. Passion ennobles, said the knights and the troubadours. Chasing the beloved makes her more and more valuable. The more inaccessible she is (it tends to be a she), the worthier to be desired. Companionate affection, another recent innovation, was blessed by Protestant husbands such as Luther and John Milton. Classical theorists of marriage, such as Aristotle or the Stoics, had been skeptical about extending the possibilities of friendship to women. The arrangement between husbands and wives was for many moralists in antiquity a utilitarian if socially sanctioned practice: true meeting of the minds had to happen between men. With the Puritan affirmation of *friendship* as one of the justifications for marriage, the marriage plot deepened, taking on a central role as guardian and supervisor of the moral goods a godly society offers its members. "I am for having everybody marry," says Sir Charles Grandison, the perfect hero of Samuel Richardson's eponymous 1753 novel.[58] Marriage is, if not "the whole duty of man," certainly a major part of that duty for the devout Protestant. Finding one's mate, one's counterpart, could be critically important to the fate of the soul. The pious conjugal couple were not to disdain sexual activity but to practice it with reverence and dignity. "Esteem enlivened by desire," was the way the eighteenth-century Scottish minister and poet James Thomson described the goal of marital friendship and love.[59] This, rather than licit copulation or procreation, gave a certain sheen to the ideal of marriage, sufficient to keep its prestige high among readers of novels and, we assume, among the married.

Narrative Desire and the Making of a Chastity Plot

Plot can also mean conspiracy or intrigue. In the seventh definition offered by the *Oxford English Dictionary, plot* means "a plan or project, secretly contrived by one or more persons, to accomplish some wicked, criminal or illegal purpose; a conspiracy." Is there a conspiracy against desire? No research into the history and currency of chastity can afford to avoid this question. No amount of research can adequately resolve it. Nietzsche and Freud, two of my constant companions in theorizing this project, would probably accept the conspiratorial metaphor, adding that the secret and malevolent purpose is one we harbor ourselves, and that the project of "civilized sexual morality" is a campaign against pleasure that gives us pleasure (even if it shouldn't), and that "ascetic" animals find their health and flourishing in some odd places. Where there is power, Foucault wrote in a related context, there is resistance. Chastity plots are emplotments of resistance, which means they can, in some ethical or pedagogical versions, assume a prior state—of indulgence, of natural carelessness, of life without shape or rigor—which the engines of resistance intend to correct. But chastity plots also create their own romance, where virtue is taken into sublime and otherworldly directions, where new heroes and heroines appear: athletes of self-denial, angelic paragons that sprinkle the history of fiction with their own dubious sheen. If one impulse of the literary chastity plot leads to the heroic virgin, majestic in his or her principled resistance, another lures it toward the saccharine precincts of the "Angel in the House." Such ambivalence within the chastity ideal is central to my case. Also relevant to it is another discovery I owe to aesthetics rather than ethics, although it is one Freud and Nietzsche made before me: frustration can be a source of aesthetic delight. There is energy in denial.

There is also, of course, energy in sex. Civilization needs the impetus of the devouring drives of the young and sexy; it needs by the same token to devour them. One of literature's great devouring machines is eros, the manifestation of sex unbridled, eros the cruel and whimsical god or the goddess who must be worshipped. Not everyone will agree to worship. The characters in my chastity plots that refuse to pay such a tribute are an interesting lot. When the chaste are sanctioned by a religious community (as are the "magical ascetics" or "religious virtuosi" of whom Max Weber writes), their renunciation of sex and marriage can be admired. Even if these deserters from sex and reproduction remain at the margins of society, they can be accepted as society's debt to those strange antierotic forces that would otherwise destroy the species. However, there is also real danger in saying no. Unsanctioned by the sacred, chastity plots lead to trouble. The veneer of civility is thin, when it is a question of the war between eros and its opponents. Renunciation, which appears to defend the self from the chaos of desire, turns against its subject. So, too, does orgiastic desire, whose ultimate irony is that extinction and consummation look almost indistinguishable. Freud discovered this duality when (with a certain push from his reading of Schopenhauer) he pushed his own thinking "beyond the pleasure principle." Freud acknowledged that his quest was full of risk. The death-drive was a discovery he wished he didn't have to make. Extirpating desire can lead to the condition of "death-in-life."[60] Here Freud believed he had located in civilization as well as in nature the prolongation of a will to deny and decline, an entropic destination. When cultural development was unchecked by life's resilience, or countered by a faith in desire and the senses, then humanity could embrace its own defeat. In a work that has deeply influenced my understanding of literary plot, the Freudian critic Peter Brooks borrows the language of Honoré de Balzac to describe the last stage of narrative desire. "Beyond the pleasure principle" is a "castrated imagination," which is "ultimately, inexorably, desire *for* the end," the decadent's desire to desire no more.[61]

Generally, the impulse of plot works to keep desire alive, to stir things up, to keep change on the boil. And that is a good thing. Under the pull of desire, situations otherwise indifferent become charged with meaning; events matter, and intentions wake up and become actions; incidents fall into place according to an organizing dynamic, for which Peter Brooks uses the grand term the "logic of narrative discourse." Yet the literary context, suggestive as it is, does not exhaust the connotations of the chastity "plot." Outside the realm of narrative or drama, "plot" means something more like "conspiracy," machination, or secret plan, usually the kind of scheme a small and furtive group concocts, for purposes that need a certain amount of concealment, as they are likely to be hostile or illegal, like Guy Fawkes's Gunpowder Plot. In our case, if there is a "chastity plot," it might be both furtive and conspicuous, deliberate and disavowed. Like Guy Fawkes's plot, the cultural swerve toward chastity has political objectives. "Everyone knows that patriarchy has always loved a virgin," writes the literary historian Corrinne Harol, "for reasons that appear to be transparent . . . virgins help patriarchy reproduce itself."[62] Minds well versed in what "everyone knows" will see in the chastity plot a grand scheme to control patrilineal inheritance, on the grounds that families who exchange their virgin daughters believe they are investing in the stability and transparency of the lines of descent: a pure maiden, expected to become a chaste (if nonvirginal) wife, won't intrude bastards into the nest and will protect the honor of the family name.[63]

The relationship between desire and plot is unstable, generatively so. Desires can be legitimate and still animate plots; they can be illegitimate and animate other plots; they can be conscious or unconscious. In the patriarchal chastity plot, accordingly, female desire must be subdued if it is too demanding, deflected if it threatens to disturb the order of the family. Some plots kindle at the merest hint of an unruly passion; others invest heavily in passion's suppression, punishing the unruly and chastening the impulsive. But in all cases the dynamics of narrative have a persistent attraction to desire. When desire is present, the succession of events generates an orientation and a force; it becomes a story.

Resisting desire has a high reputation as a philosophical ideal. It seems, however, a poor choice for a plot. That is true even when the desire at stake is not sexual. We could consider the case of Shakespeare's Hamlet, who struggled with the problem of how to get action under way. He was better at detecting plots than hatching them. Passion, Hamlet reflects in act 2, scene 2 of the eponymous play, is generally sufficient to push us here and there, into trouble and, less often, out. A tepid temper may resist longer; an equivocator can ignore the promptings of anger or desire or ambition. The moment passes, the plot remains asleep. If plot is, in Aristotelian terms, the "weaving together" of things and actions, then the good ones—the complex ones (*Poetics*, 1451b–1452a)—often show their merits by the way they use the weaving of desire to structure anticipation and reward readerly or spectatorial investment. Without the suturing of desire, narrative fictions can collapse into the merely episodic. Or worse, the static. To resist desire would be to stand still, to make nothing happen.

In laying down the rules for poetics, Aristotle made inaction into an impediment. To know, to intend, and not to act, Aristotle says, is loathsome. It is better to act without knowing than to know and not act. Eros, of course, is notorious as the motive for action whose promptings can often be at war with knowledge. Provoked by desire, one does not estimate the consequences; I chase the beloved even if the beloved's feelings about me are opaque: I wager all on a moment's reward. Eros is profligate. And the more complex the motives involved, the more the story goes on.

Morality and plotting are often entwined in traditional narratives, the hero or heroine being the one whose moral integrity survives trials or suspicion, as happens in quest romances or in the tragedies of male jealousy such as *Othello*. The chastity plot is no exception: it foregrounds a debate about morality. Some chastity plots involve the sordid business of contesting and sullying the virtue of a character put forward as a paragon. Others follow the rake's interest in offending the innocent and corrupting the pure. These rake or "seduction plots" are conventionally formulated by men exercising their power against women (Tarquin and Lucretia, Lovelace and Clarissa), less often by women against men (Potiphar's wife and Joseph, Phaedra and Hippolytus). Tragedies of seduction favor the gothic and melodramatic modes, with innocent and pure women (whether maidens or wives) subjected to violence, humiliation, or—even worse—successful persuasion.[64] I am interested in this narrative tradition (sometimes called "the tested woman plot") because of what it reveals about notions of female and male behavior, even if that revelation is predictably conventional, as are the motives for the testing of chastity. There is, by contrast, something else in the tradition that is genuinely mysterious. Innocence and chastity, we might want to say, are grander than the practiced seducer suspects and more important than the jealous husband believes. In the sociosexual plot, they figure as rare commodities, increasing the value of the women whose bodies are exchanged in a marriage market or competition for masculine prestige. But in a mythic or romance plot, they are the tokens of an integrity nobody has but everyone desires. What is important to the epic adventurer or the culture hero is "saving" a people, recovering a home, converting the unknown into the known. What is important to the romance hero is a more magical and elusive type of "safety": not mastery of the world but an inner truth, a freedom from contingency and vulnerability, a way of being true to oneself or true to one's ideal. The figure of the virgin matters because, as Northrop Frye put it, a mystery is lodged in her which otherwise would have no tangible correlative. It is the "secret of invulnerability" which is "symbolized" in the figure of the virgin:

> Deep within the stock convention of virgin-baiting is a vision of human integrity imprisoned in a world it is in but not of, often forced by weakness into all sorts of ruses and stratagems, yet always managing to avoid the one fate which really is worse than death, the annihilation of one's identity.... What is symbolized as a virgin is actually a human conviction, however expressed, that there is something at the core of one's infinitely fragile being which is not only immortal but has discovered the secret of invulnerability that eludes the tragic hero.[65]

I would like to adopt for my own purposes Frye's reading of the romance heroine, the steadfast virgin who might otherwise be banished from serious attention because of her conventionality, the triviality of the way the world imagines her moral excellence or dismisses it as prudery.

The virgin's battle against her slanderers and seducers is not, in every sense, banal. There is in it the hint of something else, the fantasy of an integrity so innate as to be untouchable, an identity resilient against all doubt, something both craved and despaired of.[66] The mystique of virginity, if this interpretation holds, expresses not so much an aversion to sex as a recurrent yearning for an autonomy none of us can sustain.

Most plots promise drama and intrigue. The chastity plot hides its explosive intentions behind a veneer of sobriety. Force will at times be called upon, but generally the incitement of chastity operates through an inward mechanism, encouraging a taste for denial that promises to compensate for other frustrated impulses. Ascetic ideals are experiments in a different register of meaning, a different way of distinguishing good from bad, weak from strong, beauty from ugliness. Here the soul, as Foucault put it, has imprisoned the body.

The first of my stories is that of a young male virgin, a prince and the son of an Amazon. He worships Artemis, the violent goddess of chastity, and he is destroyed by his contempt for Aphrodite, the violent goddess of love. The Greeks, who knew Hippolytus's myth, believed he was wrong. His story was a lesson to others not to strive for the kind of virtue that despises the social and condescends to sensual needs. (Christians, also deeply versed in stories about virgins, came to the opposite conclusion, at least for a while.) Euripides's tale of the marriage plot rejected, the virgin doomed, is where I want to begin.

✷ 2 ✷

Virginity and Terror

READING *HIPPOLYTUS*

"Naked" or "pure" sexuality is directly connected to violence. It is the final veil shielding violence from sight; at the same time it is the beginning of violence's revelation.

RENÉ GIRARD, *Violence and the Sacred*

The sexual sensations have this in common with the sensations of sympathy and worship, that one person, by doing what pleases him, gives pleasure to another person—such benevolent arrangements are not to be found so very often in nature!

FRIEDRICH NIETZSCHE, *Daybreak*

The Olympian Chastity Plot: Introducing Hippolytus

In 428 BCE Euripides won the prize at the Athenian festival of the Dionysia for his play about Phaedra and Hippolytus, the first an unhappy woman burning with love for her stepson, the second a young man passionate about wild things, smitten by the purity of nature in the raw. The story was well known to its audience.[1] Hippolytus, the son of King Theseus and Hippolyta the queen of the Amazons, was a name to make admirers of chastity think twice. Hippolytus wanted to live and die a virgin, unbothered by women, marriage, children, and the ordinary baggage of domestic existence. His ideal leads him to disgrace and ruin.

Spurning the demands of Aphrodite, the youth adores a rival deity, the virgin huntress Artemis. To humiliate the blasphemer, the goddess of love chooses a circuitous plan. Aphrodite feeds a degrading passion into the veins of a virtuous woman. Phaedra, the modest and retiring mother and wife, is the unknowing victim of the Cyprian's plot. She is a sacrifice Aphrodite does not scruple to make. If Hippolytus must fall, so must his stepmother. Both mortals wanted to be virtuous and controlled. Both loved what they understood as moderation. Their ends were also similar—violent, shocking, messy, their bodies bruised and disfigured. Does that mean that the deities they revere are also similar? On the stage, in view of the audience, are placed two statues, one of Aphrodite, standing close to the door of the palace in Troezen shared by Phaedra and Hippolytus; the other of Artemis.[2] Represented by their images, the goddesses receive the tributes offered by the pious.[3] Those who are sensible will find reasons to adore both these proud immortals. Yet love and chastity do not get on well together. Their conflict is pitiless. Sexual passion, we have often been told, can be savage and imperious. We are not surprised at Aphrodite's cruelty. Chastity is also cruel, also dangerous. This is an idea that is less familiar.

Before the action of the play opens, the audience knows that Phaedra has fallen hopelessly in love with Hippolytus, who disdains her. Unable to speak of the passion destroying her, Phaedra wants to die. She is horrified by the fact that her desire has damaged what she believed she knew about herself. If her identity rested in her unblemished and irreproachable sophrosyne, what can remain of that self now? Retreating from the eyes of others, Phaedra tries to lock herself in her room and starve herself to death, hoping that thereby her secret would remain forever concealed. Her nurse, who loves her and cannot bear to see her misery, betrays her mistress's confidence to the young prude. Shocked, Hippolytus rebuffs any idea of satisfying her desire. He loves only wild things and the hunt; he serves the virgin goddess Artemis, who will not let anyone get close. And he hates women. But he is a person of integrity. He takes an oath never to reveal the shameful story of Phaedra's incestuous passion to his father.

The situation in the palace of Troezen moves quickly from misunderstanding to catastrophe. Phaedra is convinced that Hippolytus, to whom she has not even spoken, will expose her to Theseus when the king returns to his palace. Distraught, half dead with starvation, fatigue, and self-hatred, she hangs herself. She leaves her corpse as an indictment, her offended body tied by a noose to her bedroom ceiling, a note tied to her breast accusing the young man of rape. Theseus curses his son, and Hippolytus refuses to defend himself. Doomed by the anger of his father who has called on the sea god Poseidon to assist his revenge, Hippolytus dies in agony, his body ripped apart by his terrified horses. And Artemis, coming too late to console her devotee, lets Theseus know the tragic error he has made. Now Theseus, the great womanizer, heroic vanquisher of the Minotaur, companion of Heracles, Athens's king and the Amazons' conqueror, has lost everything.

To be desired by a woman horrified Hippolytus. The crime of incest played only a minor part in his repulsion. That horror was his ruin. Sexual purity is a bitter boon: it hurts those who come into its path and deforms those who dedicate themselves to it. The medicine the pure take to purge their souls has more than one effect. Expelling the libido, it opens up a space for other moral toxins—self-righteousness, arrogance, and insensitivity.[4] Chastity's potential for mischief makes lust look benign. This is a thought Euripides makes us consider. The end of the tragedy is violent and devastating. Those who cared about their honor are dishonored—and dead. Others carry on their lives through aggression and cunning (Theseus, Phaedra's wily nurse). They are alive but grieving.

In the many years the story has lingered in the mind of the West, most of the sympathy and much of the shock has concentrated around Phaedra. For me, it is Hippolytus who matters. Suspended between the world of men and the world of women, between childhood and maturity, Hippolytus remains frighteningly alone. There was no room in ancient Greek society for the conception of virginal masculinity he held sacred.[5] Prior to marriage young women and girls were expected to remain chaste, if they came from "good" families and were citizens; young men, who often did not marry until they were close to thirty years of age, could find their sexual attachments among other men, slaves, prostitutes, or concubines.[6] But a life devoted to the discipline of virginity was unprecedented for a male: was he naïve? Monstrous? Stupid? At Hippolytus's age, the time was right to complete his education, to persevere with (in the classicist Froma Zeitlin's words) "the initiatory scenario that would have him pass from the yoking of horses to the yoking of maidens, from the hunting of game to the hunting of a wife."[7] The social life was the honorable life, and this entailed marriage and procreation, ideally to be practiced with the proper manly virtue of self-control, sophrosyne. But Hippolytus's love for chastity didn't seem so self-controlled. To unsympathetic ears it sounded like a fantastic aberration, raising suspicions of sorcery, manic possession, or—in the opinion of the more coolheaded observers—bad faith. If he had been born later, he might not have felt so isolated. History has a sense of irony. For the adolescent Hippolytus at his pagan altars, chastity proved a mirage. The Greeks looked at the passion for virginity and saw hysteria.[8] Christians found a way to make it last longer and dig deeper. But they worshipped Christ, a male virgin, not Hippolytus's beloved Artemis, the "witch-goddess" thrown out of her temples and denounced as a demon and an idol by a furious Saint Paul at Ephesus. Young men and women excited by Paul dreamed of the unsullied life. Aphrodite, if she knew, chose to ignore them.

Greek audiences went to see Euripides's play to learn that male sexual purity makes a poor substitute for a life of self-knowledge and virtue. A wise person must submit to the same norms as everyone else. That is the virtue the city needs, not wild ethical innovations like puritanical chastity. The power of eros is to be respected; it will outlive this city and the cities to come. Its rule does not admit of exceptions, no matter how high-minded. For those of us in the mortal condition, it is irreverent to dream of eros's demise and futile (or perverse) to live alienated from eros. We know why Hippolytus is considered a traitor against sexual desire. Why does Phaedra have to be a victim, too?

Phaedra's Story: Sophrosyne Divided

σωφροσύνη, (*sophrosyne*) I: *soundness of mind, moderation, discretion,* also *sense of shame, bashfulness, modesty; self-control, temperance, chastity, sobriety; a sense of shame* or *honour; regard for others, respect, reverence; awe, self-respect, regard.*

Liddell and Scott's Greek-English Lexicon

Phaedra is caught in Aphrodite's plot against the deviant who will not bend the knee. Wracked by the shame of her adulterous and incestuous desire, Phaedra cries for a death in cold running water. She wishes she could flee to the mountains and the woods; barely able to stand or walk, she calls for her bed to be moved outside the house, into the open air, where she might be broken by hunting dogs and wild racing horses (*Hipp.* 228–31).[9] She calls for Artemis, queen of the wild and innocent places (*Hipp.* 228–31). Artemis, however, can't come to her aid. For Phaedra is married and a mother. She belongs to the city and the family, and her shame is perfectly intelligible by the standards of family and city. If her secret desire were to be exposed, she would cause a scandal, disgracing the marital bed. Cretan women, according to Greek gossip, were prone to sexual excess. And Phaedra comes from a family whose flamboyant lust and lack of sophrosyne is well known. Yet it is sophrosyne that Phaedra invokes as the reason for the most criminal of her actions, when she accuses the innocent Hippolytus of raping her. Frantic as she is, she knows that her best course of action would have been to remain silent, to go to her grave repressing her desire and hiding her secret. But an impulsive wish for comfort and sympathy has made this impossible. Her nurse has found out her guilty thoughts and communicated them to Phaedra's prudish stepson. Phaedra can save her honor only by besmirching Hippolytus's, by blaming him for her shame. By this ruse she can leave her family convinced of her good reputation and good name, still a picture of sophrosyne, an example of chaste fastidiousness.[10]

As Phaedra says proudly, she is "*sophron*," an exemplar among women. But what is it to be *sophron*, and why would it give Aphrodite the opportunity for her devious revenge? What Phaedra means is that she has a good reputation, a good name (*Hipp.* 717). She has a need to be conspicuously *sophron* because, as she says (*Hipp.* 337–39), she comes from a messy lineage. Her father, King Minos, was sired by Zeus in the form of a bull, which the king of the gods considered the right way to approach Europa; her mother, Pasiphaë, in some versions the daughter of the sun, was struck by Aphrodite with a passion for a beautiful white bull that Minos refused to sacrifice to Poseidon, and her half brother was a monstrous Minotaur. Her sister, Ariadne, previously the partner of Theseus, Phaedra's husband, helped the roving-eyed hero escape the labyrinth but was abandoned by him on the island of Naxos, becoming there the bride of Dionysus.

Sophrosyne, a virtue widely admired in Greek and Roman antiquity, meant something like temperance or self-control. Etymologically it means "having a safe mind." It was commonly used to signify sexual forbearance in both men and women. Sophrosyne is a virtue claimed in Euripides's tragedy by both men and women. In the Greek city, to be *sophron* was the pride and ornament of the citizen and statesman. At the same time, sophrosyne is the virtue that protects feminine discretion and preserves the honor of husband and father.[11] It is the honor for which "good women" could be known without damaging their social position and their essential marginality. The *sophron* woman is a docile, obedient, prudent wife whose pleasure it is to remain at home, who doesn't get herself spoken about and is sparing with words, who slips away when other women are gossiping lasciviously, as they like to do.

To be *sophron*, you need to be sensitive to *aidos*, shame. Shame is crucial. Fear of shame awakens the ethical forces within, mobilizing the will to achievement and noble action; the moral life of ancient Greece would be unintelligible without it. Certainly concern for the way one appears to others is part of the way shame educates the moral character. It bonds the individual to the view and judgment of others. But since it is also experienced through a private, perhaps invisible, wave of anguish and embarrassment, shame tells me that I cannot escape from myself. Shamed, I am exposed in two directions at once. In his classic *Shame and Necessity*, Bernard Williams clarifies: Guilt looks to what I have done, how I have hurt others or let them down. Shame looks to how I have fallen short of what I hoped to be:

> The basic experience connected with shame is that of being seen, inappropriately, by the wrong people, in the wrong condition. It is straightforwardly connected to nakedness, particularly in sexual connections.... Shame looks to what I am. It can be occasioned by many things—actions,... or thoughts or desires or the reactions of others.... Shame embodies conceptions of what one is and how one is related to others.[12]

Who judges my moral success and failures? Religious and moral thought in antiquity puzzles about the duality in an ideal as central as sophrosyne. Is self-denial strong or weak? What does it mean for those who are used to mastering, or for those who are used to submitting? Is it manly to be anxious about one's reputation, to be sensitive to how one appears to others? If moderation is virile (as most experts argue), then sexual excess, cruelty, and anger are weaknesses, considered even to be feminizing. But then how does the phallic male demonstrate his undeniable prestige? Aristotle in his work on ethics has the clearest reply: it is not manly to over-indulge in pleasures. Rather, it is bestial or slavish. "Excess with regard to pleasures is self-indulgence (*akolasia*) and is culpable." Being motivated solely by one's desires for what is pleasurable is the mark of the immature. Hence persistent chasing after tasty things to eat or carnal indulgences are the habits of the lowly man. What makes the intemperate man weak (and "unmanly") is his childish inability to cope with minor frustrations, while the manly, temperate man does not feel pain at the absence of pleasure, nor does abstinence make him suffer.[13]

The two antagonists of Euripides's tragedy worry about who they are and how they appear. They want to be virtuous; they compete in the arena of self-control; they long to be proven right. But their competition destroys them. They share an ideal. And it is that ideal that divides them. As Anne Carson neatly explains, "If you asked Hippolytos to name his system he would say 'shame.' Oddly, if you asked Phaidra to name her system she would also say 'shame.' They do not mean the same thing by this word. Or perhaps they do. Too bad they never talk."[14]

Ethically scrupulous, precise in her concern for her good name and flawless reputation (*eukleia*), Phaedra is sincere in her struggle for self-control (*Hipp.* 375–81, 399) even if circumstances steal the rewards of that self-control from her.[15] But her young male antagonist also insists on his own achievement (*Hipp.* 995, 1008. 1034–35, 1100, 1364–65). Both Phaedra and Hippolytus go to their deaths as champions of a moral ideal which, the play suggests, they may have failed to understand or, as Hippolytus generously confesses in his last moments of agony, to use fruitfully (*Hipp.* 1034–35). Maybe eros could have taught them more about human limitations and needs, about abandoning oneself without calculation to emotions of care, compassion, generosity. Maybe they needed to consult Dionysus about the rights of the irrational. Maybe it is not *sophron* to resist the common lot of gods and men. Caught in the web the jealous Aphrodite has fashioned, Phaedra puzzles about our human ability to know and do what is right. More narrowly, as she argues to herself, the meaning of *aidos* is unclear and confusing. *Aidos* is the ideal attribute of those noble by nature and birth.[16] It is the virtue she yearns to represent, and the virtue young Hippolytus believed he could preserve only by fleeing society to race in uncut meadows with unmarriageable virgin deities.

The difficulty is that *aidos* comes in more than one form. There is a "fold" in the structure of shame, we are told in Barbara Cassin's *Dictionary of Untranslatables*. Phaedra "does not know in which direction (honor or dishonor) *aidos* will incline her love for Hippolytus."[17] Like the Latin *pudor*, the Greek term can mean a sense of shame, propriety, self-respect, all good things to have. If *aidos* is present, then dignity and circumspection can be expected, and the messy area of conduct is in safe hands. But *aidos*, as Phaedra has discovered, can equally refer to the very thing that causes dishonor, that "destroys houses" (*Hipp.* 385–87). As Hesiod put it, "Shame is sometimes a blessing, sometimes a curse."[18] It refers to the prudish and the erotic, to blushing and also to scandal. *Aidoia*, the plural of *aidos*, is used as a euphemism for the genitals (the "shameful parts," Homer, *Iliad* 2.262), like the Latin *pudenda*.

Ambivalent at best, the ideal of leading a life that insulates you against shame would seem to be threatened by an uncertainty about the meaning of words. For the play's antagonists, it is impossible to agree about the true conditions for moral excellence, the source and safeguards of our fragile, unreliable strivings to be good. Is it nature? Is it nurture? Hippolytus insists that modesty and chastity belong only to those who possess them by nature and birth (*Hipp.* 78–80, 400–401); Phaedra rests her confidence in her own restraint on the way she has been taught, on her training, diligence and practice, on her sensitivity to environment and culture. She knows what is right even if she cannot always do it (*Hipp.* 380–81): shame and honor are her guiding principles. For a woman, even one inflamed by inadmissible passions, it should be possible to achieve honor (*time*; *Hipp.* 329–31) through self-mastery, which Phaedra understands as the need to bury her guilty secret in silence and concealment.

The argument about the relative values of nature or nurture is a hot issue for the fifth century BCE city as it struggles to shift an aristocratic system of values into a rougher democratic terrain. Self-elected as the companion of a goddess, Hippolytus has little time for the prejudices of the crowd, the conventions of the demos. Yet it is not easy for anyone to forget the unusual facts of his genealogy, nor to be sure about the legitimacy of his parents' marriage, and such doubts are a problem for him. Hippolytus is pure by nature and from birth, he boasts. His nobility has all the extravagant recklessness of the arrogant upper classes and of youth. Never will he lie or break a vow, not to save all that is most precious in the world, nor for charity or humanity or love or even for reason. Phaedra, on the other hand, tries to adopt the strategies of the new, relativistic middle classes, so cunningly formulated for her by her nurse. But she fails. At bottom it is Hippolytus's morality that she believes in and betrays: it is that morality which provides the only inner life she can recognize in herself; he is, as Zeitlin points out, her mirror, her original self, all she depends on. It is that self that is torn from her by her involuntary erotic mania. When Hippolytus can't bear even to look at her, Phaedra acknowledges that the self she meant to be is no more. So why should his survive? Their parasitic intertwinement has sucked the life out of each of them; he, she curses, will "share my disease" (*Hipp.* 730–31).

Phaedra's final words, as she leaves the scene to prepare her own death by hanging,[19] are a bitter indictment of the young man who has rejected her with contempt and horror: "He will learn of *sophrosyne* in moderation (*Hipp.* 732)." Hippolytus dies on the stage. Since he is male, not female, he does not need to hide his agonies, but his display of them brings him closer to the sacrificial victim than to the brave hero. (Greek heroes are never shown in death or even being hurt.) In his painful speeches to his father, trying to explain himself without betraying his vow of silence to Phaedra, he reflects on the ethical instruction of sophrosyne. Now that he is aware of its ambiguity, his words show a deeper, more painful understanding of Phaedra's dilemma and his own: She showed sophrosyne, self-control, but was not able to be chaste, *sophron*; I had sophrosyne but was not able to use it in a beneficial way (*Hipp.* 1034–35). Gender divides their respective performance of this ideal and guides it with an iron hand. For a woman, to be *sophron* is, in the great majority of cases, to be sexually pure and modest. It is rare for that to be the criterion of sophrosyne for a man. Yet this is one of the messages of the play: male purity and female purity collide, offering yet another way for the sexes to be at war.

Phaedra's enigmatic meditation on the feminine propriety that has defined her life and her bid for lasting glory is prophetic. Phaedra's vulnerability does not lie in her guilty desire, as readers of Jean Racine or Sigmund Freud would suspect. Her doomed love does trouble the social order, but this is still something that order can handle; it is, like parent-child incest, a story that comes around every generation. What makes Phaedra vulnerable, and complicit in her own catastrophe, is her desire for moral rectitude, her excessive hunger for temperance.[20] Worrying about shame, about "how you appear," is certainly "the woman's part," in ancient as in modern societies. Descendant of a family who mates with bulls, Phaedra might have been at home with wild things. But she is not. Manipulated by Aphrodite, disdained by Artemis, Phaedra creeps into her corner. Her role is to be a witness to the games of the gods, a sacrifice to their brutal competitions. In the more than two thousand years since her death, Phaedra the burning stepmother has become a byword for transgressive passion. Nothing could be more ironic.

Artemis and Her Cult

Fifteen thousand people, more or less, would have been in the audience for the first performance of *Hippolytus*. If the play had been presented at Ephesus, as part of the festival of the Great Goddess who was patron of that city, Artemis could have reigned alone, her worship unchallenged. But this is Athens. Virgin goddesses have to share honors with others. The scene is polarized by sex and virginity, the bed versus the hunt. Is it a dual sovereignty? These goddesses don't get along. Jealous of their prestige, the seductress and the tomboy fight it out. One uses intrigue, the other a bow and arrow.[21]

Murderous and virginal, huntress and maiden, Artemis is the goddess of the untamed world and of the young who have not yet been integrated into society. On the other hand, she is also deeply tied to the sphere of women, whether as a supervisor and inspiration for their lives as untouched virgins or as comforter and guardian of the crisis of childbirth. Protecting "the female body, whether closed or open," this goddess is double-natured to a fault.[22] Her dominion embraces the "intact" space of the maiden—described by Greeks as the "jar" with one end "stopped up"—and it embraces the generating body of the married woman, suffering her labor pains in the enclosure of the house. Is it an oxymoron, this way of being at once inside and outside, skittish and modest, pure and violent? Or is hers one single nature that doesn't compose itself in a single place or form but hovers on every boundary, every liminal space? All cultures know things like Artemis, odd and hard to classify, things that are not altogether dry and not altogether wet, neither savage nor civilized but somewhere in between.[23] In other contexts, Artemis has also been wor shipped as a goddess of fertility, not an obvious province for a maiden deity. But it is Artemis's intimate relations with the phenomena of the threshold that are relevant here. She belongs where there are events that initiate, that are primal and originary, with nature as it is unprocessed and fresh. (In the terms made famous by Claude Lévi-Strauss, Artemis stands for the "uncooked.") As patroness of fertility and childbirth, Artemis looks after the force that brings unexpected life out of those uncultivated regions of the human or natural world, just as the stirrings of puberty quicken life and urgency in the playful timelessness of childhood, or the pangs of labor break into the sleepy world of late pregnancy. All these outbreaks of energy are essential. Yet they can also be disturbing, abrupt, and harsh. And, as Hippolytus will find out, change makes human life precarious and exposed. The peaceful continuity of pastoral is a fantasy for beasts and the immature, not men and women.

In a series of lectures delivered at the Collège de France (1974–84), Jean-Pierre Vernant studied the cult of Artemis, the virgin sister of Apollo:

> She haunts all the other places the Greeks call *agros*, noncultivated lands that mark the boundaries of the territory, those *eschatiai* that lie beyond the fields.... Artemis, then, is not wildness. She sees to it that the boundaries between the wild and the civilized are permeable in some way, since the hunt allows passage from one state to the other. At the same time, however, these boundaries remain perfectly distinct, for if they were not, men would become savage.[24]

Artemis was worshipped as Mistress of the Animals (Attic: *Potnia Theron*) in the Minoan civilization well before Homer and as the Great Goddess in the sanctuary at Ephesus, present-day Turkey.[25] As a religious observance, her cult is probably older than that of Aphrodite.[26] It is bloodier, certainly more obscure. The arts of Artemis are hunting and war, activities of young men in packs, known as *ephebes*. Unusually for antiquity, the packs who run with Artemis include young women: athletic and virginal girls who hunt and dance in her ritual rounds. She spends her time with them, lets them see her. The Homeric Hymn to Aphrodite describes Artemis running wild in the mountains, her "love for the bow and slaying wild animals," and her love for "lyres and dancing and the piercing cries of women."[27] Although she thrives in solitude, she takes part willingly in the violent doings of men. Anything to do with a bow and arrow finds favor in her eyes and quickens her mood. The beasts she is intimate with are savage like her: bears, lions, panthers, deer, wolves, and horses. Her dress is rough as well: in the temple of Despoina her statue is dressed in the pelt of a deer. Always moving fast, difficult to catch, in and out of the wilderness, she presides over the path of the wanderer in unfamiliar places, and she sometimes exacts human sacrifices from those who need her help, as she does from Agamemnon, who was required to give his daughter Iphigeneia to the goddess's thirst for blood. Intimately associated with the pains of women in childbirth, Artemis also knows the pleasures of those other painful activities: athletic competition and battle. Given her affection for untamed animals, it is no wonder that she also protects children and those who look after them. In Laconia, a "festival of nurses"—the *Tithenidia*—was celebrated in her honor, and little boys were brought to pay tribute to the goddess. She is appealed to by women in labor to ease the pain of parturition with her gentle hands, and she also bears away those who die in childbirth. At her sanctuary in Elis, near a gymnasium where the ephebes play, Artemis receives one of her most appropriate titles: *philomeirax*, "friend of boys."[28]

Artemis is a nature deity, in that she cares for mountains, forests, streams, seacoasts, and swamps, not farms and orchards. Modern conservationists should be leaving offerings at her shrines and respecting her taboos. To be just toward the wild requires discipline and control. Even the hunter cannot perform his art without cooperation, restraint, and awe. That is what distinguishes hunting from butchery. Lines have to be drawn; initiates have to undergo a process of education, training, and self-discovery. For the young Greek man, hunting is an essential element of the *paideia* that integrates him into the city."[29] On the edges of social structures and norms, religious piety still governs the Greek relationship to the cosmos. Strangers approach the city from the outside and are potential foes; the gods insist that they be treated with hospitality, if they come as supplicants. Hostilities break out between peoples, threatening a reign of unrestricted, monstrous, "pure," violence: sacrifices must be offered, codes of engagement drawn up, so that the licit, sanctified violence may be shielded from the bad, anarchic violence. Females are the gods' cruel trick, a lawless but irresistible delight. They have to be carefully nurtured from their state of androgynous infancy into the docile creatures of the household; they have to be ushered into marriage through rites of initiation and gifts of appeasement. In the hunt, which steals from the wild, as in the ransoming of a maiden to bring to your bed, if something is taken away, something must be given back.

All of these exchanges have been supervised, in one myth or cult or another, by the goddess sister of Apollo. We know that Aphrodite's power is perennial. There has been no time in history oblivious to her effects and significance. Artemis, on the other hand, is a deity peculiarly sympathetic to modern feminist tastes. Her patronage liberates the idea of chastity from the suffocating interiors of domestic femininity and brings it back out into the open air. She promotes in our cultural memory the elusive, skittish figure of the tomboyish maiden, proud of her independence from the sexual yoke. To turn this into a divine role is something we can admire as a corrective and antidote to the confused doctrines of monotheistic prudery.

Yet what we learn from Artemis is the irreducibility of violence, its significance in the settled as in the unsettled life. A civilization that never lets the savage grow near is a civilization in danger of asphyxiation. The question is how to navigate the sacred and the savage, how to find the rituals that will both open the bounded city up to the energies of nature and respect its need for enclosure, for an artifice of integrity. Worshipping this goddess is one way of sustaining the ambiguity. To honor Artemis, you have to play seriously with wild animals, get under their skin, become so close to them that they may not be able to tell which is the animal and which not. Ritual effectiveness relies on such confusions. It also relies on death, which is to say, violent death, the kind that takes the body apart. The Victorian anthropologist Sir James Frazer found that gods, too, need to be sacrificed if sacred things are to remain pure. With *The Golden Bough* (1890–1915), Frazer begins the modern study of mythological comparison, and his very first image is the priest-king—as Frazer calls him, the "King of the Wood"—who tends the cult of Diana (Roman Artemis) on the shores of Lake Nemi, and who, coming as a stranger and an upstart, wins his kingship through murder. Legend has it that fragments of the great statue of Artemis were brought from Tauris by Orestes and Iphigenia. Thus the worship of the goddess in Italy began in this very grove. The worshippers clustered around a tree whose branches can't be broken: the Golden Bough. And the King of the Wood, who is isolated and outside the world of men, is a descendant of Hippolytus, or so Frazer prefers to believe.[30] The mysterious nature of the rites at Nemi is what starts Frazer's imagination going. Why this custom of sovereignty only gained through murder? Why must a stranger and foreigner be the only one who can consort with the tree that represents inviolability? It must have something to do with the unhappy martyrdom of Hippolytus, the illegitimate son of an Amazon, an outsider, who never got to be king of Athens and died a virgin, in love with wild nature.

The city needs Artemis: there are literally hundreds of cities and villages throughout Greece, Asia Minor, Italy, and as far as Gaul, Spain, and Egypt that built temples to her. But she doesn't need the city. The outdoors is where she moves and has her being. Grown-ups in general don't seem to suit Artemis. Goat horns, bulls, and bears are more likely to find favor with her, and of course stags, dogs, and virgins. Her cultic statue in the land of the Taurians demanded an annual sprinkling with human blood—to refresh it, we may assume. In Sparta, the young men celebrating the festival of Artemis Ortheia had to steal cheese from her altar while being scourged with giant whips; again, the rite specifies that drops of blood decorate the altar. (Fraternity hazing takes its norms from these customs.) This taste for cruelty, even for crime, is not gratuitous. If you want to consort with holy things and goddesses, purification is essential, and that often involves a passage through pain and physical rupture. To expel the unclean in a religious context, you must eliminate what disturbs, say, by consecrating and destroying a victim. Pollution is contagious. The Greeks thought you needed fire to get rid of it when water isn't enough. The truly polluting, like Oedipus the parricide, must be banished for fear their stigma will spread.[31] But violence is also contagious, and to achieve a release from the cycle of blood, sometimes only more blood will do.

So we should not be surprised to discover among the customs sacred to this goddess a social and symbolic chain. This leads, all too literally, from virginity through savagery to a surrogate death and ritual purification, only to end up at a place (the marriage bed and the bed of childbirth) where virginity is no longer welcome but blood is manifestly present. Artemis shuns marriage and is quick to lash out if her virginal integrity is compromised. But she also holds the key to the mysteries of marriage, those that are hidden behind a veil and not spoken about in profane settings.[32] To navigate the path that leads to adult life and knowledge—especially sexual knowledge—exposes the young and unformed to danger. It may end in festivity and civic acknowledgment, but it is no less a crisis. Puberty is an ordeal.

At the center of the anxiety that plagues the transition from childhood to maturity, from pregnancy to birth, and from life to death, there is always a goddess, and it is very often Artemis. All female virgins intended for marriage are implicitly consecrated to her. The little girl, often no older than ten, dedicates the playthings of her childhood in Artemis's sanctuary; she offers her the maiden girdle removed before the threshold of wedlock is crossed. When a wild she-bear Artemis held dear was killed for scratching a young girl near Brauron (outside Athens), she insisted that every young girl who expects to marry must first spend a year of her life playing the "she-bear" at her shrine.[33] The deity gathers adolescents into a herd who hunt, steal, dance, and compete together; often they form choruses, run races, sacrifice goats, and live without clothes. Initiation, like most symbolic actions in the sphere of religion, mixes elements which are otherwise incompatible. It is meant to do so, as the difficult task it carries through—the renunciation of youth, the surrender of virginity—is itself ambivalent, and not everyone is willing to go the distance.

Artemis's name reflects this ambivalence: it may come from the word for "safe," healthy, or perhaps from the word for "butcher." Chastity is her ideal, but there is nothing docile or modest in the way she represents it. Her inviolability is defiant. To equate virginity and violence, purity and cruelty, you don't have to wait for Freud. Walter Burkert, the great German scholar of Greek religion, put it like this: "The serene and not entirely innocent picture of the Artemisian swarms of maidens is not without its darker obverse. . . . The ritual cruelty brings some of the harshness of precivilized life into the civilization of the polis."[34] For a virgin, Artemis takes a great deal of interest in the more extreme states of bodily experience. One needs to be careful with Artemis; like her boars and stags, she bites.

The goddess of the margins is essential to civilization; the goddess of chastity is essential to marriage. Prepubescent Attic girls, on the "cusp of adult sexuality," participate in rituals of initiation dedicated to Artemis and held at Troezen, among other places, in the name of the virgin hunter who met his death there.[35] Boys, too, needed help making the transition into adult masculinity. Youths in Crete, in practices that already were in decline by the fourth century BCE, devoted themselves to hunting, sport, and ritual contests that could include "being hunted" by gift-laden older men. But once these fun and games were finished, the youth would withdraw from the young male "herd," the *agela*, and get married.[36] Between maidenhood and marriage, or between the life of the youth and the life of the husband, boundaries have to be crossed and difficult beginnings taken in stride. It may not be experienced as "crisis." But it is not just the same as picking rosebuds. Modern romance—I am thinking of literature here rather than life—has often failed to reckon with the difficulties of this transformation, and with the fact that marriage (for women) is a loss as well as a gain.

Abandoning one's physical virginity may not be so hard to do. But even so, there can be problems. In Hellenistic times, Longus's charming pastoral narrative of Daphnis and Chloe posed some interesting questions: How do we know how to do sex if we haven't been taught? Where does desire come from, for the innocent and inexperienced? Is it obvious that eros arises "naturally" in the life of the young, that attraction knows how to find its way to pleasure and performance?[37] The Greeks appeared to understand that initiation into the physical acts of love could be alarming, and defloration could be experienced as a "wounding." A "common analogy," Simon Goldhill writes in his study of virginity in the Greek prose romances, was to describe defloration as a "slaughter that does not kill."[38] To survive the first night could be hard enough. Breaking away from something like "psychological" or "spiritual" virginity could be much harder. At least the possibility has to be considered that such a surrender could well be painful, close to what Freud would describe as a "narcissistic wound."[39] In the best cases of marital wish fulfillment, the man who desires a woman's consent also helps make the passage out of virginity a mutual adventure. In the best cases (we shall look for some) the "goddessy" airs of the woman are respected and not treated either dismissively (as prudish skittishness) or brutally (as the no that means yes). In the best cases there is an integration of the desire for purity with a desire for shared innocence and pleasure. In these best cases the virgin's claim for exclusiveness—which a cult of Artemis might protect as the purity of the young and the wild—can morph into a second and more mature innocence, an arrival at conjugal pleasure and confidence that does not annihilate or underestimate the childlike pleasures of independence and freedom. But are there any best cases?

Young brides about to be betrothed will reenact the flight of Hippolytus from the marital bed. Like ephebes undergoing initiation, maidens fulfilling their duties to Artemis will spend time segregated from society. On their own in the wild frontiers of the city, they play at savagery, play at being animals or warriors.[40] They dance, sometimes dressed, sometimes not. In a few places their ceremonies are said to involve cross-dressing. And they kill animals, although this part of the procedures is shadowy and hard to pin down. Hippolytus, the virile but bashful *parthenos* (virgin, maiden), becomes after his death the cult hero, whose ordeal and vindication "will provide the symbolic model for the physical experience of others—nubile maidens on the eve of their marriage. But in weeping for him, as they will when retelling his story of eros refused, the young virgins are acknowledging at the same time that his story is one they themselves must not literally imitate."[41]

Inexperienced maidens will linger for a time with Artemis. The process of maturation, for a Greek adolescent girl, presents a number of challenges: women, writes the classicist Helen King, "start their lives as outsiders to male society; through maturation they are taken 'inside' in order to reproduce it." Like wild fillies, they need to be tamed, broken in. Innocent and unmarried, they are like unripe fruit. But the term of their "unripeness" is short. Bodily changes will "open up" their flesh, so that it acquires the sponginess characteristic of the mature "woman"; breasts will "bud"; blood will flow.[42] And the final work of their "ripening" and "taming" will be performed through male intervention, supervised by Aphrodite. Their wildness will come to an end: they will put on their veils and enter their husbands' bedrooms, allowing the girdles of their virginity to be loosened. Hippolytus was aghast at the very thought. For his impiety he will be punished, and Artemis, who guides the virgins over the threshold, cannot save him from his fate. In the name of eros but also of life and increase, Aphrodite functions not just as Artemis's rival but as her collaborator: the goddess of love is on the watch against the arrogance of the fleshless. Her war must be won. Just as it is mad to seek to escape nature and immoral to long beyond human longings, it is hubristic to seek to escape the inexorable rule of desire. Eros conquers all.

Giving the Goddess Her Due ("Mighty Aphrodite")

> *Eros* attended her and beautiful *Himeros* followed her when she was born and first went with the tribe of immortals. She held this honor from the beginning and obtained this portion among humans and the immortal gods: the chatter of young women, the smiles and deceptions, the sweet delight and gentleness of love.
>
> HESIOD, describing the birth of Aphrodite in *Theogony* 201–6

Given the tragedy's outcome, Aphrodite, who fights for the marriage bed, comes off as the dominant force, the puppet master of the events, the avenger who gets her revenge. She has claimed her sacrifice of two innocents: Hippolytus, for refusing sexual love, and Phaedra, used and discarded as a tool in the destruction of her household. And she has ruined in the process one not-so-innocent, Theseus, who killed the Minotaur and stole an Amazon as mistress. Does the play prove her supremacy? Its evaluation is certainly not a flattering one.

Eros in antiquity was a complicated matter. It was grand as well as squalid, tragic and farcical. It made the dumb articulate and the heroic shy. *Epithumia* or *orexis*—the more common words for "appetite, lust, desire"—involve the body and are avid to possess their objects. Multiple and insistent, human appetites can drive us, inspire us, keep us busy, and even make us brave and noble. Desire fosters eloquence and numbs judgment. It jealously demands possession and inspires reckless generosity. It is often described as a delirium. Laying siege to the mind, it disturbs the rule of reason in its own domain. The Chorus in *Antigone* complains to eros: "You take the minds of the just and turn them aside to injustice."[43] Greek philosophers were divided in their attitude to the erotic. For Plato, eros must be purged of carnality if its creative powers are to fertilize rather than destroy. The pleasures of the senses are not worthy of human life at its best; what sensual desire wants is always changing, transient, and superficial. But erotic love can be purged of these inconveniences and, transformed into a more fully intellectual yearning, can be noble, pure, and lasting. Aristotle had less time for erotic idealism: for him, physiology is sufficient to explain sexual pleasure, and those who are most susceptible to sexual desire are like people who have a constant itch.[44] Epicurus taught that sexual desires were natural but not necessary; Diogenes of Sinope was known for gratifying both appetites, for food and for sex, in public and without any signs of shame.[45] These philosophers, as ever, were in a minority. But religion affected most people in their everyday lives, and religious scruples influenced beliefs about eros. To live up to standards of religious and cultic propriety in the Greek cities, it was important to take special care in the affairs of sex. The successful performance of ritual actions required specific abstinence from sex at specific times and places. The human body was sexual, and that was natural; indeed, it was as tradition and justice demand. (*Themis* is invoked by Homer in the *Iliad* 9.276, to explain how both the gods and the laws of the household govern lawful sexual intercourse.) But under the wrong conditions (childbirth, incest, rape), it was polluted and needed to be purified, to be insulated from the sacred.[46] Strict hierarchies governed the uses of sex in Athens: an adult citizen-male must dominate, not be dominated. And concern for sexual propriety did not end when Latin replaced Greek and Roman law formalized Greek norms. Certainly eros has its competitive side, which the Romans appreciated. If the founder and first of the Romans, Aeneas, was indeed the son of Aphrodite, it seems reasonable to expect heroism and not just degradation from those called to her cult. Eros, the Latin poets write, rewards the daring with glittering prizes.

All the ancient poets paid close heed to the scandals of eros even if they did not produce all their work in its shadows. Of the poets who specialized in eros, Catullus is the most tortured, Sappho the most elegant, and the tragedian Euripides the most unflinching. Euripides does not rhapsodize or mock. He analyzes. His Aphrodite is more than imperious. She is insolent. Her decisions are irrevocable, her whims devastating. There is little comfort to be expected from a rational protest. Here the claims of justice end. Jason, in his *Medea*, is shocked by the brutal intensity of his lover's desire. He puts the responsibility on the goddess: her "inescapable" shafts have pierced Medea's heart. This woman who was first his deliverer is now his murderous nemesis. Her behavior is inexplicable. Is Medea guilty? Or can there be no responsibility when resistance is impossible? Aphrodite's dictates are, tragically, absolute. Like spells, they steal away the freedom and peace of the bewitched, violating some core of personal sovereignty which we would otherwise want to guard with care. The demands of desire are also cruel, less promises of pleasure than sentences to pain: "Desire is unpleasant . . . every form of *himeros* manifests itself as an urgent, impelling need to put an end to the sensation itself. In its negativity, this sensation—to be *missing something* (an action, a condition, a thing or a place)—impels impatience and rash haste towards its own annihilation. Desire is suicidal."[47]

"Spare me from her mania," begs Phaedra's nurse in *Hippolytus*. Those who serve her know great pleasures. But their lives are exposed to forces they cannot so easily rein in, and those who defy her fare worse: they are run down by wild horses, bulls, hungry animals from the sea, all reckless mobs whipped into action by a combustible force, image of her frenzy. A black horse, wanton and scruffy, is Plato's image for the appetitive part of the soul, easily aroused to violent pursuits, resenting the bridle.[48] Euripides gives Hippolytus, the tamer of horses, an ironic death, for someone seeking to escape the savage irrationality of sex. At the very least, love's violence disturbs. It is not necessarily fatal, but it does seem to preclude calm and prudent enjoyment. A later observer of erotic upheaval, Ovid, the Roman theorist of amorous success, gave explicit shape to a popular idea among the ruling classes in antiquity. As Ovid describes it, love is a contest, a public campaign where the ambitious seducer must not hold back. Conquest in the bedroom is what victory is in the arena. If you are good at it, you can beat your rivals, or you can bend a proud lover to your will. In the games of Venus, Ovid writes, force may prevail, but the victor is as wounded as his victim (*Ars amatoria* 1.125, 165–70).[49] Love punishes and humiliates, so the pursuer is warned: your prey will be wary. The adept lover lays traps with delicate and insinuating compliments, all the better to disguise the brutality that disfigures his passion. No sooner satisfied than stale, conquest leads to possession and then to complacency and contempt.

Son of an Amazon: Hippolytus and Gender

The cycle of sexual exchange cannot be dispensed with, or cities and states will crumble into oblivion. Hippolytus's dream would turn the world into a desert. He is too young to have thought to the end the implications of his rejection of sexuality. But, neurotic or not, Hippolytus is also unusual among Greeks in his sensitivity to the injustices of gender. His fondness for such classically masculine pursuits as hunting and horse racing does not disguise a certain androgyny in his presentation and manner. And his greatest loyalty is to a female deity. In his equivocal gender identity, he resembles those sacred monsters among the gods—Dionysus as well as

Artemis and Athena—whose ambivalent presentation makes them persistent figures of the poetic imagination. The virgins among the gods are a special case in their challenge to patriarchy: protected by the Law of the Father, they line up behind Athena's words in Aeschylus's *Eumenides*: "I am always for the male with all my heart, and strongly on my father's side" (*Eum.* 737–38).[50] Absolute in their privilege because they are motherless, they exploit patriarchal license to the limit, exerting a sometimes unhealthy influence on mortals who, like them, run away from traditional femininity. When confined to special cultural performances of transvestism or cross-gender imitation, such as the adoption of hoplite clothing by the girl chosen to embody Artemis in her festival at Lake Tritonis, temporary "participation in the nature of the opposite sex" serves the purposes of the initiatory procedure, allowing the novice "woman-in-training" to test out the powers and drawbacks of masculinity before she commits herself finally to the conventional female form she has no choice but to accept. Yet the existence of such rituals testifies to an anxiety about gender and its rigidity also manifest in the Greek fascination for such extreme dissidents as Hippolytus, Atalanta, or the Amazons.[51] A girl warrior is a contradiction in terms; she is, by this logic, therefore even more savage than a male could ever be; a boy sworn to the renunciation of sexual desire is less emasculated (Hippolytus yields to no one in his brash frat-boy camaraderie with his hunting and riding band) than uncivilized and out of control. Without the tempering influence of the social institutions, maleness and femaleness alike are problematic. In their pure state, where they abjure all mixing, combination, and modification, they are forces of destruction. What the Greek myths tell us is that these pure states do not exist in normal human beings—that is, beings who have undergone the molding of identity sponsored by the civic, familial, and religious bodies and reaffirmed in the rites of preparation for adult life. But if ritual symbolizes and confirms, myth, as classicists remind us, always exaggerates.[52] As J. P. Vernant in his essay "City-State Warfare" asserts:

> Thus a girl who refuses marriage, thereby also renouncing her "femininity," finds herself to some extent forced toward warfare, and paradoxically becomes the equivalent of a warrior. This is the situation in myth of females like the Amazons and, in a religious context, of goddesses such as Athena. . . . This deviation both from the normal state of women, who are destined for marriage, not warfare, and from the normal state of warriors, who are men, not women, gives a special intensity to warrior values when they are embodied in a girl. They cease, in a way, to be merely relative or confined to a single sex, and become "total."[53]

Hippolytus's fanatical chastity exiles him from both gendered destinies available to Greeks in antiquity. In his hostility to the works of Aphrodite his misogyny comes to the surface, as Phaedra's nurse complains. But curiously it makes him susceptible to what we might call a sterile form of protofeminism. To Hippolytus, woman's business is repellent. And the "woman" he means is the one he suspects Phaedra of being: the compliant and sensual servant of man, the glue of social exchange and male arrangements, the key to and connecting fiber of families. There may be another mode of femininity he finds sympathetic, one equally ill at ease in the family foyer: the warrior, the maidenly, athletic tomboy. For that is what Hippolytus is, less apprentice male than maiden manqué, Amazonian in the wrong skin.[54] Judgmental as he is, like his patron, who is always quick to punish infractions of chastity among her nymphs, he is also protective. Once he has given a promise—to a servant, even—that he will preserve Phaedra's secret, his word is good. He does not betray the trust. Although he gives way to scornful denunciations of his passion-wracked stepmother (*Hipp.* 616–68), he shows an understanding of Phaedra's plight, and that of women in general, unexpected from a young man whose speeches express a misogyny intemperate even by Euripidean standards.

Perhaps because of his own irregular background—his mother was an Amazon queen, taken by Theseus as booty in the prize of conquest and displaced by Phaedra—Hippolytus can feel what it is like for a woman to be denied mastery of her own existence.[55] Such insight into the punitive norms of patriarchy was what Euripides was famous for in his time.[56] The first to put a maenad on stage (in the *Bacchae*), Euripides seems to know why a closeted female has no halfway place between invisibility and barbarism. Respectable females, unlike goddesses and Amazons, are prisoners of the household. The weaknesses of their character—which Hippolytus lists bitterly—stem from that social oppression. Marriage and child-rearing constitute the entire horizon of female activity; how could their intelligence flourish and their moral sense develop under such conditions? Hippolytus's rebellion against the rule of Aphrodite is solipsistic. He cares about himself, his Artemis, and his father; the plight of other men and women barely touches him. He refuses dependence, "binding," connection, everything he associates with human relationships and social obligations. In the course of the play's bitter persecution of him he is forced to experience those. But his tragedy exposes something of the callousness of sexual institutions and codes, as well as the more spectacular cruelty of the sexual drive itself, an indictment Euripides has no interest in extenuating.

Hippolytus is a young prince, but an illegitimate one. He is ardent, reckless, willfully innocent—an *enfant sauvage*. He worships the hunting goddess and runs wild with her pack. Good Athenian society found him dispensable. And he returned the contempt, saving his anger for the patron of carnal love, the goddess of eros. Aphrodite is quick to resent the insult: "He alone of all the citizens of Troezen here," she complains. "proclaims me the worst of divine beings. He says *No* to sex and will not touch marriage." (*Hipp*. 14–17) Hippolytus dies young and in agony, despite his innocence and his ascetic virtue. He is not the only one in mythology to suffer for his defiance of eros. A punishment even more apt in its poetic cruelty was devised by Aphrodite for the maiden Myrrah, daughter of the king of Assyria: refusing sexual love and insulting the goddess caused her to be visited with an incestuous passion for her father, whose bed she shared without his knowledge, producing both his fury and the child Adonis, the circuitous (and unconscious) instrument of his mother's revenge on Aphrodite, her destroyer.[57] But even if Aphrodite will come to know grief herself as a result of her intemperate hostility to those who resist her spell, no mortal has been known to get away with such resistance scot-free. As Zeitlin puts it, "Hippolytus must meet his fate in order to reconfirm the truth of the cultural dictum that no one may refuse the power of Aphrodite with impunity, not even the Amazon's child and worshipper of Artemis."[58]

Purity could not save him. Nor could nobility.[59] His wish to be exceptional is at odds not just with the values of democratic Athens but also with the will of the gods, who govern all, life and death, and who bring all, mortal and immortal alike, under the sway of sex. Even for the philosophers, who dared to think outside the borders of piety, eros showed up as a cosmic force, primordial and pervasive, as it did for Empedocles. Without eros, nothing hangs together; nothing grows; a cosmos without eros would not even be sterile: it would be nonexistent. Respect for Aphrodite is not an option, something one can take up or reject, as he prefers to think. To acknowledge eros is to acknowledge one of the "ineluctable forces of the universe."[60] As Phaedra's nurse exclaims, "*Kypris* is after all not a deity but something even mightier!" (*Hipp*. 360). To despise eros is not a mark of distinction but of impiety, pride, rebellion (*Hipp*. 84–120, 530–64). Scorning desire, Hippolytus is brought down by the deity who writes the rules of desire. Hippolytus prayed to the virgin goddess he loved to let him die a virgin, as he was born (*Hipp*. 82–87).[61] He got his wish, although not in the way he intended. An adolescent shocked by everything he suspects about the life of his elders, Hippolytus would prefer that children were bought in the marketplace or produced mechanically; the nighttime couplings sacred to Aphrodite are things he'd rather not know. Life's origins disgust him, women he finds abominable, and the virtues admired in the secular city strike him as stale and compromised. As the tragedy unfolds, Hippolytus's horror turns hysterical: everything indoors is vile. He is an odd candidate to be a leader for Theseus's Athenians, used to the aggressive style of politics on the heroic model; he is just as odd as a figure designed to appear in the civic rituals of democratic fifth-century BCE Athens, since his fastidiousness leads him to reject both private and public worlds, both *oikos* and *polis*. Hippolytus prematurely suffers from what Jean-Paul Sartre's antihero Roquentin calls "nausea," and from the world contempt of the desert monks and Christian ascetics. To Hippolytus's delicate sense, the world smells of human overuse. Words are tainted and insincere (*Hipp*. 601–55). The female in particular, who works her plots from inside the house and with insinuation and indirection, is loathsome. Hippolytus is a Spartan escaped from a prewar English public school. His fantasy is fresh air, riding, running, military drill, the world of the boy who never grows up. Is that so bad? Is it enough to destroy a dynasty, a noble house, and a civilization?

The play sees his ascetic enthusiasm as catastrophic and a crisis, an anarchic fissure too close to the city's center of power for comfort. It's also, no way to get around it, annoying:

> Figures such as Hippolytus who, in tragedy, are the embodiment of a religious insistence on total purity, are presented with such equivocal features and display a puritanism so ambiguous in its very excesses that there is a whole side to their characters that tips the scales over towards wildness. . . . He rejects carnal union with the same intransigent disdain as a vegetarian rejecting animal flesh. He is a strange vegetarian though for he also appears to be very close to the wild beasts which he devotes his time to hunting and slaughtering and which then, once the hunt is over, he shares as a meal with his male companions. . . . While he speaks of marriage only to reject it with indignation and horror, this young man, believed to be all modesty and reserve, has difficulty in masking under the artifice of a sophistic rhetoric the brutish violence of his true temperament.[62]

"I have a virgin soul," Hippolytus explains when he tries to make clear that he has not touched his father's wife. "My body is untainted by love. I do not know this act save by report or seeing it in pictures [*graphei*]. I am not eager to look at it either, since I have a maiden soul" (*Hipp*. 1005–6).

Purity and Purification in Antiquity

Hippolytus's premature Rousseauism is self-defeating. Neither for him nor for us is there a utopian virtue outside the social. The old servant who hears his first, defiant hymn to Artemis warns him: this is unwise, reckless, discourteous, arrogant; humans must honor the gods, all of them, and especially the imperious goddess of eros (*Hipp.* 102). The savage purity he desires is not for mortals. Sanctity in Greek culture is not what Hippolytus imagines it to be. It is not a permanent condition or even a special status.[63] It does not define a personal life. It is a requirement of a certain function or practice, the way wearing a helmet is for a crossing guard. Good religious practice is akin to good governance overall, in the home and in the city. Taboos govern what can and cannot be done or even seen. Prescriptions for purity, accordingly, work toward these practical ends. They are conditions that protect the well-being of society; they are barriers against its vulnerability. Water and fire are purifiers, cleansing agents, scrubbing out defilement. People hardly ever are pure in that way. When they are—those who are *hagnos*, as Hippolytus says he is—they are that way because they shun blood and death, which he cannot, or because they are consecrated as sacrificial victims, a fate he seems unconsciously to pursue. Priests and priestesses must be pure for the duration of their office, else they risk contaminating the clean with the unclean. Their contribution is for us; it safeguards our place in a shared world and protects us from impiety. "Purification," Walter Burkert writes, "is a social process." It is a matter of ritual, of cultic actions and forms that establish a group's standards and codes, excluding the outsider, the banned, the unstable. In special cases, rites of purification have a magical character. If illness, crime, and madness are mysteries that disturb and even shatter, the need to overcome them is urgent: it calls for mysteries just as potent.[64]

Sacred things must not be defiled, and if desecrated, their purity needs to be restored by sacrifice; those who desecrate are cursed or dangerous (*enages*), liable to endanger and pollute others.[65] Sacred areas, like special events and festivals, are strictly marked off, barred from all that is profane.[66] As Hippocrates of Kos writes in the third century BCE, "We ourselves fix boundaries to the sanctuaries and precincts of the gods so that nobody may cross them unless he be pure; and when we enter we sprinkle ourselves, not as defiling ourselves thereby, but to wash away any pollution we may already have contracted."[67]

Festivals break up the Greek year into sacred and profane times. During the observance of any one of the local and urban cults, mundane activities are suspended, as they are in periods surrounding crisis, times of war, the illicit spilling of blood, or outbreaks of disease. Everything to do with the gods, all that communicates between the ordinary and the religious domains, requires care and special hygiene. Statues of the gods need to be cleaned, their clothes washed on special occasions. Birth and death are naturally arising pollutions, and both sacred persons and divine beings avert their eyes from their occurrence. Yet the idea that removal from the sexual makes a person unique and to be revered was not obvious to the Greek mind. Virgin priestesses and oracles did play a special role, "part of the timeless religious landscape of the classical world," as Peter Brown puts it. The vestal virgins are the most famous, and most intriguing to the later Christian mind. But their limitation as a model for sacred chastity needs emphasizing:

> The message conveyed by such women as the Vestal Virgins at Rome and the virgin priestesses and prophetesses of the classical Greek world was that their state was of crucial importance for the community precisely because it was anomalous. They fitted into a clearly demarcated space in civic society. Though eminent and admired, they were not thought to stand for human nature at its peak. . . . The chastity of many virgin priestesses was not a matter of free choice for them. No heroic freedom of the individual will was made plain by their decision not to marry.[68]

The priestesses belonging to the order of the goddess Vesta at Rome were recruited from the upper classes; they did not choose this life as a vocation. After their service, which could end when they reached the age of thirty, they were free to marry. Their "difference" bore no challenge to the ordinary expectations that women would marry and bear children. Virginity for real people in antiquity was not a viable profession but a transitional phase, a condition meant to be terminated in the essential celebration of marriage. All we know of Greek religion confirms this fact. The demands of the sacred specify the renunciation of sexuality during a short, well-defined period of preparation and devotion, observed by the participant in the festival or the officiants at the sanctuary in respect and, almost always, voluntarily. The priests and priestesses in drama make this clear: Iphigenia guards the shrine at Tauris with her virginity and her watchfulness; Ion dedicates his childlike enthusiasm to Apollo; the citizen-wives who celebrate the Thesmophoria, the festival of Demeter, are not virgins but women who each year shun the company of men in their mysterious fasts and seclusion (although the consummation of the rite involves obscenity and phallic excess).

In part the option of abstinence is a privilege, in part it is an offering to the gods, renewing the festive contact with divinity. In other, noncultic contexts the abstinence of the warrior, the hunter, or the wrestler serves as a kind of insurance, propitiating those powers that can give or take away success. The well-being of the community relies on the integrity of those required to keep pure as part of their commitment to the festival or the rite or the shrine. Turning that continence into a law to govern everyday life would not only make no sense, it might even be disrespectful. Greek religion was, as the historian Robert Parker puts it, a "religion without a church."[69] The servants of the temple officiated part-time, raising their families and keeping the books when they were not performing sacrifices. In most of the great urban festivals, nonpriests conducted the mysteries, being purified for the occasion. There existed no caste or class of professional priests or consecrated officiants considered exceptional, ontologically set apart, unconditionally *hagnos*. Such was the situation from Homeric times up till the fifth century BCE and beyond, all through the Greek territories. Farther east, other stranger customs slipped into the cults of Artemis, Hecuba, and Cybele. At Ephesus, which was the sanctuary meant to be special to the Amazons, eunuchs served as high priests. Ecstatic castrations were known among the followers of other divinities. But these reach the mainstream much later, in the second century BCE. At the date when Euripides constructed a narrative around the ritual commemorating Theseus's young son, consecrated celibates were rare. Cultic chastity, if the gods required it in their service, was one thing. At Athens and elsewhere, priestesses who were either old or very young tended the temples of Athena and Aphrodite. They took a vow to maintain sexual purity for the term of their service. Since Homeric times, Greeks understood that priests must shun anything polluting such as death, childbirth, illicit sexual relations, or bodily disfiguration. Great care had to be taken, and the cultic practices had to be administered scrupulously. Lapses, even if unintentional, caused immediate and lasting disaster. The goal of all this effort to maintain the purity and holiness of religious business was the well-being of the community, which needed to be protected by keeping things in order. If sexual purity figured among these things to keep in order, it would be in the nature of a prescribed offering, a compliment to those gods who happened to demand it, when they happened to demand it. It was not something one would turn into the meaning of one's existence, into a special signifier of just who one is.

Hippolytus was wrong to believe that his zeal for chastity would bring him closer to the gods. He was wrong, too, to believe it entitled him to an exceptional identity, an exemption from social norms. In the name of virtue and his commitment to living "cool and clean," Hippolytus boasts about his contempt for the "filth" of "conjugal pleasures" (*Hipp.* 853) and his hatred of women (*Hipp.* 617–68). His father is disgusted. Neither the city nor the inaccessible places where the gods go are available as homes for this alien and restless young hunter. Purity does not belong to the isolated individual. It belongs to the community, as does marriage. To make a fetish of sexual abstinence and use it for one's own self-adoration is something not just baffling but alarming. Everyone who moves across the scene of Euripides's tragedy feels the tremors. What they are witnessing is a challenge for which there seems to be no precedent. Perhaps it could be, in some unimaginable elsewhere, a new religion, the law of some daimon yet to be encountered. Here and now it can be only a serious mistake, a perversion to selfish purposes of a piece of ritual and collective magic. So Hippolytus is punished, made into an offering on the altar of the eros he despises. Torn between the divine and the animal, there is no middle ground on which he can stand. The circumstances of his death are what Froma Zeitlin calls a "demonic parody of *eros*."[70] Driven mad by a bull sent by Poseidon, he is ripped apart by his own horses.[71] He dies in torment, the goddess he serves unable to console her favorite as the sight of dying men is polluting to the gods. But his cult, and his memory, are preserved at Troezen, where he lived and died, by young women from Athens who want to get married and can't do so unless they cut off their hair as an offering to the tortured male virgin who was so good with horses.

Strategies of the Eunuch: Bloody Virgins and Castrated Gods

The wise among the Greeks were under no illusions. It is dangerous to be ruled by Aphrodite. It is equally dangerous, or absurd, to think "like a eunuch," imagining that the queen of sexual love could be dethroned in such a brutal fashion, swept aside, defeated by the self-destructive strategy of castration or the harsh austerities of the ascetic. But what exactly was so desirable about being a eunuch? Could the holy arrogance of the "unsexed," the apostates from carnality, actually compete with the prior rights of love, the holy arrogance of Venus's domination?

Attis was a Phrygian god of vegetation, and one of Hippolytus's alter egos. His cult was known around the Greek world by the time of Plato. Himself the product of an immaculate conception, Attis offered his sexual organs as sacrifice to the demanding goddess he worshipped, Cybele, the Great Mother, whose priests form a eunuch brotherhood. When he awoke from his madness, Catullus writes, he was shocked to find himself bereft. Those who flee sexuality don't escape punishment, and their torture seems all the more cruel to us; it is not clear that it would have seemed so to the ancients.

> Various explanations have been given for the relationship of castration to the worship of the Mother of the Gods. The priests' self-castration was seen even in antiquity as a symbolic sacrifice of individual fertility in order to enhance the fertility of the community and even of the cosmos, and as a sacred re-enactment of the spring harvest. . . . Likewise, both ancient and modern scholars have seen the priests' self-castration as a pledge of their sexual purity. The priests' self-castration may also have been part of a renunciation of masculine identity, however, and associated with their personal dedication to a feminine deity.[72]

When Jean Racine wrote his *Phèdre* in the seventeenth century, he felt he had to change Hippolytus's character to make him less "innocent," otherwise the indignation at his fate would have overwhelmed the pity and terror. He gave Hippolytus a girlfriend and made the tragedy mainly Phaedra's. Yet there is something correct, an accusation that sticks, in these stories about the vengeance visited on the sexually innocent. Great mother goddesses don't care too much about human vulnerabilities. Nor do virgin goddesses. Titian's two great paintings *Diana and Actaeon* and *Diana and Callisto* have been called by Lucian Freud "the most beautiful pictures in the world." In the first, the angry goddess, discovered nude and bathing by a hapless young hunter who was looking for his dogs, is portrayed at a moment of exposure and repudiation: baleful, a recent critic calls her. Her shock and the terror of her nymphs lead to a swift and horrible act of violence, which the painting cannot show but which readers of Ovid will supply for it: the goddess splashes water on the unwary Actaeon, magically changing him into a stag, and his hounds tear him to bits, echoing Hippolytus's panicked horses. Diana's grace toward those who follow her rites can be bestowed, as Hippolytus so passionately wishes, and taken away, just as arbitrarily. The fate of Callisto, Diana's favorite nymph who accompanies her in Arcadia, is even worse. Wandering in a forest "whose trees no axe had deflowered," Callisto loosens the strings of her bow, lets down her guard, and is raped by Jove, who has taken on the form of the virgin goddess herself. Callisto becomes pregnant by the god in the form of a female virgin, an anomaly that should make us think. Furious at her fall, Diana banishes Callisto and Juno turns her into a wild bear.

But the most telling image to stay with is the solemn ceremony in honor of Hippolytus, the nubile girls cutting off their hair as an offering in the temple of Artemis. Before the myth came the ritual, as the Cambridge anthropologists told us. Those about to marry or, in other cases, to become pregnant for the first time—those untilled fields made ready for the plough, as the Greeks so delicately put it—must first appease Artemis. Perhaps they have an obligation to pay her back for what she is about to lose. Or perhaps they have reasons to fear their own loss, the surrender of autonomy they have only barely glimpsed as they are about to leave the nursery and the schoolroom. In the rites for Artemis, maidens play with the idea of a return to the undisciplined life of the beasts that have not known a harness. The mistress whom they honor, and who keeps exacting sacrifices, did not have to become a wife and mother. Artemis did not go through the door to the husband's home and guardianship. Mortal women, by contrast, are made to live inside, according to the Greeks and Romans. Goddesses don't agree. The goddess rules the open countryside, and she enforces the ancient hunting taboo. The hunter must be continent or the prey will elude him; lucky in love, unlucky in war, is another way to put it. The sovereignty of Artemis is anomalous; she founds no dynasty, worries about no children. And her sovereignty remained unchallenged, her separateness intact; she moves in and out of the great house of the Olympian family, and she won her exemption from sexual service by charming her father, playing girlish games.

Human girls don't have this choice. It remained for a new religion, arising in the dog days of paganism, to turn virginity into a political career. In so doing, it sapped the strength from this weird and exceptional option. The ascetic life had bewitched many, and the more it demanded, the more attractive it seemed. Monks, hermits, and consecrated virgins signed on for the charms of mortification. Asceticism was a life of extreme solitude and harsh diet, shorn of most of the ordinary markers of civilization, like roofs and walls and beds, with minimal covering so that the ascetic would be exposed to sun and rain and dust. Sexual austerity or indifference was only part of the package: the spirit of a virginal existence was a rigorous spirit, working hard and sharing labor, retreating to caves or forming communities a bit like primitive federations.[73] Christian world-renouncers challenged themselves physically in order to live in this world as if not of it, with their minds constantly on prayer, penitence, and purity. Christians who followed the ascetic call could live outside the family, outside the yoke of sex. And remarkably, this option seemed open to females as well. "Dedicated virgins," the early church decided between the third and fifth centuries, could live in communities with other dedicated virgins, closely supervised, or they could live invisibly at home, veiled, silent, charitable, and spiritually distinguished.[74] But first it was necessary to defuse the sacred awe of queenly and warlike chastity, to make it mild and meek, humble and tender, not vengeful and austere. Against the image of Artemis, who is too proud and cold to look at her devotees as they lie dying, another face is juxtaposed: the docile and submissive Mary, compassionately bent over the scandal of her own immaculate pregnancy.

With the rise of a Virgin who is a kindly, humble and nurturing mother, the game is over. Unlike Aphrodite, Mary is not sexual for anyone. She does not preside over marriage nor encourage the world to follow the law of love. Unlike Artemis, who was also a divine virgin, Mary is not proud, autocratic, or defiant, for the pure goddess of wood and hunting was cruel in her exemption from the human (and divine) passions that unite the rest of us. Mary is everything the Greek deities are not: she is feeling, caring, grieving, all-forgiving. And she has a remarkable way of focusing on the single task at hand, her infant and his needs. Mary the virgin, mother of God (*Theotokos,* bearer of God, as she became officially in 431 CE in Artemis's city of Ephesus), is exclusive.[75] She does not look for other attachments. Her breast and the warmth of her skin are available only to her child. There is no one in the pagan pantheon, not even Demeter, who is so single-mindedly defined by her maternity. Yet the aura of female fertility, nurture, and generation has somehow enveloped Mary in its magic without interfering with her maidenhood. She is no longer a child. But she has not entered the world of men.

Doing Justice to Hippolytus

Literature's first stormy male virgin wanted to replace this world with one washed clean of women. Why couldn't the gods invent a better way to replenish the species? If men could go to the market and, for a decent price, pick out those seeds that could mature into men, life would be much happier. That was Hippolytus's futile dream. The Christian god may have followed his advice: a human form, fashioned of flesh and blood, able to suffer, love, and die, was made in the Virgin's womb without sexual intercourse. Hippolytus would have approved. In his own culture he was a heretic. Refusing marriage, fleeing "the bed," makes him strange and, as he acknowledges, an outsider. The tragedy, in my view, is his more than it is Phaedra's. Defying a deity is a quick way to destroy yourself. Hippolytus's hysterical denunciation of eros, much like Pentheus's scorn of Dionysus, is sacrilegious and self-important. Like the unhappy king of Thebes, he deserves his fate, as its horror follows from his own "excellence." Euripides does not allow Hippolytus to remain unsympathetic. He may be cold, but he is also exuberant, impetuous, idealistic. The play's language permits a certain glory to this rebel, and the existence of Hippolytus's cult at Troezen confirms his stature.

For this moment in Greece's reflection on sex and its vicissitudes, an adolescent who refuses the marriage plot could be a symbol of life lived according to a different rhythm. Hippolytus is ascetic but never reclusive or cerebral. Everything he surrounds himself with is physical, vigorous, raw in the best sense. His departure from conventional norms of "proper behavior" is an adventure. The play offers him no second chances: his type of adventure is blocked, shut down, for us as well as Hippolytus. Late romantic fiction (and philosophy) played with the possibility of a return to the untouched garden and the rough charmers who inhabited it. American literature, we learn from the critic Leslie Fiedler, has had a particular attraction to this fantasy: civilization is not just an ordeal; it is an enemy of what is fresh, unscripted, raw, uncultivated, and—of course—sexless. It was civilization that got to the young Huck Finn, when he was trying to escape down the river and light out for the territories. Civilization was just as discouraging to the other primitivist American romances that tried to follow Huck, to escape into a land of perpetual innocence.[76] In Euripides's play, civilization joins forces with the sovereign deity of sex and marriage. Together they hound and hunt down the rebel. Hippolytus tried to use the sanction of religion to protect and bless his flight. He didn't succeed. There are few versions of the "antimarriage plot" that do.

3

Marriage and Mayhem

Again Gudrun paused, slightly irritated. She wanted to be quite definite. "You don't think one needs the experience of having been married?" she asked. "Do you think it need be an experience?" replied Ursula. "Bound to be, in some way or other," said Gudrun, coolly. "Possibly undesirable, but bound to be an experience of some sort." "Not really," said Ursula. "More likely to be the end of experience."

D. H. LAWRENCE, *Women in Love*

Bringing Back the Wild Times: The Antimarriage Plot

Social as well as literary traditions overwhelmingly favor the marriage plot, the ready-made structure of narrative closure and social resolution. This is our "middle way," our compromise between the anarchic energies of desire and the sedate patterns of the city. But there is also an antimarriage plot. Literature offers a number of examples; two of the most instructive were written to be performed. When the antimarriage plot takes to the stage, an essentially stable condition (marriage) begins to shake under the pressure of a passionate disagreement: defiant maidens behave in unmaidenly ways, daughters refuse to be wives, virtuous women act unruly and resort to breathtaking violence. In the name of autonomy and self-determination for women, and reinforced by a high-minded claim of immunity to the impulses of desire, the antimarriage plot would appear to subvert the sexual and social order. Except that it doesn't.

One of the first dramatizations of the antimarriage plot is Aeschylus's *The Suppliants* (sometimes translated *The Suppliant Maidens*), staged early in the fifth century BCE, the classic epoch of Athenian theater. It was known to Euripides when he wrote his two versions of the Hippolytus and Phaedra story. The story behind *The Suppliants* has a long Greek pedigree. What Aeschylus did with it, however, deserves attention. The sexual politics in Aeschylus's world are not those of Euripides, whose house of Theseus can sound almost Ibsenite. While Euripides is a skeptical, ironic, and subversive artist "preoccupied with uneasily 'modern' themes: sexual ambiguity, religious doubt, the status of women,"[1] Aeschylus's voice seems to come from another world, where raw conflicts—of men and women, revenge and deliverance, archaic memories and brittle conventions—remain unresolved. *The Suppliants* is the only play that remains from a trilogy devoted to the daughters of King Danaus, legendary ancestor of the Danaan race, a patriarch wedded to at least fifty wives who is credited in some myths with the invention of the alphabet and the building of the first seagoing vessel.[2] For a legend treating the delicate question of Greek ancestry and national foundations, the Danaid myth has some complicating features. Fifty maidens, pursued by suitors whom they consider violent and importunate, flee a mass marriage and, when their resistance fails, forty-nine of them murder in the marital bed the men who claim them as brides.

Myth also plays a role in my other theatrical antimarriage plot, *Turandot,* the story of a Chinese ice princess, also known for executing her suitors. The story comes from a Persian verse epic of the twelfth century CE by Nizami. Turned into a play by the eighteenth-century Italian poet Carlo Gozzi and first presented in Venice in 1762, it became better known when it formed the basis for the libretto Giacomo Puccini used for his last and unfinished opera (staged at La Scala in 1926, after Puccini's death). *Turandot*'s continuing popularity with audiences proves that combining Orientalism and male hysteria remains a potent recipe. In neither story do the angry virgins get their way. In Aeschylus, marriage replaces death. Husbands banished have a way of returning, if a woman is not careful. Turandot and the Danaids escape the tomb (unlike the other stubborn virgin, Antigone). But the price they pay is heavy. Avoiding one altar, they end up at another. A life outside marriage is not among their options.

These two plays, Aeschylus's *The Suppliants* and *Turandot* by Carlo Gozzi, feature feminine insurgents, stubborn virgins who go to war against matrimony rather than God. Coming from women, the resort to violence is noteworthy and the surrender to conformity predictable. We might expect things to have changed by 1939 on Broadway and in Hollywood, when a bright woman's struggle to reconcile self-respect and marriage could take place against a different background. Couverture had been abolished, the campaign for the women's vote had been won, and the climate of manners and morals was more sympathetic to divorce in the case of marital breakdown or misery. My third literary example is friendlier to marriage.

It is the Philip Barry comedy *The Philadelphia Story* (filmed by George Cukor in 1940). Its assertive heroine is an American, an aristocrat from a democratic nation, who is neither a virgin—technically—nor spousicidal, although she is haughty enough to provoke comparisons with the Greek and Roman goddesses of the hunt. Tracy Lord is a Main Line socialite with not enough to do. Smart, rich, and thoughtful, her confusions about sexual politics and chastity are a source of some distress but not a motive for bloodshed. In her story, the "Philadelphia" story, the violence in the air is psychological rather than physical. As it is a romantic comedy, the conjugal ending is on the cards from the start. Yet there is a sadness to this sophisticated portrait of a proud young woman who must learn to think less of herself before she can find contentment with a man. Consenting to marriage—indeed, to a true and happy marriage, which is the one this story promises with considerable plausibility—is perceived as a compromise, a necessary one, but a compromise nonetheless. The heroine of *The Philadelphia Story* must agree to set aside not her physical virginity (she has already been a wife) but something similarly valuable to her: her intactness, her "individual exclusiveness," something for which the cruder "fact of virginity" is a symbol or a placeholder.[3] "In comedies of remarriage," Stanley Cavell writes in the book that defined and invented the genre,

> The *fact* of virginity is evidently not what is at stake. Yet all the more it seems to me, is the *concept* of virginity still at stake, or what the fact meant is at stake—something about the possession of chasteness or innocence, whatever one's determinable condition, and about whether one's valuable intactness, one's individual exclusiveness, has been well lost, that is, given over for something imaginably better, for the exclusiveness of a union.[4]

This is the interesting lesson Cavell takes from the sparkling romantic comedies of the 1930s and 1940s, films he argues are worthy of comparison with the best European novels of the eighteenth and nineteenth centuries, worthy even of comparison to Shakespearean romances. Like the novels which first brought to full articulation the artistic possibilities of a psychological inquiry into interiority, the Hollywood comedies question the self as well as society: What do I want? Am I confused or unconfused? Am I understood or misunderstood? The novel's interest in states of mind was also an interest in the reconciliation of the individual and society and, most poignantly, the reconciliation of a woman with her social context. For such reasons, there were few themes as important to the novel as marriage.[5]

With its companion genres, the bourgeois novel and the romance, the Hollywood comedy interrogates marriage. What is marriage for? Is it the bridge between society and the antisocial, the transition from savage nature to civilization? Is it the secular form of religious ritual? Is it an economic arrangement or an affair of sentiment and passion? What does it mean for men? What does it mean for women? Literature will pose those questions differently than social science or history (for which the economic function of marriage can often take precedence). It is the moral significance of marriage that matters for literature. It is the moral significance of marriage that also matters for philosophy, or at least it seemed so for one of the first philosophical husbands in the post-Enlightenment world. Most domesticated of all the great thinkers of the Western tradition was the German G. W. F. Hegel. "Marriage," Hegel explained in his lectures on *Rechtsphilosophie* between 1816 and 1820, "is essentially an ethical relationship." It would be "crude [*roh*]" to interpret it either as simply a civil contract or a sexual relationship. "The *ethical* aspect of marriage consists in the consciousness of this union as a substantial end, and hence in love, trust, and the sharing of the whole of individual existence."[6] Marriage, taken as the honorable condition of mutuality, cannot offer happiness unless a woman's proud attachment to her own inviolable integrity is surrendered: this is the surprising message of Barry's bright comedy of love and class relations among the Main Line elite. But one worries about the nature of this surrender. Does the attachment to chastity need to be exposed as a vain and timorous fantasy? What do these feints and counterfeints, virgin and lover, resistance and surrender, tell us about the character of sexual knowledge or the ethics of sex?

Virgins in Revolt: The Danaids

Is saying yes to sexuality consenting to violation? Marriage, the state at the other side of the ordeal of initiation, is hardly a perfect option for women. In 1922 the poet Marianne Moore, who called herself a "blameless bachelor," began to write a poem on the subject, "Marriage." It is by no means easy to be a woman and a modernist. In this poem, Moore observes her position, driven by a desire to escape "this institution," as she calls it, this public enterprise. The institution she has in mind, argues Ellen Levy, is as much the field of poetic and cultural production so clearly marked by male dominance as that of wedlock. Moore's desire is an ascetic ideal, a wish to be exempt, refusing the "circular traditions and impostures" which "require all one's criminal ingenuity to avoid":

This institution,
perhaps one should say enterprise
out of respect for which
one says one need not change one's mind
about a thing one has believed in,
requiring public promises
of one's intention
to fulfil a private obligation:
I wonder what Adam and Eve
think of it by this time ...[7]

As Levy explains, "marriage is 'the' institution, the one on which all others are founded. Marriage at once confers legitimacy on our sexual desires and confirms us as members of the polity: the wish to avoid it implies a rejection of both the sexual and social orders."[8] Some women just said no. Rape was bad enough. But marriage? It could be even worse.

Renouncing their duties to Aphrodite, young women Greek and otherwise, daughters of royal blood with a strong sense of self-entitlement, have been known to take their lives into their own bloodstained hands. Probably they knew a few things about the fate of the Amazons, those alien warriors who mated only once a year with a tribe of men, or took their mates by force, keeping only the female offspring. Though capable of promiscuity, the Amazons were as devoted to Artemis as they were to Ares.[9] Violence, for them, was preferable to making their peace with the race of men. The bloodiest of literature's virgins agree.[10] Most scandalous are the Danaid maidens and the Chinese princess Turandot. These highborn girls pursue their murderous ends with passion and deliberation, defying the local standards of what counts as femininity, unless your idea of the feminine includes a great deal of beheading. "May great Zeus ward off an Egyptian marriage for me," the Chorus of virgins sings in Aeschylus's *Suppliants* (1053–54).[11] "Nessun m'avra!" ("No one will ever possess me!"), boasts the princess in act 2, scene 2 of Puccini's *Turandot*.[12] Many a good hanging prevents a bad marriage, said the Clown in Shakespeare's *Twelfth Night* (act 1, scene 5). These prospective brides took him at his word.

In *The Suppliants*—the first or second part of a trilogy built around the ancestral family of Argos and the fates of those who trace their descent to Zeus and a nervous cow—a wedding was planned that would join two royal families and unite an entire generation of cousins. The plan misfires, badly. Something went wrong between the conception and the execution. Perhaps an oracle told King Danaus to be afraid of his Egyptian sons-in-law; perhaps the manners of the young men were too uncouth; perhaps a trepidation about endogamous alliances disturbed the family. The blushing virgins fail to enter into the spirit of things. They run away, with the help of their father; they commandeer a ship and reverse their grandmother Io's path across the Bosporus and Libya; they arrive at Argos at last, they ask for sanctuary and protection, invoking the sacred rights of the suppliant; their suitors chase them, violently make war on the Argive protectors, who are defeated; the girls are caught; marriage is forced on them. When the morning after the wedding night arrives, forty-nine bridegrooms are lying in their own blood on their nuptial beds, their throats cut by their reluctant brides. One bridegroom, Lynceus, was spared. His bride, Hypermnestra, did not have the heart for the slaughter. Her sisters, a Chorus of human Furies, had no such compunction.

The violence the maidens carry out is at once commonplace and unusual. Men are supposed to defend women, often by force. Most cultures exclude women from the exercise of violence, reasoning at times that the bearing of children is strenuous enough. In the Greek tradition from Homer on (and well into the Roman era), things were different. Jealousy and revenge were considered basic to the female psychology. Women were said to resort to intrigue, cruelty, and deception to protect their children and harm those who had wounded them. Female deities were known for stormy and tenacious fits of rage. Nor was the battlefield off-limits to all women: Amazons, Platonic guardians, and Spartans fought bravely and were not inhibited by the supposed womanly repugnance toward bloodshed.

But aggression, which was highly respected as an attribute of masculinity, did not belong among the feminine ideals for Greeks in the classical age of Athens. And the code of female virtue, invoked by orators such as Lysias, Demosthenes, and Aeschines or politicians such as Pericles, was conventional in ways that Victorians would easily recognize. Respectable women were not meant to be seen in public; respectable women's names were not to be mentioned in wills or law courts. Within the house of substantial citizens, women lived in separate quarters, normally on the second floor. They did not meet strange men; they socialized only with relatives. Provisions for their education assumed the limited range of what could be "knowledge" for a woman. These are the broadest of strokes, but the outlines are reliable. In the average way of the world, for a not too curious man of antiquity, this model was nothing to complain about. Women were born and raised to become wives and mothers. That was what they were good for. Why would they run screaming from the chance to get married? Why wouldn't they decorously assent to their sanctioned and inevitable fate and enjoy being given as valuable gifts by their fathers to their husbands? Why wouldn't they be eager to emerge from a maidenly tutelage that was broadly constricting to one that, while still limited, allowed them admiration, respect, and far more sway over their allotted realm of action? For there were new arenas of power to look forward to: the reins of household management, the prestige of producing legitimate children, the pleasures of spending their husband's money and earning his gratitude.

Forty-nine of the bloodthirsty brides of Argos thought otherwise. They rebelled. Much of what we know about them is conjectural; the sources are diverse and contradictory. Only the fact of their adamant resistance to the state of marriage is a constant feature, together with the description of their bloody escape from it. The incidents are relayed, as a matter that tradition has established, in the first-century BCE *Bibliotheke* of someone who went by the name of Apollodorus. (Apollodorus's book is a "library" of myths, relating familiar and standard versions of old stories, ranging from the fights of the Titans to the homecoming of Odysseus.) The Danaids' adventures are referred to again in the *Fabulae* of Hyginus, probably written in the second century CE; they are remarked on later by Pausanias.[13]

Apollodorus has a few extra details: the grooms were killed in their sleep with knives supplied by Danaus; the reason Lynceus was spared by Hypermnestra is because he had not taken her virginity. The murderous brides buried the heads of their husbands in Lerna but were later purified from the murder by Athena and Hermes (*Bibliotheke* 2.21–22). The murder itself first gets mentioned in *Prometheus Bound*, which experts no longer believe was written by Aeschylus. What they did, and how they did it, his play only hints at; how Aeschylus would have framed and explained it, we can't be sure. The punishment of the daughters of Danaus in Hades or Tartarus is the subject of later traditions, unknown to Aeschylus: they are condemned to carry water in sieves, endlessly. Their assignment to this task may represent futility, as it has generally been interpreted. For those familiar with the vestal virgins of Rome, and the ordeal of Tuccia, obliged to bear water in a sieve to prove her purity, the Danaids' fate in the afterlife raises an interesting question: who is saying that these proud maidens are actually leaky vessels (typical insult thrown at sexually experienced women), and why are they saying that? The punishment may also represent something more positive, their indispensable role in bringing water to parched Argos, which some legends tell about.[14]

In the play the Danaids persist in drawing attention to two things: their descent from Io (*Suppliants* 40–45, 333–37) and their virginity. Most mortals seized on for sexual reasons by gods succumb with greater or lesser degrees of resistance and resentment. Io fought against her seduction;

Creusa denounced her rapist (Euripides, *Ion* 870–922). The Danaids are timid. Yet they are also assertive, most forcefully when they threaten to tie themselves by their girdles to the statues of the gods. We would know more about their motives and defense if we had access to the two lost plays of Aeschylus's trilogy, the *Aegyptii* and the *Danaids*. In our play, the young women have arrived across the sea at the shore they consider their ancestral homeland, Argos. Their cousins are hot on their heels, vowing to get them back. The women ask for protection from the reigning king, Pelasgus. Anxious about their status—are they promised to legitimate husbands who rightly are demanding their return?—Pelasgus initially refuses until he can get the agreement of the assembly. Once he does, he rises to the occasion, overcoming his skepticism and convincing his subjects to take up their cause, protecting these strange young visitors as suppliants and guests, defending them at the price of his life. With this, the play ends, incomplete and, if you like, happily.

The Danaids' story does not traditionally end there. Despite the concession of the Argives, the belligerent Egyptians do not give up, and their attack succeeds. This we know from contemporary summaries of Aeschylus's portrayal of the subsequent events. Versions of the Danaids' story that circulated before Aeschylus give varying versions, but they agree that the Argive defenders are defeated, at which point the girls' father, who has followed them to Argos, conducts negotiations, giving up his claim on Egypt and ascending to the throne of Argos, in place of the hospitable but unlucky Pelasgus. The Egyptian attackers are allowed to keep their kingdom and take their cousins as wives. But then there is a massacre, for the maidens have not accepted the need to renounce their virginity. Aeschylus, we know, would have retained this famous scene, and the surviving play prepares the ground for it. In the early moments of Aeschylus's *Suppliants* the sisters speak of wedlock as an oppressive yoke, the act of a tyrant. Their cousins, they object, are brutal hawks, bent on carrying off these weak sparrows. They are not eager lovers but insolent, immoderate, impious, furious predators (*Suppliants* 30–37, 80–81, 104). They behave like aggressive dogs; they don't respect the gods. They think of women as slaves. "Why should I buy myself a master?" the girls complain to Pelasgus (*Suppliants* 335–37). Dark hints are made of cannibalism, of birds who eat other birds. For these young women, there are no half measures: marriage offers no scope for equality, no room for mutual recognition and cooperation.

The accusation is unexpected. What is Aeschylus doing pretending to be a modern feminist? A comic provocateur like Aristophanes might have given such speeches to his characters; the audience would know how to take them. Here they are a puzzle. Are the Danaids making a claim for equal representation as citizens? They certainly win almost everything they request, being granted the status of free and protected metics (*Suppliants* 609). They have landed at the place they believe to be their traditional home, but they are clearly foreigners and look very odd to the Hellenes who meet them. Black of skin, speaking Egyptian, yet honoring the same Olympian gods, they appeal to their supposed Argive kin to extend to them the respect shown to women in Greek rather than barbarian cities. Any Greek would know that foreigners have nasty customs and don't abide by proper standards of honor and law. The locals listen carefully but take their time. They inquire about the legal status of the demand made by the pursuing suitors: Are these girls their promised property? Would Argos be in violation of the Egyptians' rights if it harbored these fugitives? At this challenge, the maidens threaten to kill themselves on the altar. Fifty virgins, hung by their girdles in the sanctuary: it is a desperate action that would bring pollution and catastrophe to the city and its citizens.

Pelasgus has no choice. He must decide how to salvage the situation, even if a proper judgment will threaten his city with invasion and war. The Argive king was not being teasingly provocative when he insisted he could do nothing without discussion and group consideration. His rule is democratic, which shocks the Egyptian visitors; barbarians were obviously going to be mystified by Greek democratic ideals and institutions. We can recall the incredulity of the Persians in Aeschylus's earlier play, unable to get their heads around the intensity of the Greek attachment to freedom.[15] Here the Argives' practice of shared governance makes even more painful the contrast to female unfreedom. It is not merely these homeless asylum seekers who can expect constraint and subordination from marriage: all women are, in one way or another, Danaids. The fact that they see the future more clearly than most may be due to the unusual attentiveness of their father, who consults their will rather than his own in many things and who supports their extreme measures. In creating such an alliance between a feminine spirit of rebellion and a patriarchal defense of justice, Aeschylus has done something very curious indeed, more complex in its way than the collision of Antigone and Creon. Could this be a father who doesn't want to give his daughters away, whose loyalty is to things other than the household and the polis? But what things might those be?

Marriage in *The Suppliants* is pushed about as far as it can go, away from the domain of the desirable and the approved, onto another, darker terrain. Certainly this play about the horror of matrimony avoids the comic structure of the "marriage plot." If anything, it is roughly comparable to the "unorthodox" or "averted" tragedies represented by Euripides's *Ion*,

Helen, *Alcestis*, and *Iphigeneia among the Taurians*. These are what the classicist Anne Pippin Burnett calls "plays of mixed reversal, mixing actions of catastrophe with others of favourable fortune."[16] They are, one is tempted to say, tragicomedies or melodramas, and they suggest the beginning of the end for the tragic form in its full classical glory. Euripides is usually taken as a sign of this change, the sign of a cultural swerve toward what we might want to call the "secular." Aeschylus is rarely invoked in this context, but here we begin to wonder. When myth is beginning to give way to politics, and tragedies of fate to tragicomedies of passionate disappointment, something different is happening in history. And something different is happening to the relation between the sexes, an event of at least some historical importance.

In several of the stories I consider in this chapter, a battered but still powerful myth makes its presence felt. It is a myth about marriage, political life, and the eclipse of violence, or if you like, the replacement of one sort of aggression by another. Marriage and slaughter are two weapons in a struggle over power between women and men. Reciprocal violence follows its own relentless path until a matrimonial pact interrupts the reign of hatred. And thereby, if I am right, the iniquities of gender are at once addressed and avoided. This pattern is, I believe, recurrent and revealing. It functions to justify marriage, while at the same time making the case for the "natural" submission of one sex to the other: the "world-historical" defeat of the female sex and of "mother-right," as Friedrich Engels termed it, is explained as a myth of origin, the primal confrontation which never occurred yet is always remembered.[17] The inauguration of marriage is one of the most important steps humans take as they pass from the natural into the civil order. For women (and probably also for men), that passage involves the surrender of childhood independence: the Danaids cherish their state of being "unbroken, unconquered, wild (*adamaton*)," and "unmarried (*agamon*)" (*Suppliants* 149–51). Think of Artemis and her cult: one stops being a virgin when one stops playing the bear. And one becomes a different kind of animal, no longer a wild one, unless eroticism allows that wildness to survive in some way or another. The social contract, for which the public institution of marriage is one of the traditional symbols, follows on from the sacrifice of virginity. Old gods give way to new ones. Virgins make their peace with fathers. In one version of the myth, as we will see with *Turandot*, the rule of the sun—a masculine enthronement—eclipses the flickering sovereignty of the moon. Yet some stories of virginal protest can be interpreted more charitably, without the inevitable defeat or humiliation feared by a number of the heroines in this chapter. Marriage reimagined might not crush the spirit of the married; it might also make a larger demand on the flexibility of the polis. And this could mean the eclipse of at least one type of gender myth: "Male and female principles locked in bloody war! Sterile feminine self-assertion relenting in favor of life and passion!" Mayhem, indeed.

There are other interpretative fictions inspired by the problem of the sexes, and one is the idea of marriage as conversation promoted by John Milton and, following him, Stanley Cavell.[18] In his 1644 tract on *The Doctrine and Discipline of Divorce,* Milton wonders whether marriage could be lived as a form of friendship, somewhat in the manner Aristotle believed to be ideal for the relations of citizens in the city: "In God's intention a meet and happy conversation is the chiefest and noblest end of marriage."[19] The arc of this chapter heads in such a Miltonic direction, hence away from tragedy, melodrama, and romance and toward a comic and conversible ordinariness, away from the sacrifice and violent memory of Hippolytus. The sublime alienation of the solitary, chaste hero and heroine in a world of compromise is Hippolytus's alienation. In his world, a tragic world, spiritual distinction is possible, but only at the cost of silence and untouchability. Hippolytus's end is not one most people would welcome. I should not be forced, by violence or ostracism, to repudiate my ideals as illusions. But I may find I need to give them up if I want to listen and be heard, or if I have a place to take up in the social world that strikes me as neither oppressed nor oppressing.

Unlike romance and unlike most modern marriage plots, myth looks backward, to origins both troubling and enabling. In this case, the mythic background of the Danaid narrative returns to a cycle of violence and retribution, a cycle that the Greeks called "barbarous" when they chose to, despite being on very close terms with it. As the rebel girls in Aeschylus demonstrate, this deadly cycle is broken only if a new and unexpected clause is written into the marriage contract, and that is the right of the bride to decide for herself, to choose her own husband rather than accept the authority of her father.[20] It is that, the requirement of consent, that brings marriage closer to a happy conversation and further away from what the Danaids feared it could only be: a rape (compare *Suppliants* 58–60, where they identify with Metis, whose husband raped her sister). For Aeschylus's democratic Athens, just emerging from the terrors of the Persian Wars, the struggle between men and women made an irresistible metaphor for the opposition between civilized and barbarian. Yet who is civilized and who barbaric? The Danaid maidens were savage in their ferocity, foreign and strange in their appearance and manners, yet they are quick to denounce their suitors as thuggish, hubristic, uneducated. We know that Aeschylus intended the outcome to be a reprimand to his

Danaids' campaign against marriage. In the lost conclusion to the trilogy, the goddess Aphrodite brings back the reign of civility and forgiveness, insisting that the duties of love be fulfilled and marriage honored.

An alternative plotline in the complex Danaid myth establishes the sisters themselves in Argos as priestesses of Hera and keepers of a sacred spring, providing fresh water to a region otherwise in danger of destruction because of drought. Blood turns to water, vengeance and rape resolve into the terms of the social contract.[21] The one daughter of Danaus who refuses to murder her husband is put on trial for her disobedience: just in time, Aphrodite comes to her aid with an eloquent and persuasive speech that won for Hypermnestra "her right to decide for herself who was to be her husband."[22] Dedicating a statue to the goddess and to Hermes, Hypermnestra and her man gratefully become the founders of the royal line in Argos and begin the cult of Hera. Hypermnestra's sisters, now snatched back from bloody virginity, marry also and introduce into Greece "the initiatory festivals of Demeter known as the Thesmophoria, in which, to be sure, legitimacy was de rigueur and the powers of the female body were exalted, but at the same time the race of women, recovering autonomy even within marriage sanctioned by the *polis*, constituted a closed city, an acknowledged and redoubtable gynocracy."[23]

Did the matrimonial pact bring an end to the era of violence and purge the Danaids' "remarkably light defilement of bloodshed"? That is what the great classicist Marcel Detienne suggests in "The Danaids among Themselves," the ingenious reading of the play in his volume *The Writing of Orpheus*. This myth of foundation, he continues, does not allow us to draw too neat a conclusion. The private sovereignty of women, the "gynocracy," happens only behind closed doors; it is a licensed aberration, a secret world from which men are excluded along with virgins. Here, in the rites for citizen-wives approved by the city of Athens and other great cities, respectable women who bleed according to the rules get a chance to shed blood themselves, to offer animal sacrifice. Detienne adds a point for all Danaids, present and future, to consider: marriage, the sexual union of a man and a woman, is a city in miniature. It is also founded on blood, resentment, and violence, and those traces will not disappear. If the success of the city allows the scars of the past to be well hidden, the same could be said of a successful marriage: the pain of what is lost becomes harder and harder to recall, the private sovereignty of women more and more a faded secret. Few are "ingenious" enough, as Marianne Moore recognized, to make their deviation permanent.

Yet the protest against marriage in the name of self-possession is essential, for the dignity of men and women alike. It cannot be denied that marriage is society's founding institution, its cement and its soul: it can still be the source of intolerable abuse. Like many originary institutions, marriage has behind it a guilty conscience, a memory of trauma. As Detienne explains, "The Danaids showed that, while the social contract of marriage could exorcise the blood and warfare between those who were closest and most similar to one another, the union between a man and a woman nevertheless remained characterized by violence, and would forever be founded upon it."[24] If society wants marriage, and it seems clear that it does, that may mean that tolerance for violence (and I mean here especially violence against women) is the drink every known social order has been willing to swallow. How ready are we to admit this?

My rebels take aim not only against the city and its norms but against the very survival of the species, a sacred (or evolutionary) obligation they suggest is compromised by the sacrifices wives are required to make in its name. The anthem they invoke is a revolutionary one: freedom versus servitude. They are also invoking a less revolutionary but equally familiar one: women against men, two "races" in violent antagonism. The story begins, in Detienne's words, "with a band of boys harassing their female cousins. There are insults, blows, violence, all the makings of a drama.... In that reciprocal violence in which males and females clash head on, what is essentially at stake is power: power in both senses of the word *kratos*—namely, might and authority." Marriage is, in the resolution of the Danaids' revolt, "the sovereign conjugality that is enforced in this territory (Argos) by Hera of Argos," who is thus endowed with the credit for finding and regulating a "new way for the two antagonistic races to live together, sharing the same bed, without violence and with each partner respectful of the rights of the other."[25] The "might" the angry girls resent is not simply that of unchivalrous and entitled masculinity: it is the "might" of marriage. Is marriage just? Is it a resolution to an eternal civil war that triumphs by concealing the infamy of defeat?

> The story had been told in the seventh century, set out in an epic, the *Danais*, and it became one of the tales that the Greeks continued to tell and that everyone accepted.... The story of the Danaids tells of a bloody war that escalated in a society whose members were related by blood. And in the horizon there can be glimpsed a space in which, for the first time, a social contract would be founded upon the conjugal relationship—a contract that would be supported by many ritual gestures and religious practices designed to guarantee particular ways of behaving, and that would constantly be safeguarded by the divine powers called upon to convert open hatred into a necessary alliance.[26]

If we look at a number of myths, we find various ways of accounting for the invention of marriage, many of them violent. For marriage to exist, says the Old Testament book of Judges, brides first had to be stolen.[27] Much later, when the most virtuous of wives, the Roman Lucretia, was assaulted in her own bedroom, the horror of rape was taken to represent the fragility of justice in a despotic system. With honorable marriage the city can be established and, indeed, marriage has to be defended if the city is to survive and to flourish. A Roman tradition has it that the first republic was founded in the uprising against a tyrant's hubristic resort to rape. Only if rape is denounced can a political order respectful of consent and conversation begin. Only then can the social contract even be imagined. Rape is, for most people, the extreme expression of a denial of consent. The literature of rebellious virginity proposes that nonconsensual marriage is a crime as vile as rape, and as politically weighted. If *The Suppliants* could formulate such a complaint, so could thoughtful virgins as far from mythical Argos as Clarissa Harlowe and her successors in Victorian melodrama. Compulsory heterosexual union sanctioned by civil and religious law is a travesty, the rebellious virgins complain, if it is imposed on us. In Aeschylus's version the maidens' protest is heard. The audience is moved. But then, in what we believe Aeschylus would have gone on to write, the nerve-racking narrative moves to its predictable resolution: marital love trumps all, or perhaps it is the victory of expedience, or sovereign fiat and dynastic necessity. The virgin's story of dissidence withdraws to the margins of the literary and theological canon.

Yet that is not the end of the story, not at least of my version. If the virgins' protest recedes, the anxiety of rape does not, as we can see in the multiple retellings of the legendary rape of Lucretia by her cousin Tarquin. As long as heterosexual marriage is the privileged subject of literature, social practice, and psychological expectations, rape will continue to be its unsettling companion. It may be men who rape, but it is also men who marry, and the city has to find a place for them. Girls who refuse husbands, and seem disgusted by the very idea of masculine sexual importunity, will not get a ready hearing in literature or in public life. Marriage, all in all, is the norm. It is the norm in monarchies and republics, in tribal communities and imperial courts. There have been some wishful utopian sketches that have imagined erotic and domestic life beyond the marital arrangement. Some scholars have argued that true paradise on earth on a socialist or Platonic model, including that true equality of the sexes, can never arrive until humans give up the habit of monogamy. They are the utopians. I have sympathy for the utopians. The ancient Greeks had less time to waste on such sexual radicalism. The skittish adolescent girl who, as Claude Calame puts it for the Greek example, "arouses desire but refuses the advances of men," provokes in them a "resort to violent action: the violence of the abduction and if the rape has to be understood as a metaphorical domestication, by force and through sexuality, of the untamed young girl."[28]

Perhaps the young girls have been reading the story of Bluebeard. Young girls get much of their knowledge of the world from fairy tales, and many of their sexual expectations come from the same place. Some Sleeping Beauties see marriage as the awakening from the narcissistic fog of childhood; some Cinderellas expect the privilege of the wife to save them from a painful disregard and insignificance. Climbing on to the pedestal of their proud and self-sufficient virginity, invoking their goddess, the untamed champion of the untamed, the Artemisian candidates retort: where's your evidence?

History, literature, and myth give conflicting accounts of how communities have reacted to distress and mutiny in the "race of women" (Hesiod), those unruly descendants of Eve and Pandora who, like their late Victorian sister Nora Helmer, try to slam the door on the doll's house. Nora has had many defenders. The Danaids, by contrast, have had trouble finding admirers, in their time and in recent times; the image of their hopeless fetching and spilling of water hardly helped their reputation.[29] Critics on the lookout for insurgency, ingratitude, or perverse prudery find it hard to admit any moral force in the argument against marriage when presented by dissenting virgins. (Disenchanted husbands are a different type of witness.) Eve, our first problem if we are committed to the idea of women's natural subservience, learned to conform and set the example. Milton, for one, liked to see her as happy in her marriage, a chastened helpmeet. The "good wives" in antiquity—Penelope, Andromache, Alcestis—confirmed the template. Women are designed to become helpmeets to men, sexual partners, housekeepers, and mothers. That was the ancient norm, and most daughters of Eve and Pandora went along. Their doctors recommended it: are young women listless, sickly, agitated? There is one answer that always works: get them married; get them into bed.

What happens when marriage is seen as the problem rather than the solution? Men of many types and many dispositions have not been idle in complaining about the concessions and compromises married domesticity requires. Since the Cynics, debating marriage as a life choice was popular among male sages and philosophers in Greek and Roman cities. The fondness for bachelor freedom continued in the scholarly world, where avoidance of marriage, if not sexual abstinence, was the rule for male scholars throughout most of Western history. Many intellectuals were attached to institutions open only to clerics, and others—such as Arthur Schopenhauer, Friedrich Nietzsche, Søren Kierkegaard, Immanuel Kant, David Hume, John Locke, Baruch Spinoza, Gottfried Leibniz, and numerous less celebrated members of the male intellectual elite—cultivated ideals of freedom, work, and solitude incompatible with conjugal entanglements.

If men can opt out, why can't women? Some of history's refusing women are runaway brides, both literal and figurative.[30] Their role models are not the female ascetics of religious tradition who yearn for union with the divine or who are exalted by the idea of self-sacrifice, but rather earlier figures from myth. The patrons of all runaway brides are those tough, willful, and strenuous dissenters from the "rule of Aphrodite," the three divine virgins Athena, Artemis, and Hestia. Runaway brides, I will argue, are trying to tell us something. The literature of defiant virginity is a subgenre with an unusually miscellaneous set of instances and conventions, and critics have only recently begun to explore it with an open mind.[31]

Marriage, the Danaids imagine, must be bloody and horrible. The modern psychoanalytically informed reader wonders why: Does this indicate hysteria, on the part of the woman? Or on the part of the man? There is something disturbing in the willingness of the Danaid maidens to anticipate a humiliating and oppressive future, should they be forced to join themselves to men physically and emotionally. It may be that their fears are sincere: Greek descriptions of the sexual union do not stint on the imagery of the male "mastering the female."[32] But we should also consider the fact that the female perspective being portrayed here is mediated through a masculine writer. The male poet is imagining the revulsion of a large group of young women, horrified by the idea of marriage.

The panic does not only strike girls. The prospective husband could also be nervous about all the ways in which this "rite of passage" can go wrong—his impotence? Her pain? The (metaphorical) disappearance of his penis? Freud and his contemporaries in armchair anthropology speak sagely of non-Western taboos surrounding the first act of coitus. It could be that the "contact" itself is dangerous, exposing each participant to sexual properties which are "contagious." Even the sacramental character of the marriage ceremony (a conception of the practice unknown to the Greeks) can only partly secure the safety of a union that breaks what could be a deep taboo. "The state of marriage," writes A. E. Crawley, a student of James Frazer, "is harmful and later, sinful, theoretically forbidden."[33] Among the Arunta in Central Australia, studied by Spencer and Gillen, ceremonial perforation in preparation for marriage is a form of proxy, to lessen the danger by magical substitution.[34] Ritual and ceremonial, acts of separation and mimicry, often performed in groups, presumably as there is safety in numbers. However dubious the methodology of ethnography's first generation of speculators, they agree on a phenomenon more scrupulous classicists since have generally confirmed. Marriage is not a simple treaty, concluded between authorized agents, whether individuals or families. It is a social ordeal, through which one passes only as profoundly changed. On the far side of the rite of marriage I may encounter someone I hardly recognize—and that stranger may not be my spouse but what used to be myself. Small wonder there were prospective brides who found the prospect intimidating.

Anthropologists try to learn more about the emotional and social meanings of marriage by looking at its rituals. On pots and cups, steles and amphora, the Greeks showed preparations for marriages, processions, sacrifices, the giving of gifts, the unveiling of the bride, the beautifying of the wedding party, even the approach to the bed. Like all important civic and religious events or crises in the fifth-century BCE polis, marriage and the preparation for it requires *sacrifice*, the spilling of blood, the honoring of the divine, a potent if limited communication between mortals and immortals, the practical and the mysterious. To understand some of the anxieties about the event of marriage that, I believe, influence Greek notions of virginity and its ambiguity, the peculiar role of sacrifice needs more spelling out.

Animal sacrificial offerings are at the core of Greek religion. In our instance and in many episodes from Homer on, untried maidens must make dangerous transitions from childhood to maturity, from the profane to the sacred and back again.[35] Strangest are the cases when a virgin girl or boy, rather than an animal, is demanded by a god: Iphigenia knew this case; so did Isaac. At times of transition between childhood and maturity, the gods are not far off; they need to be propitiated; initiation presents dangers and involves offerings of pain and blood. Yet sacrifice is also in the symbolic system of Greek thought the privileged way of marking out what is specifically human, not bestial, not divine. Killing, for mortals, is reined in with taboos. Although defloration is not death, and virgins are not animals, there are analogies. Modern theorists of Greek religious rituals describe the prevalent "bloody animal sacrifice of alimentary type" as a solemn and serious civic practice, which "simultaneously gave expression to the bonds that tied the citizens one to another and served as a privileged means of communication with the divine world."[36] Only domestic animals can be sacrificed, and of those it is almost always sheep or oxen, rarely pigs (to Demeter). The animals must consent.[37] They are purified, garlanded, treated with care; the actual throat cutting is done discreetly, quickly. The meat is cooked, generally roasted but sometimes boiled as well, and shared. The same festivals that involve sacrifices include competitive games as well as musical and theatrical performances. If the animal which was slaughtered is burned in its entirety (a "holocaust"), it is intended to be consumed by the gods alone, and this is a special case of the rite reserved for certain hero cults or cults of the dead. Otherwise mortals and immortals can eat the same food.

At one end of the line sacrifice is a meal, a compensation for brutalities committed, a sharing with the beasts who have so generously allowed themselves to be slaughtered. At the other is art, cultural display, celebration as of a marriage or a victory, and solemn political confederation. For the ancient Greeks, sacrifice is considered "civilizing," the antithesis of "barbaric." It is an offering that consecrates, a careful and cautious negotiation between the city and its gods. Hermes complains about barbarians that "they don't offer sacrifices." They kill and carve without culture.[38] But with us, the Greeks asserted, the necessary element of violence is changed, treated differently. It must be remembered that the violence enacted in ritual has its limits. Humans accept blood sacrifice as a reminder of their mortal limits and the sacrilege in their distant pasts, when Prometheus brought them fire. This is the message Hesiod inscribed into his story of the foundational sacrifices and their causes in the *Theogony*. Only in myth is there allusion to human sacrifices. History offers no substantiation of such practices (although there are rumors and hearsay). Human sacrifice? It is something we "remember" but we don't do.[39]

Tragedy tells another story. In tragic poetry the memory of human offerings to voracious gods and heroes is kept alive with a cruel persistence. And there is one situation that tragedy in the classical age never seems to tire of: the voluntary sacrifice of virgins. Animals get their throats cut, their blood spurts out as an offering to the gods. But by a strange process of association, Greek tragedies choose to ascribe the same sacrificial throat cutting to a "deviant" and monstrous offering of virgin daughters on bloody altars, as we note in the sacrifice of Iphigenia in Aeschylus and Euripides, of Polyxena in the *Hecuba* and the *Troades*, of the daughters of Erechtheus described in Euripides's *Ion*. What makes this "unthinkable" act thinkable? What makes this "abnormality" exemplary, as the French classicist Nicole Loraux puts it? It is, Loraux insists in *Tragic Ways of Killing a Woman*, a "rule ... or what passes for a rule in the world of tragedy: a sacrifice is made with blood shed, and the victim is a young girl.... The sacrifice of a virgin in the theater allows one to think the unthinkable, to question the norms from the standpoint of extreme abnormality, all the more freely since this abnormality is so flagrant."[40]

What is deviant is a sacrifice that is not an animal but a girl on the threshold of womanhood. "Of course," Loraux adds, "in real life the city did not sacrifice its young girls, but during a performance it gave its inhabitants the double satisfaction of transgressing in imagination the taboo of *phonos* and of dreaming about virgins' blood."[41] And what is it about the situation, in mythology or tragedy, that makes a virgin appropriate for this appointment with death, to be offered up in a sacrifice that breaks the rules, when the girl is pure and goes willingly to death, silently and like a warrior, as Polyxena does in Euripides's *Hecuba*? What else can she do, given the catastrophe her city is suffering? Through their courage, the heroic virgins can symbolically heal a threatened fracture that is putting the community at risk. This is the interpretation Helene Foley offers in her reading of Euripides and, like Loraux, Foley agrees that it is the interchangeability of marriage and sacrifice that makes the metaphor work.[42] Loraux puts it with precision: "When the victim is a virgin, the sacrifice is tragically ironic in that it resembles, all too closely, a marriage."[43] The girls with their throats cut are brides for Hades. They leave their own homes for an alien home, just like their surviving sisters led off by husbands. This is, writes Loraux, the "tragic destiny of the parthenoi."[44] Our dancing maidens at Brauron or Troezen, playing the bear, mimicking the warriors they can never be, are not designed for Antigonesque suicide. Yet something about that possibility remains available, and acknowledged. Is consent to marriage, for a young woman, analogous to consent to death? Is consent to sacrifice the same as losing your virginity?

Blood on the Sheets

Classical scholarship has changed in its attitude toward the Danaids. In the early years of the twentieth century their behavior was universally denounced. They were "fanatics," unnatural, repressed, exhibiting an extreme or neurotic aversion to men and sexuality. Their standing has risen in recent times. Classicists informed by feminist and psychoanalytic literature are more willing to speculate on the mystery of this female hostility to men. Perhaps we need to know about the origins of this sexual subjection which, it must be said, can provoke resentment of a kind that "never completely disappears in the relations between the sexes," as Freud puts it in his paper on "The Taboo of Virginity" (1917).[45] Could this bad feeling between the sexes stem from some primal scene of prehistory, at around the time when males and females first became differentiated? Freud's colleague Sandor Ferenczi described a possible scenario, imagining a time when copulation "took place between two similar individuals, one of which, however, developed into the stronger and forced the weaker one to submit to sexual union."[46]

The habit of domination and submission hardened into a sex-gender system and became "normal"—that is to say, a social fact. The humiliation, however, remained, even in the psychological lives of moderns. Among his neurotic patients, Freud reports women who confess to this fear of sex, and men (and women) who desire to inflict pain and to dominate. Apprehension at the very idea of the first sexual experience could be quite explicable if Freud is right that the loss of virginity for a woman "creates a state of bondage" in relation to the man who was her first lover, leading in some cases to "an unusually high degree of dependence," "the loss of all independent will," and "the greatest sacrifices" of one's "own interests"! Yet such dependence is of the very nature of marriage, Freud remarks. Some measure of sexual bondage is essential if "polygamous tendencies" are "to be held at bay."[47] No wonder, says Freud, that "primitive peoples" approach the prospect of defloration with a certain 'lurking apprehensiveness," which indeed they are believed to feel "on all occasions which differ in any way from the usual," occasions which are hard to understand or "uncanny."[48] The passage from virginity to sexual experience may be one of those "uncanny" occasions.

It is a fact that virginity is valued in most cultures. Thus it is incumbent on the psychoanalyst to offer something less flimsily conjectural in the way of explanation of this virginity anxiety than what has been produced so far. There are reasons, Freud admits, for female virginity having such a strong appeal to the sexually anxious male, who hopes to create, through the ascertainment of purity, the feeling of "exclusive possession of a woman."[49] Yet, Freud muses, there is much that is puzzling about the notion that "this right" to exclusive possession, considered so central to the institution of monogamy, is something worth extending to "cover the past." You shall have had no lovers before me. Is that the sum total of civilization's investment in sexual purity, to save the pride of a selfish, narcissistic, insecure lover? Groping about to find a less trivial explanation for the prestige of virginity, Freud picks up from some early and, by most criteria, prescientific anthropological literature, the intriguing notion of sexual dread as something that arises on the "threshold of a dangerous situation," the threshold of a psychical danger, not clearly articulated but nonetheless real. Crossing the barrier between husband and wife, adolescence and maturity, is not all doves and roses. In women it can produce a fierce resentment and will to vengeance; in men it can produce a fear and sense of guilt that can make the pursuit of less "respectable" love objects a much more rewarding choice.[50]

What do Freud's lurid conjectures tell us about marriage and the grisly lengths some people will go to escape it? Was it the prospect of brutality that so inflamed the Danaids, as they claim—the barbarous hubris of their cousins? Was it their masculinity? Was it the maidens' fear of sexual violation? Perhaps it was the idea of marriage as such, the agreement that turns a maiden into a wife, that transfers her from one protection to another, from the household of her father to that of her husband and his family. It turned her into a gift, an item of value in an economy of obligation, exchange, and benefit. Could the dread be, in fact, based on a knowledge of the real power a husband could and did wield? What *are* the threats posed to a maiden that would justify such immodest acts of self-defense?

Conventionally, marriage is the end of drama, and its celebration offers an opportunity for resolution, peace, and festivity, even finality. A wedding is the way we make a narrative hang together despite all evidence to the contrary. For much modern literature the wedding is the ultimate coordinating device, a breathing space that knits together the tangled web of plot. If marriage heals the uncertainties of literature, it does at least that much for society. Marriage is social action in its clearest form. Marriage regulations, in Claude Lévi-Strauss's famous formulation, resemble words: they form part of communication systems between men.[51] Marital agreements are the elixir of economies and the advance planning of the future. Marriage binds nations, defines families, manufactures dynasties and alliances; it mediates between the stranger and the friend, the licit and the illicit, the inside and the outside. It is the all-purpose metaphor for any attempt to translate between privacy and public meaning, between stubborn self-interest and the ever-needy collective good. Communities suffering from a marriage default would die out. Land and wealth, if not replenished by marriage and secured by the complex laws and customs that have for millennia regulated the transmission of property through marriage making, would be as ephemeral as the daylily. With the decline of the original "clan system," in which Friedrich Engels likes to imagine land as held in common, there came an increase in the accumulation of wealth and with that the habit of subordinating women. In Engels's hypothesis, males recognized the urgent need to control inheritance through the male line, and so was invented female chastity and the monogamous organization called the "family," preserved through the rite of marriage and flourishing only at the price of the "*world-historic defeat of the female sex*."[52] He explains:

> The rule of the man in the family, the procreation of children who could only be his, destined to be the heirs of his wealth—these alone were frankly avowed by the Greeks as the exclusive aims of monogamy. For the rest, it was a burden, a duty to the gods, to the state and to their ancestors, which just had to be fulfilled.[53]

The institution of marriage is responsible for the raising and education of children, the formation of subjects and citizens, the stability of everyday life, the accumulation of estates, and the transmission of name and status and obligation. In preindustrial times, the family was the basis of the organization of production. And it is the central battleground for the meeting of two races considered by the Greeks to be distinct and in unending competition: men and women.[54] Engels agrees with Hesiod, albeit in a different spirit: "The first class antagonism which appears in history coincides with the development of the antagonism between man and woman in monogamous marriage, and the first class oppression with that of the female sex by the male."[55]

If you were a woman in antiquity, you were destined to become a mother and, all things being equal, a wife. Homer simply repeated the commonplace: women are made for marriage; men for war, speech, and action (*Iliad* 6.490–93; *Odyssey* 1.356–59). Jews, Greeks, Romans, Babylonians, Phoenicians: the female fate has a certain uniformity.[56] Honor and prestige for a woman is to be found here, if anywhere. Across the Greek archipelago, in the colonies, in built-up towns and rural landholdings, from the Archaic period through late Hellenism and the entire life history of Rome, the continuity in the conception of marriage is striking. Some of that continuity may be more a matter of symbolism and ideology than legal form or definition.[57] Though there are names for many of the elements in this "change of condition" that ushers the unmarried into their new state, in ancient Greek there is famously no word for *marriage* as such, nor for *wife*. The Greek word *gamos* refers to the act of forming the couple and also to the rite of unification in its performance; it does not specify the institution in any abstract or theoretical sense. Indeed, Greek marriage is not a civic or public act, though it is a spectacle, a nuptial spectacle. There are torchlit processions, there is a ritual bath, there are sacrifices, there is the meal, the songs (*epithalames*); there is the unveiling (*anakalypsis*), and the "loosening" of the bridal girdle.

Marriage is the keystone of social structure and stability. It forms links between households and families. It distributes wealth and property: from the groom's family to the bride's—as a payment or *hedna*—in Homeric times; from the brides to the grooms, as a dowry or *pherne* in classical Athens.[58] Particularly interesting is the class of gifts called *diaparthenia dora*—gifts in payment for the taking of the wife's virginity.[59] The woman is given from one family to another, and once properly "taken" and put into the web of her new functions (sexual, maternal, mistress of the household), the action, passing from potential to actual, is accomplished; those married are *teleioi*.[60] Of unique value, this gift of a wife. It opens doors between closed households; it brings new life, a future generation. It takes charge of the well-being of bed and board. A human group is formed; a small society within a larger society. With each new marriage, as Claudine Leduc puts it, "cattle and sheep moved from household to household."[61] Goods circulated and thus created bonds of reciprocity, gratitude, and obligation. Lands were expanded. Signs of status passed on, through the auspices of the legitimate marriage, from one generation to the next.[62]

Marriage is for the girl what war is for the boy. This is Homer's time-honored trope. For each of them these mark the fulfillment of their respective natures as they emerge from a state in which each still shared in the nature of the other. Thus a girl who refuses marriage, thereby also renouncing her "femininity," finds herself to some extent forced toward warfare and paradoxically becomes the equivalent of a warrior. This is the situation in myth of females such as the Amazons and, in a religious context, of goddesses such as Athena. Their status as warrior is linked to their condition as a *parthenos* who has sworn everlasting virginity. It could even be said that this deviation both from the normal state of women who are destined for marriage (not warfare) and from the normal state of warriors (who are men, not women) gives a special intensity to warrior values when these are embodied in a girl.[63]

Turandot or Death: Cutting the Princess Down to Size

> What has happened? Nothing. Just a woman who gives up and gets married.
>
> CATHERINE CLÉMENT, *Opera, or the Undoing of Women*[64]

It is an understatement, this remark on Puccini's *Turandot* in Clément's entrancing book. At the end of *Turandot*—"Love! Eternity! Sun! Life! Our infinite Happiness! Princess! Love! Love! Love!"—the picturesque city of Peking (modern-day Beijing) explodes. Everyone is relieved about this marriage. The crowd is freed at last from darkness and night, and the taste for blood. The reign of Turandot had kept the city on its knees, dreading the next display of high-minded feminine cruelty. It was mesmerizing but a bit indecent. The law of terror and torture, now brought to a satisfying end, began with a vow taken by Princess Turandot. Incensed by the rape and murder of a long-ago ancestress, she proclaims that she will never marry until a man comes along who can answer her three riddles. Suitors who fail the test of this glamorous sphinx will be put to death at nightfall. Now the dawn breaks to see a spectacular reversal.

But there are problems. The frenzied "happy end" is a mess, narratively speaking: Puccini died before he could resolve his drama and tie up the loose ends. Everything runs headlong to a premature conclusion. "My glory is ended," moans Turandot (act 3, scene 3). The male sun rises, the moon sets, the sovereign lord of marriage and daylight wins. The rich music saves it, even if Franco Alfano, who finished the opera, rather than Puccini leaves the last impression. Theatrically, it's a scramble. Catherine Clément doubts that even the genius of Busby Berkeley could have carried off the involuntary clowning. The finale is over almost before the lovers have a chance to sing their duet. Love's victory is noisy yet anticlimactic, a dramatic equivalent of the penalty goal. The mutual passion that seals the final chorus is insufficiently motivated when compared with what preceded it: lavish suffering, heroic innocence, autocratic bad behavior, masculine heads impaled on the walls of the city. The heroine, an icy virgin, had killed anyone who tried to interfere with her chastity. Even to look at her was sacrilege. When she felt annoyed, no one in the kingdom was allowed to go to bed. Raw and absolute, her name is Turandot the Pure, and she gives purity a bad name. But now she has been swept off her feet by a kiss. Accordingly, she renounces homicide and accepts "profanation." Much ado about nothing? Her cold veil is off, her body is warm. She who dictated the lives of others suddenly yields. It's a lucky break. The marriage of the queen brings life back to the frozen world. The Ice Princess is no longer a sorceress, drawing her power from the moon and from revenge, but a votary in the new cult, one in which women rather than men are the sacrificial victims. And, as Clément observes, the mix of comedy, eroticism, and severed heads is in the mode of the grotesque, a confused generic message for this opera about feminine rebellion and the sacrifice of virginity.[65]

The Turandot story went through a number of hands before Puccini took it on. At a loss for a story, Puccini was attracted to this Persian fairy tale of a man-hating Chinese princess and the folkloric motif of the ordeal by enigma. Its exotic improbability had made it popular in an earlier generation when the Romantics discovered the rich vein of the *fantastique*. The riddles are the crux of the drama. Yet the legendary riddles and their answers are less important than the larger cultural and psychological riddle. Once you begin, it just goes on: the complex riddle of erotic ambivalence and the hostility between the sexes; the riddle of sexuality as a wound that promises to heal itself; and somewhere in the foreground, rebellious virginity as feminine protest against the eternal recurrence of the same. Onstage and off, everyone by the end of the drama knows the secret of the riddle, even though it is one which the arrogant sphinx herself has a hard time acknowledging, for the secret is love. The word *love* is sung repeatedly in the final scenes. Yet we hear other words conveying a more sinister meaning: possession, conquest, victory, pride humbled, the shame of surrender. These recur. They sound ominous to Turandot, as they sounded ominous to the Danaid maidens. Marriage is supposed to be the goal of a young woman's life. What if it means the end of every possibility she could imagine wanting?

We can speculate about *Turandot* played another way. Carlo Gozzi wrote his elegant version of the perhaps mythical old Persian fairy tale, and compared to Puccini's his is quieter, if more satirical. Gozzi the Venetian was a cynic and a conservative. He aimed his commedia dell'arte pastiche as a broadside against the upstart middle classes who were starting to write the rules of theater and ideology. His text was frank about the gender politics involved, having learned something from Shakespeare's breeches romances, from Beatrice and Benedick, from Rosalind and Orlando, from *Twelfth Night* and *Taming of the Shrew*. In Gozzi's farcical tragicomedy, the last words are those of the penitent female rebel against men and marriage who comes to beg pardon:

> TURANDOT. Heaven, I have indeed been brutal and stubborn in my hatred of men, and now I ask your pardon. Gentlemen, I once hated your sex, but I have repented. Pray, give me a sign of your forgiveness. [*She mimes applause.*] (act 5, scene 2)[66]

Gozzi's feminist princess is tough but not sinister. Less of a sadist, her flaw is that she is overly attached to her own opinions. She is smart, peremptory, and insolent, her cruelty incidental rather than hysterical. Her fantasy was independence, not revenge. Daily killings in the streets of Peking were part of the ritual because men kept failing to get the point. She did not aspire to supernatural sublimity or picture herself drinking blood. Her defiance is secular. She just had a strong, principled objection to the character and behavior of men, their way of thinking of themselves as the crown of creation, their fickleness and their lies. Her contempt for the sex is almost less important than her intellectual pride, although the two together are certainly a discouraging prognosis for a successful marriage plot. Why should someone as superior as Turandot make a fuss over some two-bit household despot? As we saw, the Greeks had a fascination for this phenomenon, too, for the spunky virgin who isn't ready to be tamed, who makes abrupt appearances in inappropriate places when you expect her to be invisibly sequestered in upper rooms. Strong-minded girls like Antigone or Macaria made interventions in the public sphere that their married counterparts would find impossible unless they were willing to be seen as unfeminine monsters like Clytemnestra or Medea.

The Greek tragedies understood that the condition of virginity endows young women with a sense of exceptionality that they may be reluctant to lose. Their purity is a kind of cross-dressing. As Jean-Pierre Vernant put it, they are not quite male, yet not quite female either, which gives them some stake in the privileges of both and accordingly a leaning toward arrogance that their detractors are quick to deplore. The virgin's mix of pride and aversion is, however, differently shaded in the two versions of *Turandot*. The Princess Turandot as she appears in Gozzi's play is the kind of spoiled rationalist that French satirists sent up as *les precieuses*: fastidious ladies, overeducated, stubborn, priggish certainly, but not castrating demons. This is the context that explains Gozzi's heroine. A woman attached to her privileges, the prospect of domination bothers her; sexuality appears only dimly on her horizon. While Puccini's princess, fixated on a traumatic memory and sleepwalking through her endless night, is manifestly terrorized by the possibility of physical contact, Gozzi's princess hardly bothers to imagine anything so tangible. What she hates is interference, the husband's prerogative. "Men want to keep women weak and useless," she objects (act 4, scene 3).[67] Marriage is bound to be an encroachment. For a girl brought up with no restrictions and no peers, marriage represents an undeserved defeat, the sad taming of a proud nature. Turandot puts it explicitly: the very name of "wife," she says, sounded loathsome to her; nothing could be more cruel than the thought of submitting to a man's authority. A thousand deaths would be better. Like Artemis arguing with Zeus, she beseeches her father to exempt her. To be under a man, that would kill her. Schiller's German version of Gozzi's *Turandot* gives her the most uncompromising words:

> Der bloße Name schon, schon der Gedanke,
> Ihm untertan zu sein, vernichtet mich.
> (act 2, scene 4, lines 1043–44)[68]

What are my choices? Turandot wonders. Marriage or death? Death at least safeguards my honor. Like the Danaids who threaten to hang themselves on the altar by their girdles if they are forced to marry, Turandot is serious. For her, marriage is not that different from rape: both represent subjugation and despotic privilege. In the Greek myth told in Aeschylus's *Suppliants*, the father supports the virgins' resentment. Gozzi's Turandot is on her own in her resistance. Her father is exasperated, embarrassed by her belligerence, and he finds his impotence unbearable. He is keen to give her away, to see her safely in the hands of another man. Marriage will reinstate the law of the father, so perversely abrogated in this feminist fantasy which borrows from the romance tradition the joke of the "petticoat kingdom," where bluestockings lecture their skeptical male subjects until sexual attraction mends the topsy-turvy world.[69]

Puccini's libretto goes several shades darker. Marriage is still a crisis that the troubled woman refuses to negotiate, choosing instead the suspended animation of the cool, uncommunicative maiden, friendless and mysterious, communing only with her long-lost relative, hiding in her bedroom. Gozzi's Turandot has female friends; she gossips and stamps her feet, a feisty, headstrong Emma Woodhouse, if a lot more dangerous. Puccini's haunted man-hater thinks of herself as a deity, a manifestation rather than a creature of flesh and blood; those who presume to get close to her commit sacrilege. Adami and Simoni, Puccini's collaborators, rewrote not Gozzi but an Italian translation of Schiller's "correction" of Gozzi (Schiller raises the tone, removing the ribaldry, making Turandot and her successful suitor Calaf more exalted and serious).[70] The traces of a Voltairean humor at the expense of proud women in love with their own cleverness are removed. Turandot becomes a fury rather than a bluestocking. The libretto adds a sinister backstory, a curse: Turandot has been made inhuman because she is haunted (possessed?) by the unappeased ghost of her ancestor, raped and murdered by a Tartar invader:

> TURANDOT. In this palace, a thousand, thousand years ago, a desperate cry resounded . . . Princess Lo-u-Ling . . . who reigned in your dark silence, in pure joy, and who defied, inflexible and sure, bitter domination, you relive in me today! (act 2, scene 2)[71]

The stage directions have Turandot speaking as if from far away. The past dwells in her; the ancient princess sleeps on in her "tomb," which has taken the vivid form of a young woman's life and actions. Turandot is a crypt in which the purity of her ancestor and her outraged pride is reborn. It is not just for herself that she wages this war. "No one will ever possess me!" she vows (act 2, scene 2).[72] Her invulnerability must redeem her ancestor, magically save her from the crime that took her life and pride.

No such distant horrors bother Gozzi's princess. Since her campaign is against the objectionable qualities of the male sex, what disarms her will not be a second sexual conquest—blissfully undoing the mischief of the first deadly one—but a recognition of qualities that are not at all objectionable. Calaf's generosity, his kindness and loyalty, the nobility and goodness of his father and his old family friend: these soften Turandot's heart, already losing its austerity in the face of these enlightened examples of the new masculinity. Puccini's Turandot is converted not by reeducation but by the magic of a sexual desire she had banished until it vanquished her: she remains a virago until she is kissed, forcibly. Gozzi's Turandot, on the other hand, is slipping all the time, trying to figure out how to save face, how to avoid being defeated in a battle of wits, reluctant to give up the freedom of the virgin in society.[73] Thanks to trickery, not to her natural superiority, she puts Calaf at a loss, but then (in act 5, scene 2) renounces her unfair advantage. Her dignity preserved, she can acknowledge him as an equal worthy of winning in a fair contest. (Shakespeare's readers will be reminded of the flirtation of Beatrice and Benedick, where the friction of the sexes is resolved through changing positions, through the shared opportunity of seeing through riddles, through a wit that allows emotion to appear but not overwhelm.) What tormented Gozzi's heroine was the unjust domination of men, unworthy beings whose transformation she had not been ready to imagine. Once she is exposed to a more enlightened type of masculinity, one compatible with a greater degree of equality and shared interests, her objections can be answered and put to rest.

The vengeful moody princess in Puccini's libretto inhabits another world, one where perversity is to be expected and authority is secured by force, not trickery. If love triumphs over adamant purity, the victory in Puccini is a brutal one. The happy end is achieved only because young Liù gives up her life, making herself a shocking sacrifice to assuage the hatred of the woman whose rival she would have liked to be. Puccini is never sanguine about relations between the sexes: Turandot elects virginity as a defense against the indignities and terrors visited on women through eros and its cruel cults. She is a heroine for a Freudian age, one that has heard about the atavistic power of eros in the unconscious, one that has been listening to sexual iconoclasts like D. H. Lawrence talk about the dark gods of the blood.[74]

Puccini is not known as a poet of feminist protest, yet he is consistently moved by the tragedies of women's sexual exploitation, the duality of female victimhood and female splendor. Love is toxic for women: that's certainly a point you could draw out of Puccini's most beloved operas: *Madama Butterfly* and *Tosca*. It is toxic for men also (*Manon Lescaut*). But for whom is *virginity* toxic? The introduction of the ravished ancestor, a character unimaginable in Gozzi's conception, gives Turandot a motive for her obsession. She values nothing more than her purity; nothing else makes her so invincible, so cruel, so coldly just and vengeful. Redeemed through marriage, Turandot the Pure resigns her sovereignty. The sun is out, the moon is gone, the altar readied for bloody sacrifice is quickly converted to a bridal altar. In opera, that last preserve of feminine passion, the outcome of the war between the sexes is continually in doubt. Marriage or death? Ransomed or condemned? Another execution? Bloodthirsty brides holding up the sheets in the morning? Men, it seems, don't care. The risk made it exciting. Winning a woman who doesn't want you is both dangerous and confirming.

Calaf, the stranger prince from Astrakhan, is hypnotized by the cold silent moon-face of the princess. He rushes to join the procession of those young men headed for decapitation: "Turandot or Death! Turandot or Death!" Either will suit him. Death also is beautiful, he sings: "È pur bella la morte!"[75] He doesn't know enough about Turandot, or death, to know the difference. In Greece, the noble virgins under the knives of priests throw themselves into the hands of death, too, but their bridegrooms did not metamorphosize. When death *is* the maiden, the result changes. Because of Calaf's willingness to die for her, the Sleeping Beauty awakes from the dark and the cold. Hatred becomes tenderness through the pressure of a kiss. Princess Turandot is both furious and delighted. That's sexism speaking, the dog-eared wisdom of misogyny. "She wanted to do it all the time." But her amour propre got in the way.

It's a male fantasy about virgins' fantasies.[76] "They talk of honor and integrity but they really want you to force them." What does this attitude tell us about the hostility between men and women, the odds against their reconciliation in the conjugal bond? History keeps going as if there wasn't really a problem. Literature and art, however, teach us to pause and wonder. Can marriage really happen? Is it only a compromise formation between violence and indifference, between hatred and need? Rape, sacrilege, pride, revenge, and domination are good themes for opera, highbrow and low. On the stage haughty women strike imperious attitudes. Audiences like to watch Clytemnestras and Medeas show off the iron in their souls, remnants of an archaic state of affairs when the pious worshipped sibyls, virgins, or witches.[77] *That* was myth, regressive, superstitious, when primitives were in thrall to a mystified nature they could only imagine as feminine and inscrutable.[78] Now that we are over magic, women usually are not allowed to dominate. In *Turandot* a woman rules for a while through terror and strength of will. She murders every man who aspires for her hand, turning the Danaids' one-night efforts into a long-running melodrama. She is implacable, her subjects cry. She is adorable, her victims insist. But she gives up and gets married in the end.

The play starts with the rumor of an unattainable virgin goddess. It ends with a royal wedding. It is hard to think of an episode in Greek and Roman literature where such a reversal could be enjoyed. In the world of Greek myth, mortal virgins are the right raw material for sacrifice, or for marrying. Divine virginity is off-limits: serious, dangerous, touchy. A semidivine figure like Turandot—absolute ruler, object of sexual fantasy—does not exist in the classical period. Those who conspire against the virtue of an Artemis, an Athena, or a Hestia get a sharp brush-off, or worse. The repercussions for those who assault those mortals bound to purity are also discouraging. Virginal priestesses who break their vows can be buried alive; punishment for their frailty must be severe because their honor at the sanctuary protects it from pollution and the city from calamity. But their celibacy belongs to their office; it is not a matter of personal choice when they are exempted from the profession of marriage. In the chronicles of the Olympians, the virgins Athena, Artemis, and Hestia argued for their freedom, and Zeus, king of the gods, saw fit to give it to them. However, what is possible for gods is not possible for humans: that's what makes them gods. Goddesses have both the right to revenge and the privilege of the single life. They are thereby awesome and admirable. Mortal women who defend their chastity with homicidal intent cannot hope for such admiration. They are seen as monstrous and grotesque. It is not a question of equity but of genre. What divides the gods from us is a strict double standard. Self-protective moral rigidity in a goddess inspires us with respect and terror; for the Chinese Princess Turandot and her would-be sisters, other conventions apply.

Turandot is a fairy tale. It holds out the possibility of an exception, a woman who thinks she is the moon and looks as if she will get away with it. She should have known better. In folklore and mythology, the stubborn girl who won't get married comes to a bad end, at least temporarily, as the Cashinawa myth revealed to Claude Lévi-Strauss:

> Once there was neither moon, stars, nor rainbow, and the night was totally dark. This situation changed because of a young girl who did not want to get married. She was called iaça [cf. Tupi jacy, "moon"]. Exasperated by her obstinacy, the mother sent her daughter away. The young girl wandered for a long time in tears, and when she tried to return home the old woman refused to open the door. "You can sleep outside," she cried. "That will teach you not to want to get married!" The young girl ran frantically about in all directions, beat on the door, and sobbed. The mother was so infuriated by this behaviour that she took a bush knife, opened the door to her daughter and cut off her head, which rolled to the ground. Then she threw the body into the river.
>
> During the night the head rolled and moaned around the hut. After wondering about its future, it decided to change into the moon. "In this way," it reflected, "I will be seen only from afar." . . . The eyes of the decap-

> itated woman became the stars and her blood the rainbow. Henceforth women would bleed each month, then the blood would clot and children with black bodies would be born to them. But if the sperm clotted, the children would be born white.[79]

Although decapitated, which could be a disadvantage (and one the moon-girl's descendant Turandot exploits against her suitors), the resistant virgin in the myth wins a splendid transfiguration, bestowing great boons on the human race. From now on humans will have lights in the sky at night. At the same time, the myth solves the problems of conception and procreation, along with the puzzle of differently colored races. Shy virgins, the interpreter of myth explains, are a problem for communities; they cling to one extreme, the feminine axis, and refuse to mingle, which is to say, they do not participate in the exchanges that unite near and far, the close and the distant (and of course the male and the female). By contrast, the counterpart to the shy virgin is a twofold threat: the incestuous man or the promiscuous woman (symbolized by a rolling head). In between, we are to understand, is marriage of the sort that Turandot and Calaf ultimately celebrate. In the play and the opera, the end is presented as the best possible result for all concerned. The couple reigns supreme. A woman's violent resistance to the marital yoke has been gloriously surrendered; a politically advantageous alliance between royal houses has unexpectedly been consummated. Rightful rulers regain their thrones. The cycle of vengeance is broken by love. A woman's pride is salvaged by a man's delicacy and a slave's suicide. Secret names have come to light, old and justified resentments no longer look important. The war between the sexes reaches a temporary lull. Tartars and Chinese unite their empires. The executioner can take a well-deserved holiday. The crowd celebrates.

The Meaning of the Maidenhead

> Few details of the sexual life of primitive people are so alien to our own feelings as their estimate of virginity, the state in a woman of being untouched. The high value which her suitor places on a woman's virginity seems to us so firmly rooted, so much a matter of course, that we find ourselves almost at a loss if we have to give reasons for this opinion.
>
> SIGMUND FREUD, *The Taboo of Virginity*[80]

Turandot and the Argive murderesses represent extreme positions in the arguments women have had about marriage. In that sophisticated form of ironic romance called the Hollywood comedy of the 1930s and 1940s, modern women have many more options than the Danaid girls. They have money, education, and driving licenses. Yet they still dither, change their minds, leap into the breach, and run away. Marry? Don't marry? It's not invariably a question of finding the right man, the perfect match, the lover who can sustain both a conversation and a life of tenderness and care. It's also, at least in this classic period of cinema when female stars briefly ruled the studio, a question about women's identity and self-knowledge. The achievement of romantic comedy (recent Hollywood versions seem to have forgotten it, to their discredit) depends on how successfully it can make us care about some of the problems interfering with the happy arrival at a state of comic or, in Northrop Frye's word, "festive" contentment. These would be problems having to do with the clash between men and women, with the manipulation and anxieties of sexual attraction and sexual barriers, and the viability of marriage, innocence, and experience. They would have to do with compatibility and incompatibility, hope and disappointment, domination and submission.[81] These are not trivial issues. That they belong in comedy as well as tragedy is central to my argument and my choice of literary examples. It is something I have learned from the work of Stanley Cavell, and which he learned from Frye. For Cavell, the genre of romantic comedy—from Shakespeare to George Cukor—is the place to observe the way society juggles between obsession and indifference in its attitude toward women. Romantic comedy is also the place to ponder the problem of how women define themselves.[82]

"The issue of innocence," "that ancient superstition," as Cavell remarks, may seem too naïve for the glamorous and fast-talking heroines of such movies as *It Happened One Night*, *The Lady Eve*, or *The Philadelphia Story*. In his book on the Hollywood comedies of remarriage, Cavell looks with some amusement at the way in which his preferred genre "pokes fun at the older problem of virginity; what used to be a matter of cosmic public importance is now a private matter of what we call emotional difficulty. We live in reduced circumstances."[83] The symbolism of virginity, and the flurry of cultural or ideological excitement around it, speaks about the significance we place on crossing the threshold of sexual maturity—exiting childhood—now that we know (perhaps we still need to learn this from Freud) not to expect its accomplishment to happen in a single night. We pride ourselves on our sophistication. We think it no advantage to worry about the protection of sexual purity, modesty, and ignorance. But are we really that different from the superstitious "primitive" of Freud's fantasies, aware that sexual intimacy is something to be approached more in dread than in laughter?

Looking back at our ancient duel between a virgin and his stepmother, it is hard to find the moment of comedy. Dread did not let the combatants of Euripides's drama alone. They both wanted to be virtuous and exemplary. But they could not see the humor in their positions. Phaedra was not a modern woman. She could not resolve the contradictions of her gendered circumstances, no matter how hard she put her mind to it. Eros was her doom, not her release. Phaedra did not have the advantage of wit nor the glamour of Hollywood and grand opera. Stuck behind the walls of her palace, Phaedra was at once adulterous and faithful, excessive and secretive, knowing and ignorant, grandchild of the sun and woman of the interior and darkness. Her fantasies, Froma Zeitlin argues, "attest to the slippage of the boundary between the chaste and the erotic."[84] That slippage may be inevitable. Does it have to be a reason for regret? The difference between innocence and experience (and the possibility of their mutual coexistence) is central to Cavell's philosophical rehabilitation of marriage. Or, more precisely, remarriage. Remarriage belongs to the comic. Here the comedy of "remarrying" differs in its conventions from the structural movement which has held comedy together since the days of the New Comedy of Plautus and Terence, a construction summarized by Northrop Frye:

> What normally happens is that a young man wants a young woman, that his desire is resisted by some opposition, usually paternal, and that near the end of the play some twist in the plot enables the hero to have his will ... the movement of comedy is usually a movement from one kind of society to another.... The appearance of this new society is frequently signalized by some kind of party or festive ritual, which either appears at the end of the play or is assumed to take place immediately afterward. Weddings are most common.... As the final society reached by comedy is the one that the audience has recognized all along to be the proper and desirable state of affairs, an act of communion with the audience is in order.[85]

The final word of comedy, especially Shakespearean comedy, is, Frye remarks, "grace." Inclusion drives out exclusion. Grace and inclusion preside over the ending of *The Winter's Tale*, that most painful Shakespearean comedy of remarriage. In the other comedies, too, there are many things that the comic festivities would like to sweep under the rug. Cavell acknowledges the purgatorial quality of the comic universe. There has been pain, betrayal, alienation. Those who once loved thought they hated. Then they loved again. Perhaps they will hate again? Moral markers had been hard to see. Virtue and purity looked like vice; innocence was unrecognizable. Between friends and lovers there had been so much doubt, so much interference, so many obstacles ridiculous as well as serious that the social order seemed to be damaged beyond repair, and all bonds of trust looked like worthless currency. Perhaps the comic turn is only necessary because everything that precedes it is so dismal, because there is so little to believe in. Comedy has to get us out of this skeptical hell.

It does so by a kind of magic—and sometimes (as in the Shakespearean romances) the magic is literal, miraculous. More often, comedy's therapeutic magic is the natural magic of welcome, that grace of hospitality that does not look for guarantees. We can all come in now. The party has begun. But not before separation, misunderstanding, and alienation have taxed our emotions and stretched our resources. The pleasures of comic resolution are not the simple satisfaction of expectations briefly thwarted, not the return to the social state of things we started with but, if Frye and Cavell are right, a "new" covenant, a better organization of things. As Cavell puts it, "The achievement of human happiness requires not the perennial and fuller satisfaction of our needs as they stand but the examination and transformation of those needs."[86] Transformation does not just happen by our deciding it should happen. It must be achieved—and achieved generally at a price. There is rupture and pain in "making things new." Romance, even romantic comedy, may exist in the atmosphere of magic and surprise, but it is not a simple wish fulfillment fantasy. The path out into the sunlight and the party includes a path down, a descent into doubt, loss, amnesia, and even sometimes a seeming death, as Frye points out:

> Whether romance begins with a hero whose birth is, as Wordsworth says, a sleep and a forgetting, or whether it begins with a sinking from a waking world into a dream world, it is logical for it to begin its series of adventures with some kind of break in consciousness, one which often involves actual forgetfulness of the previous state. . . . At the beginning of a romance there is often a sharp descent in social status, from riches to poverty, from privilege to a struggle to survive, or even slavery.[87]

The constant yet plastic story structure of romance, as Frye understands that, is a mythos the imagination requires. Romance likes things to be black and white, high and low; it likes to contrast two worlds, one above ordinary experience, one below it, so that the heroine's or hero's survival of the lonely and painful world (the "daemonic or night world") can justify an induction into the idyllic condition, no matter how implausible the parade of coincidences required to get us there. But comedy is less tolerant of a prolonged indulgence in the embrace of dream and wish. And it is less tolerant of infantile escapism, at least not as a way of life for adults. Comedy, as we know, tolerates—indeed, welcomes—disillusionment. It rejoices in mockery, the discomfiture of moral pieties, especially priggishness. Its eyes are open to the messiness and complexity of sex. Does this mean it leaves no room for innocence? Not necessarily. For Cavell, the notion of innocence is up for revision: "One consequence of our sophistication is that if we are going to continue to provide ourselves with the pleasure of romantic comedies, with this imagination of happiness, we are going to require narratives that do not depend on the physics of virginity but rather on the metaphysics of innocence."[88]

Although this Cavellian turn from the crudity of the physical to the rich ambiguity of the metaphysical is, for my purposes, just what the doctor ordered, it is perhaps too quick. This question of innocence is more persistent than it looks, and it proves to have some important things to tell us about problems that Cavell, and I, believe to be central to the work of philosophy as well as the flourishing of social relations. The most obvious link is to the question of knowledge, or better, the experience of knowledge and how that can be shared, how the existence and content of my mind can be part of the world for you, even part of your experience, despite the daunting impenetrability of something philosophy calls metaphysical privacy. Cavell recasts the old issues of epistemology—How do I know that I know? Can I trust my senses? Can I know the mind of another?—onto a terrain better called moral, insofar as skepticism is not just a professional deformation but a moral failing, a refusal to acknowledge and be acknowledged, a mean-spirited insensibility.

Enemies of the overvaluation of virginity are quick enough to denounce a comparable lack of generosity in militant chastity, which is, as Frye nicely puts it, "seldom likable."[89] In George Cukor's 1940 romantic comedy *The Philadelphia Story*, a divorced heroine is subjected to a series of trials, meant not to test her virginity but to unseat it. As she has been married, and has fled her marriage after some not entirely specified disappointment (only her husband's drinking is mentioned) to return to her childhood home, we can assume she is not a maiden, literally speaking. But there are problems. It is something Cavell decides to call "psychological or spiritual virginity" that the heroine, Tracy Lord (played by Katharine Hepburn), has been unable to shed, and that psychological maidenhood may be interfering with her ability to be happy in marriage. Those bizarre rites of passage the Greeks prescribed must have been interrupted prematurely. Accused of passing herself off as a "virgin goddess," a Main

Line Diana, Tracy finds her moral and epistemic confidence shattered. Unwilling to tolerate the failings of others, Tracy can grow into married womanhood only by falling.

As a Freudian would recommend, the perfection of maidenly narcissism needs a bit of wounding. Tracy's admirable sharpness of character and nobility of appearance have put her on a pedestal; a few bits of marble have to shatter. This is indeed what happens. Before she can seriously remarry, Tracy has to go astray and come back. Her "wonderful, marvelous, beautiful virtue" is not allowed to survive intact, symbolically at any rate. *The Philadelphia Story* is a modern retelling of *A Midsummer Night's Dream*. It applies itself to the business of getting its proud Titania properly married and freed from a kind of ethical frigidity, or metaphysical purity, which the film calls "priggishness." At the end of a bumpy or Dionysian night, Tracy awakens to what she thinks, in her first confused suspicions, to be sexual experience. Chastened by her "fall," she has sacrificed something we may, again provisionally, call unmarried, or Diana-like, independence. Read through Cavell's eyes, the film ponders the question of the meaning of marriage as mutual acknowledgment, since what is required to make a marriage is clearly something more than a man's having the opportunity to have sex with his wife:

> Our genre emphasizes the mystery of marriage by finding that neither law nor sexuality (nor, by implication, progeny) is sufficient to ensure true marriage and suggesting that what provides legitimacy is the mutual willingness for remarriage, for a kind of continuous reaffirmation, and one in which the couple's isolation from the rest of society is generally marked; they form as it were a world elsewhere.[90]

Marriage, as the life embarked on after the initial barrier of sexual innocence has been crossed, belongs on the side of acknowledgment and acceptance rather than Cartesian skepticism. That is, if it is successful, if the marriage is happy. The aesthetic sign that such happiness has been secured is, for Cavell, less erotic than conversational. Marital happiness is a life in words that can be shared, a community of consciousness, as Milton recommended. Against this background, virginity poses a problem, if virginity is taken as the cult of the modest, shamefaced maiden, secluded in her self-regard. Virginity is, I'd even want to say in a Cavellian mood, an epistemological problem, an invitation to solipsism. However splendidly mythology presents the figure of the virgin armed and quivered, the goddess of the wild, or the pure vessel of Mariolatry, we detect in the ideal of virginity more than a trace of narcissism, as Freud was not slow to point out. Or of a frigid arrogance, a fantasy of invulnerability or self-creation, as our sophisticated comedy for grown-ups lets us know.

I want to take this set of associations a bit further, although its full implications will not be visible until we turn to some of the post-Christian ordeals of chastity in chapter 8. One of the most disturbing features of sexual purity as an ideal and a requirement, specifically of women, is its indemonstrability. How do I know that my wife isn't a whore? Physical virginity is difficult enough to ascertain. Hellenistic doctors suggested urine tests; earlier experts, convinced that female bodies (on the inside) resembled bottles with two openings or "mouths," thought a powerful scent could, in a sexually "opened" woman, pass from one end to the other.[91] The bloody sheet is widely popular as a proof, though not for the Greeks; the Middle Ages tried the experiment of dropping the female in dispute into a deep body of water to see if she would float. Fidelity in a wife is even more elusive, as Othello raged when he called for an impossible "ocular proof." If men are maddened by the fact that the inner truth of sexual honesty resists explicit confirmation, the situation is even more dire for women. Can innocence be knowable when its possession implies the absence of knowledge? What does it mean to believe in the existence of what cannot be seen? Can't purity be counterfeit? But isn't it precisely that which destroys all counterfeiting? The dilemmas have been known to drive suspicious lovers mad. Infidelity leaves some traces, or the profession of the private detective would lose its practical rationale. But how much knowledge is enough? Is knowledge really what is required?

If *The Philadelphia Story* is to succeed as a comedy, it needs to find some way to resolve the anxieties about innocence and sexual distrust, self-doubt and honor, that make the "passage from virgin to bride" the perilous transition I take it to be. Athens, with its tragedies and its deities, had a number of options: placate the goddess with sacrifices; use coercion, abduction, rape, or the threat of rape. My outraged female rebels, the Danaids and Turandot, tried violence to protect their virginity. In 1930s America, the passion is muted. No suicides are threatened, no beheadings performed. Nonetheless, female chastity suffers a variety of attacks, some gentle, some cruel.

By the rules of comedy, marriage is the default position. Its consummation should be deferred, so that there is time for tension, misunderstanding, and reconciliation. Society, however, has to have the final world, and society "must be peopled." Society, of course, isn't always sedate. Anarchy is enlivening, and rebellion is necessary from time to time. Hence comic disruption must be tolerated—indeed, encouraged—in order that the values of coherence and conformity (for comedy is generally a conservative operation) be reaffirmed in a festive spirit. Defiant virgins who would rather kill—or die—than marry are not easy to integrate into the accommodating spirit of comedy. Cavell, who tries to create a common space where marriage and antimarriage can meet on mutually tolerable terms, acknowledges that the resources of comedy have to be supplemented by the resources of myth. There is tragedy in Tracy Lord's makeover, a process through which the haughty Diana comes to believe in her own frailty, in her ordinariness, her fleshiness, her "easy virtue." That process can be read in terms myth would understand: to become a wife, the wild virgin must be tamed. The girl must die and then come back as a woman. A sacrifice, yes, but an accomplishment, a growth in stature and understanding. Or it can be read as something uglier: why would a woman accept marriage, given its insult to her autonomy and integrity, unless she had already become disappointed in herself?

The presence of myth and mythic patterns in the film permits larger claims, the largest of which is Cavell's idea that it shows the heroine undergoing a kind of death and revival, "her death as goddess and rebirth as human."[92] *The Philadelphia Story* involves a syncope, a blackout, an amnesiac episode that is at once convenient, safe, necessary, and, as one of its onlookers concludes, an awakening, a coming-of-age. Thus this blackout, with all the mischief and "mess" that can occur during it, is to be welcomed, according to the men in the film and the male critic who thinks about it. Tracy, they suggest, should be glad. Her falling and recovery constitute an essential moment in the recovery of a second innocence, a condition the philosopher and the other male observers call "being human," or that they might less discreetly call "being sexually available." The syncope in this film is also a test, a test of moral discrimination, a way of sorting the sheep from the goats. Tracy's night of glorious drunkenness either ends in a wild episode of extramarital sex in the garden—or it doesn't. It is quite likely to be viewed in the wrong way by the wrong man, the man she was about to marry (the unappetizing George Kitteridge), a man who lacks moral vision and is blind to everything but "breaches of common decency." The heroine's syncope can invite the most conventional and vulgar cynicism. Is she guilty or is she not? Is she chaste or is she not? How one interprets the unconscious, or, as in this case, the lapses that allow the passage from innocence to experience and back again, can be crucial.

Tracy Lord has passed her life as a paragon of aristocratic virtue, hauteur, beauty, and wealth. She is a shining example of what her first husband, C. K. Dexter Haven, calls alternatively an "American Married Maiden," a "virgin goddess," and an "unconquered citadel." But she has a habit, when she has drunk too much champagne, of changing from priggish paragon to abandoned bacchante, a transformation of which she, like Titania roused by Puck, remembers nothing the next day.

The definitive and clarifying instance of this habit occurs on the night before she is to enter into her ill-judged second marriage. Swept up into a giddy flirtation with someone else's boyfriend, Tracy spends a long and carnivalesque night, concluding with a naked swim and a kiss for the eye of the camera. And then . . . She does not remember.

The trials of this modern queen are explained as arising from the fact that she is unable to admit her fallibility—she calls it her weakness—or that of others. Because we know that the stakes in our investigations are those of chastity and the threats to it—for good or evil—we should not be surprised to hear that Tracy's imperfection, the human stain she has been unable to admit, is desire, or more precisely, lack of desire. She had failed in her first attempt at marriage, it is suggested, because she had trouble not always being an untouchable goddess. The few times she was able to shed her veil of Diana, as it were, are times over which she draws a very thick veil indeed. Crudely, Tracy has a problem with sexuality.

Virginity, in the terms this film insists on, is a problem, an obstacle between us and our humanity, a threat not just to sensual fulfillment and happiness but to moral integrity and self-knowledge. Dexter, the husband she has been unable to accept as a lover, calls it the obstacle to her "becoming a first-class woman" (as if there are classes in women?). Tracy's spiritual virginity is the subject of repeated lectures by the men in her life: father, ex-husband, friend. She is described as being unable to become "more of a person," a being of flesh rather than bronze, until she has passed through this moment in which her virtue is in question. This particular moment is, as our understanding of the syncope should now allow us to see, a moment when her consciousness was suspended, until, for all intents and purposes, she has given up her virginity. For, although we are told and given every indication that the men involved are wonderful, courteous, and honorable, Tracy knows that her "wonderful, marvelous, beautiful virtue" being still intact "is no thanks to her."

At the end of the film, we see her basking in the glow of general admiration, having survived exposure to the ordeal of public examination of her virtue. Believing herself to have succumbed to a casual if agreeable seduction under the influence of alcohol, Tracy had claimed, with rueful pride, the title of "Miss Easy Virtue." No longer a goddess on a pedestal, she describes herself to Dexter as an "unholy mess of a girl." She is now allowed to take off the veil of Diana and give up the dubious pleasures of holiness for the more tangible, if risky, pleasures of mess. Second innocence, the outcome of knowledge, experience, and loss, is not immaculate innocence. It is compatible with a bit of soil, a bit of dissension, and a certain amount of sexually amused bickering. Call that remarriage.

Is Virginity "That Old Superstition"? Marriage and Surrender

In the terms of romance, and of comedy, the achievement of marriage averts madness. Dionysian temptations are acknowledged, even permitted their night of oblivion. The sophisticated husband, who values his wife's intelligence more than her doll-like docility, has an intelligent response to her sexual escapades or her occasional flights from the enclosure of the domestic and conjugal yoke. He gives them an amused, knowing glance and then moves on. Love can also be ironic, if it is grown-up love. It does not expect simplicity. It has a large vocabulary. We are not all Cary Grant. Or Oberon of Shakespeare's *A Midsummer Night's Dream*. But we don't have to be as obtuse as Henrik Ibsen's Torvald Helmer, the patronizing guardian of his doll-wife Nora. Before a woman is ready for marriage, she has to be ready for herself. If there is a *Bildungsroman* designed specifically for the young woman in search of herself and a place in the world—the Maggie Tullivers, the Isabel Archers—this issue of the right emergence from childish self-preoccupation is central to it. Rites of passage, ordeals to usher the initiate from immaturity to maturity, are central both to the romance plot and to the ancient religious surveillance of social life and its difficult transitions. And husbands have their appropriate place at the end of that journey toward maturity, not on the bridge to it. Until then, men and women may play with various forms of identity, acting out, as Cavell suggests, a return to childhood. Just as licensed priests were entrusted (one hears) with the dangerous task of defloration, so in fiction, a trickster or a weaver with the head of an ass or a poet (as Tracy's one-night boyfriend is) can perform the work of presenting the goddess with her feet of clay, which she is now smart enough to recognize as happiness, or as desire. It will be a "virtue" of the genre's heroes and heroines, Cavell writes, "to be willing to suffer a certain indignity, as if what stands in the way of change, psychologically speaking, is a false dignity."[93] Remarriage comedy rejects innocence but replaces it with a conversation that knows when to stop, what to leave unspoken in the face of a couple's demand for grown-up independence, even for a certain escape from being known.

Cavell entrusts Hollywood comedies of the 1930s with a very high standard of philosophical achievement. Remarriage comedies, he argues, represent a central case of the aspiration to self-transformation, an Emersonian theme Cavell has identified with the quest for the representative human, or further self; they show us something about the perfectionist desire in a secular age.[94] Perfectionism here should not be confused with the interest in making one's life into a work of art, for that interest fails by emphasizing the individual life at the expense of that of society. Marriage is the trope for the realistic and domestic mise-en-scène of moral perfectionism as Cavell understands it: its promise of happiness requires the individual to affirm the life of society, call that the alignment of private with public interests, of inner feeling and public visibility, the Romantic version of the Lockean social contract.

But Cavell adds something quite different to the practice of comic romance. The way he reads it, the romance form—quest, daydream, journey, and education—does not shirk looking in the face of madness, into the abyss of metaphysical doubt which is normally reserved for tragedy or at least melodrama. In the disillusioned romances of our remarriage comedies, our confused brides learn to recognize the taint of villainy in the noble face of the savior, the perfect suitor, the knight who comes in the dark and disappears. They learn to accept what the Marquise von O in Heinrich von Kleist's tale calls the devil in the angel. Cavell relates this detour of romance into moral horror to his central philosophical problematic, that of epistemological skepticism and its hyperbolic inflation of what *knowing* must be. The desire to know is more than a temptation. It can be an invitation to madness, when I acknowledge that I cannot know with certainty the external world, or myself, or others in that world, and when that admission shatters all my confidence, exposes me to hollowness and disgust. Metaphysical doubt is a kind of defense against the slipperiness or partiality of my everyday ways of knowing, and it can lead to a prolonged attachment to negation. The skeptic's despair over finding an adequate language and an unconditional, undefeatable relationship between mind and world is represented another way by the trauma of the perfectionist in imaginative forms such as myth, film, and literature. If I cannot know with certainty, how do I know what my own history has been? Am I really married? Can anything be sure?[95]

Kleist's virtuous Marquise von O, Cukor's Tracy Lord, and Trudy Kochenlocker in Preston Sturges's comedy *Miracle at Morgan's Creek* are all survivors of a night of oblivion that steals a central portion of their identity away. If remarriage has a moral code, it is forgiveness; this is like the answer we are often tempted to give to the skeptic: Wake up. Get a Life. Cavell turns to Ludwig Wittgenstein's advice here: bring words back to their homeland in the everyday, give them a chance to be used and thus believed. In the darker cases, it is rape that needs to be forgiven, if ordinary life is to be redeemed. Even in the lighter cases, *The Philadelphia Story* and

Miracle at Morgan's Creek, there is darkness enough in the recurring presence of sexual transgression, distrust, social ostracism, betrayal, and insult.

Let me finish by indulging even further, more blatantly, my (or, rather Cavell's, with my additions) allegory between philosophy and remarriage. A philosophy that forgives metaphysical excess does not flee from the truths of skepticism (the truth of skepticism being the fear that our words don't mean anything, or don't mean what we say), nor does it remain mired in empty demands for purity. Philosophy as a romantic and ordinary occupation is still worth the trouble, although I would like to see its future as containing a few of the assignations with literature that it has neglected in its long and settled marriage to science. Philosophy, in its marriage to science, runs the risk of being patronized as well as bored. Spending time with the literary could be a refreshment to the argumentative mind and even a serious recall to an ethic of necessary indecision. The virgin is, often, too rigid, too smug, and too averse to compromise. But the wife has different nightmares.

Nietzsche called the philosopher the man of tomorrow and the day after tomorrow. That suggests that it is the unfinished, the provisional, the suspension of final judgment which are relevant to the ethics philosophers need. This is something like philosophy's commitment to a prolongation of naïveté, a refusal to become too *knowing*, too sophisticated, which saves philosophy from some of the excesses of the art world or the newsmaking world of scientific research. In philosophy we are all amateurs. This is also the conclusion reached by the romantic comedies of remarriage. The time to make up your mind about people, Tracy Lord explains, is never. Forgiveness is the way comedy accounts for that suspension of the cruelty of the law and moral judgment. If remarriage is comic, it is because betrayal, falsehood, and failure are, strangely enough, not the final word condemning human relations or philosophical projects. In comedy, and in philosophy, we can always start again.

Neither philosophy nor literature, however, is the agency most responsible for civilization's long case for and against the sexual instinct. Our great nineteenth-century demystifiers of culture's perverse successes, Nietzsche and Freud, made strong arguments indicting the demands of civilization for their ill effects on the sexual happiness of human beings. Is there any point in expecting sex to bring happiness and pleasure, at this stage of the game? Freud was not optimistic, as he wrote in 1912:

> We may be forced to become reconciled to the idea that it is quite impossible to adjust the claims of the sexual instinct to the demands of civilization; that in consequence of its cultural development renunciation and

> suffering, as well as the danger of extinction in the remotest future, cannot be avoided by the human race. This gloomy prognosis rests, it is true, on the single conjecture that the non-satisfaction that goes with civilization is the necessary consequence of certain peculiarities which the sexual instinct has assumed under the pressure of culture.[96]

Yet however often the "gloomy prognosis" was delivered in the history of civilization, humans kept trying to pretend it could be averted. Law and love, order and desire, *should* be moldable into a shape conducive to human flourishing. All it needed was a certain willingness on both sides to compromise. The urgencies of libido could be talked into accommodation and restraint, if they were promised licit opportunities for expression without intervention. The repressive weight of law and civilization could be distracted at key moments by producing the anarchic energies of eros in disguise, as was done through comedy, romance, and joke telling. Marriage was one resolution of the case civilization brought against what Freud calls the *Sexueltriebe* (sex drives), and by far the most popular. The sex drive, which at its most unchecked ran families, friends, and cities together and into conflict, could be tamed. Taboos against incest, fitful schemes for regulating promiscuity or punishing its results, were partially effective, especially in tandem with the preferred legal and social strategy—the conjugal confinement of desire. Another strategy has been less popular. But it has played a key role, as the next few chapters will show. This was the strategy favored by several of the world religions. Instead of settling for a domesticated and regulated sexuality, why not ban it entirely? Sexual renunciation may not do much to avert "the extinction of the human race in the remotest future," of which Freud warned in 1912. (Why he said "remotest" is a mystery.) But Christianity was willing to take that risk.

4

The Dangerous Mystique of Continence

And when will there be an end of marrying?
I suppose, when there is an end of living!

TERTULLIAN, *De exhortatione castitatis* 9

Toward the heavenly light you too have been summoned, illustrious bride, and to the lifestyle of the angels, as also their companion on account of the brilliance of the lofty beauty of virginity and the perpetuity of the unending glory.

PSEUDO-ATHANASIUS, *De virginitate*, ch. 42

In the same way when he urges us not to live according to the flesh, lest we die, but to put to death the deeds of the flesh, in order to live, the trumpet that he sounds certainly makes evident the war in which we are engaged and inflames us to struggle keenly and put to death our enemy, so that it will not put us to death.

AUGUSTINE, *De continentia* 3.9

Christianity and the Dream of Sexlessness

The Church combats the passions with excision in every sense of the word: its practice, its "cure," is *castration.*

FRIEDRICH NIETZSCHE, "Morality as Anti-Nature," in *Twilight of the Idols*

In the period between the travels of Saint Paul and the High Middle Ages, a new dream came to plague the souls of Europeans. That dream is best called "the romance of renunciation." An ideal, a program, a practice and a fantasy, it was one of the most remarkable of the intellectual innovations of the ancient and medieval worlds. Its story is not that easy to tell. Its evolution was not entirely smooth and its objectives are often unclear: sometimes, as Nietzsche notes, the goal was to find ways to spiritualize the passions; at other times, nothing less was demanded than extirpation—castration as a universal dream. The renunciatory program—morality as "anti-nature"—was a new form of madness, one whose success continues to amaze. The church, Nietzsche grumbles, put a curse on health, on life, on spirit, a suitable "cure" for a species it believed to be degenerate.

Despite all the efforts of saints, hermits, fanatics, and monastic administrators, renunciation's conquest of the spiritual field was never complete. It won the hearts of its adherents in varying degrees. The more extreme degrees of self-mortification were reserved for those with a special vocation, the spiritual athletes who pursued a life of sustained martyrdom, who made denial a career. For the rest, moderate forms of sexual refusal or avoidance were prescribed, and it was those customs and practices that made the greatest impact on the culture of the West, for at least one millennium and maybe two. However you lived under a Christian sky, whatever were the compromises you made and the varieties of desire you accepted for yourself, you could not ignore the fact that there was a war on the flesh, and in this war there would be winners and losers. In a brilliant and quirky book called *Pagan and Christian in an Age of Anxiety*, the great E. R. Dodds looked at the flamboyant behavior of late antique ascetics, hermits, flagellants, and anorexics, at saintly and celebrated feats of fasting, prayer, self-accusation, and sleeplessness, and asked, "Where did all this madness come from?"[1] It is worth trying to give an answer to Dodds.

In this chapter and the next, I want to explore the case for radical sexual renunciation, Christianity's most original contribution to the chastity plot. Radical renunciation was a strange exercise in human self-fashioning. Engendering perfection was, as we shall see, its explicit aim. At times a vow of celibacy is required, as for monks and, eventually, for all the clergy of the Latin Church. In this case, abstinence is key to the freedom and self-abnegation of those dedicated to caring for the souls of others: perfect being is more likely to be found through the practice of a life totally without sex, devoted to prayer, to poverty and humility. At other points, admiration for sexual purity is still strong but expresses itself in less prescriptive ways.

While I do want to underline the significance of Christianity's turn to a sexless sublime, I am aware that the novelty of this dream of renunciation can be exaggerated.[2] Christians were not inventing anything when they warned their neighbors about the dangers of carnal appetites. Those attracted to intellectual or physical asceticism could find much encouragement from Greek and Roman philosophers. While marriage was the norm, for almost anyone born around the Mediterranean before or after the birth of Christ, there were always exceptions, runaways from the norms of domesticity. On the margins of ancient culture, competing with traditional and elite patterns of excellence, there lurked the "others": sages, misfits, solitaries, defiant maidens, and athletic monomaniacs, the spiritually ambitious or the diffident. They were never in the mainstream, but they existed, Hippolytus-like anomalies, drawn to an "antimarriage" ideal, an ideal that is at times sharpened by something else, by an awareness of the divine violence of virginity and a taste for the powerful fantasy of *innocence*.

Christianity's founder was probably one of these outsiders, a young Jewish holy man who avoided his community's social and familial traditions and urged those who could handle it to become eunuchs for the kingdom of heaven. His recommendation (in this instance as in many others) acquired a different meaning when it was adapted to the needs of the institution—that is, when the new movement grew large enough to need a well-defined formula applicable to all who wanted to identify with the Messiah from Galilee. "Eunuchs for the kingdom of heaven" was a club only a few could expect to join: so Jesus seems to say in Matthew 19:12. But did the call to enlist in the coming kingdom imply something more ambitious, a wholesale transformation of the conditions of time, eternity, and the social order? Did Jesus mean to draw everyone into the rebellion against sex and marriage? It was not clear.

Over a number of centuries, and with many bumpy moments, powerful figures in the church made doubt about sex a way of life. But they didn't do that quickly or without controversy. There were, from the start, critics disenchanted with Christian asceticism. In company with many thoughtful pagan observers, critics within the Christian fold tried to uncouple the ascetic imperative and the quest for moral perfection. Suspicious of the cultish pretensions of those groups who came to be known as Gnostics, many self-styled "orthodox" Christians condemned the absolutism of charismatic teachers such as Valentinus or Marcion, who viewed the material universe as tragically corrupt, beyond recuperation by anything "less than a definitive modification of the sexual drive."[3] To the opponents of the Gnostics and the radical Encratites, these proposed cures for carnality were a disease worse than the excesses of the flesh, and a faith that battled too stubbornly against the body was a faith at odds with the divine blessing of creation. Moderation in the name of health or philosophical improvement is one thing; criminalizing the erotic is another. The upper-class Roman monk Jovinian suggested that the church had erred in promoting an encratic discipline, arguing that celibacy and fasting should not be ranked higher in the scale of virtues than other important goods and that virgins, widows, and married women could all achieve the same merits. (It is interesting to note that the statements for which Jovinian was condemned by Pope Siricius in 395 CE are now principles in the official catechism of the Roman Catholic Church.) Clement of Alexandria, a thoughtful apologist much impressed with the Stoic reserve toward sexual activity, put a great deal of effort into the arguments against abstinence and denied the idea that "sex was somehow connected with the transmission of original sin."[4]

We don't need to remember every struggle between ascetic and anti-ascetic to recognize the themes. The case against Christian sexual ideology is familiar; its abuses well known. By the time Christianity had done all it wanted to do with the idea of chastity, sex was a battered and furtive affair, tainted by its associations with the perverse will, the unruly body, and the human inclination toward sin. The rise of clerical celibacy (with its long history of abuses) made the church's intentions clear. So did the church's position on the value of virginity, an issue much more compelling to the theological giants of the third and fourth centuries. With the consolidation of strict sexual abstinence as a rule for the Christian elite, propped up by immense literatures on monastic discipline, penitence and spiritual direction, confession and mortification (a body of material Michel Foucault nicely describes as the Christian "technologies of the self"[5]), something new certainly had arrived: a new way of ordering the self's relation to itself, a new terrain of experience, a new battleground for moral and intellectual warfare.

When monks and nuns, priests and bishops, added to their vows of humility and poverty a promise to extirpate the sexual from their lives and feelings, the Christian world committed itself to a strange equation. The good person was no longer to be the moderate and self-controlled person. Only the sexless were innocent; only a physical and spiritual repudiation of erotic pleasure and attachment could reconnect the errant human creature with the lost state of innocence and integrity. As clerical celibacy gained hold in the Roman church, an old anticonjugal ideal of sexual purity and otherworldly heroism was reshaped and ultimately institutionalized. A form of achievement previously reserved for the extraordinary and the exceptional now became the badge of office, the price of entry into the administrative class of a religious empire in the Latin West. Those who preside at the services of communion, who can administer the sacraments and hear confessions, who accompany the believer through birth, life, and death will be recognizable as holy because they are virgins; those who devote their lives to sanctity, women and men alike, inspire our awe and shame because they can be sexually pure, even if we cannot. At the Council of Elvira in 305 CE, continence within marriage was declared mandatory for the clergy, while bishops and other higher priests were told to abstain absolutely. It looked clear. The prohibitions, however, did not take. Priests and monks continued to live with women, to father children, to support concubines. Pope Gregory VII in the eleventh century found the need to reinforce the rules. As confirmed in the Gregorian Reforms, the Latin priesthood was to be distinguished by its embrace of celibacy, its authority over the laity marked by its exceptional discipline and denial.[6] Those who chose a religious life were also expected to choose purity. Marriage was allowed for most other believers, but only if they conformed in their sexual practices to procreative, heterosexual, and marital norms.

How had this happened? Was this swerve against sex one of the reasons God had become man? The development of an ideal of committed chastity—in the sense of strict continence, ideally including a virginal life from birth to death—took time, and a certain amount of strong rereading of biblical and philosophical traditions. Theologians and converts to the exacting discipline of bodily renunciation recognized a rare and difficult conception of human perfection in the few remarks Jesus made about the lives of those keenly awaiting the end of time, those in a hurry for the coming of the Lord. From the few puzzling hints left by Jesus, a series of gifted writers, preachers, and ecclesiastical politicians fashioned a cult of continence. The married man and woman had long been the bearers of social value, the responsibilities and conduct of the family the subject of moral teaching and religious supervision. No longer was this to be assumed. A new model of moral excellence outshone the conjugal pair and the pious family. The virgin's day had arrived.

Promoting the virgin as the superior instance of the moral life created for Christian civilization a "two-story" world, demarcating the pure and the impure. Its effects on everyday life, even on history, went far beyond the distinction between cloister and marketplace, sanctuary and world. Principled and perpetual sexual abstinence was a way for those who aspired to holiness to imitate the martyrs: the mortification of the flesh might not produce the spectacular glory of dying for the faith, but it delivered a daily reminder of ordeal and challenge. Sexual abstinence—difficult to achieve, rare in a world where procreation and marriage were the norms—severed the chaste and the virginal from everyday and profane reality. Hippolytus would have been delighted. Sacred chastity is a new kind of magic, sacrificial and purifying. The eunuch and the virgin can be admired, noble figures of healing and power, in a culture where even a bully like Theseus would have to confess his sexual abuses and feel ashamed.

The history of Christian chastity from the first to the twelfth centuries shows how the ideals of a minority, a self-appointed elite infatuated with the "angelic life," became a central theme in European culture.[7] Sexlessness was a strange and improbable notion, not an obvious element in the constitution of the virtuous and commendable man or woman. Ethical theorists such as Aristotle wondered whether the extremes of *enkrateia* (self-control) were ever found in human form. Yet the possibility of leading a life untouched by libidinal urges spoke to a certain kind of imagination. The renunciatory theme fed Western notions of spiritual aspiration. It shaped Western literature and aesthetics, controlled the limited way women could enter the political sphere, and infected Western emotions with a toxic strain of guilt, anxiety, and impossible idealism. For the clearest picture of the scope of this ascetic culture, and the most damning diagnosis of its symptoms, any modern observer has to defer to Friedrich Nietzsche, above all to his *Genealogy of Morals* of 1887. If I find myself more sympathetic than Nietzsche wanted to be to the ascetic spirit and its influence, it could be because the Christian turn away from eros reveals something that I believe is unavailable in any other context: it tells us about the disorders of gender and about the way those same disorders have shaped the special dilemma of femininity, a dilemma I think my sex still faces.

Nietzsche called Christianity an ascetic disease. He also described it as a "feminine condition." In both cases he meant to be insulting. Do we have to accept his insults? The Christian community in its early period was a strange association of persons unrelated by blood or birth claiming to be a "corporate" body through its uncanny participation in the passion and death of its incarnated God. It offered ancient Mediterranean society a new model of solidarity. Eventually the church found lasting accommodation with the Rome it began by resisting. But for its radical exponents—and they were many—it offered alternative forms of social grouping. The exceptional Christians who chose to enlist in the corps of the continent had abdicated from ordinary kinship structures and retracted their involvement in the social contract. Living as "abstainers" on the outskirts of imperial and colonial society, they adhered to a different image of the soul and the body, of freedom and power and detachment: an "abnormal" one, "largely because it was, by normal categories, profoundly asocial—it did not belong to society as naturally defined."[8] And this "abnormality"—for how can human bodies withdraw from society?—meant that "one form of human solidarity" was treated as dispensable; as Peter Brown explains, "The common bonds of society, expressed at their lowest common denominator in terms of sexual needs, of sexual joining, and of the natural forms of union that sprang from such joining: family, offspring, kin … for mere human beings, the impetus of the notion of virginity had been precisely to evaporate all such merely natural bonds."[9] And with "natural bonds" went natural reasons for men and women to continue their traditional norms of dependence and subordination.

For the early Christians who warmed to the apostolic and then patristic calls to perfect purity, the old laws of gender and social subordination might become things of the past. As long as there are women and men, bound to one another in the chains of lust and dependency, this mortal earth will go on, exacting its penalties of suffering, illness, injustice, and death. But if that carnal order could be overcome (and who was to say it couldn't be?), neither time nor death would be the last word. In this new heavenly order, masculine precedence could not necessarily be assumed. Montanists in second-century Phrygia spoke excitedly about the generalized spread of the prophetic spirit and the extension of charismatic gifts to women as well as men, women such as Prisca and Maximilla, leaders in a movement which called itself "the New Prophecy."[10] Under the old dispensation, ordained in Eden and reinforced by the disobedience of Eve, the male was the head, the female the subordinate. Humans who lived as angels, however, might not belong to the old Adamic dispensation. Christ, the Prince of Angels, lived without sex, as far as we can tell. In some obscure way he also lived free of the conventional codes of sexual difference, or so mystical readers of the salvation narrative suggested. Most of his first followers were Jews accustomed to traditional divisions between male and female, traditional expectations of female dependence. Women had their important role to play, bearing children, caring for their husbands and relations. Active participation in religious matters did not belong to the "woman's part." Yet here, in the Gospel narratives, in the Acts of the Apostles and in the noncanonical accounts, women clustered around the savior and his disciples, recognized in some instances as disciples themselves, asking questions, paying attention, joining the movement. Something unusual was going on.

The Slander of Femininity: Going Down-Market with the Early Christians

Did Christianity appeal in a special way to women and the socially inferior? Suspicions circulated early, even in the lifetime of Jesus of Galilee. The mockery continued over the next few centuries after his death. Lucian the satirist of the early second-century CE makes fun of the Christian brotherhoods in his parodic "biography" of a missionary and wonderworker, *The Death of Peregrinus*, in which Peregrinus's association with the Christian "charlatans" and "quackery" is just one of his many follies, topped by his throwing himself into a pyre at the Olympic Games of 165 CE.[11] While less inclined to the farcical, the Greek philosopher Celsus in the later second century was equally shocked by the tastelessness of this religion. He judged it a scandal, this worship of a man arrested by the authorities who died the shameful death of crucifixion. Who would be convinced by this but "the foolish, dishonourable and stupid, and only slaves, women and little children."[12] Upper-class pagans transferred their social prejudice to the secretive congregations of Christian worshippers they began to hear of in the late first and second centuries. Only those denied access to the real centers of power and importance could give in to the resentment and rebelliousness these cultish groups encouraged. To be taken in by these magical practices and outlandish claims would be shameful to a man of learning and taste. Indeed, it would be demeaning, as Celsus suggests:

> Their [the Christians'] injunctions are like this: "Let no one educated, no one wise, no one sensible draw near." For these abilities are thought by us to be evils. But as for anyone ignorant, anyone stupid, anyone uneducated, anyone who is a child, let him come boldly.... Moreover we see that those who display their trickery in the market-places and go about begging would never enter a gathering of intelligent men, nor would they dare to reveal their noble beliefs in their presence; but whenever they see adolescent boys and a crowd of slaves and a company of fools they push themselves in and show off.... In private houses also we see wool-workers, cobblers, laundry-workers, and the most illiterate and bucolic yokels, who would not dare to say anything at all in front of their elders and more intelligent masters. But whenever they get hold of children in private and some stupid women with them, they let out some astounding statements as, for example, that they must not pay any attention to their father and school teacher, but must obey them ... the more reckless urge the children to rebel.[13]

Religion has its place, and a gentleman will not neglect public observance or respect for the gods. Upper-class Greeks and Romans wanted their piety to be seen; only a few daring philosophers risked acquiring reputations as atheists. But too much enthusiasm for mysteries and cults is a bad sign, inappropriate for those whose minds are more carefully trained by philosophy and whose responsibilities to active, public life will usually outweigh their interests in spiritual curiosities. It was a commonplace in

Greco-Roman antiquity that religion was woman's business, and it was not a compliment. Strabo of Pontus in Asia Minor said it most clearly: "Women are the chief founders of religion (*deisidaimonia*) ... women ... provoke men to the more attentive worship of the gods, to festivals and to supplications, and it is a rare thing for a man who lives by himself to be found addicted to these things."[14] Celsus spoke for many educated Greeks and Romans in his diatribe against the Christians and their appeal to the socially inferior. Later Europeans were more sympathetic to the association between the oppressed and the religion of a humbled, crucified God. Christianity's call for social change allowed interpretation in radical ways, usually with an eye toward the abolition of private property, the fall of the class system, and the vindication of the low.

As Celsus feared, the unlearned and the socially insignificant heard a message oriented more toward them than to their privileged masters, in parables such as that of Matthew 20:16: "The first will be last, and the last will be first." Christians rising up against an entrenched social order may not have been the only political grouping the church inspired, but they made themselves felt at many times and in many places. One can think of the mystical anarchists of the Middle Ages or John Wycliffe's Lollard followers in the fourteenth century, of Thomas Müntzer during the Reformation and the Levellers and Diggers in seventeenth-century England. At many moments of crisis and social upheaval, Christianity has known its millenarians and godly agitators. They are its outliers and its conscience; they kept Christianity from falling entirely into the hands of the owners and the bosses. Friedrich Engels is one who saw primitive Christianity as a religion for the dispossessed, observing, "The history of early Christianity has notable points of resemblance with the modern working-class movement. Like the latter, Christianity was originally a movement of oppressed people: it first appeared as the religion of slaves and emancipated slaves, of poor people deprived of all rights, of peoples subjugated or dispersed by Rome."[15]

Engels leaves the gender of the oppressed people unspecified. But other observers have not been slow to link the socially insignificant to the lesser sex, and both to the population in which early Christianity found its members. The church historian Wayne Meeks draws some interesting conclusions about "the first urban Christians": "By virtue of their birth, or their citizenship status, or their inclusion (or exclusion) from the various Roman *ordines*, many new Christians ranked low in the Greco-Roman prestige system."[16] Did women find a special relevance in the preaching of Christ?[17] Certainly there were a number of women named in the letters of Paul (Priscilla, Phoebe, Julia, Tryphaena, Tryphosa, Junia, Apphia, Lydia, and other "sisters" and "friends" who are deaconesses, fellow workers, leaders of house-churches; Rom. 16:1–12). There are women appearing prominently in the book of Acts, in the Apocrypha, and in the Gospels themselves. The texts from the Nag Hammadi corpus that became known as the Gnostic Gospels are particularly attentive to the presence of women, although it is true that many of these figures are described as sinners, fallen far from their original integrity and virginity, and yet in the course of their stories (their "romances of the soul") are restored to knowledge and salvation.[18] In the *Gospel of Philip,* fidelity and truth cluster around the figures of the three Marys: the mother of Jesus, the mother of James and Joseph, and Mary Magdalene, companion of Jesus (*Gospel of Philip,* 59:7–10).[19] Gnostic literature indeed differs from that of Jewish and Christian texts of the same period in its lavish use of feminine metaphors for the divine.[20] Norea, a mythical figure who struggles with the "rulers of this world" in *Hypostasis of the Archons,* is a virgin and a daughter of Eve, and perhaps the "mother" of all the Gnostics.[21]

Many episodes of the second- and third-century Apocryphal Acts of the Apostles stage encounters between a charismatic apostle and a shocked (but often receptive) outsider. Frequently these outsiders are female. Won over by the teaching, young women and old women abandon or betray the men who are their guardians, to throw themselves into this "new age" cult. The apostles come to know where their market is: attracting men through their skills at healing, the miracles they perform, their bravery and intransigence; attracting women through other means. Some of these women are widows, some maidens, some bolting wives: Peter and Xanthippe, Peter and Eubala, Paul and Artemilla, Paul and Stratonice, and most famously, Paul and Thecla. As the editor of these apocryphal texts comments about Paul's activities, "Evidently events thus took the same course at Philippi as at many other places: the preaching of continence met with success among the women, but aroused the men against the apostle."[22] And other versions of these romantic stories of the brave and persecuted apostles continue to emphasize their relations with female converts. The canonical Gospels show a keen awareness that Jesus was fishing for more than one sex: in some of the most popular stories in the canon, Jesus is portrayed with Mary and her sister Martha, with the Samaritan woman by the well, the poor widow with her two mites, the woman taken in adultery. He is linked in profound fellowship with Mary Magdalene. The texts on the margins of the canon are even more attentive to women, who are shown asking questions, leaving their homes, infuriating their husbands and fathers, courting the fury of the state, seeking martyrdom.

Beyond that, all is speculation. Reliable figures showing the proportion of women to men among the early congregations do not exist. To guess without any accurate demographic information, in the absence of sources or firsthand accounts of the early communities, is pointless.[23] There is some evidence that women were teaching and preaching, that they enjoyed a freedom from attachments to fathers, spouses, or children that their Jewish or pagan neighbors hardly knew, even that they were angling for authority. Certainly there were women performing clerical offices, consecrated women called deaconesses assisting bishops with women believers and catechumens.[24] But were they more welcome in the churches than they had been in pagan cults? According to the historian Ramsay MacMullen, non-Christian women in the period after 200 CE "enjoyed access to a great range of activities, experiences and authority among traditional cults," in which they could serve as priestesses and even preside on their own over cults and initiatory rites.[25] This prominent level of participation was uncommon in churches, and unknown in synagogues. Yet women are mentioned again and again by the male churchmen who observe and sometimes cultivate them, conspicuous among the charitable, giving to the poor, establishing sanctuaries for the sick:

> The Christian church not only redefined the bounds of community by accepting a whole new class of recipients, it also designated a new class of givers. For women had been the other blank on the map of the classical city. It was assumed that gift giving was an act of politics, not an act of mercy; and politics was for men only. By contrast, the Christian church, from an early time, had encouraged women to take on a public role, in their own right, in relation to the poor: they gave alms in person, they visited the sick, they founded shrines and poorhouses in their own name and were expected to be fully visible as participants in the ceremonial of the shrines. By the end of the fourth century, the traditional view of the place of women in upper-class Roman society had come under strain.[26]

Luke-Acts (probably written between 80–90 CE) and Paul's Letters (53–70 CE), some of the earliest texts in the canonical New Testament, mention rich women as benefactors of the ministry and of the churches: if they could hand over useful amounts of gold or supplies, it would be difficult to deny them a voice in church matters. And women accompanied the apostles and their descendants on their missions. Members of the first churches were well aware of the challenge they offered to conventional codes of masculine and feminine behavior. Gender trouble was there from the start. One could read for many years in a library of Greek and Roman literature without noting the presence of women in the social and intellectual arena. A few women entered the Stoa and the Garden; a few were visible around the Cynics and the Platonists; Pythagoreans would not even consider them for membership. The voice of Roman poetry and political discourse is a masculine voice. The implied reader of pagan philosophy is a masculine reader. It is curious, then, to see the changes in language as well as practice from the start of the Christian campaigns. Wherever Jesus went, women are mentioned in his company, or as joining a crowd eager to hear him. Women are the first people to discover the empty tomb (Mark 16:1–8; Matt. 28:1–8; Luke 24:1–11; John 20:1–18). It was a woman, Mary of Magdala, to whom Jesus first spoke after the resurrection (John 20:1–19; Mark 16:9–11). It is probable that women were among the first disciples.

It was men who molded Christianity. But, Gillian Cloke points out, there were "large numbers of extremely active women of high-profile piety at this time, some of them enormously wealthy, powerful and influential, the stars of their contemporary Christian stage no less than the men."[27] And it was not just upper-class women. The celebrities did come from privileged backgrounds, as other women lacked the freedom to dispose of their time and their resources: Macrina, Marcella, Melania the Elder, Melania the Younger, Olympia. Products of rich and powerful families, famous heiresses, these women devoted their fortunes, their houses, and sometimes their lives, often abandoning their children and spouses. There were also women among the hermits and anchorites whose names are unknown, wrinkled emaciated women in the desert living for years unvisited, sometimes by passing as men. These "holy women" entered history when they were significant enough to be written about by "holy men"; if they wrote their own stories, none have survived, and there were reasons male leaders of the early Christian church preferred to underestimate the participation of women. To cite just one vivid example, Augustine's sister was the founder of a monastery for women and pursued a life of service and spiritual achievement comparable to her famous brother's, if not quite on the same world-historical plane. Her very existence is unmentioned by him; appreciation of her work figures nowhere in his immense body of writings, whether private letters, autobiography, or publication.[28] Just as obliterated is Ambrose's sister, prominent in the same monastic career.

Historical evidence about the extent of female participation in early Christianity is sketchy. Nonetheless, it is clear from many sources that the language of male and female had shifted. Sexual difference becomes more slippery. Symbolically loaded, curiously inflected, it is an element in the way the new kingdom is imagined, especially in the allegorical language popular with a number of church fathers and medieval divines. Pagan philosophy had skirted around the question of the soul's gender, even when it laid down recommendations for the different social and moral educations of boys and girls. Plato, at least in the *Republic*, offers an out: intellectual enlightenment bypasses the messiness of the gendered body; the guardians are both female and male, even if the intellect sounds suspiciously as if it were formed in a masculine school. But when Christians spoke of the soul and its salvation, they used a more sexually differentiated vocabulary. For Paul, Jesus was signified as the "Bridegroom." His followers were his virginal "brides" (2 Cor. 11:2). While the image had rich scriptural authority—Israel is the bride of God as well as the fickle harlot (Isa. 54); the bride in the Song of Songs awaits her spouse with joy and erotic excitement—it was also startling. Male converts must have wondered what this meant for their sexual status. Including all the church in its scope—men, women, virgins, wives, and widows—the metaphor turned the repentant, keen to leave their sinful lives for a better one, into a mystical army of the betrothed. They were promised an eternal and heavenly marriage in exchange for renunciation or sexual restriction on earth. Their white clothes might signify the purity to which they aspired, but such clothing was also appropriate for the celebration of a nuptial rite. How far was this rite expected to go?

Church fathers enlivened their ascetic exhortations with allusions to the embrace of both men and women by their divine Bridegroom: "The man who is courting the spiritual alliance," writes Gregory of Nyssa, will want to show himself at his best, not decorated by his worldly wealth but with the treasures of his mind, taking for his "life-companion" the wisdom that will embrace him, then "he may prepare himself in a manner worthy of such a love, so as to feast with all the joyous wedding guests in spotless raiment." Both men and women will be eager for such a marriage, Gregory explains, for the soul wants to "cleave to the undying Bridegroom," and will not be as happy in a "marriage of this world" (*De virginitate*, 20). Erotic language was not spared: just as a young girl in secular society would want to keep herself a virgin for the greater pleasure of love with her licit partner, so the Christian will want to stay pure (or the widow avoid remarriage) to enjoy marriage to Christ.[29] Just like his Father, Christ was of the male gender: Jesus's circumcision was carefully attended to by his (biological?) mother and (adoptive?) father. His intended companions were presumably female, as Judaism and its Christian offshoot scorned same-sex marriage. Did that make Christian masculinity a strange condition? Was it shaped by its image of the mystical marriage of Lord to his church into a sacred masquerade, a little too reminiscent of the cross-dressing ceremonies of the Galli and other worshippers of Isis, Cybele, or Astarte?

What kind of men (and women) would this celibate and divine Bridegroom want to marry? The church, wrote Tertullian, Jerome, Cyprian, and Ambrose, was a virgin bride awaiting its spouse, modest and pure but decidedly feminine, unlike Israel, who often "played the harlot."[30] Members of this church might understand their betrothal mystically and enjoy the sensuous imagery from the Song of Songs without fear that their masculinity was henceforth irrecoverable. But to participate in this allegorical marriage to God, which led to spiritual rather than corporeal procreation, did one need the accidental features of gender at all? What was the physical union between a man and a woman doing in this new chapter in the history of humanity? Was it not doomed to obsolescence?

When Christians looked to Jesus or Saint Paul for advice on how to live their lives, they were confronted with an apocalyptic horizon. Marriage and procreation might make sense in a world for which no end could be seen, but a different and more radical sexual ethic was appropriate to a community living in expectation of the coming reign of God, the Parousia. In the world to come, our bodies will not be what they are now. Family and kinship will be irrelevant. *Husband* and *wife* will be words without meaning. To a question posed by the Sadducees, Jesus replies, "The sons of this age marry and are given in marriage; but those who are accounted worthy to attain to that age and to the resurrection of the dead neither marry nor are given in marriage, because they are angels and are sons of God, being sons of the resurrection" (Luke 20:34–36). And Mark's Gospel makes the same point: "For when they rise from the dead, they neither marry nor are given in marriage, but are like the angels in heaven" (Mark 12:25). In the kingdom of God, Paul explains in the biblical letter to the Galatians:, "There is neither Jew nor Greek, there is neither slave nor free, there is neither male nor female; for you are all one in Christ Jesus" (Gal. 3:28).

The statement from Paul's letter to the Galatians has great potential to provoke: There will be, in the better world to come, "neither male nor female." But then, what? Will there be a third sex? Will the questionable female sex, those unreliable daughters of Eve, became sanctified as holy, or will the entire "race of women" (as the Greeks preferred to conceive it) slip into irrelevance, once the function of wife and mother recedes in favor of the sister in Christ, the companion in arms? Church historians in the nineteenth and early twentieth century choose to leave such issues unexplored, for the most part. The hierarchy of the church was male; presumably it had always been so. Women had a role to play in the past, present, and future life of Christendom and no doubt useful talents to offer the church, as anyone who studied the medieval flowering of powerful abbesses and headstrong female visionaries could not help but notice.

But the fact that Christianity made sexual difference problematic, that it "placed a question mark after marriage, sexuality, and even the differentiation of the sexes,"[31] did not echo for scholars in the past with the same resonance it has come to enjoy today.

Christianity and Its Romance with Renunciation: From Eros to Angel?

The movement inaugurated by the preaching of Jesus was influential among Jews in the turbulent outposts of Palestine. Soon it was converting non-Jews in all the territories governed by Rome. The message it brought came in the shape of an announcement that the kingdom of God was at hand, that Israel would soon be free, not just of the yoke of Caesar but of all earthly rules and alliances.[32] It promised salvation and new forms of life. It demanded that the lovers of God and of their neighbors forgive and forgive again. And, as it spread in the years 100–400 CE from Galilee to Rome and Corinth, Antioch, Carthage, and Damascus, many who were dissatisfied with conventional social, class, and family arrangements had a chance to hear it.[33] Listeners to the first Christian missionaries made up an audience whose character and composition we know a fair amount about from contemporary observers, some hostile, some merely curious. Many converts to Christianity came from the educated elite.[34] But there were many others, who had various reasons to sever themselves from families and the dominant social environment. Some were poor, some were slaves or recent freedmen, some were itinerant, some were women, some were religiously restless or themselves charismatic, in love with the new possibilities of a prophetic vocation.[35]

As the movement attracted more interest from those outside Judaism, strengthened by compelling missionaries like Paul, its "romance with renunciation" blossomed.[36] Indeed, this fondness for world rejection and ascetic detachment may have been the secret of its success. In some respects the Jesus movement was not particularly unusual. Wonder-workers and healers were a fairly familiar phenomenon around the eastern Mediterranean. Another small sect of itinerant miracle believers from the tempestuous circles of Judaea would under normal circumstances attract little attention. There were a number of unusual beliefs that the early Christians publicized, the most remarkable of which was the idea of a dying and rising God-Man whose intervention in human history could combat the finality of death. But the ascetic refashioning of the natural conditions of the body, and its partnership with a stubborn withdrawal from the values and pressure of the "world," represented something else: a vision of an alternate life that must have sounded convincing to many people unsatisfied with the options on offer.[37] It was a vision of a life where the constraints of gender seemed lighter or less significant, a life equal to that of the angels. "Do you grasp the value of virginity?" John Chrysostom writes to his flock in Antioch. "It makes those who spend time on earth live like the angels dwelling in heaven. It does not allow those endowed with bodies to be inferior to the incorporeal powers and spurs all men to rival the angels."[38] And it was a vision of ascetic transcendence, where freedom from sexual desire was reimagined as a kind of transformative magic, an empowering change in the old and weary makeup of the human creature: "The ideal of the untouched human body came to the fore. In the imagination of the time, it acted as a charged joining point of heaven and earth and, on earth itself, as the symbolic rallying point for a rapidly expanding church."[39]

Was it obvious in the early history of Christianity that sex would be so fatefully on the agenda? I suspect that the warning signs were inconspicuous. "Sex-negativity" was not the main event in the preaching of Jesus, nor in the missions of the apostles. The earliest Christians were divided about marriage and celibacy, some indeed indifferent to the entire question of asceticism; there were other battles just as urgent as the fight for chastity, the "great war of continence."[40] To "derive a consistently ascetic message from the Bible," Elizabeth Clark notes, was a challenge for those early Christian writers who wished to find scriptural authority for their "renunciatory program."[41] The movement that began around the magnetic figure of Jesus had other objectives. Its hopes for reform, for the kindling of a new life and a new way of living in community, only tangentially brushed up against the conventions of Jewish and Roman notions of sexual propriety. About these, as about many other things, Jesus spoke with a freedom and authority that was provocative. Jews, of course, were used to being accused of backsliding. The prophetic books of the Bible contained a copious diet of angry allegations, disappointed scolding, and threats to God's fickle but still chosen Israel, the "virgin Bride" who so often threatens to cheat. Israel was a lax and unreliable lover of the deity; her infidelity was manifested in moral lassitude, failures in the performance of ritual and cult, and in centuries of obliviousness and complacency. While reminiscent of the sharp solicitude of the prophets, who called on sinners to return and repent, Jesus's tone was different. It was more enigmatic, more personal, its accusations more intimate. Those who are sure they are adhering to the form and command of the Law, Jesus was saying, are failing to hear it properly, failing to love it in spirit and in truth. They let themselves off too easily. And the consequences are there to be seen: political impotence and disgrace for the Jewish nation, decline in prestige and independence, physical tribulations, exile and humiliation.

The inspired young reformer from Galilee was all too conscious of this disappointing state of affairs. He did not place his hopes in any of the political movements of the time, ones that were mobilizing at least some Palestinian Jews to revolt against the Roman Empire. Like the Zealots and other insurgents from Israel's stormy history of exile and frustration, he wanted the Jews to raise their standards, to cease being a compromised and downtrodden people. This would, in his view, require dramatic reorganizing, both personal and collective. Jews were in a wilderness, but it was one they had made for themselves; they had built the pit, and the pit was moral. Straightforward political upheaval would be of no use. Only a transformation of the inner man would change it. Much of this call to reform was uncontroversial. Judaea had heard versions of it before. What was new was the radicalism of Jesus's ethical demand. Equivocation has no place in the moral life (Matt. 5:29–30). There can be no excuses, no lukewarm approximations of fidelity to the "greatest commandment," the commandment to love (Matt. 5:44). Jesus's clarification of the Mosaic precepts was simple but rigorous. Reasonable discretion in matters of marriage and bodily purity was not good enough. Avoiding outright adultery was a sham if you could not keep yourself from lascivious private thoughts. Conformity to the strict letter of the law was no guarantee of excellence. What passed as respectable conduct, Jesus announced, too often shrouded a hard heart and a hypocritical disdain. The adulterous woman is not the shameful secret who should be expelled and hidden from view: she is you, she is everyone. Jews' pride in their high moral standards was ridiculed. How are you honoring marriage and chastity if you allow divorce and polygamy? Divorce, approved as a convenience and a necessity by state and temple, is a contradiction of the God-given meaning of marriage. Wife and husband are no longer two; they have become one body. Only God can take them apart, not men.

The time is short, as Paul was to reemphasize thirty years after the departure of his master. Concern for the fine details of relationships within the household and the bedroom would be a luxury that those on fire for the kingdom of God cannot afford. Your kin, your brethren, your dependents on this side of the abyss that separates those mired in time and those redeemed from it, they may all be vanishing shadows. There is little point in accumulating ethical credits for a world that could soon cease to exist. Marrying and giving in marriage, sexual virtue and its cultivation, these may be concessions to a society that believes it will endure: those concessions are obsolete, if such endurance is a phantasm. Old moralities will not apply, in the presence of God. The stringency of Jesus's preaching shifted the focus of attention away from the concerns of social reproduction and cultic purity, such as the Jews along with many of their neighbors understood those. A sharp wind from the heavenly future stirred up longings for a kind of independence from the demands of society and the body, an independence strong enough to cut all tired links to life as it has been known. Marriage was one of those ties.

The eschaton, as we know, was delayed. Apocalyptic fervor did not long remain a factor. But its decline did not erase the new dream of a sexless existence. On the path of Christian thinking about sex in the postapostolic age, there were a number of detours and eccentric adaptations as the church gradually acquired, first, a place in the Roman world, and then, dominance. From being a persecuted minority, Christians became a tolerated and then a triumphant majority, closely affiliated if not in many instances hand in glove with the imperial power. The story is not clear-cut. But there is one thing that emerges from it, a stress that is hard to overlook. Greco-Roman pluralism in sexual matters—the public accessibility of prostitutes, the inclusion of youths as desirable sexual objects, the easy accommodation of divorce and remarriage—was doomed. Where moralists in the pagan world called for control and, for a few, dignified austerity, Christians went all the way for prohibition. Sexual excess was not simply shameful, to be avoided by rational and well-bred people. It was a sign of human nature perverted, of the rule of evil spirits, of unholiness and damnation. Aphrodite must be slain.[42]

Once puritanism was let out of the bag, it was hard to seal it up again. This is still true. For as long as Christian idealism has haunted the conscience of the West, finding a congenial home in the literature and in the art of Europe and its colonies, there has always been an audience for what Friedrich Nietzsche rightly perceived as the slander against sensuality.[43] To appreciate the novelty of Christian asceticism, it is useful to return to Nietzsche's writings of the 1880s.[44] Here the philosopher develops a hypothetical narrative about the twisted origins of moral ideas. With a malicious delight, Nietzsche documents the absurdities of renunciation. The ascetic is placed under the harsh light of the psychologist, who is trained in the diagnosis of deviance. What are the symptoms displayed by the ascetic? They are found in his very success. The ascetic is a high-functioning but toxic form of life. Asceticism turns a deficiency and an emotional incapacity into an advantage all the world comes to envy, to the world's discredit. Weakness is made to look like strength; denial to look like plenitude. Nature is pushed aside in favor of the unnatural. This is what the West calls morality.

Morality, all morality, not simply altruism and the ethics of disinterestedness, is really a mutation in the body of culture. The trouble is, this mutation is seductive. Christianity is only one of the many "slave mentalities" to benefit from it. The "slave revolution in morality," as Nietzsche describes that, triumphed under the sign of the spirit. The *spirit* is an odd organ for the human organism. It does not seem to like the belly, and it particularly recoils from the genitals. As spirit sees it, natural man is vulgar man. The spirit has a low threshold of disgust and has specialized requirements for its health: thinner air, a less robust diet, sedentary occupations, shaded rooms, and bloodless ideas. Christianity arose as one of the spirit's frequent historical victories in its war against life. It demonized what it called the "old animal," the sensual man at ease in his own flesh and with his own appetites. When Nietzsche takes on Christianity in the first essay of *The Genealogy of Morals,* he portrays it as adopting the Jews' fight against nature and the human race. The Judeo-Christians had somehow mislaid the crude instincts of other more successful races. Their ill-tempered "ressentiment" was the physiological reflex of a temperament unable to thrive in a healthily competitive milieu. It found a congenial atmosphere in a psychic condition best called masochism, a condition some might be tempted to ascribe to the early Christians in the desert. Slave morality digs out the most tenacious of all pleasures, the pleasure in pain. It reverses all commonsensical norms to make passivity and impotence seem noble and pure. This was the genealogy of ascetic values, the fatal darkening of our "ascetic planet."[45]

The Jews and their offspring, the Christians, discovered a new and even more dangerous kind of hatred, Nietzsche asserted, "the deepest and most sublime hatred, capable of creating ideals and changing values." Then they called that subtle monstrosity "love."[46] The Christians were the worst: they burned incense in front of ascetic ideals; they besmirched sexuality with their ugly creed of self-denial, and they made guiltiness into a deeply rooted human habit.[47] Nietzsche did not predict the association between ascetic styles of conduct and modern capitalism that Max Weber made famous. But he did identify the tendency of ascetic scrupulousness to foster mediocrity. Asceticism is more dangerous to the flourishing of the human species than crime, illness, or greed, because it does not just attack a healthy organism, a living society, weakening its defenses and undermining its resolve. Asceticism, complains Nietzsche, has warped our taste and seduced our intellect. Any hope we can resuscitate our old, natural selves is an illusion, one that sexual radicals and liberators from Rabelais to Reich continue to indulge.[48]

If Nietzsche is right, Christianity won the battle for values before Constantine ever painted a cross on his battle flag. Undoing asceticism's victory would mean undoing the human mind, in some fundamental way that even Nietzsche's call for the birth of a new kind of (Zarathustran) human could not accomplish. Science, Nietzsche insists, leaves the terrain of puritanism pretty much untouched; even feminism has done little more than muddy the waters, mixing demands for sexual liberation with demands for censorship. Sex had become too important to be fixed by the forces of reason and good sense. This is something Nietzsche helped nineteenth- and twentieth-century critics of morality see. Enlightened faith in a naturalistic explanation of moral judgments failed to make much headway against the culture that had swallowed the ascetic pill. The belief that there was something intrinsically wrong with sexual pleasure would not go away. It was incoherent. But it was indelible.

The period of late antiquity, into which Christianity intervened with its propaganda against eros, is an interesting case. It would be convenient to interpret late ancient attitudes toward sexuality as positive and relaxed, but as Paul Veyne and Michel Foucault have argued, the pleasant picture of pagan sensuality is full of holes.[49] Drawing from another tradition, that formed in the stricter styles of the Jewish Bible and Law, postapostolic Christians developed a mythology of sex as something powerful, domineering, and possibly diabolical. Insults and denunciations became the normal language for speaking of sex. Preachers and theological writers were not shy in stirring up anxiety and distaste with their talk of acts and appetites as defiling and polluting. Working on a susceptibility to shame that played a considerable role in late Roman moral life, the Christians went to new lengths: sex was, in most cases, sinful. The original sin of the human race, banishing us from our original condition of felicity, is in some mysterious way bound up with sexuality.[50] Sexual love in pagan antiquity, however girdled with expectations, taboos, and norms, was not sinful because sinfulness—as opposed to transgression, disgrace, and shame—is not a Greek or Roman concept. Sex in pre-Christian antiquity did not represent the entrance of darkness into a world of light, the cosmic and existential wound that destroyed innocence and turned the will away from its intended objects. On the other hand, sex in the lands that spoke Greek and Latin was a complicated business. Erotic passion causes suffering; it can unman a manly man and expose anyone to ridicule and violation. But, however destabilizing, it had a grandeur in Greek and Roman literature, if not in life or law.[51]

The passage from pagan constraint to Christian sacred virginity is what I hope to make perspicuous. However thin it is in external events and grand, destiny-shaking spectacles, this is a passage that marks a break in history. A new shape of religious and moral life unveils itself, and so does a new and odd idea: that a sexual identity could be created by abjuring sex.

Yet that novel type of sexual identity ("holy asexuality," if you like) is best understood as a new direction in the metaphysics of the subject, as more significant ontologically than for the history of sexuality, as a recasting of myth rather than a variation in the activities of the libido.

An anonymous homily on virginity, written in Greek in Syria in the early fourth century, advises fathers that they should rejoice if their daughters express a desire to remain a "virgin for Christ."[52] Your young plant, the homilist explains, will be glorified like "a bunch of grapes amid thorns and briars." In your undefiled daughter you have a real treasure; do not be careless in guarding her, make sure her comportment is measured, her appearance and gestures modest, her habits abstinent, her devotion to fasting strong and consistent; keep her at home, do not show her off to men, "do not allow anything wicked to approach the pure temple." Follow the discipline with your sons, "do not be remiss in persuading the males to sanctify their own bodies"; turn them away from the passions of the flesh; persuade them of the value of virginity by describing the miseries of marriage. If your daughter chooses the virginal life and remains faithful to it, do not regret that her beauty is not being offered to a husband, for her Bridegroom is the eternal one, not the one who can die or remain absent, filling her life with worries and sorrow. The virgin is the pure and perfect fruit, "a sanctuary dedicated to God, temple of Christ, pure altar to the King, Holy Spirit become flesh, amulet of the law, student of the Gospels, pride of the Church of God, triumph over Eve's transgression, revocation of banishment, reconciliation with humanity, bride of the Heavenly King, pledge of life." If you, the parents, fulfil your office as priests to this immaculate temple, you too will be rewarded, "admitted to the bridal chamber of the heavenly kingdom." Just as temporal marriage of their young, involving complex negotiations for the upper classes, delivered status and security to the proud parents, so this betrothal to Christ will advance your credit in heaven. Your household, which guards this paragon, will shine.

The images the homilist uses to praise the privileged virgin, and exhort others to join the cause, are the same ones appearing in one after another fourth-century treatise on virginity. Once established, the rhetoric seemed too satisfactory to admit of much change. Virginity was "the perfect life" and the tonic of immortality. It was reserved for a privileged elite. "These are our angels," John Chrysostom says of the gaunt holy men living as solitary hermits in the mountains around Antioch in the fourth century. The elite was male and female, aspiring indeed to a state wherein sexual distinctions would no longer apply. Though the homilist addresses the young of both sexes, via their parents, it soon became clear that the female virgin had a special role. Her body was a sanctuary, and the metaphor here was exploited as far as possible. Since the female body was adapted in most cases to the natural and social function of conceiving and nurturing a child, if it renounced those offices it was available for a more sacred function. A house on the Sabbath is swept and washed (so the Jews believed) to serve as the proper dwelling place of the Lord. Why shouldn't an ardent girl be a dwelling place for a divine bridegroom?

Encouraging pious Christian parents and their daughters, the writer is optimistic: with the consecration of female virgins, centuries of attacks on women's carnal weakness might be rendered obsolete. The virgin's purity could wash clean millennia of sin and error. A virginal woman is a second chance for humanity, the final reparation for the crime of Eve: her modesty and sexlessness undoing the stigma borne by the entire female sex. Eve was a shadow that remained on the reputation of the female sex. Because of their ancestor's weakness, women were suspected of sensuality, shamelessness, and incontinence. And the homilist finds much to agree with in the traditional imputations against womankind. But the virginal woman, he rhapsodizes, marks an exception, an emergence from the history of shame, slander, and treachery: no longer will one see a woman and say "Jezebel, Eve, Herodias." The virgin, triumphing over the curse of Eve, shows that the sex can compete with males in the contest for self-control. Sophrosyne operates in the world to protect the vulnerability of the wise and reflective from the uncertainties and tribulations of life. But *enkrateia*, the more extreme renunciation of the immaculate and virginal, shuts the world out entirely. If you convert to its discipline, you will be living in the body as if within the walls of a sanctuary, as if this earth in all its reality had already passed away: the virgin is not a person but a temple.

Such a life would become the elite way of being a Christian, the exceptional calling that allowed undisturbed concentration on the love of Christ, the condition from which introduction into God's presence could most readily occur. But did such a promotion of the elite form of the Christian life necessarily mean that the "rank and file," who continued the conventional use of sex to reproduce and found families, were still bound to corrupt, even demonic practices? Some of the patristic vitriol on the subject of the filthiness of lust and procreation is of course exaggerated for rhetorical effect, as any Roman orator would have advised: your opponent is always a scoundrel, a dirty dog, selfish, impious, and a liar. Any good lawyer would have a pile of insults handy for such disputations. And church fathers like Tertullian, Jerome, and Basil fell easily into the prosecutorial mode. When an advocate for chastity wants to recruit, say, wellborn maidens to a life of permanent virginity, he makes the alternatives look bad: marriage is full of woes, parenting a prolonged ordeal, admiration of your sexual charms doomed to dissipate, and sexual pleasure (graphically described to alarm the innocent) a brief, humiliating release. Yet if the struggle for continence is to look heroic, a noble exercise in overcoming a powerful foe, then sexual pleasure cannot be entirely belittled. If the sexual temperament of a prospective female, or male, candidate is lukewarm or temptation an insignificant and rare occurrence, then the triumph of chastity will be less dazzling.

Christian propaganda for virginity had to deal with these divergent elements of the program, and the rhetoric sometimes shows the strain. On the one hand, chastity is the authentic and original state, what Adam and Eve would have enjoyed if they had not been corrupted. It is beautiful and pure, restoring human nature to the likeness of God. It is an imitation of Christ, himself a virgin. Just as an earthly husband wants his bride to be his alone, so Christ the spiritual and immortal Bridegroom wants us to come to him untouched and autonomous. On the other hand, lust is a wily and persistent antagonist, one that the Christian must continue to fight as long as life on this earth continues. The Christian thinkers who wrote and preached in favor of dedicated virginity played on both registers, speaking with great sweetness and intimacy about the glorious stature the continent Christian achieves, while at the same time not sparing the brutality in describing all the temptations and disgraces of nonvirginal backsliding. Christian chastity, it must be said at the outset, was never considered identical with physical integrity: a virgin who has kept her body unavailable to sexual use is not a virgin if her mind and manners are unchaste. Rather, she is a false virgin and deserves cruel contempt from Christians. In the late fourth century, John Chrysostom writes sternly of the virgin who "has reversed the meaning" of virginity "by wearing the glory on the exterior but being entirely dishonored within":

> Even if her body should remain inviolate the better part of her soul has been ruined. What advantage is there in the walls having stood firm when the temple has been destroyed? Or what good is it that the place where the throne stood is pure when the throne itself is defiled? No, not in this way has her body escaped pollution.[53]

To be a true virgin, John Chrysostom continues, is not a matter of sexual abstinence on its own. It involves a continuous struggle. "You need a soul fond of strife, one forceful and reckless against the passions. You must walk over coals without being burned, and walk over swords without being slashed." You must be a sound reasoner, unafraid of fasting and sleeplessness, alert and armed with arguments. It is challenging: "Our battle is against natural compulsions," as "we emulate the life of the angels" and "race with the incorporeal powers."[54] Another expert, Pseudo-Athanasius, wrote a Greco-Syriac treatise on virginity that synthesizes many of the admonitions favored in this genre: no true virgin cares for her looks or pays any heed to adornment; she renounces all anxiety about worldly things. For what use is it to preserve the integrity of the body if you have not preserved the purity of the soul? But if you do, you deliver a gift that is precious to all:

> Let chastity and serenity rise upon her, just as those who are not steadfast, but debauched, will arise and be ashamed when they see her. Just as a good ointment and a precious liquid, even if put in vessels, fills those in the house with its sweet fragrance—not only those who stand within does its sweet fragrance delight, but all those outside it fills with its sweetness!—so too when the sweet fragrance of the virginal soul flows onto her body through chastity and serenity, the excellence that lies within is made manifest.[55]

The language of "altar" and "temple" and "sacrifice," as well as that of the "sweet scent," which purifies the house and everything about it, shows how the Christian advocates of chastity adapted to their own uses the Jewish connection of sacramental holiness to bodily purity, of sin to pollution.[56] The virgin's body is a sacred vessel and an altar, as Ambrose also emphasizes (*De virginibus* 2.4.27). This is what all Christian bodies, virginal or not, should aspire to be, as Paul insisted: "temples of God" (1 Cor. 6:19). Virginity in its Christian sense stands for a state of perfection, not for a condition of the body. Those who understand it will not confuse virginity in this religious sense with a young person's inexperience, something passing and temporary that is surrendered for the sake of initiation into social adulthood. In many of the treatises devoted to the virginity gospel, widows or the married who have renounced sex aspire to have a purity and integrity equal to that of their sexually inexperienced fellows. The crucial criterion is choice and commitment. Becoming a virgin is an act of the spirit. But it does mean that the flesh will have to be transformed—not only tamed but remade, born again in newness of life.

Christians were prepared to go to great lengths in their war against the flesh. Sexual desire is a dangerous force, something to be feared and guarded against. It is a burning fire, said Paul to the Corinthians, a restless and intractable ache that wants always more. Corruption is waiting at all times and in all places: it can enter through the eyes, the skin, the lips, and, easily, your thoughts, dreams, and fantasies. Keeping busy is a good idea, as is segregating yourself from the opposite sex, avoiding the sight and touch of your own body, and remaining inside. But if you can wean yourself from the excitement that female bodies bear—here not that different from young male bodies, as Paul acknowledges (Eph. 5:5; 1 Cor. 6:9–10)—then you are the lucky ones.

Making the Two into One: Virginity and Gender

It is good for a man not to touch a woman.

1 CORINTHIANS 7:2

In the treatises and letters of the third- and fourth-century Eastern and Western church fathers, female virgins change the very nature of the human. The virgins who will fill the choirs praising God in his heavenly courts are female virgins, rarefied beyond any earthly kinship. No longer mothers and wives, these are figures of femininity who redefine the category, replacing all its traditional elements (carnal, reproductive, and economic, being a helpmeet and yokefellow of man) with unfamiliar ones. Women, once they are introduced to the benefits of Christian celibacy, will be powerful allies and recruits. They have been destined for subordination and service. Can they discover a greater freedom and spiritual authority in lives of withdrawal, austerity, hardship, and sexual abstinence? Many women thought they could.[57] Perhaps the limits of their gender would be transcended when they entered a new community of love, undefined by any of the functions so far assigned to the female. Clement of Alexandria, late in the second century, gave them reason to be optimistic (reasons quite possibly adopted from those Plato had advanced in redesigning the *Republic*'s system of social organization):

> Pregnancy and parturition belong to a woman as she is a woman and not as she is a human. . . . As far as respects human nature, the woman does not possess one nature and the man exhibit another, but the same: also with virtue. If, consequently, a self-restraint and righteousness and whatever qualities are regarded as following them, is the virtue of the male, it would belong to the male alone to be virtuous and to the woman to be licentious and unjust. But it is offensive even to say this. Accordingly, women are to practice self-restraint and righteousness and every other virtue, as well as men, both bond and free; since it is a fit consequence that the same nature possesses one and the same virtue. (*Stromata* 4.8)[58]

In his first letter to the church at Corinth, Paul addresses women who might be recruited for the cause of total continence by listing some of the aggravations the wife will experience in marriage. If a woman espouses God rather than an earthly husband, her mind and heart will be focused without interruption or distraction. She could be free in a way pagan or Jewish wives can only dream of. When Paul addresses men, his tone changes. Undoubtedly the higher choice would be to embrace a sexless existence. That, however, is not going to be easy. There are some whose temperament is well suited for it, or—better—who have the gifts for continence, and they are strengthened by divine grace. For the others, sexual desire can continue to gnaw; sexual thought and fantasies can becloud the mind and shame the anxious Christian even if he refrains from acting on them. For males, a frank appraisal of the self is in order. How realistic is it for you to believe you can expunge sexual arousal from your constitution? Good intentions are useless if the urge to fornicate continues to hold its sway. If this describes you, the only valid response is to marry soon and conduct your marriage with sobriety and decency. The same applies if you are betrothed to a virgin. If her youth makes her restless with sexual desires, then do not keep her in an unstable state of denial: marry.

When he speaks to the Corinthians, Paul knows he has women and men in his audience. The first generation of the Christian ministry expected that males would be its leaders and its role models. But women's cooperation mattered even more, since they held the reins of reproduction. Descendants of Eve, they had the power to reverse the old association between the female body and temptation. In the language spoken by the early church, women were the weak link, the devil's gateway. Yet for that very reason they were the ones who could rebuild the bridge between God and man. Daughters of Eve could become daughters of Jerusalem. Brides of men could become brides of Christ if only they would keep themselves out of men's beds and minds, if only they would give up admiring their own bodies and making themselves desirable, if only they would stop enhancing their flesh with baths and scents, inviting with their glances and alluring with their movements.

By the time of the great flowering of Christian asceticism in the fourth and fifth centuries, the age of Melania the Younger, Macrina, Olympias, and the famous virginal "friends of Jerome" such as Paula, Blesilla, and Eustochium, outstanding women had become a major part of the story. The fourth century was female virginity's "golden age," when the allure of continence became practically a fever, exciting and winning away daughters, wives, and widows in the East and in the West, in Constantinople and Caesarea, Nicomedia and Antioch, Alexandria and Ancyra, Rome and Jerusalem. Consecrating yourself or your daughter to a life of strict and austere celibacy was hardly a universal practice in ancient cities and communities. But it was an idea that inspired the pious and the spiritually ambitious. For just a minor sacrifice here and now, of a life that was often difficult, compromised, or even miserable, you could be set aside for an undefiled communion with the Lord in silence and tranquillity. The training for chastity was, it must be said, exacting. Instructions to the naïve virgin were stern. Purify the senses: keep yourself untouched by any unfitting sounds, sights, tastes, and smells; the hands are particularly vulnerable, as are the feet. Make sure hands are used never in violence or in greed but only "uplifted in prayer" or reached out to help the needy.[59] You have been crucified to the world and all its bodily desires; keep your hair short and covered with a band and veil as symbolic of affliction and the pure life, your clothes "dark and mournful," eating very little and without gusto. "It is shameful for the virgin to put on a tied sandal that is carefully decorated in order to attract the gaze of those who see her." The virgin's footwear is provided not by shoemakers but by God, for the Gospel is an "incorruptible and enduring sandal."[60] You could be useful—caring for fellow ascetics, giving your goods to the poor and needy, tending to the sick and old. And you could learn—studying the Bible, thinking on the holy truths, even attempting to write in Latin, Greek, and Hebrew as the great Marcella did. And in the long run, as a compensation for bowing out of the social routines of marriage, household management, and child-rearing, you would win the bridal crown as the most blessed spouse of the divine Bridegroom. And all your friends, who had not chosen this holy career, would look on with envy after death when they see "holy virgins clothed in the garments of immortality, holding in their hands the Psalter that is engraved in their hearts, singing the triumphant hymn of virginity, and wearing on their temples the wreaths of immortality in return for which they renounced the human groaning here below, dancing in front of Christ under the leadership of the angels, with delight arising in the merriment."[61]

One encratic paragon, the apostle Andrew, is described as traveling through Asia Minor and Greece, working miracles, banishing demons, fortifying his disciples with the example of his ascetic rigor and courage. No less impressive, if more irritating to his opponents, was his effect on women: Andrew was particularly good at converting women to virginity. In the view of the author of his romantic story, Andrew was the kind of spellbinding and charismatic male that elite Roman husbands particularly detested. Wherever he went, he attracted those ready to break free from the captivity of the body. Listening to him, they found they wanted to secede from the world of marriage and procreation; they yearned to live in poverty and self-denial. Who were these converts? What was their social status? The Acts makes large claims for the success of the apostle, recounting how he draws to the cause both women from brothels and women from great families. Running from the "filth" of sexual intercourse and the norms of their city and land, they become converted to sexual abstinence. For this new life is something extraordinary. It is said to be a way of being a champion (*athleta*). In Patras Andrew converts Maximilla, wife of the proconsul Aegeates, so that she refuses to sleep with her husband and cares for nothing but her "inner husband." Her husband is furious and remonstrates eloquently with her: how could you, who had received so much from me, who warmed my bed and raised my children, love someone else more than me? Despite Aegeates's threats, which are far from hollow (he gets Andrew executed), Maximilla runs to kiss the hands of the apostle who continues to solicit her for the unblemished chaste life of the consecrated virgin. Although her husband has the social superiority, Andrew's moral superiority is the clincher. And he offers her the chance to heal both herself and him, to redeem them from the "ignorance of Eve" and the "acquiescence of Adam."[62]

There were women who took up the challenge with determination, dedicating their lives to the pursuit of an ideal that was increasingly specific: to become a saint, a divine human being. One who succeeded in becoming a saint was Macrina (325–380 CE), the daughter of a wealthy and distinguished family from Cappadocia. Her family had been Christians and landowners for several generations, and both brothers became important figures in the early church: one, Basil, bishop of Caesarea (370–379) and promoter of monasticism, the other, Gregory, bishop of Nyssa (371–395). Macrina was destined to be extraordinary. According to her brother Gregory, who wrote a hagiographic story of her life and works in 383, even her birth demonstrated her vocation to the life of sacred virginity. Shortly before the birth of her daughter—indeed, while she was in labor—Macrina's mother had a dream:

> She fell asleep and seemed to be holding in her hands the child still in her womb, and a person of greater than human shape and form appeared to be addressing the infant by the name of Thecla. (There was a Thecla of much fame among virgins.) After doing this and invoking her as a witness several times, he disappeared from sight and gave ease to her pain so that as she awoke from her sleep she saw the dream realized. This, then, was her secret name. It seems to me that the one who appeared was not so much indicating how the child should be named, but foretelling the life of the child and intimating that she would choose a life similar to that of her namesake.[63]

Macrina became a teacher, a spiritual guide to other women, living quietly and apart from the politics of the church, devoting her inheritance to the convent for women she established and ran at Annesi, in the hills of Pontus. Her physical integrity was only part of what made Macrina special. Yet the fact that her virginal body was manifestly something that had remained in its original and untouched state, a direct link to the purity of Adam and Eve before temptation arrived, demonstrated her closeness to Christ, her chosen Bridegroom. Other upper-class women with fortunes like Macrina's were not so privileged: they had to marry; she was lucky enough to lose her fiancé to death before the wedding. Without retreating to the desert, or living a vagrant's life as a pilgrim, this refined woman achieved the freedom she desired.

Among Christian congregations in many parts of the Eastern Mediterranean, North Africa, and all over the late Roman world, young women were leaving their homes. Sometimes they took their betrotheds, husbands, or brothers with them. Often, sensibly, they brought their female servants as well. If they could, they signed up for the harsh conditions of the ascetic life. Otherwise they lived at home, as long as their parents were in tune with the Christian concept of household monasticism. Careful female converts avoided the conversation of strangers, but they still sought to spread the word, encouraging others to join the cause. If home was not suitable, the zealous might cultivate the company of other dedicated virgins or widows and form collective households for support and protection. There were some women who threw caution to the wind, following men such as Eustathius of Sebaste into unconventional communities where men and women lived as brother and sister, in chaste or spiritual marriages—as *syneisaktes*.[64] These unusual choices, however, aroused concern. In many cases gossip went viral. What could a "spiritual marriage" be? Surely it was an excuse for high-minded promiscuity. The anomaly of a sexless union was difficult to believe. Those who championed it claimed that a male who could cohabit with women without falling victim to sexual temptation had climbed even higher than the average ascetic on the ladder of holiness. Others were scornful: how could this secret chastity be proved? Undoubtedly it was exploited. Young women who wished to hide the parentage of their illegitimate children began accusing anchorites.[65] What was going on in these communities? Just how *loving* were the agapaeic feasts of the Christians? Worried bishops met at synods to figure out how to crack down without weakening the fire of ascetic enthusiasm. Was it worth provoking the scorn and suspicion of outsiders who would be quick to interpret the abnormal Christian styles of behavior and social organization as a hypocritical alibi for fornication and impropriety?

Whether living privately with their families or in the new protomonastic communities, female virgins became more and more visible, the subject of considerable discursive investment as the case for chastity built up steam, leading ultimately to the founding of large and successful communities in Egypt, Syria, Armenia, Turkey, and Palestine. They also became more controversial. Paul and his companions, when they were traveling around the coastal cities of Asia Minor, Greece, and Syria, had to deal with questions about the social composition of their fellowship: married women often joined up as couples with their husbands (Priscilla and Aquila, Claudia and Linus) but other converts to the touring movement were widows (prominent in Acts) and young women of an age to be married.[66] Paul and his associates took particular care in how they guided the women attracted to their ministry. That care, and the responsibilities that accompanied it, would become more and more contested. Virgins in particular were a source of anxiety. If they too wanted to reject marriage, where were they to live? In communal households shared with other virginal males? In communities presided over by older and more responsible women, widows who were coming late to the career of virginity or who were leaving marriages for this sexless form of fellowship? Was it safe for young women to attach themselves to an apostle like Paul, even a celibate one known for his chastity? What risks did this create for the group and the individual? What sort of tensions, and embarrassments, could the visible presence and patronage of women pose for a church that was trying to make itself more mainstream? Gillian Clark addresses these questions:

> For male ascetics, female company, even the presence of a woman, was held to be particularly distracting. Years of hard spiritual struggle could be thrown away in a brief encounter, and even old and experienced monks were afraid. . . . The construct of woman as sexual temptress, as desire personified, was apparently so powerful that even men committed to a life of prayer could not think of women as human beings with the same commitment. An abbess once said to the monk who had carefully avoided her sisters, "If you were a perfect monk you would not have looked at us, and you would not have seen that we were women."[67]

"During the fourth century," writes Aline Rousselle in her *Porneia: On Desire and the Body in Antiquity*, "discussions of virginity became something of a fashion."[68] The genre of the virginity treatise, which achieved its distinct and substantial form in the hands of church fathers between the late third and early fifth century, wavered between the trite and the ecstatic. Its language was often dramatic, full of dire foreshadowings and fears about the imminent degradation of the fickle, righteously outraged over the abundant evidence that women as a sex deserved all that their reputation promised. Males all, the cheerleaders for virginity subscribed to the misogynistic clichés of their antique forebears, yet tempered them with the strange idea that this special class of women, if it could hold to its vows, might bypass the veniality otherwise assumed for their sex. Women and their male protectors did not have to look far to discover the consensus about female sexuality: while the Bible explained that women were to be saved through their bearing of children, the judgment of the patristic authorities and their descendants was that the safest course for a pious woman was to take a vow of virginity.[69] Elizabeth Castelli gives a list (organized alphabetically) of the most important treatises: Ambrose, *De Virginibus*; Athanasius, *De Virginitate Sive Ascesi*; Augustine, *De Sancta Virginitate*; Basil of Ancyra, *De Vera Virginitate*; Pseudo-Clement, *Epistolae 1–2 ad Virgines*; Eusebius of Emesa, *Homiliae* VI and VII; Gregory of Nyssa, *De Virginitate*; Jerome, *Adversus Jovinianum* and *Ep.22*; John Chrysostom, *De Virginitate*; Methodius, *Symposium Decem Virginem*.[70] Beginning in the third century in Africa, they soon became a speciality of the times. It was a new genre with women primarily its subject. The treatises and letters were full of advice and caution, admonition, cheerleading and even admiration. Even the gruff, self-involved Jerome occasionally turned full-blooded in his compliments to these remarkable women, especially once they were safely dead and no longer potential rivals to his authority. These discourses—all could be called "On Virginity"—can best be understood as propaganda; they are a bit like the recruiting literature sent out by colleges interested in attracting high-quality applicants. What they were promoting was the way of life of virginity as the more rewarding alternative to marriage.

Making Mary Male

> When Salome asked the Lord: "How long shall death hold sway?" he answered: "As long as you women bear children."
>
> *Gospel according to the Egyptians*

> They say that the Saviour himself said: "I came to destroy the works of the female," meaning by "female" desire, and by "works" birth and corruption.
>
> CLEMENT OF ALEXANDRIA, *Stromata* 3.63

That Christian celebration of virginity concerns women may now seem obvious. It was not always so. The flow of chaste women into the church is an interesting phenomenon, and it altered the shape of ascetic exhortation. The asceticism-gospel was originally presented to men for men. Susanna Elm makes this clarification in her *Virgins of God: The Making of Asceticism in Late Antiquity*:

> That "virgins" are not always women, has also become clear. Grammatically, the Greek term *parthenos* is of ambiguous gender, as long as it is not accompanied by an article. The canon of Ancyra as well as the homily referred to leave little doubt that men as well as women dedicated themselves to a life of virginity.[71]

Ascetic renunciation made men more masculine, tougher, less receptive to the softening influence of women and the domestic sphere. Did it do so for women? Elm cites common fears about the perils of unrestricted (and unsupervised) female asceticism and the reactions of church fathers—Eusebius of Constantinople, Armenian bishops at Gangra, Athanasius. Influenced by controversial leaders, men and women in places like Syria, Cappadocia, and Carthage have taken *anachoresis* to extremes, these church fathers asserted. Eustathius of Sebaste, a formidable ascetic, presided over groups of men and women who lived out a literal interpretation of the New Testament. Leaving families, marriages, property, and political life, his followers were said to dress strangely in a unisex philosopher's cloak as the Cynics did. They refused to pay taxes; they showed no respect for the official clergy and revised the procedures of worship as they saw fit. Social distinctions the rest of the world considered unimpeachable were treated by these groups as frivolities, obstructing the freedom and purity of the life of withdrawal. Authority meant nothing to them, and hierarchy had no place in the service of Christ. Slaves should be equal to masters, women to men; marriage should be abolished.

Most unconventional of all, women were "assuming the appearance of men," cutting their hair short or even shaving their heads, wearing male clothes all "under the pretence of asceticism."[72] Even a mainstream church father such as Basil of Ancyra subscribed to the radical view that ascetic chastity, when practiced by women, lessened the female aspects of the body and made such women "through their virtue, like men, to whom they are already created equal in their souls": "And while men through *ascesis* become angels instead of men, so do women, through exercise of the same virtues, gain the same value as men." Both men and women, united in the incorruptible virginal life, have "castrated the female and male desires to cohabit."[73] If God made two distinct sexes out of one, this was a concession to the need for the earth to be peopled. In our time, after baptism has canceled our debt and death is no longer the all-consuming power, the two sexes may become one again. Given that sexual difference is structured around the complementary positions of masculine and feminine desire, the renunciation of desire could create a new kind of being. Perhaps the human to come would be a strong and spiritual androgyne, a eunuch by choice who suffers from none of the liabilities of either sex. Christians claimed they could undo the feminine weakness of the virginal soul. But this hope was not merely a Christian one. Porphyry, the Neoplatonist disciple of Plotinus, who wrote a stinging attack against the Christians, could not be more explicit if he were a campaigner for gender fluidity. He writes to his wife Marcella toward the end of the third century, consoling her on their separation (in terms it is unlikely she found reassuring) and urging her to remain "pure and virginal" in her soul as in her body. "Pure," in this case, means "masculine":

> Thus the presence of my shadow, that visible phantom, will profit you not, and its absence will not pain you if you earnestly try to leave the body far behind.... Do not consider yourself as a woman: *I am not attached to you as to a woman. Flee all that is effeminate in the soul as if you had taken on a man's body*. It is when the soul is virginal and when the intellect is still a virgin that they produce the finest offspring.[74]

The ideal neuter state, as both Neoplatonists and Christians imagined it in the period from the second to the fifth centuries, reveals many more of the qualities of the male. In this prejudice they were recycling an old philosophical trope. Greeks in the classical and Hellenistic eras had their own way of responding to the occasional challenge to the hierarchy of the sexes when raised by a Platonist or a Cynic: the exceptional woman who thinks and reasons is probably sheltering in her composition an extra share of masculinity. Women who engage in philosophy, at least those who appear in a few philosophical texts such as Xenophon's *Oeconomikos*, are praised for having a "manly mind" (*Oec.* 9–10.1). Similarly, the exceptional woman who stands out in the contest of asceticism is portrayed as passing from one sex to another—as Perpetua does on the eve of her martyrdom—or as at least discarding a number of the marks of femininity. Masculine toughness was essential in the battle of holiness against sin and calumny, just as it was essential to the philosophical sage fighting distraction and irrationality. Through asceticism it was also available to women, whose deficient wet bodies could also be rendered more dry by their ascetic exercises and singleness of mind. The ascetic woman is a manly woman—unsurprising, given that the deprivations of a rigorous asceticism would indeed interfere with menstruation, and ascetic women, anxious not to be a temptation to men, often tried to make themselves look haggard, unattractive, and dirty. Female ascetics, according to Basil of Ancyra, would find their voices had grown more firm; other manuals on ascetic life or hagiographies of esteemed ascetic heroines point out how near they have come to men in their courage, their physical stamina, and freedom from undignified tears or cares for the body.

By the end of the fourth century, the ascetic preaching was extending its reach among women, and their enthusiasm made church leaders take notice. If the message was to be carried on from generation to generation, female influence mattered, and female defection from the old norms mattered even more. It was women's purity that Christianity had to secure. Women's bodies and their triumphant release from pollution through the elixir of virginity were the symbol of a society transformed, the sign that its members could through conversion and baptism hope for an inviolable new being. The virginal body was a light in the darkness, something even the heathen could notice. And it was women, those frail vessels of vulnerability and temptation, who stood for the imminence of a rectified creation. They had, in Eve, been the cause of shame. Now they could pay back the debt. Masculine conversion to a life of continence was heroic, a badge of honor and defiance just as glorious to a Christian as the soldier's sacrifice was to the pagan. But feminine conversion to dedicated virginity opened up another dimension: a reworking of the natural and social order. It may sound an ambitious inference. But the mutual dependence of woman and society is hardly a novel thought in the world where Christianity was born. Pagans, Jews, and Christians agreed on the basics: women were inferior but essential. Woman stood for biological life, the needs and cares of the family, the reproduction of society. As an anthropologist would put it, the exchange of women is to society what the circulation of the blood is to the living body. A virginal and willfully sterile woman snaps the thread. If she stepped out of these roles, the architecture of reality could well totter.

Yet the females of the ascetic tribe could not easily be released from their secondary status, no matter how energetically writers such as Basil promoted their cause. Male virgins were the top, the crown of creation. The leaders of the apostolic community were men, despite some acknowledgment of Jesus's intentions to leave a female disciple (Mary) as his preferred replacement. Similarly, the leaders in the campaign for sexless existence were the male writers, teachers, gurus, and bishops. As men, they had the authority. They could travel freely, ask for money (often provided by rich women sympathizers), engage in polemic and disputation, and perform public works of healing. Even the spread of monasticism in the early Middle Ages, supported by such towering figures as Cassian and Benedict, strengthened the masculine dominance of the highest ranks of asceticism, "the elite corps fighting as the vanguard of a Pantocrater Christ," as John Bugge expresses it.[75] The heroes of heaven in the book of Revelation, the 144,000 redeemed from the earth who will fill the first ranks of the blessed around the throne of the Lord, "singing a new song," are *males* "undefiled by women" for "they are virgins" (Rev. 14:4). Their perfection—they are "without guile"—is related to their abstinence. Enthusiasts for strict male chastity, such as Jerome, Ambrose, Gregory of Nyssa, and Athanasius, searched in the books of the Old Testament to find favored figures before Jesus and John the Baptist who were also famous for living without sex. Elijah and Moses were the most popular. It is true that Israel had been almost entirely immune to the spiritual tonic of chastity. But where it did acknowledge the power of the abstinent exception, the paragon was always male.

Is Marriage Bad for You?

Be the eunuch! Paul had made the suggestion with circumspection: a good thing, if you are like me. But for those who are differently constituted, something to avoid. And do not deny your spouse the pleasure of the bed, he continued, or if you do, make sure it is only for a brief time and by mutual agreement, to pray or do something else important. I have from the Lord, Paul said clearly, no command concerning virgins (1 Cor 7:25). His fine distinction fell on deaf ears. For the next millennium the honorable state of marriage was treated with scorn by the loudest voices in the church. By 500 anyone who aspired to higher office was well advised to keep their distance even from their legally wedded wives; by the Gregorian Reforms of the eleventh century, clerical celibacy was assigned even to the lower orders of parish priests.[76] The sacred army of the ascetics had won. Even in the teeth of the Protestant Reformation, the Council of Trent would affirm its hard-line position: "If anyone says the married state is to be preferred to that of virginity or celibacy, and that it is no better or more blessed to persevere in virginity or celibacy than to be joined in marriage: let him be anathema."[77]

Marriage, although not the bar to salvation that Priscillan and the Montanists had claimed, was meant to be for Catholics a second-best option. Certainly not sinful, for a Christian could be a decent representative of the faith even with a wife or husband and a brood of children. It was the heretics, Tertullian writes in *De monogamia,* who repudiate marriage now, in this day and age: the right to marry will be abrogated, Tertullian is sure, when the Paraclete arrives. Then we will all be as eunuchs. And creation will go back to the way it was in the beginning, according to the integrity of the flesh, like Christ, the virgin who has but one spouse, the church. But it made getting to the upper ranks of sanctity all that much harder. Looking back from the reaffirmations of the Counter-Reformation and the present-day Catholic opposition to relaxing the rules of celibacy, it can look as if what James Brundage calls "a peculiarly Western sexual ethos" was intrinsic to the success of the new faith from its earliest days. Yet it was not obvious all along the route that the antimarriage camp would carry the day. If "Christian," as Brundage writes,

> means what Jesus of Nazareth is reported to have taught, then there is not much Christian teaching about sexuality to discuss. Jesus was in favour of marriage (although apparently he did not practice it) and he opposed adultery (which is a special case of his general condemnation of deception and infidelity). He also seems to have disapproved of promiscuity and commercial sex, although he scandalized some of his contemporaries by befriending prostitutes. But it remained for medieval Church authorities, confident of the authenticity of their own beliefs, to wrap their views on sex and the family in the mantle of Christian orthodoxy.[78]

Even during the controversies over the propositions of Jovinian, which inspired the most vitriolic of all Jerome's bad-tempered polemics, there were real and understandable fears expressed by many onlookers, wondering whether the church was painting itself into a corner. As David Hunter has shown, the condemnation of Jovinian could be taken as a vote in favor of that uncompromisingly ascetic elitism that, in an earlier day, was enough to get one condemned for heresy, as Priscillan of Avila and other radical Encratites had discovered.[79] One of the most interesting questions of ancient history is this one, as Kate Cooper reminds us: "Why did the early Christians alight on the ideal of virginity," when an intelligent or even just a suspicious Roman could see that its adoption would "undermine the very fabric of ancient society"?[80]

It was such a different kind of idea of what human excellence could and should be. Unmarried women (a status viewed with shame by Jews and most pagans) were now cherished members of the Christian community, essential to its flourishing and, in particular, to its financial health. A wife might be the highest status a devout Jewish woman could aspire to. Christianity offered a new possibility of social climbing: those who renounced marriage and childbearing were no longer to be pitied or scorned; they were candidates for the elect, "our angels." The sociological reasons for the popularity of this new position are not hard to understand. But its symbolic resonances are more bizarre. Peter Brown refers to the "explosive" debates about the value of asceticism and the married life that inflamed so many, prolonging into the fifth century the dramas of the early years of desert and wandering, keeping the cult of bodily mortification alive. Not everyone believed that the angelic career of the celibate was exemplary or even possible. The laity continued to marry, and the spiritually exalted continued to scorn that conservative option. And yet the ordinary and the extraordinary were obliged to coexist, even appreciate one another. Tales of the intrepid apostles entranced their admirers: as exciting as the pagan romances they resembled, the narratives collected in the Apocryphal Acts showed how far the challenges of ascetic self-denial could be taken. Physically daring, spiritually unflinching, stronger than the beasts they faced down and the rulers of this world they defied, these were models to wonder at.[81] Equally electrifying were hermits "perched in the open air near their villages or, a little later, on the top of great columns," whose very existence pushed beyond the boundaries of comfort, barely retaining any ties to the earth. Without family ties, shunning the continual reminders of sexual identity, these were beings of an austere and frightening freedom. It was a hard act to follow. One might not have the chance to battle a lion or fast for forty years. But self-control in the presence of carnal temptation was within the reach of many eager Christians.[82]

Continence was a virtue recognized by many upright pagans and even, as a dedication to extreme forms of the life of piety, by Hellenistic Jews. Yet rabbinic Jews, by far the largest party in the Jewish communities of Rome in late antiquity, had a very different attitude to what Daniel Boyarin calls "carnality": they invested moral and spiritual significance in the body, unlike the Hellenistic Jews, Platonizing angels, who invested it in the soul.[83] Chastity before marriage was essential for women in Judaism, and the sanctions were severe. Abstinence from sexual relations, together with fasting, was expected during certain festivals (the Day of Atonement) and periods of mourning; they could continue for as long as a month, to allow a married man to concentrate on Torah study. Unusually, many of the Jews in the Essene communities renounced marriage: in the burial sites at Khirbat Qumran the remains of more than one hundred adult men have been found, but only a handful of women and children.[84] But the idea that permanent virginity promoted one to a higher class of excellence, or could endow its practitioners with a special kind of integrity and heavenly authority, this could only have come as a surprise:

> That it should have been this particular form of heroism, liked to a particular form of sexual renunciation—the preservation of a virgin state in the strict sense—which increasingly caught the imagination of all Christians, is a development we should not take for granted simply because it happened with seemingly unquestioned rapidity.[85]

The dark cloud that enveloped sex in the thoughts of many Christians (some taking it better than others) was a problem. How could human life continue without some accommodation to the actualities of biological reproduction? Was there a contradiction between the divine blessing of the intimate companionship and prospective parenting of Adam and Eve ("Be fruitful and multiply") and the new wariness about the corruption potentially infecting the soul unable to break from its carnal fantasies? Could sex have been skipped, if God had taken a bit more time designing the world? Perhaps the Creator instigated sexual relations and procreation as a concession, after Adam and Eve have disobeyed, when it became clear that humans would not abide in the paradisal condition where they lived like wise and simple children, brothers and sisters unaware of the provocation their anatomy presented. In the beginning, Genesis says, there was no death. Our first parents would have had no need to perpetuate themselves; yet if God chose to make two sexes, with distinct sexual organs, there must have been some plan for them to be used. Some theologians faced this difficulty by distinguishing between the corruptible character of human natural bodies (meaning not their moral frailty but their susceptibility to change and division) and the incorruptible character of human souls. With the blessing of nature in the work of Creation came the divine blessing of generation: it was good, but it was good as long as it took place without sinful concupiscence. God's scolding of the postlapsarian Eve demonstrated that an initially serene procedure could become darkened and difficult: now all women would bear children in pain and be subject to their husbands.

Augustine, as we shall see, was unusual in taking on the question with all its provocative complications; others who read Genesis with care recognized that it was difficult to deny that sexual relations had their place in Eden. Because the act of disobedience came so quickly, Adam and Eve did not have the time to try out their privileges. So we can only speculate about how lawful, tranquil, voluntary, and untroubled the necessary couplings would have been. Other early church fathers (Foucault for one believes they were the majority[86]) were drawn to the theory of a post-Edenic accommodation to make up for the loss of immortality: with death came sex, the argument went; some, such as Gregory of Nyssa, added that the first and best version of the creature God created in his own image was one without sexual differentiation.[87] In Gregory's important treatise "On the Making of Man" (*De hominis opificio*), the "image of God" is described as still present in humanity, although obscured. It was ours once, and the prototype of the human was, like the angels, genderless. Marriage and reproduction were unknown in the Garden of Eden. As Teresa M. Shaw explains, this was Gregory's hope, that we, like God, might have had "no sexual differentiation, passion, taste, sight, or mortality."[88] If sex disappeared, maybe death would, too. Ascetics who renounced sex would be first in line for the new way of being, beyond the flesh's decay and sex's cloying reminders of the short distance between human and animal. Those who are in a hurry to enter the kingdom of God can dispense with God's afterthought. While marriage is honorable and the fruits of conjugal union are not shameful, sexual desire is a bruising reminder of our assignment to an endless cycle of generation and death. Those who imitate the angels and the ascetics can be free from some of the more demeaning effects of the human condition by voluntarily giving up the pleasures and pains that anatomy provides. And they will be practicing to live as they will in paradise, since in the life to come, there will be neither female nor male, neither marrying nor giving in marriage.

Why not speed up the process? Principled commitment to a sexless existence could restore the androgynous simplicity. Even better, it could promote the abstinent soul to a higher class of achievement. All Christians, writes Robin Lane Fox in his sweeping 1986 study, *Pagans and Christians*, "faced the same final test, but while the majority hoped only for a modest pass, a few aspired to congratulated honours."[89] If you can show you possess what Saint Paul had received from God—in Peter Brown's words, "the prophetic gift of continence"[90]—then you too can share the undistracted life of the vanguard, free from anxiety about the affairs of the world, prepared to take flight at any moment when the shortness of time yields to "no time," and "the form of the world passes away" (1 Cor. 7:29–30). The married and widowed will not be left behind, but you will be ahead of the march, in company with the angels, contends Lane Fox: "From its very beginnings, Christianity has considered an orderly sex life to be a clear second best to no sex life at all. It has been the protector of an endangered Western species: people who remain virgins from birth to death."[91]

The extent and the nature of disagreement about sexual desire among the early Christian communities and thinkers were not fully clear to the very Christians most interested in the topic. It was common to assume that all, except the wild-eyed Gnostics, were on the same page. But divergences were sharp. Soon they could not be denied. They emerged most concretely over the question of marriage and divine intention.[92] To a large extent, these debates did not acquire their content or their argumentative shape from specific religious commitments but from the myriad philosophies of the Greco-Roman world, many held in great affection by the church fathers, even if their admiration had sometimes to be disguised. It is usually not hard to discern the philosophical allegiances hiding under the Christian veil. Clement of Alexandria was a philosophical and cosmopolitan defender of marriage. He did not consider his views incompatible with the Christian idealization of chastity. The product of a pagan family, born in the middle of the second century and possibly in Athens, Clement put his heart into proving that the church will do best if it drinks long and respectfully from the fountain of Greek philosophy. Those who take fright at Greek learning and logic are like children afraid of actors wearing masks, he writes in his book *Stromata*, or *The Miscellanies.*

With Clement's love for the philosophers went a fierce impatience with the errors of the Gnostic sects, who he believed failed to recognize the benevolent genius of God the Creator. Their errors were serious: they disparaged both the world and human powers, denying the significance of free will and despising marriage in all its forms. Extreme asceticism, reasons Clement, insults the intentions of God who created Adam and Eve free to fall but also free to stand, competent to use their sexual makeup to just purposes as long as they remained obedient. Marriage, in Clement's view, could be no disgrace. Indeed, the Gnostic Valentinians, unlike the Tatianites, approved of monogamous marriage. But Clement had heard about many extremists who worried him gravely. If the radical ascetics misconceive married love and procreation, then their crazy alter egos, the Gnostic libertines, are even worse: the Carpocratians, who may have been wayward followers of Valentinus, practiced principled promiscuity and held sexual partners in common. Both the contempt for marriage and the violation of it, Clement argues, come from too deep a pessimism. For Clement neither the material world nor the human will is tainted and unreliable: man can rise and be superior to nature; he can serve both his fellows in community and his God. Yet there was nothing of the easygoing sensualist in Clement. Everything he has learned from Greek philosophy supports his understanding of Christian moral strictness. The highest form of life will still be a life sealed against the chaos of the passions. Sexual relations may be natural; here Clement agrees with the Stoic philosophers such as Musonius and Epictetus. But are they necessary? Couldn't a good married couple perform the dreaded act a few times, just to ensure their progeny and do their social duty, but without allowing lust and desire to settle into their souls? Couldn't a commitment to continence accommodate an extremely limited experience of marriage while cultivating in the pious couple an ardent friendship, a brotherly-sisterly love that will aid their salvation and inspire all who know them?

> In general all the epistles of the apostle teach self-control and continence and contain numerous instructions about marriage, begetting children, and domestic life. But they nowhere rule out self-controlled marriage. Rather they preserve the harmony of the law and the gospel and approve both the man who with thanks to God enters upon marriage with sobriety and the man who in accordance with the Lord's will lives as a celibate, even as each individual is called, making his choice without blemish and in perfection. (*Stromata*, bk. 3, 12.86)[93]

For the goal, to persevere in the contest for continence, is the work of the whole man or woman, the achievement of a life, not the mere suppression of sexual activity. The Greek philosophers, Clement notes, teach the human ideal of continence as do the Christians, and that is well and good. Philosophy encourages us to fight against desire and not be subservient to it. But "our ideal," he explains, is greater: "Our ideal is not to experience desire at all" (*Stromata*, bk. 3, 7.57). And it is not purely sexual desire that is the problem. The contest Clement urges the Christian to engage in "applies also to the other things for which the soul has an evil desire because it is not satisfied with the necessities of life. There is also a continence of the tongue, of money, of use, and of desire" (*Stromata*, bk. 3, 1.4). Stoic reserve, or *apatheia*, he argued, is the best possible prophylactic against the dangerous effects of irrational libido as against all other corrupting desires. It is not the mechanism of procreation as such that is the problem, Clement argues: the Gnostics who believe sexual reproduction is bestial and revolting are blaspheming against the Creator. Marriage can be used rightly or wrongly, in chastity or in fornication, in obedience or in transgression (*Stromata*, bk. 3, 17.104; also 6.45–50). Living sedately and with discretion in a respectable, appropriate marriage, a disciplined household of believing husband, believing wife, and their well-brought up children, would have been for Clement the ideal. Sexual relations would have their place, but a limited and instrumental one, charged only with the responsibility for procreation, not pleasure or mutual love. Passions need not disturb the exemplary Christian, who is methodical in his monitoring of every detail of his life, as Peter Brown explains: "What mattered for Clement was that married intercourse should be approached in the Stoic manner, as a conscious action, undertaken in the service of God."[94]

Other voices in the early church took a line that was compatible with Clement's, if less elegantly expressed. One was Tertullian, writing at Carthage in his pre-Montanist days. "Of course we do not reject the union of man and woman in marriage," Tertullian writes in "To His Wife" (*Ad uxorem*):

> It is an institution blessed by God for the reproduction of the human race. It was planned by him for the purpose of populating the earth and to make provision for the propagation of mankind.... We do not read anywhere at all that marriage is forbidden; and for the obvious reason that marriage is actually a good. The Apostle, however, teaches us what is better than this "good" when he says that he permits marriage but prefers celibacy—the former because of the snares of the flesh, the latter because the times are straitened.... It can be said that what is merely tolerated is never really good. (*Ad uxorem*, bk. 1, 2–3)[95]

"Every contest is a straining for the first prize," Tertullian continues like the competitive Roman citizen he is. If you come in second, you have consolation, but you don't have victory. Because of the weakness of the flesh, married couples have the right to "exercise the functions" of the flesh. Yet they cannot help envying the better lot of those pious widows who, by remaining continent, belong even while still on earth "to the household of the angels (*Ad uxorem*, bk. 1, 3–4)." Christians who marry other Christians can be assured that God has consented and the church gives its blessing; that must not be denied.

A century later, John Chrysostom, the "golden-tongued" orator of the Eastern Church in Antioch and then (disastrously) in Constantinople, could describe marriage as "a great mystery," a bond ordained by God, that makes two into one, and that "through the bridge of the child" creates a single flesh made of three persons (*Homily 12, On Colossians* 4.922–27). Marriage is honorable and must be entered into by Christians with great awe and sobriety: all the pomp is to be relinquished, all the dancing and cymbals and ostentatious dress that pagans consider necessary to a wedding. Do not use the institution of marriage to chase wealth or attention or public admiration. That is wholly alien to its spirit. If you are arranging a marriage, invite only those of good character, and invite the poor. Before all the rest, invite Christ.[96] Not everyone can be "crucified to the world," Chrysostom explains helpfully. Those of a moderate degree of virtue—temperate, grave, in control of themselves, who care for and serve the poor (John's particular concern), are also worthy of the highest admiration. It is of course good if you can abstain from marriage, but only if by doing so you are using your freedom to serve God; if you reject marriage out of a dislike or condemnation of the state, you are as guilty as the worst of the unbelievers. And a virgin who thinks she is better than her married sisters, privileged to condemn marriage as accursed and impure, should be shunned. False or vainglorious virgins dishonor the name of continence.

Only a genuine vocation justifies disappointing family and city by throwing away everything to flee to the desert, or go on pilgrimage, or join a monastery. If you truly believe you have the gift for renunciation, why shouldn't the privacy and seclusion of your bedroom be a sufficient sphere of operations for your virtue? If it is status or power you are secretly seeking, there is no piety in your sacrifice, only a fraud and a delusion. Most Christians will go further in the direction of purity by entering solemnly into a faithful and discreet marriage. The couple is united in spirit as in flesh; they will instruct and strengthen each other in the faith. They face difficulties and prosecutions together, share the consolations, and have no secrets from each other. Tertullian prefers to picture the married singing psalms and giving alms rather than paying the conjugal debt. His hymn to the "beauty" of Christian marriage is silent on the proper sexual exercises of the Christian couple. But in this treatise, before he joined the extreme ascetic Montanist sect, he gives no arguments to preclude sex within marriage.[97] Marital sex is permitted. One does not, however, have to take advantage of a permission. Tertullian sounds as if he regrets the existence of the institution, and *An Exhortation to Chastity* (*De exhortation castitatis*) speaks passionately about the superiority of a life outside marriage. The choice is acknowledged. Together with most of the church, Tertullian accepts the compromise position. In many ways the existence of marriage is a shame, but its utility cannot be denied.

Married Christians would continue to do their duties in a modest and solemn manner. The way Tertullian outlines it, they would bear children, keep their episodes of sexual activity to a minimum, observe periods of abstinence, march on to middle age, and then step up the conditions of their continence, achieving with luck a postmarital celibacy (*De exhortation castitatis* 1.5–7, 10.81–82). If widowed, they would not seek to marry again, he explains in *Monogamy* (*De monogamia*):

> We, however, who are deservedly called the *Spiritual* . . . consider that continence is as worthy of veneration as freedom to marry is worth of respect, since both are according to the will of the Creator. Continence honors the law of marriage, permission to marry tempers it; the former is perfectly free, the latter is subject to regulation; the former is a matter of free choice, the latter is restricted within certain limitations. We

> admit but one marriage, just as we recognize but one God. . . . Now we no more outlaw marriage when we prohibit its repetition than we condemn food when we fast frequently. Prohibition is one thing, moderation another (1.5–6; 15.189–90).[98]

This gentle if rather bloodless conception of the "marital debt" might have satisfied Paul. It was nowhere radical enough for Gnostics and Manichaeans, Tatianites, Montanists and Encratites, Marcionites and Valentinians, or for the semimythical apostles portrayed in the Apocryphal Acts who were so gifted at converting Roman women to the new and antisocial "doctrine of purity," much to the dismay of their fiancés, husbands, and fathers (*Acts of Paul and Thecla, Acts of Peter*). Many of the early church fathers proudly proclaimed their divergence from the Jewish conviction that the marital bed is blessed and that God intended husband and wife to have "joy." Even among certain Jewish communities like that at Khirbat Quamran or those described by Josephus and Philo, there was those who compared their holy celibacy to the purity God requires from all who would enter the temple. What the pious now acknowledge as the necessity of ritual would be the rule in the eschaton. A thought occurring to a few nonrabbinic Jews gained traction in the minds of Christians eager to hasten the end of time, proud to do Adam one better and avoid profaning the sacred. As in the *Endzeit* (end time), so in the *Urzeit* (before time): for those entranced by the Paradisal analogy, the conclusion seemed clear. The original condition of the Garden of Eden was one of continence, Gary Anderson explains:

> The Garden of Eden was not simply a story about the primeval world; it could also function as a metaphor for the world-to-come. Hence the Garden was a paradigm for the ideal world of the eschaton, a world one should attempt to actualize or bring into existence now. Because Christians believed that the next world was devoid of marriage (Luke 20:27–40), it followed that the Garden was as well.[99]

The radicals represented the extreme fringe of the virginity movement; for them any indulgence in the marriage bed would drive the soul back into the mud. Turning away from Clement's accommodations to reality, "a younger generation of leaders were simply not interested in rethinking the issue of the sanctification of the married, as Clement plainly felt himself obliged to do."[100] Those converted to what Brown calls "the dangerous mystique of continence" had a new slogan and a new aesthetic of virginity.[101] It was addressed to men and to women. It would reverse the scale of values ancient society took for granted. To be barren would no longer be a disgrace. To be ignorant of sexual passion, as young Hippolytus was, would no longer amount to hubris and madness. There are some men who have made themselves eunuchs for the kingdom of God, said Jesus. If this calling is for you, then take it. Jesus made no further suggestions. But he left a large, yawning space open for a new and strange identity: Be that eunuch!

The Chastity Plot Assessed

One way of explaining the interest in sexual renunciation is to point to its functional utility, not in restricting the population or keeping fortunes from being frittered away in brothels or extramarital liaisons but in giving the signals through which a community can recognize itself. Sacred chastity could be the church's bid for an identifying sign, a way of distinguishing those inside the church community from those outside. Even as late as the fourth century, the role of renunciation as such a signifier was both widely recognized and subject to fierce disagreements. When the great ancient historian Ramsay MacMullen asks, "How complete was conversion?" he notes the fluid and uncertain character of Christian practices even at the time of Augustine:

> For Christianity had not developed its own particular way of doing everything. On many a corner even of religious life it had still to make its mark.... How broad a conformity to the practices prescribed by the church was needed to make one a Christian? And what difference did conversion actually make anyway in the various zones and areas of life?[102]

"What difference did Christianity make?" This remains the right question. To spread and take root, the new cult needed a number of things. Which ones were more important, historians have never been able to agree. Did it need to preach a distrust of sexual relations and physical desires? Certainly that distrust already existed, as the inclinations of Greco-Roman ascetic writers demonstrated. Christianity added to the ascetic plot a novel idea. What if marriage—the linchpin of social life—were unnecessary? What if the celibate life was superior and ennobling? Christians must be different from their neighbors and rivals. Being continent did not just make them look different—they could do that through simple clothes, communal homes, any number of unusual customs that early churches adopted. Some of those customs caught on and were formalized: avoiding animal sacrifice and food sacrificed to the Roman gods, fasting at special times, the shared meal; others attracted a few practitioners but did not make the cut. Sexual renunciation may not have been the most successful in helping to make the new cult a wise choice for the average Roman, but it was, in my view, one of the most significant of the religion's innovations. If Christians needed to make visible their special relation to history, eternity, and time, this was perfect. Followers of the Crucified God expected a dramatic transformation, when God's kingdom would replace the secular kingdom of this world and its powers: chastity was a way to live as if one were already an angel, unhampered by the heaviness of life, the obligations of posterity and estates, as well as a way to revive the purity of God's original conception of human being: free from care and sin, sickness and death.

Christianity made its way into history on the strength of several dramatic plots: models of meaning and value that reshaped the possibilities of nature, time, power, and the human "stuff." One was the odd but intriguing story of a God who relinquished omnipotence and impassivity to become a "Man of Sorrows," a creature sharing the human condition in all its weakness and pain. Another was the story of fall and redemption, error and recovery. Another was the dream of life restored beyond the grave, with a condition of bodiless eternity promised as a reward for a life of denial and faith. The one that inspired this book was the story about the purifying powers introduced through the sacrifice of human sexuality—the story I have called the chastity plot. All of these stories are odd. That they succeeded in convincing so many people—that they were plots in which so many individuals wanted to invest their lives and hopes—deserves attention, even from moderns who think themselves immune to their appeal. Christianity's romance with sexual renunciation was not inevitable. That it was a successful romance, each member adapting to the other's strengths and weaknesses, may have been a matter of chance rather than intention.

Controversy and dissent about all the ingredients of the Christian confession were intense during the years when believers were gaining strength and presence in the Roman world. The Christian policy about sex and marriage was no exception. Smart Romans, alerted to the dangers of the new movement, took these disagreements as a good sign. It may not be necessary to use strong-arm tactics to minimize the threat to the Roman order, they thought. This religion has some strange features. These Christians are very good at hating each other, and they love to fight about their beliefs. Leave them alone, and they will cancel themselves out. It was a fair prediction, yet in this case it proved excessively optimistic. Equally smart Christian bishops worked out ways to accommodate both the ascetic rigorists and the less ambitious. Fracture could be avoided. Virginity is pleasing to God, but so is sober marriage. The body was made by God, who designed even its sexual parts and purposes. The act itself is innocent and good in its purposes. It is the desire, rather, that is reprehensible and dangerous. And that desire might be dispensable. According to many church fathers of the first six centuries CE and beyond, sex is accompanied by desire only because we have been punished for the Fall. Christians could attend decently to their marital duties without risking sin as long as they didn't succumb to passion (even for their licit spouses). It is unclear how many of the faithful managed to follow this advice. What is clear is that marriage survived in Christianity only under a cloud: there was nothing sacred about family values, and the love within the couple that modern Christians look to with apparent approval was far more suspicious to their ancestors in late antiquity. Christianity may not have destroyed sex, as some of its detractors believe, but it was no friend to romantic passion.[103]

As a foretaste of the kingdom of heaven extended to the early Christian, chastity could be loved and admired. As such, it was open to all who could, as Jesus said, receive it, and that included the sex whose spiritual character was widely belittled by the communities Jesus came to provoke. Women were believed by pagan and Jewish cultures to have only a secondary place in the scheme of things. They were fashioned to bear children and serve the males in their families. With the gospel of chastity they got a second chance. In this respect they were on a par with men. They too could be virginal and abstinent. Their bodies could be recovered for a different purpose, removed from the cycle of generation and increase, mortified and sanctified, made offerings to the god like the bodies of devout men schooled in ascetic purification. Maybe biology would not impose the boundaries of their existence. Maybe the "art of virginity" about which church fathers like Basil of Ancyra in the fourth century wrote with such painstaking practical detail could interrupt the regime of natural procreative desire that had long made women the passive object of masculine need. Then through the vigilant chastening of the body and the senses it could teach the soul how to acquire its longed-for incorruptibility. For from the vantage point of nature, the feminine part occupies a privileged and strategic position: "A magnet for sexual attraction but herself immobile, woman may interrupt that motion which nature has inscribed in all things. This is what the virgin can do. She can be the point of rupture within the overall process of attraction."[104] Virginity represents a foretaste of existence emancipated from corporeal and procreative necessities. Ascetic monks, their spiritual directors taught, would be able to leave the flesh while staying in the body, enjoying a suspended state between life and death, but only if they labored continually and penitently to expunge from themselves all sexual impulses, thoughts, and sensations. Female virgins, repelling the attentions of men, despising the temptations of luxury, adornment, and ease, were even a step ahead: sober, fearless, self-possessed, the heroic race of famous virgins transcend gender and astonish those fortunate enough to encounter them. They are, as their celebrants agreed, a mystery. Through the figure of the virgin, whose kinship to the angels makes her suspiciously androgynous in the eyes of the skeptical and the conventional, those curious about the secrets of inner purity can look through a window into the integrity of the soul.

Chastity offered freedom and acceptance to special Christian women. In many respects, as I have argued, Greek myth had already gone part of the way toward justifying the special role of the virginal female. Cults and oracles made space for pure maidens and also for abstinent older women. Standing (even if temporarily) outside the common condition of women in society, such females were suitable to serve in some special cultic practices and, in some contexts, were believed to have mediumistic powers. Virgins in Greek religion and Greek medicine were described in terms of their emptiness and their enclosedness: since they had not yet been "opened-up" by a man, they were "water-tight" and thus, in a certain sense, reliable conduits, free of external interferences. And matrons, when they practiced abstinence before performing in the most solemn of the religious festivals, were similarly purified. Yet nothing further was made of these exceptional conditions. If there was any connection between such religious offices and the sexual lives of women in general, neither Greeks nor Romans saw it. Chastity, most thoughtful pagans believed, was good because it demonstrated self-control. But self-control, restraint, and modesty were fully manifested and proven in the life of the virtuous married woman. A woman who eschewed marriage had nothing sublime about her.

As role models for the Greek and Roman city, sexually self-controlled women enjoyed solemn respect. In the exemplary case of Lucretia, the image of a chaste woman provided a site for political identification in the ideological struggles between republic and monarchy, and the argument for republican rule celebrated this singular triumph of purity over impurity. Sexual immorality was a sign of despotic decline, argued the fans of Lucretia: what was wrong with the tyrannical or monarchic concentration of power was made clear by the potential for abusing and forcing women into sexual relations. Republican liberty, in this Roman scenario, found its emblem in the virtuous woman, the *pudica,* whose modesty and self-respect defied the licentious predator and rapist. Lucretia went to the extreme of self-murder to wash out the shame, to show the superiority of her will to that of Tarquin. She was a fighter. Her choice was not one Christians could embrace. But the idea that suicide might be the right choice if you were threatened with sexual dishonor and coercion had entered the cultural consciousness with her story. It would play a significant part in the fashioning of a new, non-Lucretian myth: that of the virgin martyr, her blood spilled, the horrors of her torture, mutilation, and death painstakingly described.[105]

The chastity plot has its flamboyant ingredients. Virginity and violence were bonded in the stories of Artemis and those inspired by her. In Christianity, chastity could join you to a divine and noncarnal spouse, and the nuptials could be celebrated beyond the grave. Death was perhaps just the next step in the virgin's shedding of the burdens of the flesh and, as the cult of the virgin martyrs taught, it could serve as one fast track to immortality. But if the extravagant side of the chastity ideal were the only one in play, it would be hard to understand how female sexual purity became such an effective ingredient in the long and successful subordination of women to men. I have tried to describe the formation of the chastity ideal within early Christianity and the remarkable ways it diverged from pagan models of exemplary behavior. At crucial moments in its formation, this ideal did make possible a freedom and autarchy for female Christians inconceivable for any but the most privileged and exception of pagan women. Allowing an escape from marriage and social reproduction, dedicated virginity as a profession gave women somewhere else to go.[106] They had honor; they were holy women, blessed, sometimes workers of marvels, controlling their own institutions. That power of self-determination possible through monasticism was always contested and, in the Protestant Reformation, taken away. But the message is clear: consecrated chastity put women on a different footing.

And the remarkable vision of a virgin mother as bearer of the very Godhead played its own part in exalting one particular aspect of femininity: the asexual woman. This is certainly the most questionable of all the Christian innovations, an ideal difficult to take to heart. Its perniciousness must have been obvious well before feminists in the nineteenth century argued about whether sexual restraint (Mary Wollstonecraft, the Shakers) or sexual freedom (the Utopian and Saint-Simonian feminists) was more conducive to women's power and self-determination. What we see in the history of Christianity is the way women came increasingly to be the object of the enthusiasm for chastity. If modern feminism has judged this concentration as bad for women, bequeathing them an impossible choice between sexual expression and moral worth, the effects have also been bad for men. Feminizing chastity created an unpalatable and incoherent object of desire, even a sexless one. For heterosexual men, the message was confusing. The object of your love could be valuable only if she didn't want to love you. Barred from passion, she punishes your desire and rewards it only with resistance. If she does return and meet your desire, there must be something wrong with her. The damage wreaked by the chastity ideal on the erotic and affective lives of human beings is incalculable. It is in this sense that one does not exaggerate in saying that there is a chastity plot.

Was this what Christianity had in mind? Were the miseries of "civilized sexual morality" at all noticeable to the founders and shapers of the virginity ideal?

✵ 5 ✵

The Pure and the Impure

PASTORAL AND THE REVERSAL OF NATURE

Purity, in everything, is rejection of and abstaining from multiple and opposite things; it is singling out and taking that which is natural and appropriate. This is also the reason why sex pollutes, for it is the coming together of female and male.

PORPHYRY, *On Abstinence*, bk. 4.262

And how could the Soul lend itself to any admixture? An essential is not mixed. Or to the intrusion of anything alien? If it did, it would be seeking the destruction of its own nature.

PLOTINUS, *Enneads* 1.1.2

Then those times followed when the too superstitious admiration of celibacy became prominent. After this came frequent and unrestrained rhapsodic praises of virginity, so that scarcely any other virtue was commonly believed to compare with it.

JOHN CALVIN, *Institutes of the Christian Religion*, 4.12.27

Chastity "plots," along with many other complicated stories, do not always end up where they intend. Not even the most coercive plot is entirely in control of its options. Interruptions happen. Dissonant voices acquire confidence. What seemed virtuous at one juncture looks vicious at another. The early Christian program for a sexless existence did not persuade everyone. Nor was it meant to. While the institution of marriage serves the interests of society, the chastity plot is in principle and practice antisocial. The chaste may be impressive, but they are also, more often than not, awkward. That awkwardness is something I want to explore in this chapter.

A radical movement like Christianity, a minority cult with its gaze looking ahead to the imminent end of all things, becomes something else when it becomes a "church," a community among other communities. The early Christians, as Wayne Meeks argues, "developed 'a unique culture' in an extremely complicated manner," separating themselves from their Greek and Roman neighbors on the one side, imitating them on the other. To understand themselves as Christians, they needed boundaries, sharp indicators of belonging and difference.[1] This unfamiliar practice of sexual abstinence was certainly a good candidate for such a boundary marker. It was convenient to have a way to distinguish the faithful from the lustful and impure outsiders. Simply to recommend sexual decency—monogamy and restrained participation in marital sex, the preferred option for most early Christian preachers—would not do the trick because all good Jews accepted a similar sexual norm, as did most respectable Romans. Most people, however temperate they believed themselves to be, engaged in sex and valued the continuation of the species through sex and marriage; a number also accepted the need for a certain tolerance of casual or commercial sex, at least for males. The Christians, on the other hand, spoke glowingly of perfect continence. Enthusiastic for martyrdom, they found in the idea of "charismatic virginity" an alternative technique of self-sacrifice.[2] Presenting their passions and their bodies as offerings to the glory of their deity, who in his human form had chosen virginity, they turned sex into a trial, a test in which competitive achievement could be ranked. The winners were those who had purged their desires entirely, who became "dead" to carnality. The losers were those who found such an annihilation too much to ask, that is to say, the everyday run of humanity. They too would need to be given a place in the church. Just what it could be was a matter of debate.

Ascetically gifted Christians experimented with various forms of monasticism, within private houses, in caves and deserts, and in well-endowed institutions. Even some high-ranking Romans who were mystified by their extremism gave them credit for ethical rigor. But their ideals were also a problem, making them look intolerant. That appearance was no illusion. Even more than the Jews with their anxieties about contamination, Christians took seriously the threat of irregular sex. Prostitution was off-limits, as were divorce, adultery, and homosexuality. And celibacy—keeping oneself pure for the kingdom of heaven—was the best. The eunuch ideal made the stakes clear. It provided a symbol of intransigence, shining a light on those who refused to be assimilated into the ways and means of the everyday and the normal. Yet if they committed themselves exclusively to radical renunciation, how could Christians hope to extend the bonds of brotherhood and voluntary kinship, the network of associations, pious households, active community? Society needs sex and marriage. Embracing continence while at the same time propping up marriage, Christians learned to define themselves as both inside and outside society.[3] Purity, as the third-century Roman presbyter Novatian declared, ennobles both the virgin and the wife, the celibate and the married. Like his descendants in the Europe of the sixteenth and seventeenth centuries, Novatian believed there was such a thing as conjugal chastity, although it did not stand as high as lifelong virginity, which is sublime, equal to the angels.[4] The purity of the married, he continues, arises from the fact that man and woman were created of one flesh and in their union, that singleness of being returns. The loving dyad combines into one person, a perfect harmony, reminiscent of the trinitarian unity of persons; to achieve this is to achieve purity in the flesh, as Novatian understands that:

> Purity does honor to the body and is an ornament of virtue. It sanctifies both sexes and is the bond of marriage. Purity guarantees parentage, defends modesty, and is a font of chastity. Purity brings peace to our homes and crowns harmony. Purity is full of concern to please no one but itself. Purity is always modest because it is the mother of innocence. . . . Purity seeks no ornament; it is its own splendour.[5]

Ascetic Magic: From Abstinence to Pastoral

Religious ethics differ from secular ethics. The distinction is one that struck Max Weber with great force. Religious ethics defy the theorist's expectation of rationality. They derive—often—from stranger norms of conduct, from beliefs and performances that are mystical rather than logical; to understand their function and significance, the critic has to put aside utilitarian prejudices. Nor would a Kantian ethicist be equipped with the resources to appreciate religious ethics when they approach what Kant would call the "sublime": to feel the urgency and the extraordinary "communion with a higher nature" that the religious enthusiast feels, may seem to be a privilege, a singular achievement. Kant thinks it means that you are in danger of falling into fanaticism: your mind "inflamed beyond the appropriate degree"; you may feel inspired but, Kant grumbles, you are probably deranged.[6] Kantian or utilitarian, most modern theories of morality fail when they try to consider the sexual ethics formed under a religious sky. Early Christianity was a movement of converts, of individuals and small groups who had discovered that the lives they had been living and the moral concepts that seemed well suited to those lives were now no longer valid. New stories, new moral intuitions, even new emotions came with the experience of conversion to Christ the crucified. Entering the special community, joining the order of initiates, meant a change in social practice, as well as a change in identity. To make that change perspicuous, members of the cult turned to rituals of purification and rebirth.[7] If baptism into the converted life was one kind of "magical" transformation, so was the spiritual transformation of putting off the carnal self and becoming pure: "We who formerly delighted in fornication now delight in continence alone; those who formerly used magical arts have dedicated themselves to the good and unbegotten God."[8]

This brings us to a split in what I have been loosely referring to as asceticism, that dual creature described by Max Weber. There are ascetic features, Weber argues, in most successful forms of Western rationality: economic rationality, political rationality, bureaucratic rationality, ethical rationality. The ascetic rechannels energy into intellectual or worldly achievement by, as Weber puts it, "holding back on naïve surrender to the most intensive ways of experiencing existence." Rational and active rather than mystical and quiescent, the worldly ascetic has everything required for a culture that values stability and adaptation. (Thus, as Weber famously argues, the inner-worldly ascetic is perfectly adapted to capitalism as it developed in Western Europe.) Unmoved by rapture or despair, this sort of ascetic triumphs by being "negative" toward the urgent and sensual self.[9] Even in his religious conduct he can be methodical. Revolution is not in his blood. And then, on the other hand, there is the ascetic sublimity of the priest and the prophet. Their passions and renunciations are better understood within the framework of magical practices. Theirs is a way of life that makes radical demands on the practitioner who seeks salvation and often an eschatological or chiliastic transformation. Withdrawing from and "hating" the world, the exemplary ascetic in the religious context accomplishes "the extraordinary, acquires the charismatic ability of forcing God's hands and of working of miracles."[10] Both ascetic forms of life are, in a sense, sacrifices. But their meanings are very different, as are the experiences they sponsor. Asceticism, viewed through one of what Weber calls its "Janus-faces," is a tool for mastery of the world or of the self.[11] That mastery develops, and is developed by, active concentration, rational conduct, and industrious application. What he terms "inner-worldly" asceticism does not remain a manifestation of the extraordinary, exalted vocations of the holy and the enlightened. Rather, it reappears in a desacralized form, as economic and professional discipline, "routinized" as rational self-control, ethical dedication to a "worldly calling."

It is the sacrificial and unworldly context of asceticism that matters most to the formation and success of the chastity plot. Early Christians drawn to the unworldly discipline of abstinence and its magical, miracle-performing powers formed religious communities seeking to define themselves in opposition to the world. Chastity's very impracticality increased its attractiveness to those who cared more about salvation than survival, who were ready to believe that heavenly acknowledgment outweighed the praise of the public or the glory of a household. Early Christians, as Weber puts it, made a principle out of rejection: they lived in a "permanent state of tension in relation to the world and its orders."[12] Magic, not management, was key to their breakthrough into another order of being and feeling. "By virtue of the magical powers obtained by abnegation," they would put themselves beyond the world of social relations, discarding marriage and the networks of kinship in favor of inner, elected relations, mystical ties. And in so doing they would put themselves beyond hurt, since the mystic dies to the world and its worries. Ascetic renunciation of sex, Weber suggests, belongs to those techniques valued by the mystic, the prophet, and the charismatic, techniques that lead to a state of invulnerability. Their significance resists rational demonstration. If secret forms of knowledge are best left to priests, prophets, demons, or deities, the religious ethics that command a purity of body as of soul are also best left to the extremists, the virtuosi. Whether or not one is a Weberian, this concession is a good one to accept.

But not everyone will be content with turning sexual ethics over to unreason and priestly magic. The peculiar virtues of the eunuch exerted their greatest appeal in a time of eschatological impatience: how better to usher in the millennium than through the dramatic repudiation of "the triviall and vulgar way of coition," as Sir Thomas Browne called it in the seventeenth century?[13] Church fathers, even while accepting that the earth, including all the marriages and families that fill it, has a surprising tendency to continue, tried to remain true to the ascetic ideal. "Virginity's resistance to reproduction," observes the literary historian John Rogers, "only contributed to its efficacy as a trigger of apocalypse."[14] The chaste and the pure on principle are not simply reaching for higher marks in a moral examination. Their sacrifice of "vulgar coition" is intended to save the world, if in the process ending it. It was this redemptive and prophetic context that made sense, for early Christians and for their admirers in early modern Europe, of the radical version of the doctrine of sustained virginity. A universal embrace of absolute celibacy will mean an end to the human race. Such a prospect will not, should not, please everyone. To its fans, it is glorious, exciting, challenging, a revolutionary promise that will overturn the corrupt order of time and human degradation. To its detractors, it is irrational at best and perverse at worst.

Is it even possible? The loudest voices praising continent women and ascetic men were also the most aggressive in seeing signs of an unextinguished sexual itching everywhere they looked. In the calm words to eager virgins of Basil of Ancyra, one of the less squeamish of the fourth-century church fathers, there is a deep sense of sexual danger. One can live in the desert; one can boycott the womb; but are the senses ever dead? Basil had a sympathy for the significant ties between men and women that was unusual for a churchman of his time, and was unusually frank. Sexual feelings helped men and women care for one another, he recognized, but they also kept a degree of tension in play, and there was no avoidance of the physical reality of sex, no matter what your religious advisers might tell you: "In this life, there can be no such thing as an asexual relationship between a man and a woman."[15] The anthropologist Mary Douglas, whose work on purity, pollution, and danger has transformed the way these notions are understood, finds in the importance attached to virginity in early Christianity an absurd rush to extremes. Why are no other social relations considered so explosive, so in need of constraint and interdiction? Why were the Christian anxieties about sex so exaggerated, and why did they engender such an array of institutions and practice, symbolic but also material? Her answer is hard to quarrel with:

> In its effort to create a new society which would be free, unbounded and without coercion or contradiction, it was no doubt necessary to establish a new set of positive values. The idea that virginity had a special positive value was bound to fall on good soil in a small persecuted minority group. For we have seen that these social conditions lend themselves to beliefs which symbolise the body as an imperfect container which will only be perfect if it can be made impenetrable. Further, the idea of the high value of virginity would be well-chosen for the project of changing the role of the sexes in marriage and in society at large.... The idea of woman as the Old Eve, together with fears of sex pollution, belongs with a certain specific type of social organisation. If this social order has to be changed, the Second Eve, a virgin source of redemption crushing evil underfoot, is a potent new symbol to present.[16]

The Christian call to purity was a siren call, and many people listened. Interrupted by a heavenly light and a voice in the middle of his life's journey, Paul caught the fever (Acts 9:3–9). He would become a perfectionist, discontent with an ethics of law and obligation. Paul called for the grace that would deliver unclean and sinful man from "the body of this death," from the "old Adam" that had driven us out of the Garden of Eden, banished us from pastoral plenitude (Rom. 5:12–21). That nostalgia for the garden was to have a long career, absorbing both romantic beliefs (the original condition is the best, the primitive state the most virtuous) and pessimistic, reactionary assumptions (all human efforts are vain, when not impairments of whatever came before). The biblical suggestion that corruption arrived with knowledge was a troubling element in the theory of originary purity. What exactly made the fallen Adam and Eve impure? Paul had not resolved the issue, so church fathers continued to debate. Augustine assailed concupiscence, which deforms the will (or better: in which the deformity of the will makes itself obvious).[17] Mystics in the Christian and Jewish traditions invented sometimes violent ascetic techniques for mortifying the body and the senses. Physical impurity or material stain was often construed as the last, most insinuating barrier keeping the holy one from the dissolution of the self, something a true mystic should desire. The conception of impurity here is a tricky one. Ritual cleanliness was not a new or an unusual idea for ancient religions. Just as disease, something that invades the body and defiles it, is a danger, so practices of the sacred are vulnerable to many equally noxious, if unclear, agents of pollution.[18] Vigilance in performance of ceremonies and rites was crucial, as pagans and Jews never forgot. But the idea of a being that could be "ethically immaculate," ontologically untouchable, redeemed from the mess and contingency of nature and time, this was a Christian innovation, and a strange one.

I suggest that this strange innovation is related to an aesthetic category, that of the pastoral, which similarly promotes the fantasy of an intact and changeless condition, a world of natural sweetness and light, perhaps a world that does not know reality. The mystic is drawn to a condition of self-dissolution in which the chains of nature come unstuck. The seeker of purity wants to undo the defilements that living makes unavoidable. At some level, both want to stop human development short. Innocence is an escape from complexity. But so is nonbeing. The Christian pastoral, when it promoted sexual innocence as a sign of sublime felicity, often failed to distinguish between passivity and perfection. That failure is an interesting moment in chastity's history.

As pagan civilization slipped into a more Christianized form, the genre of pastoral held its appeal. Jaded urbanites in Hellenistic cities liked to imagine rural peace and simplicity: wouldn't it be nice to live like a shepherd, out on a hillside, singing to pretty girls? In some significant cases, this same conceit found itself reemployed in service of a theological vision.

Eden before the Fall was the model. The first self-conscious Christian pastoral, or theological idyll, was set in a well-tended garden. Methodius's dialogue *The Symposium*, written probably around the end of the third or the beginning of the fourth century CE, takes place at a decorous garden party attended by grave and beautiful virgins. Methodius, said to be the bishop of Olympus martyred during the reign of Maximinus Daia in 311, borrowed the apparatus of Plato's *Symposium* and populated it with female innocents who compete to praise not love but chastity. No amorous dalliance of shepherds is allowed here, no sophisticates playing at being rustic. The sweetness of the idyll must be matched by a moral fastidiousness. What gives Christian pastoral its character is the image Methodius adopts for his dream of holy innocence: virgins in a garden. The virtuous bodies of these sober and eloquent virgins are healing and ennobling to all those who contemplate them. Because they renounce sex, they can be safely adored; they can preach, teach, and chastise, nurture and console. The garden they never leave is a place of blessing and safety, a revived Eden where innocence is now conscious and voluntary, and is reaffirmed.

In the background hovers the grandest figure of the medieval church's chastity cult, the Virgin Mary herself. Mary is an enclosed garden, a pearl and a fortress. A still point in a turning world, she is a fountain that brings forth while miraculously remaining intact. Mary is the place where pastoralism meets devotion. Simple, at home with nature, untutored, quiet, and patient, Mary represents a special type of adult maidenhood, more a literary trope than a vocational model. Other people take chances, learn the hard way, pursue their desires, get into conflicts; she waits, serene and childlike, a bud that will never become full-blown. Despite her sadness and her unfailing compassion, she is (to borrow the words of Vladimir Jankélévitch) "happy innocence." Jankélévitch is not an enthusiast for this dream of sweetness and light. Happy innocence, sadly, is for all practical purposes useless for others; at its worst it is a license for "vegetable unconsciousness."[19] As Jankélévitch recognizes, the "zero" degree of "originary" and "naked" innocence that belongs nowhere else but in a "décor de pique-nique," or pastoral arcadia, is a chimera: it is an image of the present "nettoyée à la grade lessive" (scrubbed squeaky clean) and projected back into the immemorial past. Impossibly transparent, this innocence is a vanishing condition that evaporates with self-awareness. Jankélévitch discards the notion of pure innocence as irrelevant, a "presque-Rien" (almost nothing).[20]

Such is the fate of diaphanous innocence. The literary conceit of "le coeur simple" (the simple heart) exists only to inspire torturous self-accusations from worldly sinners (Tolstoy) or ambivalent tributes from sophisticates (Flaubert). Most of us would rather not be clear crystals or enclosed gardens. "Happy people," Hegel remarked, "have no history."[21] The same is true of innocence. Ethical life begins when consciousness loses its naïveté. The literature and spirituality of the West choose to imagine human purity in the shape of a Virgin Mother, a child-woman faithful and incapable of guile, a simple heart. But she is, as Mariolaters never fail to mention, unlike all her sex.

Christian theologians under the spell of the Virgin Mother decided that the female sex might be saved through the humility and obedience of Mary.[22] Nonetheless, womanhood remained a worry. Women in the Christian tradition are "daughters of Eve" even when they take the veil and become "brides of Christ." Placed beneath men because of Eve's disobedience, women are told that their sexuality is a temptation and an obstacle in the path of humanity's pursuit of virtue, despite the fact that a woman's womb sheltered God on earth. The contradiction here is largely responsible for the peculiar intensity with which chastity is enjoined on women. On the one hand, women's sexuality is the reason they are valuable. It is as a biological and social means of reproduction, to put it crudely, that a woman named Mary is chosen to serve in that small and distinctive way in the drama of incarnation and salvation. Yet that same sexual talent bears a stigma: it is a power women are taught to despise as well as enjoy, and Christian ascetics were often quick to join in the vilification. Women and their desires had few friends in orthodox Christian circles, and sects such as the Manichaeans were even more contemptuous. Would it require a sacrifice of her sexuality, a suspension of her gender, for a woman to be taken as equal to a man?

Against Innocence: Hegel's Complaint

> I have never wanted to extirpate innocence. I don't want to thrust the facts of life on children of four or five. What I'm against in a quite visceral, loathing way, is the sentimental vision of childhood you get in books written in the so-called Golden Age of children's literature. Peter Pan, who thinks it's better always to stay a child, some of A. A. Milne's verses, I can't bear them, they make me sick! . . . So when you get people like C. S. Lewis in the Narnia books lamenting the fact that children have to grow up it makes me very angry.
>
> PHILIP PULLMAN[23]

One of the oldest myths is that of an original innocence. We started pure; impurity came later, by mishap or design. As a habit of thinking, this one is hard to shake. Early stages of anything—life, marriage, education—are straightforward and untroubled; what succeeds them, for better or worse, adds complications, mutations, qualifications. Pushed to an extreme, this becomes a prejudice in favor of inactivity. Resting inert may be unproductive, but at least nothing has been taken away, no perfection marred. "Bare earth is best," writes Wallace Stevens.[24] Why add to a pristine condition? Yet innocence does not appeal to everyone. Hegel had no time for innocence, or indeed for anything that smacked of what he called "immediacy." As a thinker of mediations, he preferred the complications. By performing any act at all, the self sunders what might have been whole. The simple certainty of immediate truth is given up, lost in the very moment of action. The self who acts is no longer an innocent self. "By the deed, therefore, it becomes guilt." Guilt is life. Or life is guilt. For Hegel there is nothing to be gained by holding back, so you might as well accept it: to act is to violate. Ethical innocence is a pointless and inconsequential clinging to an empty ideal of existence without content, without division: "Innocence, therefore, is merely non-action, like the mere being of a stone, not even that of a child" (Unschuldig is daher nur das Nichttun wie das Sein eines Steines, nicht einmal eines Kindes).[25]

What is it about innocence? For Hegel the very notion is vacuous. For those who are more sympathetic to the charm of innocence, it is well registered in the tone and the allure of pastoral. *Pastoral* refers to a poetics (rather than a lifestyle). If pastoral's foundational fantasy is to be credited, it was invented by shepherds, to "re-create themselves in their leisure whilst they fed their sheep," as the seventeenth-century critic René Ragrid puts it in his *Eclogues*.[26] The literature of pastoral speaks of sheep and olive groves, of peace and immunity to the nagging pressures of ambition, wealth, and struggle. Its mood is nostalgic; its world a never-never land, a place of beauty and simplicity for which the poet claims to long as a lost homeland, a beloved memory.[27] Once there was peace and plenty, once humans lived as simply as beasts, unaware of tension and alienation. Latin writers such as Virgil and Theocritus established the conventions of grass and trees, water and fruitfulness: the *locus amoenus*. Here sheep may safely graze, unafraid of wolves, bears do not threaten the deer, and palms or olives may give a gleam of exoticism to the scene.[28] Here lovers can lounge on the ground, spades and tractors out of sight, playfulness unscolded. Here nature shares in the divine, the blessed dead live in eternal spring, and poetry comes unbidden to the lips.[29] The pastoral program is gentle, a vision of beginnings where conflict and correction remain offstage. From Theocritus and Virgil to its revival in the Renaissance and the seventeenth century, its moral beliefs remained constant.

Rural pleasures are the true pleasures. The country is the soul's homeland, the restorative elixir that brings tranquillity and a sense of the true order of things and their importance to a mind overtaxed by stimuli and distraction. Corruption is unknown here. In the timeless world of rural simplicity, only eternal values prevail. It is the illusion only a city sophisticate who does not make a living on a hillside could cherish. For others, it might be better if poetry had come up with another way to unite elegance and simplicity, one that skipped nymphs weaving garlands and the entire bucolic apparatus.

Hegel sneers. But the art and literature of the West would be bereft without a pretty picture of this undisturbed condition, so unlike our own that we have pushed it way back in time or transferred it to islands beyond the known world. Once upon a time there was a garden where everything presented itself for the taking, where pain and discord were unknown. "Taking" here did not require compensation: this was a world without reciprocity or exchange, without economics, without debt. In those days the earth, like the sun, was a place of absolute plenitude, without the possibility of degradation or decay. Purity in this sense also signified immunity, and it precluded reflection. It is a world gone by, which can only be approximated by the imagination today, and even imagination must eventually succumb to hunger and desire.

The book of Genesis calls it "Eden." The humans who inhabited it were like creatures in a "spiritual zoo," Hegel adds ungraciously. Lacking in self-awareness, they could be called "innocent but hardly good."[30] But they were, he admits, at one with themselves. They just didn't know it. They needed to fall. Only after a long wandering through many shapes and ruptures can the self return to itself and "digest the entire wealth of its substance," recollecting all that it has been through.[31] You have to take reality on, Hegel insisted: "Contrasted with the simplicity of pure consciousness ... this reality is a plurality of circumstances which breaks up and spreads out endlessly in all directions, sideways into their connections, forwards in their consequences."[32] You can't stay where you start from. To resist mixture, confusion, alienation, is to remain stupid, hypnotized by the monotony of immediacy. Turned into a moral stance, the innocent attitude is in danger of expiring on the altar of its own spotless perfection:

> It lives in dread of besmirching the splendour of its inner being by action and an existence; and, in order to preserve the purity of its heart, it flees from contact with the actual world, and persists in its self-willed impotence to renounce its self which is reduced to the extreme of ultimate abstraction.... The hollow object which it has produced for itself now fills

> it, therefore, with a sense of emptiness. Its activity is a yearning which merely loses itself as consciousness becomes an object devoid of substance, and, rising above this loss, and falling back on itself, finds itself only as a lost soul. In this transparent purity of its moments [*in dieser durchsichtigen Reinheit seiner Momente*] it is an unhappy, so-called "beautiful soul," its light dies away in it and it vanishes like a shapeless vapour, dissolving into thin air.[33]

The pastoral mode is also a philosophical position, although a strange and self-dissolving one. Its image of purity is a powerful fantasy, and Hegel admits that. This myth of the beautiful soul untainted by actuality maintains its grip on the history of ideas. Better a life "evaporated," evanescent (*verflüchtigen*) and abstract than a life stained by specificity or incriminated by decision. Such a fantasy recurs in every generation, in the avant-garde as among the classicists. As Hegel sees it, it turns up as the favorite ideal of the absolutist and the Romantic, the poet or mystic, who prefers the impossible to the proximate and concrete: suffering from a desire that no object can satisfy, the absolutist prefers unhappiness and earns from Hegel a title that sticks—"unhappy consciousness," *unglückliches Bewußtsein*.[34] The unhappy consciousness is hopelessly enthralled by its vision of emptiness, by the beauty of the white, the untouched, the transparent. But if there is one niche in culture specially designed to accommodate the dream of spotless perfection, that would have to be religion, and religion's close relation, the "angelic imagination" of the Platonists. Plato's big idea, presented in the *Republic*'s allegory of the Cave, is that the intellect, withdrawn into its own abstractions, could fly directly to the truth, without passing through the gate of the senses and the ambiguities of experience.

The Angelic Illusion

> "*Angélisme*," masculine noun: "désir de pureté extreme et d'évasion hors du domaine charnel."
>
> *Grande Larousse encyclopédique*, 1970[35]

In the history of religion, such a rarefied intellect is usually reserved for angels. But even nonsaintly intellectuals and some political radicals have been known to believe themselves superior to the humdrum way of the world. The angelic vocation, for those beguiled by it, arouses a taste for the absolute. Limits constrain us. Angels, created in time but with a being that is endless and free of spatial determinates, sweep across barriers that hold us back. Angelic intellection, explains Thomas Aquinas the Angelic Doctor, is immediate and intuitive. Ours is discursive and approximate. Angelism borrows both from Aquinas's hierarchical metaphysics and from Plato's myth of the soul that grows wings. Pure Platonic intellects have their vision fixed solely on the radiance of the Ideas; our senses are entangled by similitudes and reflections, metaphors and mirrors. On this side of the upper heavens, all is mixture. Generation keeps altering and adjusting the substance of these human animals who are meant to be guided by the reason which is their pride. This could change. Once we are admitted to a realm in which reason alone would be enough, surely the drawbacks of generation and biology could also be suspended.

Angelic imaginations are puzzled by the mutability of the finite. So are idealist philosophers. The view from eternity beckons. Why shouldn't philosophy satisfy this yearning? Its objective should be the provision of simple and immutable and self-evident propositions. We should want to be in the sun, not the cave. Some thinkers believe in a mind unimaginably lucid and a knowledge that would be universal and perfect, like God's. René Descartes, Jacques Maritain says, wanted such a science: "the very science of God and of the angels."[36] Nothing in his education measured up; perhaps only mathematics knew what certainty and clarity were. Everything else in history was a poor simulacrum of systematic knowledge, a chaos of straggling villages and badly proportioned cities instead of method and organization.[37] If philosophy is to deserve the name, it needs to demand a more elegant and simple structure for knowledge. It must be clear. It must be certain. But is it possible? Is anything we can assert about human life or nature fit to withstand such a withering gaze? Shelley's "Adonais" gives the canonical expression:

> Life, like a dome of many-coloured glass,
> Stains the white radiance of Eternity.[38]

Life will always stain. And there will be those who will go on finding its offerings too sordid. Spotlessness is an admirable aim—for a mop. Human beings are more likely to fall into a Pascalian shape: double, tangled, contradictory. Blaise Pascal saw "the misery that is man" as inseparable from his greatness. Man is all these: the "repository of truth, sink of uncertainty and error, glory and garbage of the universe" (depositaire du vrai, cloaque d'incertitude et d'erreur, gloire et rebut de l'univers).[39] When he tries to be an angel, he makes himself into a brute. The angelic temptation in its Platonic form is a poisoned chalice, for Pascal and for a fellow traveler such as Michel de Montaigne. Angelism is a constitutive obsession of the unhappy consciousness. It makes everyone who reaches for it dissatisfied. But it is also the engine of the sublime.

The angelic temptation is what the American poet Allen Tate castigated as a "hypertrophy" if not a perversion: "It is the incapacity to represent the human condition in the central tradition of natural feeling" and "the thrust of the will beyond the human scale of action." Angels disdain human carnality. That is all very well for them. But for us it would mean the destruction of the world. Angelic knowledge is perfect, hyperrational, omniscient, but, Tate objects, it ultimately exhausts itself "because in the end it has no real object; it is wedded to nothingness."[40] Paradisal innocence, indeed, was a brief possibility before transgression made us what we are. Jews included as their founding myth the story of a garden where there was no death and no work. How you evaluate this nostalgia for the primeval depends on your opinion of the history that superseded it.

Some Jews and their Christian heirs were in no doubt: the demons are in control. A cosmos balanced by the beautiful coherence of divine Logos, such as the one imagined by the Stoics, was to their minds a pathetically naïve notion, contradicted by every instance of pain and confusion, both natural and human. Mortals live in darkness. Their powers of reason are unreliable, their physical powers insignificant. Why wouldn't anyone who can see realize that this condition is a far cry from the blessedness promised in the first days of Creation? History since the banishment from Eden is a history of corruption and decline. That the human race had lost its way was the conclusion of early and late followers of Christ's call to a new life. The Hebrew prophets had already awakened Israel to the infamy of sin, denouncing Israel's bleak history of disobedience and idolatry. Christians returned to the fray with new prophetic zeal, only now widening the circuit of judgment to a universal measure: all humanity is the race of Adam; all have betrayed; all require redemption. Human error was the cause of human misery. Like the rebel angels, we have lost our original stamp, our unity with purity and light. Once we radiated the image and likeness of the divine. Now nature itself is ashamed of us; the ugliness of our soul disfigures our body and our society. But that can be corrected. We can, through God's graciousness, become angels again, despite all our flaws, if we freely will to cooperate in the program of Providence (Matt. 22:30; Luke 20:35–36). And through continence, the spirit, so long dulled or coarsened by sensual indulgence and intellectual confusion, can be reborn in God's original image. This was the eschatological and paradisal hope of the great Christian champions of the angelic life—the orthodox (Origen, Clement, Gregory, Methodius), the unorthodox (Tatian, Marcion, Valentinus, the anonymous authors of the Gnostic Gospels and Acts), and also the solitaries, the hermits and desert dwellers (Anthony, Dorotheus of Gaza, John Cassian). All wished to join the angels, and perhaps some did: the records of the afterlife do not tell.

Non-Christians also dreamed of the angelic life and the state of spiritual purity, but without the allegorical drama of the serpent and the wayward couple in their nakedness and fig leaves. In Rome the philosopher Plotinus said that matter lacks ultimate intelligibility. His *Enneads* 2.4 describes the entrapment that leads the mind astray. True virtue purifies us from incontinence and corruption and draws the soul toward intimacy with the One, the Good beyond Being.[41] "Quite as much as Origen," writes Peter Brown, "Plotinus was haunted by spiritual longing for the gracious beauty of the One."[42] Plotinus's brilliant disciple Porphyry traveled from Tyre to the city of Caesarea to hear the famous Origen lecture. Although Porphyry (then a young man) shared Origen's passion for allegorical interpretations and had himself a mystical bent, he was not impressed by the Christian version. The biblical texts, which Porphyry studied with care, irritated him because of their contradictions and inconsistencies. There are many gods worth taking seriously, Porphyry argued, and he was willing to expand their numbers to include human beings like Jesus who had apparently been elevated to a god after his death. But even Jesus worshipped and was subordinate to the one God who is above all, and whom Porphyry agreed that all the wise should worship. The error came from Jesus's disciples, who tried to turn their teacher into something he had never claimed to be, and who spoiled his legacy by imposing their own cruder ideas. Christianity was a superfluous religion. (Perfectly good religions were already available in the Roman Empire.) Indeed, it was less a religion than a superstition.[43] Porphyry was interested in something more intellectual, a religion dignified enough for a man of his philosophical caliber. Such a religion should dispense with the need for a historical mediator and for the founding myth of the biblical religion, the myth of humanity's fall into sinfulness through Adam. The Bible of the Jews and Christians, Porphyry objected, left spirit enchained. Lacking all respect for intellectual virtue, it could not understand what the purity of the philosopher could be. Plotinus, that godlike man, had drawn from the Platonic fountain a much deeper and richer insight. With the right discipline, the vigilant and purified soul might return to the realm of spirit, unhampered by the body and its needs.

Porphyry's protest against the "monopolization" of soul salvation by the presumptuous Christians is a key moment in the parting of the ways between Greco-Roman and Christian dreams of ascetic purity. Despite some mutual recognition, there are important differences in the character of what I am calling these two "angelisms," the philosophical and the Christian. And there are important differences in the practical consequences of their separate doctrines of perfectible purity. Called to the seat of final judgment by a divine and omnipotent authority, Christians had anxieties that philosophy could not alleviate. No amount of insight or contemplation would do the work of sundering a yoke that had made the frail, generative human body a slave of its perverse will (as Augustine and Paul believed) or of the demons in their clamor (as Gnostic mythmakers held). In Adam's fall the human condition acquired a kink that human efforts cannot undo. Repentance and renunciation might make the soul less heavy, less truculent and disobedient: this was the best that could be expected from ascetic exercises of mortification, abstinence, and humility. But to become like the angels would take God's supernatural grace, not man's spiritual excellence. Sacrifice—to the point of the martyr's joyful death, the abrupt farewell of soul from body—imitated the unmatched obedience of the Son of God. It was the right image for transcendence as the Christians understood that.

But torture, crucifixion, willing surrender of the body to the executioner's knife, the fire, the beast—what benefit could a philosopher draw from these? The violent metaphors used by the Christians could only repel a Neoplatonic angel, however readily he could admit the shared commitments to abstinence and the pious advantage of cultivating indifference to the flesh. Even the incessant harping on lust and the appetites as proof that the unregenerate soul was mortgaged to shame struck such observers as Porphyry and Julian the Apostate as overkill, opening the gates to moral and intellectual servility. Porphyry himself was as inclined to ascetic celibacy as any man in history. A convinced vegetarian, he married at the age of seventy, but only to cultivate a companionship based on philosophical interests, no nonsense about children or sex. Porphyry could find no coherence in the Christian theory that the weaknesses of the senses and passions were due to a moral pollution traceable back to the eagerness of Adam and Eve to know more than they were allowed to know. For a Platonist, the relation of spirit to the senses was different: the senses and the appetites were simply accidents, or perhaps misdirected judgments. They are intrusive for the ordinary man and little problem for the superior man. One could happily do one's duty for the city by having sex and reproducing, by eating moderately with one's fellows: these were transient matters, flickers on a more important horizon. Becoming too preoccupied with the details of everyday life was unseemly.

Christian perfectionism opens the gate to a new type of experience, a different relationship between the self and its inner voices, a space within the soul where constant scrutiny, questioning, and examination take place. No mind is ever exempt from this relentless doubt and probing; no moment of life is free from this work of discrimination. One's duty is to fight with oneself, with the willed and the unwilled, the known and the unknown. This is the combat worth fighting, the "technology of the spirit" worth cultivating.[44] The Christians, like the Jews before them, lived under the shadow of defilement: the senses and the organs might at any moment be maliciously usurped by Satan. Every detail of life was open to the eye of God. It was all too easy to be wrong. In the battle of the soul with corruption, angel and beast never ceased to struggle. Only a leap outside the world itself, through the unexpected and undeserved intervention of a redeeming God, could restore the efficacy of the human will and human reason. In this life the soul is confused—morally, metaphysically, psychologically. Apprised of the possibility of enlightenment, it awakes, remembering its better origins. What can a Christian do to become perfect? How can the great error that was the Fall of Man be undone? The curious form that Christian thinkers in the first four centuries gave to this problem is what interests me here. The image of God has been defaced, they argued. Those who believe and struggle for faith need more than the stuff they were born with: they need the lost image that humans once had. But to regain that innocent shape, they need to unravel the history of the world. To return to the Garden of Eden and see God as he wants to be seen, perhaps they need to give back the privilege he so generously offered then to Adam and Eve—the privilege of sexual love and reproduction. To be sublime, be a child again, or even better, be the eunuch.[45]

The strange search for an asexual sublime is what made Christian perfectionism an anomaly in the history of moral ideas. It is, I want to make clear, a deeply un-Hegelian search. In Hegel's view, the Fall was the best thing that could have happened to the human race. Without a constitutive tension, an appetite for the fray, perfectionist ideals will do more harm than good in a Hegelian cosmos. Eden is for the animals. Or, as Hegel's student Heinrich Heine articulated the spirit of the new revolutionary age, better immanence than transcendence. Better a world we can see and taste than the ghostly delights of the fleshless. In a Feuerbachian spirit, Heine writes his satirical epic in verse *Deutschland: Ein Wintermärchen* (*Germany: A Winter's Tale*; 1843). At the time, the failure of the German revolutions of 1848 could not have been anticipated. The children of the Enlightenment had every reason to be upbeat. Let's have new green peas for everyone, writes Heine, spring peas fresh from the pods, and leave heaven to the sparrows, unless the angels want it. Empty the celestial academics; make theology anthropology. It was a brilliant slogan, and young

Hegelians including Ludwig Feuerbach knew what they were doing when they coined it. But sublimity proved hard to eradicate.

Created Male and Female: Augustine, Manichaeism, and Human Imperfection

Common to the Jewish and Christian stories of the origin of the world is the worry about evil. Augustine's anguish in book 7 of his *Confessions* is the classic statement. "Burning with anxiety," he turns the thoughts over and over in his unhappy mind:

> So then where does evil come from, and by what route did it crawl in? What is its root, and what is its seed? . . . Where does evil come from, then, since a good God made all these good things? The greater and the highest good did make lesser good things but nevertheless both the creator and all created things are good. So where does evil come from?[46]

Cosmic or human evil, natural or moral evil: however it is defined, it can hardly be denied. Its presence needs somehow to be explained and possibly, with the right amount of contortions, justified. Could the Creator have intended nature to be so deeply flawed, so full of pain and loss? Or if not, was he too weak? "Could evil have existed against the will of God?" Augustine asks desperately.[47] And was God, who knows everything, responsible for human perversity? Whether the plans for Adam and Eve included marriage and sexual relations (pleasurable or otherwise) was a subject of passionate argument for Jewish and Christian exegetes. The issue, as we shall see, dominated the theological arena in the age of Jerome, Jovinian, and Augustine. It is impossible to understand Christianity's interest in sexual purity and continence without referring to the biblical background. And here things get complicated. The source is, as we might expect, the book of Genesis. In its first lines there is a contradiction embedded in the doctrine of Creation itself. In the Priestly version of Genesis 1:1–23 (called the "P" text), Elohim, on the sixth day, after creating the rest of the animal world, in their varieties of male and female, chooses not to make one but two sexes, and the plan was put into action all at once. In the second version, the Yahwist text (Gen. 2:4–2:24) God created a male human named Adam, then the animals, and then woman as an afterthought. The two forms of humanity represented by the couple given the top position in the garden were much alike, but there were small and significant differences in their design.

All Jewish and Christian thinkers took heed of the puzzle posed by this twofold creation of the ancestors of the human race, none more energetically than Augustine. Even before his baptism and conversion to Catholic Christianity in 386, the brilliant and ambitious young man from the provinces was preoccupied with the meaning of creation. Attracted to the high-sounding theories of Mani and the nobility of philosopher-sages such as Cicero and Porphyry, Augustine found the language of the Old Testament unappetizing, its sentiments seeming to come from an unfamiliar world, and one he was in no hurry to inhabit. Could an omniscient and omnipotent deity really have designed such a spectacle of discord and error? The Genesis account of the origin of evil, death, and sexual difference made it difficult to understand how to save the reputation of God. Augustine turns the problem over and over again in *Contra Julianum*, his rhetorical war against the Pelagian Bishop of Eclanum: concupiscence is an evil, even if marriage makes good use of it in the propagation of offspring (bk. 3, 16.30). Yet this is what Julian was challenging, in declaring that God cannot be the author of an evil (bk. 3, 7.16–9.19) and that, accordingly, the sexual urge, implanted by God, was an instrument that could be used well or badly; the main thing was to be virtuous and refrain from excesses through the free effort of the will (the Pelagian maxim). If God creates two sexes, their members, and their union of bodies, how could human sexuality be condemned as sinful? "The evil that is in man" cannot be denied. It is contracted by generation and must be healed by regeneration (bk. 4, 1.1–2.13). Yet how could this "evil" be the result of a sexual embodiment which is from God alone?[48]

Initially it seemed to Augustine that the difficulty arose from the biblical insistence that the original condition of humans was indeed a physical, and hence a sexual, one: paradise had included marriage. The genitals were there from the beginning, and their purpose was clear. But such a view—the literal reading of Genesis—troubled the ascetic mind. Originary humanity, perfect and radiant, must have been different! Everything Augustine had absorbed from his time as a Manichaean auditor in Carthage suggested as much. The world according to Genesis and the world according to Mani could not be the same world. Mani taught that the two principles of darkness and light are born separate and mutually shunning, their mixture in our world (the "middle time") representing a deep error that must be undone.[49] Humans were a sorry mixture of two opposing forces. Yet they were not doomed to remain so shamed: the visible world, Manichaeans taught, was like a gigantic "pharmacy," "in which the pure essence of the ruined fragments of the Kingdom of Light would be distilled."[50] Trying to free himself from the Manichaean theory of salvation he had earlier found so compelling, Augustine returns again and again to these themes in his commentary on the *Literal Meaning of Genesis* and in his *Refutation* of his former Manichaean colleagues, a refutation he published in 388, well before the works of his maturity, the *Confessions* (397–401) and *The City of God* (413–437). For Manichaeans despised the book of Genesis as a naïve and anthropomorphic portrayal of the divine, full of crude implausibilities, whose entire realist spirit was alien and incoherent to the philosophically mature. Why would the divine be interested in the material world, which must have been the product of a hostile, darker force? Human souls were, indeed, conceived as images of divinity, but they have been trapped in material bodies. They still preserved a spark of the light, but their bodies, Mani taught, had been traps, framed originally by the Prince of Darkness. That bit of light needs to be rescued. If one avoided certain kinds of food, especially meat, the release of light was made possible. Sexual acts, however, only imprisoned that light deeper within. To win out against evil, procreation should be avoided; indeed, everything associated with generation and material nature is to be viewed negatively. Only a God of love could have sent his Son to atone for us, and that God had nothing in common with a Creator responsible for the cloying banality that is the "present world." The Hebrew Bible, which recounted the barbarous deeds of this so-called Lord, must be a travesty, an insult to the refined intelligence, and Adam and Eve, far from being the beloved creatures of the true God, were fashioned by demons who had seen the image of God and knew how to travesty it.[51] Or so the Manichaeans reasoned.

The young Augustine, enraptured by the wisdom and beauty of Cicero's exhortation to philosophy, the *Hortensius* (*Confessions* 3.4), felt a shock like that of the Manichaeans when he opened a Latin Bible.[52] The style seemed primitive, the sentiments barbaric, the deity portrayed was a bully uninterested in his worshippers' higher aspirations. Nothing in the Old Testament gave sustenance to the philosophical mind, Augustine concluded; it offered little but rigid regulations and bizarre myths, offensive to a sophisticated and educated mind. Much more coherent were the Manichaean doctrines Augustine's biographer describes as "irresistibly mysterious."[53] The Manichaean missionaries Augustine encountered in Carthage in 371 CE had all the aura of a secret, esoteric society. They could foretell eclipses of the sun and moon, they had the skill to understand the movements of the heavens, the patterns of the stars, even though they were ignorant of mathematics and rational science (*Confessions* 5.3–7). And they rejected all self-indulgence, Augustine reports with admiration. Their lives were ascetic, their judgments exacting, and they scorned literalism in interpretation just as much as he did, saving their most withering contempt for the idea of God who takes on a human body and converses with men and women. Following their teacher, the Persian "apostle" Mani, who had been executed by the Persians in 276, the Manichaeans seemed to Augustine to understand the pain of our mixed condition. Against the seediness of human life they offered a route to salvation, a liberation of the spiritual man from the dark imprisonment of evil and matter. Mani, an austere and charismatic figure, claimed the authority of Jesus. And he added a potent supplement of Gnostic themes to his respect for the Christian Messiah.

Christianity, whatever its attractions, had not catered so explicitly to the pessimism of the late Roman world. The religion of Mani, as Owen Chadwick puts it, "expressed in poetic form a revulsion from the material world," and in particular, a revulsion from the "baseness" of sexual life, which was, to Manichaeans, the invention of the devil.[54] Interpreting the prophetic message and the passion of Christ to his own symbolic tastes, Mani expunged from the Christian teaching all elements of the Jewish Bible and history. The virginal Seth, rather than the married Adam, was the preferred ancestor. Female sexuality, never easily absorbed into the religions of the ancient world, did very badly in the hands of the Manichaean faithful. And many, if not all, of the heroes of the Hebrew scripture—patriarchs, prophets, priests, and kings—found themselves banished. Jesus himself remained. He could fit into Mani's complex mythology. He was taken to be a symbol of humanity's struggle between the Light and the Dark, the preeminent bearer (before the arrival of Mani himself) of all the sparks of divinity scattered throughout the world. But this Jesus was different from the Jesus of the Gospels. The Manichaeans wanted a Jesus who wanted nothing to do with Israel. For the Manichaeans Jesus could not have been a Jew or a carpenter, or anything so banal. He could not have been a suffering servant who knew the pains of the flesh and shared them with us. Thus expurgated, most of what is most distinctive about the biography of the Christian Messiah seems to disappear in the Manichaean whitewash.

As Augustine moved closer to the Catholic religion of his mother, Monica, he began to be less persuaded by this Manichaean absolutism. Jesus was, after all, born from the womb of a mortal woman, a woman like other women. If our flesh is defiling, then his flesh is also defiled (*Confessions* 5.10). Manichaeism accepted only a certain version of Christianity, one that dispensed with the doctrine of Creation and the Jewish Law and, as far as possible, did without flesh and blood. Looking back, Augustine believes that what he found most sympathetic in the Manichaean rejection of the Old Testament was the alteration of all the passages that had, he complains, "been death to me" when taken literally but delighted him when read figuratively (*Confessions* 5.14). Figurative interpretation was just what Manichaeans most appreciated. It helped them around all sorts of awkward issues. Divinity, they insisted, must be conceived as pure spirit alone. To affirm the visible universe as the work of such a spirit was implausible. Instead the cosmos was to be understood only symbolically. It looks real. But it is simply a theater in which inner spiritual dramas are staged. Mani's revelations were exotic. But they were evasive. Mani had tried to look away from the contradictions that the Bible depicts in every generation of human history. Gone in the Manichaean religion was the vivid tension in the human will between obedience and disobedience, between the servile destiny of humanity in history and its hope for a redeemed world order. Manichaeism averted its eyes from an oppressive past and a sin-ridden present, from the reality Jesus and Paul had forced the descendants of Adam to acknowledge, preferring to look instead at the skies. No longer troubled by the crucial ambivalence of the biblical belief in a God who affirmed both the low and the high, body and mind, who both judged and loved, the Manichaean seeker after purity

> would realize vividly that he was not free. He could identify himself only with a part of himself, his "good soul." So much of him plainly did not belong to this oasis of purity: the tensions of his own passions, his rage, his sexuality, his corrupt body, the vast pullulating world of "nature red in tooth and claw" outside him. All this weighed on him. It was obvious that what was good in him wished to be "set free," to "return," to merge again into an untroubled, original state of perfection—a "Kingdom of Light"—from which it felt isolated.[55]

For Manichaeans, the Israelite Jehovah was a false god. Like all the other enemies of the Light and the good, this Jehovah needed to be exposed and defeated. As Manichaeism saw it, the human heart is a small repetition of this cosmic battle. We, like the universe, are the playing field of two incompatible wills. Evil arose from one side and exercised a quasi-physical activity in the world. Goodness, and Light, came from the other side, with which the enlightened mind can become united.

Methodius: Versions of Pastoral

Flesh without taint: for Augustine, that was the gift we had lost. The genre of pastoral, as I have tried to think about it in this chapter, agrees with Augustine that the better state was the earlier state, and it is this remnant of classical pastoralism within Christian teaching about sex and chastity that I want to explore further now. A "green world" of natural innocence becomes an element in the Christian imagination with the help of Augustine's determined efforts to think sex without sin, fertility without concupiscence. In happiness, in serenity, and with no experience of pain, men and women in the Edenic condition could have given birth to blessed children, conceived piously and without the remotest hint of agitation or tension. As C. S. Lewis commented in *Allegory of Love*, medieval Christians remained faithful to this paradoxical view about the state of the sexual act within marriage: "On the one hand, nobody ever asserted that the act was intrinsically sinful. On the other hand, all were agreed that some evil element was present in every concrete instance of this act since the Fall. It was in the effort to determine the precise nature of this concomitant evil that learning and ingenuity were expended."[56]

Love without licentiousness, sex without pollution: Augustine's singular vision of the prelapsarian Eden imagines how the sexes could cohabit in a condition of perpetual innocence.[57] And that is not all. There are other miseries troubling the physical and sexual lives of men and women which are absent in the Augustinian Eden, miseries that are less cosmic and theological—ones like remorse, impotence, embarrassment, jealousy, and misogyny. If the Fall had not occurred, Augustine concludes, then our emotions would have been different. But now what hope do we have of returning through that closed gate to the garden? It is clear that, for the Christian thinkers of the fourth century, only vowed virginity deserved that privileged pastoral exemption. It was here that the "Paradise-myth" (in James Grantham Turner's felicitous expression) adds its peculiar twist on the conception of human nature.[58] Human nature is flawed by carnal knowledge, yet it is capable of returning to its pure and blessed shape. Everyone outside the virginal fold must know regret and shame. For concupiscence has damaged the human power to love and has introduced a sour taste into our natural affections. Concupiscence was, for John Chrysostom, a consequence of the Fall, of that diabolically instigated disobedience, and although it is not as such a sin, it cannot help but be immoderate.[59] For Augustine, it remains in our postlapsarian souls and bodies like a wound which seems never to heal. Against the British Pelagius, who held that the human will is strong enough to combat sin, Augustine saw in the inflexibility of lust a mark of our inherited tendency toward intemperate acts. Libido reigns in us, even if we have sworn marital fidelity and have every intention of keeping to that. Sweetness and light have gone out of love. Since our banishment, we yearn for love to reunite us with our lost innocence, and that is a cruel trick because it is love itself that causes suffering and pain. The carnal pleasures we experience only remind us of how unreliable our moments of satisfaction are, how ambivalent and compromised are our erotic successes.

Paul was the first of all Christian writers to take on the problems of reconciling sex with salvation. He did not waste time in wondering what could have happened if Adam and Eve had remained secure. The big news was that a new Adam, both God and man, had broken the chains of guilt, released us from the bondage to death, and given Adam's heirs the promise of a new creation. In the Pauline conception, this was not a paradisal return to innocence but a vivid and militant hope for what is to come at the time of the Parousia. A resurrected body in all its perfection, spiritual and glorious, this is what Paul envisages as the Christian's victory over death, which will come with the fulfillment of the kingdom, when the Lord returns in the fullness of time. Not a liberated spirit (*pneuma*), airy and immortal but shorn of any personalizing traits, but a body (*soma*) that would fully express our freedom and our redemption from evil, a body that would be neither male nor female, married nor single. Pauline flesh redeemed is ever living and incorruptible. It has survived the welcome death of the clinging, rotting, needy flesh (*sarx*) of Adam's heirs, whose every move and every appetite awakened painful memories of their disinheritance. Can the human body be regenerated? Those who repudiated marriage and the "flood of the passions" said it could: "And so God took pity on us in our plight, incapable as we were either of standing or rising again, and sent down from heaven that excellent and most glorious auxiliary, chastity, that we might bind our bodies to it, like vessels, and moor them in calm beyond corruption."[60]

This is the message of divine chastity celebrated in Methodius's *Symposium: A Treatise on Chastity*. Virginity in the third to fifth centuries of Christian practice had its orators, its homilists, its propagandists and polemicists. What it did not have was a literary form that suited it. That form did arrive, and it was Christian pastoral. Its most brilliant flowering was missing in the patristic period. To appreciate the imagination of Christian pastoral, we have to wait for the Middle Ages, and for the second flowering, later, for Renaissance humanists, whose imagination (says Renato Poggioli) was "haunted by the idea of a Christian pastoral."[61] But there were early experiments. As a literary novelty, Christian pastoral began to show what it was capable of even before Gregory, Athanasius, Ambrose, and the other champions of virginity had weighed in on the superiority of continence for the ambitious Christian. To invent Christian pastoral required an imagination eager to feed on the classical and on the Christian diets, someone who could wed Paul to the more appropriate partners in the Hellenic and Hellenistic camp. That honor went to Methodius, writing perhaps a century earlier than Gregory, Jerome, and Ambrose, the bishop of a Greek town in present-day Turkey, a critic of Origen, and a martyr.

In response to Porphyry's learned polemic against the Christians, Methodius wrote his own polemic defending them, sometime not long after 270 CE. Methodius had read Plato and Aristotle, and he shows some engagement with the Stoics. His *Symposium* is a pastiche of Plato. It is set in a landscaped estate, a villa outside the city on a steep hill, rich with gardens and fruit trees, at the center of which is a fountain springing up from a stream. The guests, invited there by the Lady Arete, are all women and all virgins; they gather and converse under the shade of a "chaste-tree" (*agnos-castus*), an herb long thought to have antiaphrodisiac (and abortificant) properties if its blossoms are carried, eaten, or brewed.[62] After enjoying a (nonalcoholic) banquet, eleven of the ladies participate in a dialogue on the subject of chastity. After they have finished their "contest of words," the crown for the best speech describing the virginal ideal is awarded to Thecla, who leads the circle of virgins in a hymn, composed by Methodius who probably also composed the music to accompany it.[63] There are numerous allusions to Plato, in style as well as content, and echoes of *Phaedrus, Alcibiades, Hippias Major,* and of course the *Symposium*. Although the philosophers' banquet is the excuse for the dialogue, Methodius's own mystical conceptions and his delight in allegory drew him again and again to a different dialogue, the *Phaedrus*. From the *Phaedrus* he borrowed the pastoral setting, off in the peaceful, semisuburban outskirts of the city, under the shade of some sympathetic trees—a plane tree and a fragrant chaste-tree—and cooled by a spring (Plato, *Phaedrus* 229b–230b).

Philosophical pastoral is the genre that governs the conversation between Socrates and Phaedrus about the soul, mania, love, and oratory. It was, Methodius must have noticed, ideal for suggesting the soul's conversion to a love for spiritual beauty. Methodius adopts images from the myths with which Plato adorned his theory of the soul (the cave, the craftsman, the sprouting of wings), and he does so with a frank enthusiasm for the pleasures of symbolism and the mysteries of the allegorical mode. What we miss in Methodius, however, is the spirit of Plato's *Symposium*. There are no jugs of wine, no flute-playing girls. Instead of an elegant and urbane house, well equipped and smoothly run for the benefit of the cultured ruling classes, the scene is a suburban garden. Appreciation of the beauty of young men makes no appearance, nor does any appreciation for the excitements of male achievement in the theater, the political sphere, or war. The atmosphere is sedate and lofty. The drink on offer is water, the bodies are primly concealed in white dresses, and almost nothing is said about food. The guests at the banquet in Methodius's scenario are women, young virginal women, and the love they compete to praise and expound is not erotic love, nor even the idealized love for the Truth that Platonists aspire to, but virginal purity.

In Plato's *Symposium*, the guests were invited to show off their knowledge of love. Corrected by an oracular woman, whose lesson Socrates delivers (Plato, *Symposium* 201e–212a), they quibble about the etiquette of power or age difference in love, about passion versus friendship, about physical beauty versus wisdom as aphrodisiacs. Only men could have such a discussion. Nowhere in antiquity are privileged women presented with the opportunity to debate the meanings of love. It is important to the history of love in the West that when women finally do get the chance, they are invited to do so under the white veils of intact virgins. This would have seemed ridiculous to Plato. For the men at Plato's banquet, love begins in the flesh and is kindled by the senses. The soul desires what appears to it as good, and physical beauty entices the eye and the appetites, making us want not just to gaze but to possess and enjoy. The movement toward that promised pleasure is what we call love, ordinarily speaking. But why do we love? Plato's guests speak about the loves they know or about those they can describe with the inventions of the imagination. Carnal loves are inspired by lovely forms and bodies. The grasping of limbs and the exploration of skin makes the soul eager, hungry for more, unsure of its satisfactions. Yet love is also inspired by the qualities of those who become our beloveds. A more searching and cultivated lover turns to beauties of achievement and admires the courageous, the eloquent, the intelligent. And even these are not the end of the quest. As the process of loving immersion continues, the lovable qualities that belong to a cherished person are revealed to be little more than a lure. At the source of eros's magnetic pull is a divine being who is manifest in the beauties of that which is loved but who at the same time remains elusive. Love could be any number of things, and the symposiasts consider many: possibly a god, as myth teaches; possibly a demon, a philosopher, or a joker. Love is always hungry. Where will it find the gratification it seeks?

Plato's *Symposium* invented a way of seeing love and idealization as one movement, one impulse that both knows and does not know itself. This idea, once absorbed, has never left the poetry and philosophy of love. Using the persona of Diotima, Socrates's wise teacher, Plato offered a parable about the ladder of fleshly and spiritual loves, a ladder by which the lover might ascend to the nonempirical form, the light of beauty itself.[64] While carnal love impregnates bodies, this Platonic love impregnates the ardent soul with the love for virtue and truth. Casting aside lesser rewards, the educated lover requires nothing less than philosophical illumination. Passing from one rung of the ladder to the next, mortal illusions are gradually discarded. The soul becomes what it loves. More precious than any partial beauty is the presence of Beauty itself. To experience beauty undivided where before only individual beauties were known, even to be joined to this sublime object in a state that cancels all separation, is something the lover of beauty longs for. That would be ecstasy. Plato's invention was an image of transcendence that proved irresistible to religious mystics—and to the mystical wing of Christianity from the third century to the late Middle Ages.

By the time Origen wrote his seminal *Commentary on the Song of Songs* in 240–244 CE, the Gnostic suspicion that a perfected existence is a life of mind alone had insinuated itself into Christian sensibility, and with it the Platonic preference for spirit over matter, the eternal over the temporal. If Platonists could think about the return of mind into Mind, if Plato could portray (say, in the *Phaedrus*) the upward journey of the embodied soul as a search for its lost and disincarnate origins, so too could Christians with an education in the Greek and Neoplatonic masters. If Plato could endow intellectual purification with an erotic glow, why couldn't this be shared by the pious Christian soul, whose heart's desire must be what Origen, in his *Commentary*, described as "the truer, close, holier kiss which is said to be given by the lover, the Word of God, to his beloved, the pure and perfect soul"?[65] From Origen the Christian theology of spiritual apprenticeship acquired its form, and its core symbol—the mystical marriage. The Song of Songs described what looked like a real amorous encounter between a virginal betrothed and an ardent masculine lover. Shedding these fleshly obstructions, a mystical tradition attaching itself to the interpretation of this text translated the erotic terms into spiritual ones. There is great pleasure in the prolonged courtship of lovers who know their consummation will arrive: every type of foreplay, emotional and carnal, anticipation, caress, kisses, and intercourse, all deliver the bride and bridegroom into each other's arms, between the divine lover, the Logos or Holy Spirit, and the pure and faithful soul who is his beloved. When interpreted by idealizing Christian readers, and indeed by comparable mystical readers in Judaism, the Song of Songs seemed to speak of a union between the virginal and enamored soul and her divine or otherwise mysterious beloved. Probably the apotheosis of this vein of interpretation arrived in the time of Bernard of Clairvaux (1090–1153), the Cistercian monk of the twelfth century. Bernard imagined the invisible God wanting to be loved by carnal men in the flesh,

> to converse with men as a man. He wanted to recapture the affections of carnal men who were unable to love in any other way, by first drawing them to the salutary love of his own humanity, and then gradually to raise them to a spiritual love.[66]

Through the stages of love (or "charity"), our carnal affection for Christ leads us to desire more. Etienne Gilson finds that, for Bernard, the union with God "may be effected [to] demand no less than that the soul itself shall be interiorly changed, purified, clarified, and restored to the likeness of its Creator."[67]

Methodius, then, was not an outlier. His Platonic inclinations connected him to the great Alexandrians who were his near contemporaries, such as Origen and Clement, but also to the Jewish philosopher Philo and the Hellenistic thinkers influenced by Plotinus and the Neopythagoreans. Methodius's uninhibited glorification of the virginal life also had precedents. It rested on several generations of zeal for the practice of asceticism, at that point well into its third century as Christians in the late Roman cities differentiated themselves from their Jewish and pagan neighbors by advocating such unusual behaviors as fasting, community of property and households, modesty in dress and language, avoidance of games, shows, and sacrifices, and of course, sexual continence. What is interesting about Methodius's dialogue is that virginity is not just one of the goods but the summit of all that can be imagined as good. Virginal renunciation of sexual life and bodily reproduction is the ideal human condition and one which any variety of perfectionism must recognize. Here Plato's twofold ladder finds itself reduced to a simpler and cruder soul map: what for the sophisticated artists in the game of love and enlightenment is a sublimation of the sensual and a rich cultivation of the intellect is, for these young girls, the prudery of the innocent.

In Methodius's dialogue, the maiden Thecla, given the name of Saint Paul's famous follower, applies Plato's famous myth of transcendence to the virgin soul, whose wings are impregnated with *parthenia* (virginity) and thus can resist any earthbound force pulling them toward the shadows and illusions of mundane appearances. "The wings of chastity soar aloft into the pure ether and to the life that is close to the angels."[68] The glorious virgins see with their own eyes the "Forms of Justice, Understanding and Peace." Since Christ had brought back into creation the original human substance, untainted by sin, there has been a return of the power to display that first "image of God" by means of which humans were modeled. "Christ the Archvirgin" has put error to flight.[69] By practicing virginity, the body can be rendered immortal and purified. It is newly espoused not to men but to the Word. "By chastity," one of Methodius's symposiasts reports, "they have been emancipated from that condemnation, *Earth thou art, and unto earth thou shalt return*."[70]

The self-discipline of the virgin, like the rock salt mixture that gives the salmon its extended and luscious life, is a "cure" for nature's sensual wastefulness. Learning the "science of virginity"—every bit as demanding as the *paideia* of the strictest philosophers—allows the convert to progress in holiness, to advance from incest to marriage and from marriage to fidelity and from fidelity to continence (sophrosyne) until the final perfection is reached: the safe harbor and peaceful haven of virginity.[71] All else pales in comparison to virginity. If not the summum bonum, it is the mirror of holiness. Holiness, here, is corporeal as well as intellectual. Through the life of immaculate chastity, the makeup of the human person can be changed. Not even skin, bones, and muscles will continue in their original form. Lightness will replace heaviness, as the body becomes "dry" and semitransparent. From a natural and carnal being can be born a transformed one. The changes in physical constitution, produced by the healthy discipline of virginity, translated into spiritual metamorphosis.

For the most part Methodius's philosophical theology is orthodox and uncontroversial. Human beings are put on the earth to progress, as far as they can, toward the contemplation of God. They can do so through knowledge and moral perfectionism. They are not doomed to error. But they will not progress in holiness on their own, without grace and guidance. This was a picture of the Christian destiny, merged with its sibling image of high-minded Greco-Roman self-fashioning, that the charismatic Alexandrian father Origen had done much to advance. Despite Methodius's doubts about Origen's theory of the resurrected body, Origen's guidance has endured in Methodius's thinking. In this indebtedness, Methodius was not alone, Brown observes: "Origen's view of the spiritual struggle entered the bloodstream of all future traditions of ascetic guidance in the Greek and Near Eastern worlds."[72] Origen's conception of intellectual spirituality, steeped in the Platonic atmosphere of Alexandrian theology, is here fused with another tradition of the human "becoming-divine." For Christian athletes of sanctity—whether desert monks or protected anchorites—the improvement of the individual and the restoration of the human race depend on the ascetic "No" to ordinary human flourishing.[73] In the effort to wean the soul from the body the virgin was a key player.

Methodius's curious text is one of a kind. It contributed only indirectly to the early church's preparation of an intellectual and emotional world safe for the consecrated virgin. As far as we can tell, imitators did not rush to offer similar poetic treatments of doctrinal debates. Was it original?

Its derivation from the Platonic and other philosophical dialogues was patent. The use it made of imagery already significant in Christian interpretations, especially of scripture, was elaborate but not radical. Perhaps the most successful was Methodius's contribution of a stately and flowery language to honor the "nuptials" of young women joining themselves in spirit and destiny to their heavenly spouse. The Gnostics of second-century Rome and Egypt, themselves masters of the labyrinthine uses of mythic imagery, had already applied the Jewish motif of the mystical marriage between Sophia and God to the process of redemption.[74] In one of the central Gnostic myths, Sophia, the errant spouse, had rebelled against God and succumbed to the most unimaginably vile desires, leading her to create a grotesque material world, base and cursed by corruption. This is our world. In it things are bad. Yet as a Gnostic like Valentinus announced, hope was in sight. The "good" God has arrived to drive out the "bad" God. The universe could be restored and the soul, imprisoned in its unsympathetic body, could return to its original purity. A remarriage, like that of the repentant Sophia to God the Father, could still happen.

A mystical marriage, surpassing the earthly unions it makes irrelevant, sounded irresistible not just to outliers but to many mainstream thinkers. It had impeccable scriptural references to support it. The Gospel according to John, relating the speech of John the Baptist, has John comparing himself to his master Christ: "He that hath the bride is the bridegroom" (John 3:29); I am only the friend of the bridegroom. The Pauline letter to the Ephesians uses the nuptial metaphor to defend the subordination of women to men (Eph. 5:22–23). Just as Christ is the head of the church, so the husband is the head of the wife. Methodius, to his credit, is not interested in the arguments about the inferiority of women. For him, women are supremely fitted to serve in the first ranks of the holy. His adaptation of the nuptial imagery plays down the patriarchal insistence just as it lowers the wattage of the mystical vision. The "marriage" of his virgins to their divine spouse is a privilege and a prize, not a burden and a chastisement. Like the marriage of the Shulamite to the Bridegroom in the Song of Songs, it promises ecstasy and adoration. And, like the newly fashioned identity whose possibilities were the subject of experimentation among small groups of ascetics in the first four centuries after Christ, virginal marriage represented freedom. Paul, in the First Epistle to the Corinthians, had brought sharply into view the freedom of the unmarried woman, virgin or widow, who can devote herself unstintingly to God, in contrast to the lesser position of the married woman, bound to the duties and worries of husband and family. The distinction was convincing. The rewards of virginal dedication could seem obvious, to those who bothered to observe.

And there were many among women of all classes who responded, seeking an alternative arrangement in their social and worldly lives as well as a greater stake in the blessings of the kingdom of God.

Methodius's *Symposium* is, in Brown's words, a "muted idyll."[75] It is hailed by Michel Foucault as "the first great elaboration of a systematic and developed conception of virginity," foreshadowing the monastic innovations in what he nicely calls "a technology of virginity," which those who search for "incorruptibility" would need to practice along with their works of penance, meditation, poverty, and humility.[76] Its place is beside two other late ancient pictures of feminine love: Longus's *Daphnis and Chloe,* on the one hand, and the image of the Virgin Mary, rose without thorns, on the other. Women, if they are wise and chaste, belong in gardens. Their purity has the power to heal and to inspire. But they are only ennobling in this manner if they exclude themselves from sexual activity.

Secluded, protected, inaccessible, virginal women are lamps of truth and vessels of regeneration. Society requires them and admires their renunciation, their exemption from the complex adult life of challenge and dissension. The innocent maiden is a cultural prize, as church fathers such as Jerome and Chrysostom understood. Making committed converts for the church involved separating women from their social duties and enlisting them in the cloistered life of holy virgins, winning their hearts as well as (often) their fortunes. But Jerome, Augustine, Gregory of Nyssa, and all the many admirers of perfect continence had little that was positive to say about femininity as such. It was only Methodius who, consciously or unconsciously, saw that a sweet maiden in a bucolic setting made a powerful case for the charms of chastity. She was more than a commendable recruit for the cause. She was a symbol. What she symbolized, I want to argue, was the lost but longed-for state of pastoral innocence. Her sexual reticence returned her to the perfect condition of human understanding without guile and without corruption. Her purity and her withdrawal cast a reflection back to nature itself, in its integrity and wholeness. Thus her proper setting is the ideal landscape Renaissance painters and medieval tapestry workers discovered for the Virgin Mother, eyes cast down, modestly looking into her own heart. The cultural move here may have become familiar, but its singularity deserves emphasis. Pagan philosophy, when it attempted to give a face to contemplation, thought of the sage, in his simple clothing and disdain for worldliness. Christian philosophy gave contemplation the face and manner of a virginal girl in a country landscape, a pastoral nymph with a prayer book. The theological case for sexual renunciation acquired something more than it deserved: it acquired charm.

Courtly Love and Its Lady

Perhaps that is the best that can be expected from pastoral, that its fantasy of a place apart—tranquil, bucolic, gentle—will disguise difficult emotions and strenuous experiences. With pastoral, charm entered the chastity plot. And there it remained, even as unsophisticated shepherds and innocent country girls were superseded by more urbane, well-dressed figures in elegantly refined landscapes. Out of the tensions of life (of sex, of spiritual struggle, of human relations) pastoral creates an illusion, that grace is possible. All here is as it should be. Nature and mind need not resist each other, nor ambition fight against pleasure. The Christian pastoral was one of the many moments at which poetry was pressed into the service of religion, and the effects in this case are worth noting. Not only does poetry have a tolerance for paradox, something Christianity could not do without; it also has a sympathy for women, something the Judeo-Christian traditions found much more problematic.

Christianity always had some room for exceptional women, as fearless ascetic disciple (Saint Thecla), as martyrs to the violence of God's enemies (Perpetua and Felicity, Saint Agnes, Saint Lucy, Saint Catherine, and hundreds more), and as miraculously inviolate nursing mother (Mary). These female paragons were rare. The hierarchy of the church kept free of the influence of women. Divinity, while imagined in a nonsingular form, connected three persons, none of whom were female. The power to preach and the power to teach were very early on restricted to males. Such restriction was, however, not entirely predictable: early Christian practice had appeared to some members of the communities as offering a greater opening to equality for women, an opportunity Thecla was quick to seize. There are feminists today who believe we should be pursuing such a reading, asking Christianity to recognize the opportunity it wasted. Looking back at the history of the religion and its growth as an institution, few would deny that the doors slammed shut very quickly. Women were as much the second sex in Christianity as they were in Judaism, the religion out of which it grew. Instead of a world of disciples anticipating the heavenly condition of the sexless angels, the church re-created the same social hierarchies found in towns and cities from east to west. Indeed, the Christian drama of degradation and grace positioned women in a particularly culpable role, a demotion only to acquire an even more blatant form in the misogynist clichés of the Middle Ages, prone to depicting women as carnal traps, stumbling blocks set by the devil to lure the confused soul away from the path of holiness.

Yet if the medieval imagination was, in more ways than not, "antifeminist," it was also capable of some creative contradictions in its discourses about the female sex, about love, death, and transcendence as played out through the female body and its erotic appeal.[77] However slippery the idea of *courtly love,* however resistant to clear formulation and historical verification, it introduced a paradoxical aesthetic with significant implications for the understanding of chastity. Something happened to the familiar ideologies of gender inferiority when medieval troubadours took earthly women and claimed to see in them the signs and tokens of beauty, truth, and eternity. However little we know about that mysterious substance, *amor cortois* (courtly love), we know it is responsible for a persisting notion of the ideal beloved as a "Lady" who remains lovable as long as she remains at a distance, as long (in effect) as she refuses to love. Like the virgins subjected to the scolding of Jerome or Tertullian, the courtly lady can barely be thought about without besmirching her purity: to appear is already to be reduced to the conditions of material and mundane reality; the ultimate perfection is, if not to disappear, to approach as nearly as possible the state of abstraction and emptiness. "A vacuum towards which man is drawn," observes Howard Bloch.[78] Some would say the same about God.

The elevation of the woman to pure Idea is an odd compliment, to be sure. Noble ladies were represented as alluring and elusive. Falling in love with them could save that soul, awakening it to something fine and morally transfiguring. All that was required was humility and service—and the unwavering devotion of the faithful lover, a devotion that needed to be tested again and again. "Frauendienst"—the troubadour's invention—made a difference to the look of European idealism. It probably began as a game: see what happens when you glorify the objects of your sexual appetites rather than despising them; see if passion can be prolonged and intensified if you include distance and fear in the techniques of courtship.

The "ennobling" of love language that became a fashion at some Provençal and German courts toward the end of the feudal epoch was not a revolution in the history of morals. It was, nonetheless, a shift. What was worthy of love might also be worthy of respect. Woman might be soul as well as body, and as soul, her conquest was even more of an achievement. Upgrading the moral character of at least some special women (differentiated by class, by marital status, or by inaccessibility) meant that a reconsideration of the sex was in order. Femininity and virtue began to appear as more closely allied than ancient cultures had chosen to believe.

Between Methodius and the highly wrought pastorals of Renaissance poets such as Sir Philip Sidney and Edmund Spenser, something interesting happened that allowed a meeting between the beauty of the senses and the austere exaltations of asceticism. On the face of it, asceticism was not a likely source for aesthetic rapture. The purity of the desert was harsh; the self-fashioning favored among those who pursued its discipline stressed mortification, fasting, the avoidance of bathing and changing clothes, and also the repudiation of social niceties. Such harshness had little place in the elaborate make-believe of courtliness—C. S. Lewis's "allegory of love." Courtly poets developed the skills of ambivalence, flitting between faith and ambition, penitence and indulgence. They claimed to believe that they could love both God and themselves. This confidence separated them from the spiritual warriors—the eunuchs, the anchorites, the mystics—for whom the ordeal of solitude was necessary to keep at bay the temptation of worldliness. In the fiction of courtly love, a European aristocracy and its hangers-on played with the idea that worldliness, refined into an art, could determine its own moral code: a kind of self-conscious and refined performance of courtesy that has deep but indirect relations to the pastoral. "Courtly love," writes Roger Boase in his refreshingly demystifying study of the various theories about "the origin and meaning" of this slippery phenomenon, "was certainly a fantasy or fiction shared by the aristocracy of medieval Europe from the twelfth century onwards." Its affinities with mysticism (both Christian and non-Western) may have been exaggerated by scholars impressed by what sounded like a Neoplatonic model of Plato's "ladder of love." But, Boase argues, we do not find in troubadour poetry a movement from individual to universal beauty of the sort so dear to Dante, nor is there any vision of an ascent from the human to the divine.[79] An absorption of theological exaltation into the more rewardingly carnal fantasies of sophisticated male poets: this well-loved theory of courtly love as "sex religion" still tempts many interpreters. The hints are there. What we do with them requires some care.

The literature of courtliness is my last example of Christianity's pastoral. In it the sensual threat of "woman"—of female sexuality faced head-on—is both permitted and canceled. Venus is chastened and allowed to return as Diana. This time she has learned how to look down demurely, if necessary, to withhold her favors and to reward those of her suitors who know how to flatter her with their indifference to vulgar satisfactions. This is a different way of negotiating the relations of denial and amorousness. Hippolytus in his one-dimensional austerity has not been reinstated. Another youth whose innocence and ardor Hippolytus prefigured has come back in a new shape, even if still a pastoral one, now willing to taste the delights of a twofold goddess, at once virgin and wife. In the medieval legend of Parsifal, such an uncompromising and pure male virgin is shown as initially flawed, damaged by his own ignorance and sexual disdain. He must be tamed. Either through monastic discipline or the chastisements of an angry mistress, he will learn modesty and compassion, in place of the fatal arrogance of Hippolytus. The Tannhausers of the courtly code are both sinners and saints. They also aspire to purification. But the discipline they submit to includes carnality. That is the paradox of the chivalric code.

Complication and contradiction were of the very essence of the chivalric ideal as it ostensibly emerged in the southern French courts of the eleventh century.[80] Here was a "religion of love" that claimed to be modeled on the feudal system of service and obligation, yet added an elaborate device of rules, codes, and exemplary conduct, all in the name of governing the lover's subjection to his impossible Lady, whose word was law and whose whims must be obeyed abjectly.[81] In courtly love, erotic obsession (as the formulae must assume it) has the power to refine that same appetite of the loins that piety and society will insist is degrading and to be kept in the dark. The courtly lover is above such vulgarities. His passion is virtue, and his lust is chaste. The paradoxes are deliberate and irreducible. The lowly are exalted, loss is gain, pain is pleasure, death is life. The lover flirts with idolatry, turning his beloved into something sanctified and miraculous, yet also mocks the piety found in hagiographies that depict the torments and struggles of mystical suitors of the divine. A poetic imagining—and loud announcing—of wishes that might indict one of dishonor instead does the opposite.

Erotic sentiment (even the sexual act itself, teasingly described in some of the troubadours' poems) passes through an intricate machinery of allegorical play, turning what ordinary minds would construe as shameful into something refined, esoteric, and deflected. The illicit status of the pleasures renounced—for the poet-suitor usually claims to be in love with a married woman who is out of his class—also seems to make this ideal of passionate love all the more romantic and spiritually exalting. At least in Lewis's well-known thesis on the courtly love code as an idealization of adultery, the fact that this love cannot and must not culminate in marriage is what renders it free, noble, stylized, and impossible, an enigmatic exception to the Western devaluation of the female sex, and a long hymn in celebration of suspended action.[82]

And the fiction of renunciation was part of chivalry's serious play: just as the monks and clergy of the tenth to twelfth centuries were finding their obligations to celibacy ever more rigidly demanded, so the courtly lover proved his value and nobility by the degree to which he could abstain and subjugate himself. Lewis provides the most celebrated (if contested) definition of the courtly sensibility: "This is love of a highly specialised sort, whose characteristics may be enumerated as Humility, Courtesy, Adultery, and the Religion of Love."[83]

"Ennobling love" was a social ideal favored by the aristocracy of the European Middle Ages, C. Stephen Jaeger observed: "It is primarily a way of behaving, only secondarily a way of feeling."[84] It distinguishes the fine from the not-so-fine, the courtly insider from the base outsider. "Only the courteous can love," continues Lewis, "but it is love that makes them courteous."[85] By any account, courtly love was a literary artifice, bearing little resemblance to love affairs as they were conducted during the time of Ovid, Catullus, and the other erotic poets of antiquity. The amorists of the Roman Empire knew that love outside of marriage was a game, even a dangerous one. They could portray passion as both infuriating and amusing, as a joke and a nightmare, and even if it was one of the greater enjoyments life could afford, still something without intellectual gravitas or religious potential. The mistresses they cajoled and swore at, who alternately invited them in for hours of delight and locked them out to entertain other lovers, were not perfect, sublime, aristocratic beings. They could be proud and brilliant, educated and sensitive. And they could also be not too much better than whores. In the hands of courtly poets, such erotic games change more than their clothes.

"Courtesy" is what the true and faithful lover owes to his Lady, and no demand she makes can be too much. The Lady is not divine, but the lover is happy to pretend that she is, or nearly so, in what Lewis calls love religion as a "parody" of the "real religion."[86] Like the Christian religion, the religion of love aims at absolutism. Good manners are crucial, but the pressure put on them is of an unusual kind. Rules are supposed to regulate the expression of the courtly passion and ensure its pristine quality. The object of desire must be without imperfection or lack; she must be whole and complete unto herself.[87] One loves her without expecting to be loved in return, offering to be her hostage and vassal, suppressing vulgar lusts and indeed willing her coldness, as Bernart de Ventadour writes in *Lancan vei*: "Let her by no means love me with her body, that doesn't fit."[88] How to remain constant in an erotic worship that defers consummation and rewards the faithful with pain and rejection? Are the poets alluding to an eros that "takes place at the border of the illicit," all the while insisting on the significance of courtly chastity and reverence?[89]

The puzzle of this courtly code has inspired a number of theories, the earliest of which was that of Violet Paget in the 1880s, suggesting that a surplus of landless noblemen, often young and underemployed, excluded because of their lack of estates from marriage, needed a function, or rather, needed a cultural cover for their otherwise dependent status as hangers-on at feudal courts, and found that in the poetics of chivalric devotion.[90]

Courtliness arose where marriage could not. In this respect it is less surprising to notice the similarities between this teasingly extramarital erotics and a devotional cult dedicated to the mystical love of the Virgin Mary, like that perfected by Saint Bernard of Clairvaux and the Cistercians. It is true that the soul on fire with the love of God or the Virgin cannot expect to have the physical consummation earthly lovers experience.[91] But the "nuptial song" in which Christ celebrates his marriage to the church does promise to the soul who loves chastely a union in every sense of the erotic word: the rewarded lover receives a kiss from his mouth and a drink from his "sealed fountain"; neither the feet nor the hands of the divine lover are neglected. Bernard's meditations on the Song of Songs address without flinching the carnality of the soul's love for the God-Man. Did not God deliberately choose to come close to humans in the flesh "so that he could capture their affections" by "first drawing them to the salutary love of his own humanity, and then gradually to raise them to a spiritual love"?[92] No material marriage can compete with this. Christ binds himself to his earthly spouse, and she is transported, "sick with love" (Song of Songs 5:8). In Bernard's imagination, the individual soul mingles and converges with the mystical body of the church and the figure of the Virgin Mary, waiting virtuously in her chamber. Loving the Madonna is a mystery: the love of a celibate for a mother whose womb is at once fertile and pure injects a spiritual meaning into eros that, once absorbed, retains its power to expel the cruder versions of sexual yearning.[93] Marina Warner observes that in Bernard's mysticism, "one expression of love—carnal desire—disfigures the pristine soul, but another expression of love—the leap of the soul towards God restores the primal resemblance."[94] Bernard discovers a new use for personal and mystical love, which can attach itself to the heavenly femininity of Mary, a virgin who "bore love itself in her womb"; as she rises to the highest courts of heaven, so goes his adoration with her; her union with her Son is consummated in eternity, just as he hopes his soul, affected by his love, will melt away and be poured into the will of God.[95]

Courtly love played with the ideal of love without an object, in which the beloved must always withhold, test, and demand but never fully deliver.[96] The pleasures of loving, of devotion and praise, were what *fin'amors* was about, for the Occitans and Provençal poets: the myth of love's obstacles and obstructions was essential to its charm; the suitor's continence and self-denial were the very least he could offer his "friend." What if the joy of wanting outshone in any possible world the joy of possession?

Courtly Chastity?

From the tenth to the twelfth century, poets perfected a dual language of "erotic chastity" and ascetic transcendence of the flesh. Like the renunciations expected from a clergy now strictly enjoined to celibacy, the knightly poets claimed that their amorous worship of an unattainable Lady could purify and ennoble. The "service" a courtly lover offered his ideal Sovereign had nothing to do with appetites of the body; the vanities and egotism of the Ovidian amorist had no place here. Passion so obsessively concentrated, so selfless and oblivious to mundane considerations or even hope of reciprocity, must transform the very nature of passion, transferring it to the realm of the symbolic, the sacramental, and the mystical. Courtly love is, in a way, a "discipline."[97] Defying the logic of sexual conduct, the love exalted by the poets is neither repressed nor permitted, neither adulterous nor conjugal, but something in between. Any real, fleshly woman disappears, as René Nelli explains, in favor of an imaginary being, a symbol of amorous transcendence, which sustains the fiction of purity and chastity under the most contrived of circumstances.[98]

Courtly romance lingered in "semi-Platonic" dreams of a longing infinitely extended, snatched away from the realities of sex and the flesh, and transferred to an object described as unattainable and purifying. The mistress whose cruelty wounds and tortures is also a sovereign patron and moral educator: her pursuit sanctifies the questing and courtly knight, redeeming him from all things mundane and vulgar. And what confirms to the reader that this fictional domain of adventures and magic (this "Faeryland") is not at odds with Christian faith and decorum is the pervading atmosphere of soft plenitude.[99] The landscape of courtly romance is the world where animal and man lie down together, overseen by the good shepherd; where the birth of new life in the timeless garden happens magically, without the groaning of the flesh or the pain of labor but rather as mysteriously as the phoenix reanimates itself in fire. The same ideal landscape lends itself, if I am right, to less flirtatious, less playful purposes when pressed into the service of religious edification. Methodius of Olympus (unlike his fellow Christians Dante, Petrarch, Jacopo Sannazaro) does not appear in histories of courtly love literature or pastoral. He would be surprised to see himself designated as the first among the Christians to realize how the classical "romantic idyll" or pastoral mode could be adapted for the celebration of Christian chastity. But his unapologetic Platonizing pushed him into the company of those medieval and Renaissance Europeans moved by both their classical learning and their religious aspirations. In more skilled hands than Methodius's, Greek and Latin poetic conventions, myths, aestheticism, and sensuality were passed through a Christian initiation, giving us the grander designs of Dante's *Vita Nuova,* Petrarch's *canzone,* Spenser's visionary wanderers, and Milton's epic pastorals. The poets knew that love, rather than piety, was what poetry was about. But they, like Methodius, hoped that eros and idealization, spirituality and sensory beauty, could be reconciled. Contemplation of the beauty of women had to be key to this dream because there had to be a way to save the female sex from the condemnation and distrust the Christian tradition so readily produced; if woman was not to be a temptress, on the one hand, or a household convenience, on the other, her nature needed to be imagined better. The pure and innocent lady of the poetic and spiritual tradition I am describing was one way. It had its disadvantages, but its role in creating a new vocabulary for the emotions, and in particular for eroticism, is neither trivial nor crude. The poets of Christian eroticism wavered between love for women as they were and women in a fantasy; they lingered on the flesh, and they spent time elaborating the glories of an impossible being (a Madonna, a cruel and inaccessible beloved). To hold these contradictions together, they injected new life into the old theological virtue of chastity or sexual abstinence and purity. Chastity, for them, could be an image of plenitude and grace rather than repression and prudishness; it could free rather than imprison, and inspire rather than constrain. That belief is what they shared with Methodius.

✵ 6 ✵

A Virgin Enthroned

POWER, PERFORMANCE, AND POETRY IN THE ENGLISH RENAISSANCE

That very time I saw (but thou couldst not),
Flying between the cold moon and the earth,
Cupid all arm'd. A certain aim he took
At a fair vestal throned by the west,
And loos'd his love-shaft smartly from his bow,
As it should pierce a hundred thousand hearts;
But I might see young Cupid's fiery shaft
Quench'd in the chaste beams of the wat'ry moon,
And the imperial vot'ress passed on,
In maiden meditation, fancy free.

A Midsummer Night's Dream, 2.1.154–64

She reminds one of Hippolyte rather than Phaedra.

ROGER ASCHAM

Shepherds, Ladies, and Our Lady: A Frame for Elizabeth

Methodius understood that virgins belong in a garden. Enthusiasts for the church's great Virgin, the mother of Jesus and queen of heaven, followed him in surrounding their Lady with trees and flowers, shepherds and animals. There is a deep cunning in Christianity's adaptation of classical pastoralism. Like that first garden in which Adam and Eve discovered one another, garden settings in literature and art promise sex without danger, fertility without strain, love without loss. Spiritualizing the erotic may have begun under the guidance of Plato and his homoerotic sublime, but centuries of Christian piety, especially in the Middle Ages, took this interesting fruit and made it their own. The pastoral mode allows sex to be held at a distance. The unicorn, magical beast that cannot be captured, comes to lay its head in the lap of a virgin. That is pastoral's idyllic suspension of violence and desire. Strife and stress make only ripples in a stream; loss may intrude, yet the final separation that is death can remain forgotten, just out of reach. It is always spring in the pastoral. Virginal flowers stay unplucked, as beautiful as ever. When Gregory of Nyssa writes the hagiography of his adored sister Macrina, he turns to the language of pastoral, as Peter Brown notes. Removed from the difficult life of the city, excused from "the roles imposed on the normal woman by marriage and childbearing, Macrina was the ancient 'uncut meadow.' Her body was a clear echo of the virgin earth of paradise—untouched earth that bore within itself the promise of undreamed-of abundance."[1]

Macrina's life of secluded simplicity took the innocent nature longed for by Hippolytus onto a new level. Her pastoral had no room for indulgence, and her brother confesses his awe in the face of her strict and selfless devotion. Bawdier paradises were known, even in Christian times. The poems collected sometime in the thirteenth century at a Benedictine cloister in Bavaria and called the *Carmina Burana* mock the ideals of sublimated love. The monks who wrote these "songs" knew that knights raped girls who herded flocks. Spoiled clerics engage in any amount of sexual indiscretion, when they can spare time away from their incessant eating, drinking, and carousing. But the songs are not always debunking. Nature in its feminine tenderness appears, as do the conventions of *fin'amors,* describing the service the lover offers willingly to a cruel mistress. Some songs in the collection are pastoral through and through, like this one, from number 25 of the *Carmina*:

> The earth now lays open her breast to spring mildness which she had closed up before the hard cold in winter's fierceness. With spring comes the west wind in its sweet rustling; the north wind breathing cruelty now ceases to blow. Whom can this pleasant freshness of things allow to be silent?
>
> Look, all things now declare spring with new burgeoning, now that the harmful cold has been repulsed by mild weather. The pregnant earth brings forth great beauty as its offspring, the sweet-smelling flowers of many colors.
>
> The grove is dressed in foliage, already the nightingale sings, while the meadows are charming with various colors. It is sweet to walk through wooded places, sweeter to pluck lilies and roses, sweetest to dally with a lovely girl.[2]

Rarely in Christian writing was nature made so welcoming. These uninhibited monks had learned from literature and not from the pulpit. They allowed their imagination to linger on a place where lover and girl were fully at ease, free from admonishing eyes. Such moments of blessed fecundity rarely appear in theological reflection on salvation, sin, and human fallibility. Medieval Christianity had a daunting agenda, and the systematic intellect could not afford to relax. All of heaven and earth needed to be woven into a complex order: the incarnate God, the threat of the demons, the particular union of substance and accident in the Trinitarian economy, the relations of time and eternity. The pious had little time to stop and smell the flowers. They had to exhort themselves and others. The time was short; the balance sheet of error and sin was long. Christians had to repent, to think about their failings, to maximize their opportunities for penitence and mortification. In the demanding work of Christian perfectionism, it was difficult to sustain the pastoral's image of peace and plenitude.

Yet there was one chapter in the chronicle of Christian experience that lent itself to the idyllic mood, to the memory of childhood, rustic life, simplicity. The Incarnation was a mystery. It was also a wrinkle in time, an interruption in the history of violence and plunder. Nature and human society paused, attending to the birth of a sacred infant. According to the nativity tradition, it happened in a stable, with sheep and goats as audience. There was little in this birth to indicate the presence of celebrity. Everything was the way things happened among the poor. A young maiden had been chosen by God to mother his child. And the task, of considerable importance, was accomplished. The only odd thing was how.

Mary begins her career in history and myth when she is asked to become a mother through a strange and supernatural act, one which we would now classify as artificial or surrogate reproduction. Avoiding all mortal lovers, Mary of Galilee concentrated on the mystery of her womb and the care of the child she bore. European painters of the fifteenth century found the means to put this moment before the eyes of believers. Still and silent, protected from the storms of the world, Mary appears alone with her child in a walled garden. Artists and admirers portray her as the human equivalent of the season of spring. She is fertile and generous, blooming immaculately. Biology in Mary's case was refashioned to the measure of spirit, as if generation could happen without sex, passion, or even insemination. Her example was unique. She was "alone of all her sex," the handmaiden of the Lord. Did Mary's election mean that the female sex had a second chance? She was an ordinary young woman, exceptional only for what she hadn't done, yet she is described as if her trust and obedience were extraordinary, sufficient to restore those condemned by the curiosity of Eve. Mary was neither educated nor wellborn. Her physical bravery was not conspicuous. The Gospels and Acts tell us nothing about heroic deeds or wise sayings. Indeed, they say almost nothing about her at all, except that she rose to the occasion, enabling the remarkable event of the birth of God in human form and accompanying that human God on part of his journey in the world.[3]

Mary's profile is very thin. It is perhaps her emptiness as a character that allows so much to be invested in her. A maiden and a mother, she has no parallel among the virtuous symposiasts at Methodius's banquet who are learned and gifted, eloquent and confident. Imagined always with her child at her breast, except for the mournful occasion when she may have held him in death, Mary is the bridge through which humanity and divinity come back together. The "workshop of the union of natures," she can contribute nothing of her own, lest she disturb that "untarnished vessel" which is her body.[4] Like nature in its mild pastoral aspect, she is a frame for all our fantasies, a mirror in which the desire for purity can behold itself.

Poetry and panegyric, otherwise kept on the fringes, came into their own in the rapturous evocation of one pure and unreachable woman, the Mother of God. In the life of the sinner, exiled through the Fall of Adam and consigned to a harsh passage through an unfriendly world, there had to be moments when the soul's tension could relax and tenderness could be allowed some space. Marian pastoral, for the Christians of the Middle Ages, is that moment. It could even bring theological viciousness to a temporary halt. On the Sunday of the Feast of Mary in 429, a priest from Constantinople named Proclus (ca. 390–446) delivered a sermon in his home city. Constantinople was the epicenter of a violent clash over the ontological status of Mary. Alexandrians, Syrians, and Romans were engaged in fierce rivalry about how to understand the girl described by the Gospels as the virginal vessel in which God chose to bring his Son to flesh. Proclus's Homily is a wonderful text:

> She who has called us here is the holy Mary;
> The untarnished vessel of virginity;
> The spiritual paradise of the second Adam;
> The workshop of the union of natures;
> The market-place of the contract of salvation;
> The bride-chamber where the Word took flesh in marriage;
> The living bush, of human nature, which the fire of a divine birth-pang did not consume . . .[5]

Mary is the bride and the mother, the daughter and the vessel. Her frail body was the home of a second paradise, where God's natures came together and made human flesh blossom again. She is not herself the means of salvation, but without her, salvation would lack a welcoming face and a nurturing presence. And her odd role as exceptional Jewish woman in a culture known for its uncompromising patriarchy distinguishes her from other female figures in myth and literature (secular and sacred) who have made themselves celebrated for their sexual purity. Goddesses like Diana and Minerva could also be called "untarnished." They refused sexual indulgence and claimed exemption from the conjugal norm. But they represented a more severe, unaccommodating use of the virginal privilege. Crowned and adored, Mary does not intimidate. She is placed above all earthly women, past and future. God has elected her for honor and recommended her to receive the tribute of Christians' love and wonder. Her prior qualifications for this role are unclear in the Gospels, although noncanonical Mariological traditions go to great lengths to elaborate on them. She is a mother. And she is a virgin, meaning that at the time of her impregnation by the Holy Spirit, she had never been with a man or presumably, although little evidence is offered, with a woman. Abstention from sexual knowledge and sexual experience is key to her exceptional status. Sexual purity makes Mary special, admired by angels, greeted in the beautiful words of the *Magnificat*. Why virginity has this power is not something the Gospel narratives say much about. They communicate the fact and comment on its oddity. For Mary to be the woman who bears the son of God, it is enough that she is a virgin, *betulah, parthenos*.[6] More crudely, it is exclusively as womb, not as person, that Mary enters sacred and secular history. This womb, this fertile female body, this procreative being, had something worth consecrating, worth the divine trust and election. If the earliest Christian writers did not bother to speculate about what that "something" was, the field was all the more free for others to occupy.

Mary's power was devoid of menace. Patriarchal norms would remain unchallenged. The hierarchy of gender survived her reign as queen of heaven without a moment's doubt or concern. Nothing in her glory competed with masculine privilege. The notion of an immaculate mother, a woman whose womb was without taint and whose body was untouchable, is astonishing enough. Yet however bizarre the situation, we do not hear of males either pagan or Christian succumbing to a crisis of confidence, or fearing that their conventional sexual roles were seriously under threat. Mary only achieves her glory through her maternity. Giving birth to her son, God in the flesh, she rose higher than all the rest of the stars, wrote the poet John Milton in his 1629 "Ode on the Morning of Christ's Nativity."[7] Now she sits with her infant at her breast, "meanly wrapt," in a house of "mortal Clay," the clay of a poor farmyard and the clay of human flesh, her naked body modestly covered by the "Saintly Veil of Maiden white." And all of antiquity, in all its pride and splendor, submits to her superiority. The "Oracles are dumb" (line 173), the Nymphs mourn (line 188); Osiris, Isis, Ashtaroth, Cynthia, Pan, the Lares and Penates, all banished: this holy child makes no distinction between devil and deity (lines 189–212). Mary's almost invisible chapter in history signifies that meekness and humility are raised to the highest position on heaven or earth. Milton, a Christian but in love with the beauties of the classical past, feels the reversal keenly. The Virgin's rise signals the death of myth and the extinction of pagan wonder. When the old gods are displaced, even the powers of nature retreat.

We might compare the accommodating charm of Mary to the virtues of another powerful virgin, the English queen hailed on her death as the "Second Maid."[8] Elizabeth I was, from her earliest childhood, the target of attack, rivalry, and intimidation. As she matured, she learned how to convert those fickle instruments into the service of her own authority. Was her virginity an insult to the collective manhood of her realm, or even of Europe? Let them learn to live with the insult. This lady would be sexual without ceasing to be pure. She would be the master of all and the mistress of none.

Mary and Elizabeth were both alike and utterly unlike. Mary of Galilee was a fruitful virgin and by all accounts a complaisant wife. Elizabeth I chose virginity for herself and turned her celibacy into a symbol of her care for her people. Her Bishop Jewel, who understood Elizabeth's pretensions, hailed her as "the only nurse and mother of the church of God within these your majesty's noble dominions."[9] The unmarried sovereign was represented by her poets and her propagandists as a counterpart to the pagan goddesses, a rival to the Muses, a supreme example of those unreachable Ladies whose love tormented the troubadour poets of the Middle Ages. But you didn't need a long memory or even a classical education to notice that this majestic woman shared some qualities with the only woman for whom the old church was willing to make an exception. If Mary the Mother of God was "alone of all her sex," so (in her own distinctive fashion) was Elizabeth Tudor.

Elizabeth I was the daughter of King Henry VIII and Anne Boleyn, the only surviving child of a marriage that Catholics and other enemies of the Tudors denounced as incestuous, bigamous, and adulterous (and which had caused Henry to establish his own Church of England in defiance of the Roman Catholic Church). Her own father had Elizabeth declared a bastard. In 1559, against the odds, the Protestant Elizabeth ascended to the throne on the death of her Catholic older sister Mary, who left no child. For many years after her coronation, Elizabeth's right to the throne was contested, and her legitimacy as daughter and heir was the subject of bitter disagreement. The legitimacy of the Catholic Virgin was also subject to attack. Mary of Galilee's unusual status as virgin and bearer of a divine child had also provoked insult and skepticism. She did have a husband, Joseph, willing to protect her and, unlike Elizabeth, she was not free to determine either her role or her destiny. On the margins in the Gospels, given a few more moments of action in *Luke Acts*, Mary had to wait for enthusiastic church fathers and medieval Mariolaters to receive her own form of adoration. Elizabeth's involvement in the events of her drama was, by contrast, direct and decisive. But her liabilities were considerable. Her control over the succession was squandered by her refusal of marriage, and her reluctance to provide an heir was bitterly resented; her intervention in religious affairs was halfhearted when not divisive. She was sometimes canny and sometimes tone-deaf, and always high-handed. Because she resisted numerous plots seeking to secure her marriage, her service as woman, mother, and protector of the realm was, at the very least, incomplete. What in Mary is described by religious tradition as perfect obedience has no counterpart in the life of Elizabeth. Mary's virginity was a miracle, an act of piety carried out by submission to an imperious call. Elizabeth's virginity was an act of defiance and self-assertion. Mary was demure and compassionate; Elizabeth was haughty, willful, theatrical, and jealous. Mary, it must be admitted, achieved greatness through her womb. Elizabeth achieved hers through her will. I cannot help thinking this is a greater accomplishment.

At her zenith, Elizabeth was hailed as the godly empress who would restore the true church, which Protestant Reformers in Britain argued was the church in its purity, the primitive church long damaged by the machinations of the "Bishop of Rome." On the frontispiece of books published during her reign, she holds an orb and a scepter, symbols of sacred empire.[10] Sometimes there hovers above her head a phoenix, the immortal bird who regenerates itself from its own ashes, a bachelor father to itself. In the great portraits that hung in her castles and those of her aristocratic servants and protégées, the queen was depicted in the stiff and splendid style of an icon, bearing a sieve in token of her virginity or an ermine, the animal famous for its purity.[11] In a pageant, the *Descensus Astraeae*, designed by George Peele and given in London in 1591, an emblem of Elizabeth appears in the shape of Astraea, the Roman virgin who brings justice to the universe. Unusually, Astraea was dressed here in the outfit of a shepherdess, feeding a flock, and showing them her care:

Feed on, my flock among the gladsome green
Where heavenly nectar flows along the banks,[12]

An empress, a monarch whose shield holds the nation safe and whose displeasure can make the proudest tremble, she is also a maiden of mild manners and rustic appearance, guarding her charges with a "sheep-hook." The mysteries of sovereignty come here into close, if curious, involvement with a different range of spiritual, mythological, and literary associations. The queen is a "nymph"; yet the sexual attentions nymphs are so often subject to seem not to disturb her pastoral composure. Sent by Jove to banish cruelty, war, and envy, Astraea-as-Elizabeth is courtesy incarnate for Peele:

Whilom, when Saturn's golden reign did cease,
And iron age had kindled cruel wars,
Envy in wrath perturbing common peace,
Engendering canker'd hate and bloody jars;
Lo, then Olympus's king, the thundering Jove,
Raught hence this gracious nymph Astraea fair:
Now once again he sends her from above,
Descended through the sweet transparent air;
And here she sits in beauty fresh and sheen,
Shadowing the person of a peerless queen.[13]

Pastoral's influence among the courtly poets of Elizabeth's regime allows the timeless woods and landscapes of a Virgilian golden place to decorate the backdrops of a formal theater of power and display. This "Astraea" shadows "the person of a peerless queen." A "gracious nymph" with a Tudor rose and the legitimate orb of empire, Elizabeth restores the empire to its pristine and original condition. Pagan imagery screens out memories of Catholic worship; this virgin is just as virtuous as her heavenly rival, and she too is modest, not too proud to sit on grass. The queen is a "May Lady," a shepherd's mistress dressed in wildflowers. But she is also a chaste "Flowre of virgins." That is how she is addressed in Edmund Spenser's rhapsodic "Fourth Eclogue," the celebratory "April" verses from his *Shepheardes Calendar* of 1578.[14] "Fayre Elisa, queene of shepheardes all": Spenser greets her and entreats her favor. She may not grant everything to her faithful servant, "Colin Clout." Spenser will need to compete with many wellborn rivals, with better pretenses to aristocratic status and knightly honors: Sir Philip Sidney, Sir Walter Ralegh, and Robert Lacey, the Earl of Essex. But he will be the most effective of his queen's panegyrists in creating a cult for his "Faerie Queene," she who was to be the last virgin in the history of Western power.

Against Matrimony

On November 17, 1558, Mary Tudor, the last Catholic queen of England, died, lamented by very few. When Elizabeth, her sister and successor, convened her first Parliament, the two Houses awaited with relief the recovery of the kingdom for the Reformation.[15] This new sovereign, educated by Cambridge scholars and humanists, would surely clear the way which Mary and her unpopular Spanish consort had done so much to obstruct. There was a great deal of business to handle. A Protestant Settlement must be worked out; war with France must come to an end, leaving a relatively poor island nation free to negotiate within its limited political options; and a mate must be found for this twenty-five-year-old spinster, who was, all agreed, "the best marriage in her parish."[16] The first Elizabethan Parliament met Monday, January 23, 1559. It moved with alacrity. The afternoon of February 6, leading members of the two houses and the Privy Council went to the queen with a delicate mission. As politely as possible, in simple but unmistakable terms, they put their petition. Would the queen please get married?

Elizabeth gave her answer in writing. Her preference since "her earliest years of understanding," as she put it, was for the single life. It had always been the one that most "contented" her and, in her opinion, had been "most acceptable to God." Her attachment to the maiden estate was strong: she had clung to it, she reminds them, throughout threat and danger from her previous "prince," that is to say, her sister Mary. In those years of her adolescence, her views of marriage remained firm. No rival ambition drove her to seek a grand or important spouse, not protection and not pleasure. But now, as she clarifies her position, the public good must be considered. Despite her fondness for celibacy, she presents herself as free to act undeterred by earlier preference or vow. Providence, which has so graciously preserved her so far, will be her guide. When and if God will be pleased to "incline her heart to another kind of life"—a married life, for instance—she declares herself determined to do nothing that will harm her realm; they can trust her in that: "I will never in that matter conclude anything that might be prejudicial to the realm, for the weal, good, and safety whereof I will never shun to spend my life."[17] God may be happy to allow her to continue a maiden. Or He may prefer her to adopt the married state.

Elizabeth never stinted when it came to rhetoric. Her inclinations as politician, on the other hand, were cautious, toward the avoidance of any precipitate decision. "Averse to innovation," Francis Bacon called her in matters of religion; in matters of policy her style was the same.[18] Her "witty godson" John Harington spoke with affection about her wiliness and her deliberate ambiguity, again and again slipping away from the grasp of her counselors who "tried to know her mind." Writing to his cousin Robert Markham after her death, Harington remembered Sir Christopher Hatton's remark: "The Queene did fish for men's souls, and had so sweet a baite that no one coude escape hir network."[19] On the question of marriage, her performances were particularly interesting. Speaking as a young and untried woman to an impatient male audience of Parliamentarians, Elizabeth launched a career of evasion, vacillation, and mystification.[20] Let them wonder. Will she or won't she? Among the "legion of her remarks on the subject," writes Sir John Neale in his 1934 biography of the queen, some "are false, some true, and some betwixt and between—and which were which no one really knew."[21] Is it a matter of waiting for the right man, or is her resistance to marriage adamant and impregnable? Is she a maiden whose coyness hides a desire to be pressed and cajoled or an Amazon defiant in her distaste for a husband's privilege? Modern scrutiny of Elizabeth's complicated matrimonial negotiations tends to raise other suspicions: How much was the bizarre performance policy and how much was pathology? Were her evasions motivated by skepticism in the face of a state that did so little to make her mother and father happy? Was she influenced by the miseries of her various stepmothers and the recent observation of a sister spurned by a husband? Was her sexual development arrested by her early experiences as a fifteen-year-old pestered by the amorous attentions of that very dubious character Lord Thomas Seymour, uncle to Edward VI, who had married Henry's surviving widow and saw yet another way to get close to the throne, through the skirts of young Elizabeth?[22] Was she ruled by frigidity and fear? Or simple fondness for her own will and authority?

Penetrating the secrets of a consummate political actor like Elizabeth is neither fruitful nor discreet. But the patterns she used and those used by others for her to mold, glorify, and make sense of her image and role are interpretable, obsessively so.[23] Canny observers of her time such as Bacon and Harington tried to make sense of the freakish reality of a queen regnant—a single one, to boot—who asserted her absolute right to rule and yet sued for the affection of her nobles and people, an affection that needed to be ever renewed, ever tested, ever reaffirmed, poetically as well as politically. Harington was impressed and amused. Despite the closeness of his brush with disgrace during his time as an officer and friend of Essex in Ireland and at home, Harington appreciated the way the queen wove together cunning and coquetry, affection and imperiousness, and he describes these qualities with verve in his diary and letters. Through the power of her royal and divinely approved "state," she could always and under all circumstances command. But she preferred, as she stated on many occasions, to be loved willingly and warmly than to be obeyed out of duty and demand. Harington recognizes stereotypical traits of her gender in her political methods, as does Bacon. Safely retreating from the envy-ridden Stuart court in 1608, Harington notes with nostalgia the erotopolitical character of Elizabeth's reign. True, she was vain and hungry for admiration. Harington admits that some Elizabethan subjects found the spirit of "fantastic coquetry" a worrying reminder of women's "weaknesses" in a ruler who possessed gifts "that would have adorned the greatest of men." Comparing her to her successor James, who wanted to talk to him about the devil, witchcraft, and the royal mastery of Latin, Harington frankly preferred the Elizabethan flirtatiousness to the Jacobean pomposity. Yes, the queen was manipulative. But she was so good at manipulation, Harington recalled:

> I could relate manye plesante tales of hir Majeste's outwitting the wittiest ones, for few knew how to aim their shaft against her cunning. We all did love hir, for she said she loved us, and muche wysdome she shewed in this matter.[24]

Francis Bacon, in the middle of his own successful "courtship" of Elizabeth's successor, was more circumspect—and less witty. He writes his tribute to her "fortunate memory" to praise her as "a wonderful person among women, a memorable person among princes," conventional compliments that no one could gainsay.[25] There is caution in his tone and a clear avoidance of gush and idolatry. If he seems begrudging, we can remember that glamorizing the predecessor sovereign was not a policy favored at James's court, and the comparison between their respective popularities could have been damaging. Bacon, to be sure, had been rebuffed time after time by Elizabeth in his search for place and preferment, and his own political moves invite some skepticism. The son of Elizabeth's Lord Keeper, he had been denied the office of solicitor general, attorney general, and lord chancellor and had been prominent in leading the prosecution of Essex, his former friend and ally.

Other accounts of the poetry of the queen's ongoing "romance" go far beyond Bacon's in their willingness to play with the idea of her as the beloved "Shepherdess," the beautiful and unattainable paragon of all the virtues, the powerful Diana who will turn on her votaries if they transgress and reward them if they are faithful knights in her "Faery" world. For Elizabeth and her cult, it was possible to imagine an ideal (or at least convenient) alliance between eros, authority, mystery, and female will. The notion of "romance" and courtship offered an image of shared political advantage. Operators such as Sidney, Spenser, Ralegh, Christopher Hatton, and John Lyly, as well as the noblemen Robert Dudley, the First Earl of Leicester, and Fulke Greville, the First Baron Brooke, all understood the rhetoric of amorous praise and the fictions of romantic sacrifice. Some—for instance, the Leicester–Sidney–Sir Francis Walsingham faction—were on the lookout for the radical Protestant cause and hoped flirtation with the queen would yield benefits in the form of military campaigns to support continental Protestants against their Catholic enemies. Others were interested in status, economic advantage, or propaganda for the national interest. But Bacon cast a colder eye onto a history of royal charisma and erotic potency dislodged from their proper, which is to say masculine, positions. This was, at the time Bacon was writing, a history to be contemplated with some reserve. The image of the eroticized virgin, mistress of herself, master of others, to be wooed and made much of, is an allegory whose seductive powers have, in this instance, fallen short.

Bacon is well aware of the extravagant courtly fictions responsible for the energy (and blunders) of Elizabeth's courtiers and, as he explains, aware that serious political work, and successful policy, managed to flourish with the aid of these romances. Political culture was, in this age, filtered through a lens of pastoral romance and knightly adventure. It was also, as Bacon sagely observes, shaped by a religious ideal that had been translated into literature. For the queen might be one of the "Seven Lamps of Virginity" and a pious servant of the Lord. But an ideal of female sanctity anchored in the cloister and blessed by the special grace of the Virgin Mary had become questionable during England's years of struggle for self-definition as a religious nation under a new dispensation. Before Elizabeth, Tudor politics had found little use for the special wonder of female virginity. Matrimony and reproduction, the everyday norms of social life, were what mattered, as Elizabeth's father found to his distress. For all of Henry's efforts, marital success eluded him. Despite Henry VIII's ostentatious virility (there were a number of natural children, to prove it, Henry Fitzroy the most favored), his standing as leading patriarch of the realm had received injury after injury. The king's troubled bedchamber was haunted by a fear that divine approval had passed from the line. His anxiety would have been even greater if he could have foreseen the genealogical results of the next two reigns, as neither Edward nor Mary produced an heir. If part of the success of an early modern dynasty is its ability to unite sex and power, then the Tudors failed. Now, with the young Elizabeth asking to lead the single life, the family was proposing a different definition. A deliberate exemption from the conjugal and reproductive norms presented itself as deserving of honor and awe. The queen, after all, was unlike all the men occupying the throne before her and after. Unmarried, independent of "brother, uncle, husband, kinsman," she was a woman who "would have her glory entire and proper" to herself. Elizabeth's celibacy meant that she was, in Bacon's words, "ever her own mistress." "The reigns of women," he writes, "are commonly obscured by marriage; their praises and actions passing to the credit of their husbands; whereas those that continue unmarried have their glory entire and proper to themselves."[26]

What to Henry had been misery was to his virgin daughter "felicity." This is the point Bacon circles around. Without ever making the comparison between Elizabeth and other women, he makes it clear that his former sovereign's violation of usual gendered practices and customs is as much a victory for her radical policy as a curiosity that disturbs him. Bacon's attitude is not that of a worshipper. He distances himself from the ambitions of some of his peers, such as Spenser, Ralegh, or Sidney, with their Horatian or Senecan fantasies of being the "poet-politician" and "counsellor of kings."[27] Service to the queen could certainly lead to financial reward; whether it would also stimulate courage, civility, and religious fervor was not so obvious. Men such as Ralegh, Leicester, Essex, Hatton, Walsingham, and William Cecil, Lord Burghley, hoped to shape policy and perhaps control (in some manner or other) this unusual woman on top. If they had to play the part of the lover to do so, that did not seem too much of a sacrifice. James's lord chancellor wants to criticize the queen while admitting her remarkable features. Freed from the need to flatter her to her face, Bacon captures the aestheticism and the moral force of the Elizabethan romance:

> As for the lighter points of character,—as that she allowed herself to be wooed and courted, and even to have love made to her; and liked it; and continued it beyond the natural age for such vanities;—if any of the sadder sort of persons be disposed to make a great matter of this, it may be observed that there is something to admire in these very things, which ever way you take them. For if viewed indulgently, they are much like the accounts we find in romances, of the Queen in the blessed islands, and her court and institutions, who allows of amorous admiration but prohibits desire [*quae amorum admirationem recipiat, lasciviam prohibeat*].[28]

A heroine of romance: that is how she liked to be treated, although no one would forget for a moment that this heroine also bore the sword of rule and the crown of judgment. Bacon's shrewd judgment deserves a closer look. This is no blushing, timid maiden grateful for the strong arm of the knight to whom she owes so much and whose right to call the debt in was recognized by all chivalric romances. The queen "allows" amorous admiration. Presumably, then, she arouses and deserves it. Lascivious desire, on the other hand, she prohibits. Love may be inflamed. But it will not be indulged. The queen's erotic codes are unique to her, Bacon suggests: she plays with the fictions of amorous service, and suspended sexuality was understood by all who had the brains to deserve her patronage as part of the rituals of state in the Elizabethan court. Ladies in waiting could not afford such flirtatious games, as a number of Elizabeth's circle found out when their betrothals or affairs came to the queen's attention. Her chastity was the model they should have studied with more care.

Politics and a Virgin Queen: Making a Myth

1st Old Man: Are you then travelling to the temple of Eliza?
2nd Old Man: Even to her temple are my feeble limbs travelling. Some call her Pandora: some Gloriana: some Cynthia, some Belphoebe, some Astraea: all by several names to express several loves yet all these names make but one celestial body, as all those loves meet to create but one soul.
1st Old Man: I am one of her own country, and we adore her by the name of Eliza.

THOMAS DEKKER, "Prologue at Court," *The Pleasant Comedie of Old Fortunatus,* 1590–1600

"The purpose of myth," Claude Lévi-Strauss wrote in 1955, "is to provide a logical model capable of overcoming a contradiction (an impossible achievement if, as it happens, that contradiction is real)."[29] The contradictions investing the performance of power in the reign of Queen Elizabeth I were as real as any in history, which is not to say they weren't also fantastic, metaphorical, and elaborately inflated. Elizabeth was a problem from her birth. Born a disappointment to her parents, who urgently needed a male heir, troubling her advisers and her people throughout her life by her failure to marry and provide for the succession, a challenge to the unquestionable belief that a woman's excellence lay in fulfilling her reproductive duties, Elizabeth the virgin died as the greatest queen of England, by many reckonings the greatest of any who wore the crown.

The Virgin Queen succeeded politically, and she triumphed no less as myth. "Our eyes are dazzled by Eliza's beams," the 1st Old Man in Dekker's play exclaimed, in the hearing of his sovereign, for whom the play was presented, probably in December 1596. Lucky the Englishmen who can visit the temple of Eliza. The humblest subject, the most ambitious poet, can have no higher objective than to view the spectacle of this great goddess, a modern Diana.

> See (if at least thou dare see) where she sits:
> This is the great Pantheon of our goddess.[30]

To be far from her presence is to be banished from all light and all glory. Hers is the "celestial body" her subjects contemplate "hourly." She has many names, many personae. She is our "Great landlady of hearts," he continues; just as all her names combine like deities in one "Pantheon," so our loves meet in her. "Eliza" made amorous worship into a civic duty, and she did so, I will argue, with the help of her unexpected asset, her chastity. The queen's chastity is her greatest performance. It represents her homage to herself and to a special conception of female privilege. It granted her a considerable exemption from the disability of her gender, a disability of great concern to those troubled by female rule and unsure of how to compensate for the effect of a female "Head" on the national body. "At the beginning of her reign," Louis Montrose writes,

> Elizabeth formulated the strategy by which she turned the political liability of her gender to advantage for the next half-century. She told her first parliament that she was content to have as her epitaph, "that a Queene, having raigned such tyme, lived and dyed a virgin"; and she assured her second, "that though after my death yow may have many stepdames, yet shall yow never have a more natural mother than I meane to be unto you all."[31]

Admiring modern critics, like the dazzled subjects Dekker puts into his play, have seen a rare brilliance in the queen's embrace of a religiously resonant and erotically charged role, or "strategy," as Montrose puts it. In the complex evasions and negotiations that connected Elizabeth to her ministers and her Parliament, a code evolved, with its own rituals, protocols, and affectations. The lady could be courted. She was far from indifferent to flattering attentions, and without such attentions, political life at the court of Elizabeth was inconceivable. Her favor was crucial: it could advance a proposal for foreign or domestic intervention; her patronage would bestow a trading monopoly or promote a career; her approval could bless a religious innovation, dismiss a bishop, or reestablish a traditional cultic practice. When necessary, she would be England's "natural mother," nursing the realm at her maidenly breast, and at the same time a loving spouse (of ambiguous gender), tempering justice with equity, as, for example, apologist Thomas Norton explained in chastising the 1569 Northern rebels who sought to overthrow her: "She is the most loving Mother and nourse of all her good subjects . . . the Husband of the common weale, married to the realme."[32] At other moments, she could enter into competition with her ambitious subjects in their efforts to direct and script her, intervening as an aggressive player in their real and their symbolic power struggles.[33]

In the story that eventually solidified around the unmarried Elizabeth, the liability of the queen's gender was converted into strength. Her failure to produce an heir was covered over by the myth of the phoenixlike virgin goddess, who would somehow magically deliver the nation into safe and Protestant hands. The pleasures of an ordinary woman's life—and its compromises—were what she was prepared to sacrifice. Her devotion to her people excluded all competing loves. This strategy was not, however, enforced from the very first days of her reign. Elizabeth and her advisers were keenly aware of the realm's need for a clear line of succession, and like her sister Mary, Elizabeth was expected to marry. Advisers and members of Parliament besieged her with requests. To their surprise and annoyance, she expressed reluctance, always ready to find reasons for rejecting this or that suitor.[34] Her courtiers implored her to act like Juno. She replied that she preferred to be Diana. Is it right for Diana to take a husband? What mortal can compete, after all, with the love of a nation? The newly anointed Elizabeth offered herself as loving mother and kindly "nurse" to her people; thinking of the bond Christ established between himself and the church, she would be a true and faithful spouse.[35] If the 1st Old Man in Dekker's play speaks for the people in their warm love, the erotic buzz she aroused at court was ardent, assuming we can trust the extravagant rhetoric. In that erotic mythmaking, the queen was a willing participant.

In the collective work of imagination devoted to Elizabeth I, a monarch with a precarious hold on power became a "kind of historical fiction" and "an allegorical figure invested with the visionary body of the state."[36] It is not hard to understand how literature shapes memory or reputation. Remarkable about the Elizabethan age were the parts literature, performance, poetry, and pageant played in shaping political history and the affairs of state. She might appear frail and female, lacking in those impressive tokens of virility in which her father put so much trust. But the ideal of the realm as immortal, intact, unchanging, mystically sustained as if by the grace of God, was incarnate in her. It made a big difference what kind of body that could be shown to be. Without representation, without theater, there would be no ruler. In this case, the clothes were the empress. "Monarcholatry" was not a graceful compliment offered by the Renaissance public relations industry with some nudging by a vain or narcissistic royal client. It was the pattern through which the governed and the governor were allowed a place to work out the terms of their mutual bond, terms that in the case of Elizabeth were flamboyantly romantic. Was it always a perfect relationship, inspiring the enthusiastic devotion and amorous adherence the queen allowed herself to crave? No canny political observer would go that far. Romances need a fair amount of make-believe, a strategic ability to turn a blind eye to certain defects and contradictions, and mutual willingness to admit ambivalence without succumbing to a fatal anxiety. The "work of art" jointly admired by queen and subjects—the state as elaborate artifact with its public face a beautiful and chaste lady—needed hard work to survive. It needed ships and armies, money and coercion, stamina and manipulation, as well as smoke and mirrors—and charm.

Its survival deserves respect. The court of the "Faerie Queene" may have had its share of absurdities, and the jockeying of such knightly suitors as Leicester, Hatton, Ralegh, and Essex to win the favor of their virginal beloved can look like an elaborate farce, however serious were its stakes. The central absurdity—the anomaly of the queen's gender and the anomaly of her sexual status—is what intrigues me. How did these twinned anomalies go from being liabilities to being strengths? Many people have wondered. One answer is to be found in the flexible imagination and political cunning of the queen herself. Elizabeth's theatrical and ideological gifts should not be underestimated. Her patronage of the arts, although it was often not direct, paid off. Despite the constant complaints about the queen's lifelong parsimony and calculated deafness to financial solicitation, her court was a magnet, and the artistic culture of Elizabethan London (a mix of professionals and gifted amateurs) gave signs of rivaling the city-state of Florence in the fourteenth century. "Belphoebe, Gloriana, Astraea, Eliza," the queen's personae and the nation's allegorical images, were kept in circulation through the efforts of poets and painters. The "struggle for social dominance," as Susan Frye puts it in her revisionary study of the queen's representations, meant that a great deal of cultural energy had to be expended in refining and redefining the iconography, playing variations on the stories in response to the changing demands of political events and the changing pressures on a woman whose very existence at the top threatened male presences and traditional beliefs about the hierarchy of the genders.[37] Yet the "adoration" Dekker's 1st Old Man claims is the common currency of all those "of her country" was not manufactured out of thin air. Louis Montrose has said of the queen that she was "as much the creature of her image as she was the creator"; "her power to shape her own strategies was itself shaped by her society and constrained within the horizon of its cultural assumptions."[38] She shaped her culture's fantasies, but she was also shaped by them. If anyone in the English Renaissance established the precedent for "fashioning the self as a work of art," as Stephen Greenblatt famously put it, it was this queen:

> She believed deeply—virtually to the point of religious conviction—in display, ceremony, and decorum, the whole theatrical apparatus of royal power. Her gorgeous clothes, the complex code of manners and the calculated descents into familiarity, the poetic tributes she received and the poetry she herself wrote, the portraits and medals she allowed to circulate like religious icons or the images of the Roman emperors, the nicknames she imposed upon her courtiers—all were profoundly theatrical and all contributed to the fashioning of what was perhaps the greatest dramatic creation of the period: the queen herself.[39]

It is worth noticing that political theater, no matter how enthralling and extravagant, is not the same thing as religious worship. Since Frances Yates published her brilliant lecture on "Queen Elizabeth I as Astraea," delivered in 1945, students of Elizabeth's success have tended to talk about a "cult of Elizabeth." Hard to overlook was the practice of celebrating the queen's birthday with much of the pomp previously dedicated to honoring the birthday of the Virgin Mary, which also happened to fall on September 7—much to the chagrin of Continental Catholics, alert to what they considered an unacceptable arrogance. Yates encouraged the conflation between Mary, Virgin of the Old Church, and Elizabeth, Virgin of the New, in the way she describes the Elizabethan Accession Day Tilts, celebrated with knightly jousts on November 17:

> The annual pageant of Protestant chivalry, in honour of the holy day of the Queen's accession, skilfully [*sic*] used the traditions of chivalrous display to build up the Queen's legend as the Virgin of the Reformed Religion (witness [Sir Henry] Lee's "Imperial Vestal Virgin" set-up at the Resignation Tilt) and to present the spectacle of the worship of her by her knights in the ritual of chivalry as a new kind of regularly-recurring semi-religious festival.[40]

The dramatist John Lyly (1553–1606), an eager candidate for the queen's patronage, strayed very close to the edge of idolatry, and certainly obsequiousness, offering in 1580 to create a "Glasse" in which Elizabeth's perfection can be glimpsed, although her virtues are frankly beyond human representation.[41] If she is Venus, queen of love and beauty, she is also Virgo, celestial virginity: for the lucky Elizabethans, Diana comes appareled in the garments of Venus, just as once Venus appeared appareled in the hunting garments of Diana when she greeted her son Aeneas in Virgil's imperial story. Lucky is the empire that is ruled by such an "earthly goddess," lovely enough to "allure all princes" but strong enough in her chastity "to refuse them all," an outcome vividly on the minds of Protestant Englishmen like Lyly who in 1580 were panicked by the strong possibility that Elizabeth would marry Francis, Duke of Anjou, the Catholic suitor she seemed so much to favor. Lyly's panegyric to the English queen is worth quoting at length:

> If Uirginities hath such force, then what hath this chast Uirgin *Elizabeth* don, who by the space of twenty and odde yeares with continuall peace against all policies, with sundry myracles, contrary to all hope, hath gouerned this noble Island. Against whoem neyther forren force, nor ciuill fraude, neyther discorde at home, nor conspirices abroad, could preuaile. What greater meruaile hath happened since the beginning of the world, then for a young and tender maiden, to gouern strong and valiaunt menne, then for a Uirgin to make the whole worlde, if not to stand in awe of hir, yet to honour hir, yea and to liue in spight of all those that spight hir, with hir sword in the sheth, with hir armour in the Tower, with hir souldiers in their gownes.[42]

Despite Lyly's protestations, Elizabeth did not perform miracles or cancel the weight of sin. What she did is more impressive. She maintained a throne, on her own, unmarried, refusing to be the tool of any man or party, refusing to be the female façade for a masculine exercise of authority. The "weak vessel" that is this "young and tender maiden" came up with the prowess to defend her island. She wrote the book in a different way. Chastity, the old sexual weapon, through which weakness can appear as strength and denial become a form of assertion, worked in her favor. But she also did a great deal for chastity. At a time when sacred virginity was on its way out, she prolonged its life and gave it her patronage. If sexual abstinence is not what the era of the Elizabethans is most famous for, the fact that the most famous woman of her day was a virgin has a special, if puzzling, significance. In her dazzling person, the argument went, love and chastity were equally at home. The royal evasion of matrimony did not send sexual love into exile or promote a rash of ascetic retreats. But it did put a specific pressure on the practice and understanding of erotic idealism, a well-established Renaissance doctrine advocating the ennobling and heroic effects of the passion of true lovers. Could the queen be an exception, the one object prohibited to masculine desire, without deflating the reputation of poetic eros, and without imposing her standard on all others?

"What greater meruaile hath happened since the beginning of the world," Lyly rhapsodizes, "than for a young and tender Maiden, to gouern strong and valiaunt menne?" If Elizabeth did not always make the "whole" world stand in awe of her, she kept the realm safe and prosperous and shielded the virtue of the kingdom's women. Lyly is speaking to the happy (and assumedly male) people who enjoy the grace of this miraculous sovereign, who "hath borne the sword with such iustice." Lyly (in his guise as his character, Euphues) compares England's virtue and excellence under this reign with the vice and misery of "other" countries. Truly the "lyuing God is onely the Englysh God," and he has "annoynted a Uirgin Queene." Most significant of all is the superiority of this "blesst island" in the matter of sexual virtue. English women are just, as it turns out, outstanding in their chastity and their modesty; foreign women, to whom Euphues is addressing himself, cannot hope to compete. Men of this island have reason to be grateful to their chaste sovereign, for it is through her patronage that their wives are kept "without daunger, while others are defamed, their daughters chast, when others are defloured."[43]

In the "Epistle Dedicatory" to *Euphues and His England* (1580), Lyly insists that it is impossible even to portray someone so miraculous:

> O fortunate *England* that hath such a Queene, vngratefull if thou praye not for hir, wicked if thou do not love hir, miserable, if thou loose hir.... As this noble Prince is endued with mercie, pacience and moderation, so is she adourned with singular beautie and chastitee, excelling in the one *Venus*, in the other *Vesta*. Who knoweth not how rare a thing it is (Ladies) to match virginitee with beautie, a chast minde with an amiable face, diuine cogitations with a comelye countenaunce? But suche is the grace bestowed yppon this earthlye Goddess, that hauing the beautie that might allure all Princes, she hath the chastitee also to refuse all, accounting it no less praise to be called a Uirgin, then to be esteemed a *Venus*.[44]

Loving the Queen

One of the key oddities of the aristocratic fiction of order and degree is that the natural order, in which male superiority is daily reaffirmed, can be overridden, given the marvelous exceptionality of certain exalted women. Medieval and Renaissance *fin'amors* or *amor de lonh* (the type of courtly love of which Jaufré Rudel is the most famous exponent among the poets) allowed the scandal of service to a female to be hidden under the veil of idealization: no one is as perfect as my mistress who will never be mine. Far from being insulted by her refusal to grant me her favors, I am elevated by her cruel resistance. Her inviolable chastity confirms my superiority as a lover, through the perverse magic of what R. Howard Bloch has called "the pervasive poetics of virginity," essential to courtly eroticism's distinctive character.[45] Masochism may contribute to the distinctive character of courtly eroticism, since the fiction requires that the male suitor chooses to be abject, eclipsed, or scorned. Yet is it inadequacy that deprives him of conquest, or rather her inviolable and "rare chastitee," in the compliment Spenser gives his Diana-like heroine Belphoebe, Elizabeth's "glasse"?

John Lyly was a dramatist at the court, ambitious for preferment. But his mixture of abasement and rapture was not unusual. Sir Walter Ralegh also drew attention to the fortunate condition of Elizabeth's English subjects, gazing at the wonder of the maiden who held them captive. Petrarch or other Continental poets admiring of their angelic and beautiful mistresses can only "weep," Ralegh wrote, when they recognize the stunning preeminence of the "Faery Queene."[46] In his "Commendatory Sonnet" to Spenser's *Faerie Queene*, Ralegh describes his own vision of the "Faery Queene," one Spenser had overlooked. Petrarch (not just a poet but a former priest) pined for the impossible love of his Laura, a beautiful and pure married woman he barely knew, but whom his canzone made immortal. Yet could she, Ralegh suggests, be more admirable than the beautiful and pure Elizabeth? The sonnet, ostensibly written to celebrate Spenser's publication of the *Faerie Queene*, books 1–3, twists to become a compliment to Ralegh's royal mistress and a partial chastisement of Spenser's failure to appreciate her as fully as he, Ralegh, can do. Ralegh imagines himself visiting Laura's tomb. Then he sees something unexpected, his own queen entering the temple where the dead body of Petrarch's Laura lies. At Elizabeth's approach, the soul of Petrarch weeps, and the "vestal fire" burns more brightly, acknowledging a virtue "more fair" and more deserving than Laura's, who will henceforth suffer oblivion because of the unfavorable comparison.[47] Ralegh was happy to compete with other languishing poet-lovers in his worship of the divine "Cynthia." But to compete for her political favor proved trickier. Adoring a vestal virgin means one has to remain abstinent oneself, or risk infidelity. When Ralegh pursued other erotic opportunities with Elizabeth Throckmorton, one of the queen's maids of honor, and the young noblewoman became pregnant, Elizabeth was unforgiving. Sent to the Tower of London, Ralegh implored her to accept the penitence of her inconsolable lover. He wrote to Robert Cecil (son of William Cecil and successor to Walsingham as the queen's spymaster):

> My heart was never broken till this day, that I hear the Queen goes away so far off, whom I have followed so many years with so great love and desire, in so many journeys, and am now left behind her in a dark prison all alone. While she was yet near at hand, that I might hear of her once in two or three days, my sorrows were the less, but even now my heart is cast into the depth of all misery. I that was wont to behold her riding like Alexander, hunting like Diana, walking like Venus, the gentle wind blowing her fair hair about her pure cheeks like a nymph, sometime sitting in the shade like a Goddess, sometimes singing like an angel, sometimes playing like Orpheus; behold! the sorrow of this world once amiss hath bereaved me of all.[48]

To have lost her is to have lost the world. Denied her presence, I am exiled from the golden age of pastoral perfection, from the dazzling world of the gods and nymphs, even from the paradisal grace I should only expect to receive from a much more patriarchal deity, but which some (think of Dante in paradise) hoped to receive through the interventions of the Virgin Mary. Ralegh alludes to Orpheus pining for the dead and compares himself to those frustrated male followers of the English Eurydice. The abjection he claims to feel is annihilating; one wonders whether the savvy Cecil would have also noticed that it is ridiculous. In context, however, it is appropriate. Exalting the Virgin Queen was what an ambitious poet would do, certainly. Ralegh's excess is only different from Lyly's or Spenser's or Sidney's because he seems to be describing a love returned and then withdrawn. But the bold and amorous courtier, the famous and risk-taking adventurer with big plans for British colonialization and imperial rule, is also, in this device, a seeker of salvation who, for crimes against chastity, has been thrown off the ladder of spiritual ascent, banished from the garden in every sense. The courtly cult of Eliza—like the poetic address to heavenly Astraea and the forbidden pursuit of the chaste Diana and her votaries—refigures a classical and Christian model of the soul's purification. Sacrifice and discipline, not just pleasure and aesthetics, claim attention here. Loving the Venus-Virgo to whom all hearts are pledged is a translation of political loyalty and aristocratic service into the language of elegant compliment. But it is also a description of serious pain for the suitor. In extolling the radiance of her chastity, he is also confirming his isolation and failure.

Certainly the courtly tradition satisfied the needs of an Elizabethan male elite, especially the elites who saw themselves as responsible for the nation's political culture and statecraft. Courtliness's polite and extravagant rhetoric permitted the covert expression of deep ambivalences about female sexuality, ambivalences the queen's preference for virginal celibacy helped appease. But it is in politics that the genius of courtliness, with its affectation of awe at the very idea of a pure and sexually unavailable woman, proved most useful to the Elizabethans. C. S. Lewis is the most explicit about the cultural contradictions courtly love helped keep in a potent ideological tangle. "Cynicism and idealism about women," he explained in the *Allegory of Love*, "are twin fruits of the same branch . . . that . . . may be found anywhere in the literature of romantic love."[49] It is through the devious strategies of courtly love that a class accustomed to privilege and to the unquestioned precedence of the male sex worked out a way to accept "the monstrous regiment of women." But they would not have been able to do so without the superior skills of that "monstrous" political phenomenon, the Virgin Queen. If her alacrity in playing the part of the adorable and unyielding courtly mistress was essential to the success of the game, her creation of herself as a paragon of chastity—a Diana in the halls of power, combining in her own persona the sacred triangle of *Virgo Astraea*, *Virgo Maria*, and *Virgo Regina*—was her most consummate performance.[50] The nation, or at least those members of it responsible for the royal "political-theological theory" and its success, agreed.[51] For the good of the empire she symbolized, no encomium was too lavish, no declaration of erotic service too implausible. In a chapter on Spenser and "Sexual Politics," the poet and critic Linda Gregerson clarifies:

> The tradition of combining encomium and tutelage in courtly address is as old as monarchy itself. What distinguishes the public ceremonies of praise and petition in England during the second half of the sixteenth century from those of parallel cultures and times is first and foremost the sex of the reigning monarch. Those accustomed to speak and be heard in Tudor England, to voice opinion on matters of state and religion, to urge action and shape popular sentiment, to seek and bestow public favour, all, with one notable exception, were male. And this, rhetorically, made all the difference. Addressing his monarch, the Elizabethan courtier spoke across a gender divide, and spoke in a language heightened not merely with the usual doses of deference and hyperbole but with the fervour of eros.[52]

Accepting graciously this "fervour of eros," Elizabeth encouraged courtship while maintaining the distance of the Petrarchan mistress, who, as the poet admitted of his Laura, was "Idea" rather than woman.[53] In the case of the beloved royal mistress, the fiction allowed the incongruity of her gender to be absorbed into the greater mystery of her sacred purity, through what Frances Yates memorably describes as "the cult of the imperial virgin."[54] If "Love" moves the sun and the stars, in England between 1558 and 1603 it also moved all lovers around their lodestone, their "Dread Souerayne Goddesse," as Spenser addressed her in book 5 of the *Faerie Queene*. All virtues are summed up in her. All power and majesty come together in her rule as vicar of God, restorer of the true and original church which she delivered from its "wicked" Roman captivity. Virgo had come back to earth to begin a new golden age, protector of justice and living embodiment of the celestial goddess Astraea, the queen.[55]

Mystery and Romance: Virginity as an Affair of State

It was not a novelty to ascribe erotic power to a sovereign, for good or for ill. Philosophers and poets in classical antiquity worried about the tyrant's erotic aggressions and what they implied about the character of his rule.[56] This sovereign was, however, a different sort of animal, a novelty on the map of sexual and gender politics as on the map of nations and their games of rule. Elizabeth was neither predator nor prey. She was, and remained, a maiden, a noble and inviolable lady expecting courtship but refusing to be anyone's prize. Not a priest nor the votary of an order, she played the role of a secular deity whose piety could be publicly acknowledged and whose care for the new English church was welcomed with enthusiasm. But unlike the virgins of the church who preceded her, she neither needed nor asked for heavenly authorization.

There is, I want to claim, something unique in Elizabeth's use of the myth of chastity. For her it was not a private and personal matter. Nor was it a way of achieving religious excellence or philosophical and ascetic mastery. Chastity became in the hands of this "politique" a political performance, a way of maintaining power as a woman besieged by ambitious men, as a woman on top whose legitimacy and authority would never be beyond doubt. Elizabethan chastity was a cultural decision and a symbolic choice; it was, as many of her recent critics have noted with some admiration, a governing strategy for an uncertain time. There had been martyred virgins who achieved glory. There had been sages of the church who idealized sexual renunciation and the magic of pure flesh. It did not take Elizabeth's avoidance of marriage to prove that the idea of virginity is powerful: I hope my previous chapters have helped convince those who still need convincing. What the queen did was to make a public fact out of a secret that theology and philosophy had tried hard not to acknowledge: chastity is sexy. It took the poets to make this palatable.

Whether Elizabeth's lifelong celibacy was a deliberate, even ideological, commitment or the result of circumstances that might well have gone otherwise is undecidable. The symbolism is important. The intentions are less so. Observers of Elizabeth's virginal policies disagreed then as they do now about the controlling vision and, particularly, about the timing and dates of what Montrose calls her strategy: a strategy that, in retrospect, can be understood as antimatrimonial, a bid for an identity as a virgin queen, wed only to her people, a loving mother and nurse whose body was too sacred to be shared. But was it actually formulated at the beginning of her reign? Since 1615, when the historian and antiquary William Camden (1551–1623) printed his version of the speech Elizabeth made to Parliament, critics and interpreters of the age have credited the idea of an early preference for perfect royal chastity, stubborn in its resistance to demands she provide the realm with a consort and an heir. "The secular cult of the virgin was born," Stephen Greenblatt remarks with respect.[57] It was, he continues, the most serious and elaborate of the age's experiments in political theater and political theology. Other Renaissance players in the game of power and influence would craft identities that allowed them to move with agility from patron to patron, crisis to crisis. To remain ahead of the game, their monarch had to do something different. "Virginity enthroned" was the queen's "supreme fiction" (to borrow Wallace Stevens's phrase). Its function was transparently political: it enabled her to stay at the center, the gleaming pivot of the turning world, the still point around which all else revolves. Compared with the cult dedicated to Pandora and Gloriana, Astraea and Belphoebe, marriage and maternity seemed very thin rewards.

It is true that the queen equivocated, in this as in most of her dealings with the political nation. On a number of occasions, she declared herself ready and willing to wed. But there were always complications: most eligible suitors from the royal families of Europe were Catholic; Robert Dudley, the queen's favorite, was one of her subjects, however noble, and had his own matrimonial difficulties; Francis, the Duc d'Alençon and later Duke of Anjou, provoked the greatest enthusiasm from Elizabeth, and the greatest hostility from just about everyone else, when he rose to the surface as the likely contender in the courtship wars of 1578–1581. By the late

1580s, during what some historians call her "second reign," the program was clear.[58] She would "live and die a virgin." Early in her reign the queen's maidenhood could be welcomed for what it promised for the realm: her nubile suitability for a brilliant and politically strategic marriage leading to the happy result of a legitimate and unquestioned heir to the throne. Now that royal maidenhood had become something else. Anointed and adored, the unmarried queen was as close to an idol as the Tudor body politic could handle. And she lent herself to this casting in a variety of ways, sometimes accepting the definitions of her imperial chastity on offer, sometimes resisting them. Myth, as Lévi-Strauss also suggests, is a flexible discourse. While the elements of a mythic cluster may remain intact, the narrative that unfolds them is a shifting and multiple affair. Elizabeth favored the versions which saw her as a loyal and loving spouse to her realm, to whom she was joined by a kind of mystical marriage, or as a good and wise mother sharing her care and counsel with those subject to her, with whom she is, in a special sense, incorporated.[59] Exclusive as the bond is between queen and people, sovereign and commonwealth, a further attachment could only be, in a disturbing sense, unfaithful. Elizabeth's reluctance to marry, then, demonstrates the generous nature of her care, not the lack of it. Once the language of her preferred political myth offered itself, the queen found many occasions for its display, from her earliest rebuffs to Parliament up to her late stubborn refusals to settle the succession. But the discourse of royal chastity was not entirely hers to monopolize.

The royal virginity was a mystery lending itself to a variety of contradictory forms of devotion: the only requirement was that it remain, at some level, ambiguous or, as E. C. Wilson put it, "paradoxical." Wilson asserts, "Almost to the very last she paradoxically wedded amorousness to virginity. Hence she held the fancy of poets who read *Hero and Leander* one day and celebrated the charms of chastity on the next."[60] As virgin, the royal body was taboo, even potentially disturbing. But as courtly beloved, Amazonian heroine, sympathetic mother and diligent housekeeper, the queen's myriad contradictions worked in her favor, as Montrose observes:

> Throughout the reign, the queen and her subjects habitually articulated their political relationships in conjugal, amatory, and maternal-filial metaphors.... The vestal virgin, consecrated to the service of God; the beautiful mistress, desired by, but necessarily forbidden to, her courtiers; the thrifty spouse, married to her nation; the loving and careful mother, sacrificing herself for her subject's welfare.[61]

She is "our Eliza," "our Astraea," our "second Maid" hardly inferior to the Virgin Mother of God. Dekker's Old Man may sound effusive, but greater minds concurred. In the final scene of *Henry VIII* (1613), written during James I's reign and performed ten years after Elizabeth had left her "blessedness" behind, Shakespeare (or some collaborator) allowed Thomas Cranmer to prophesy at the cradle of the newborn princess.[62] Cranmer tells her father what is to come:

> She shall be
> (But few now living can behold that goodness)
> A pattern to all princes living with her, and all that shall succeed . . .
> Truth shall nurse her,
> Holy and heavenly thoughts still counsel her.
> She shall be lov'd and fear'd [. . .] but she must die,
> She must, the saints must have her; yet a virgin,
> A most unspotted lily shall she pass
> To th' ground, and all the world shall mourn her.
> (*Henry VIII*, 5.5.20–62)

Whether Henry was delighted to hear about his daughter's destiny as an "unspotted lily" is something Shakespeare doesn't mention. In a play written after a monarch's death, one is allowed to exaggerate. As the king listens, the far-seeing archbishop of Canterbury surrounds the infant princess with the flattering light of religious mystery and Marian imagery; even Protestants, we are to conclude, adore virgin saints who can unite a godly nation around the throne Cranmer seems already to see in Elizabeth's future. Who needs the first Maid, the humble Jewish daughter of Galilee, when you can have such a splendid and wellborn second Maid? The special demands of a Protestant realm, newly deprived of much of its former sacramental apparatus, may have encouraged the forty-year fashion for hyperbole and courtly reverence: "the cult of Elizabeth," the imperial virgin. Where theology had been, now there was politics, and political poetry: an ornate theater of masculine diplomacy, of aristocratic jockeying for power, pleading for favor and influence, was presided over by a Lady compared to the Laura of the Italian poet Petrarch, the heavenly Beatrice of Dante, the Diana of Olympus, and the pastoral sovereign adored by her shepherds. Some students of Elizabeth's mystique insist that the triumph of this chaste and imperious lady responded to the recent vacancy, and the borrowing of Marian associations to bedeck this virgin has to be taken seriously:

> Many of the symbols of this virgin—for example the Rose (the Tudor Rose, badge of union, of peace, of mystic empire), the Star, the Moon, the Phoenix, the Ermine, the Pearl—were also symbolic of the Virgin Mary. There is a good deal of evidence that some Elizabethan did not flinch from such a comparison ... one begins to ask oneself whether the cult of the virgin queen was, perhaps, half-unconsciously, intended to take the place of the cult of the Virgin, one of the most abiding characteristics of the ancient faith.[63]

"The bejeweled and painted images of the Virgin Mary had been cast out of churches and monasteries, but another bejeweled and painted image was set up at court, and went on progress through the land for her worshippers to adore." So Yates argues, introducing an interpretation formidable in its influence even if its details are controversial. Yates's appealing characterization needs to be accepted with some qualification. Elizabeth was not, in fact, prayed to and viewed as the performer of miracles; those in fear for the fate of their souls after death did not propitiate the queen or expect to meet her enthroned in heaven. "Theological politics" is a business of metaphor, and most users of metaphor understand the difference between highly charged flattery and outright worship. Yet there is no doubt that the language of Elizabethan panegyric courted idolatry, as Yates suggests. Since the possibility of devotion to a pristine and holy mother was taken away, mythological and poetic glitter, if not religious awe, could be directed toward the image of this "pattern of princes."

Not everyone was dazzled all the time. The affectionate versions of the queen and her political relationships need to be treated with some skepticism. Her subjects, her allies, and her critics did not immediately respond to the wisdom of the young queen's celibate plot. But they came to accept Elizabeth's exemption from the common lot of womankind and acknowledge the legitimacy of their "Faery Queen." As headstrong as Titania, Shakespeare's queen of fairyland, she was more worldly than any sovereign lady of romance. She had flaws. Her political and personal judgments were not always impeccable. Her vanity was breathtaking, and her whims could be as stubborn as her prejudices. Yet she turned out to be a skilled, if slippery, politician and a magnet for symbolic as well as affective investment. When the crowds of London packed the streets to cheer the queen's "Majesty" for her coronation progress, it may have been convention and protocol to acclaim her a "Queen of Hearts," beloved spouse of the nation, but in her case the convention held firm.[64]

Her cult, like the aristocratic custom of paying her courtship, was more than a convenient fiction. Even skeptical observers acknowledged that she was something out of the ordinary. Looking back on her reign from a vantage point of some intimacy, Francis Bacon wrote in 1608, "The government of a woman has been a rare thing at all times; felicity in such government a rarer thing still; felicity and long continuance together the rarest thing of all."[65]

That a woman would rule was, in the words of the Scottish Puritan John Knox, a "prodigy," something monstrous. But by the logic of myth, as Lévi-Strauss describes its power, sacred things are "monstrous." They defy nature and nature's laws. For them, special categories need to be invented, metaphysical exceptions, conditions of valid transgression.

Elizabeth the Virgin Queen, "Mother" of her realm, "Queen of Sheapheardes," and maiden prodigy, was that sort of exception. Paradox, rather than disabling her, worked in her favor. She did not reform the rules of gender in her time, nor challenge assumptions about female subordination. That was far from her intention: divine providence may have mysteriously intervened in her case to provide a sacred monarch anointed to authority and reverence, producing (as her jurists explained) the "theological fiction" of a "King's Body" politic joined to the natural body of a frail woman.[66] Elizabeth did not choose to monopolize the privilege: divine providence could also intervene to legitimate other women of royal blood. Elizabeth defended the rights of her cousin Mary Stuart to the last imaginable moment, even supporting the claims of this rival who sought to usurp her. Any skepticism directed toward the mystery of kingship was also a potential challenge to Elizabeth's authority, one she would not tolerate. But challenging society's placement of women in the broader scheme of things was not what she had in mind. Nor, as we shall see, was it the objective of those who assisted in her political production, in the complex imagining of her public spectacles and policies, especially her marriage policies.

To allay fears that a woman ruler, a dread virago, could be only a whimsical, oversexed and irrational tyrant, crying out to be "bridled" by a masterful man, Elizabeth needed to challenge the common conceptions of what femininity amounted to. This she would do. To be the beloved that no suspicion could mar, and no mere mortal usurp, she would be a beloved virgin, a Venus in the modest but austere attire of a Diana. "At a profound level," writes the historian Anne McLaren, "the insistence on Elizabeth's absolute chastity defused some of the tensions inherent in this reading of the incorporated queen."[67] She was helped by the application of the medieval legal principle of the "king's two bodies," first articulated in writing by Edmund Plowden in the fourth year of her reign but drawn upon in her first speech on her accession, November 20, 1558:

> And as I am but one body, naturally considered, though by His permission a body politic to govern, so I shall desire you all, my lords (chiefly you of the nobility, everyone in his degree and power), to be assistant to me, that I with my ruling and you with your service may make a good account to almighty God and leave some comfort to our posterity on earth.[68]

Marrying Diana: The Domestication of Chastity

Were these privileges available to anyone else? Elizabeth's example did not inspire a rash of conversions to the cause of virginity. Nor did it undermine the institution of matrimony. I do not for a moment want to generalize the queen's career: the exception made for a female ruler had few implications for any other conceptions of female value, female authority, or female autonomy. But I do want to use the case of the Virgin Queen of Protestant England to raise some questions about the period and to consider the place of Elizabeth in a larger history of chastity. I want to argue that there is something distinctive—even unrepeatable—about the Elizabethan variations on the themes of sexual relations, sexual identities, sexual "idealism," and sexual "pessimism." The English Renaissance was no paradise of gender equality. On the one hand, under the influence of imported humanist ideas through widely read books such as Baldassare Castiglione's *The Book of the Courtier*, opportunities for women to pursue secular and religious education did increase. A number of Protestant divines urged greater equality within the household and greater access to learning for intelligent girls. From Puritan and Anglican pulpits, others pointed approvingly to the moral benefits honest and noble women could bring to their partnerships with men. A godly woman in a godly household raised the standards. Servants could take their bearings from her; children absorb her good qualities; husbands temper their attitudes to hers; and the public be edified by her example. On the other hand, historians of the early modern family such as Lawrence Stone point to the sixteenth and seventeenth centuries in England as a time for the "public reinforcement of the despotic authority of husband and father—that is to say, of patriarchy."[69] Faced with the prospect of great freedom for women, the social satirists had little positive to say, mocking the absurd attitudes of the times and the prospect of a world turned upside down with strong women running estates, managing their own wealth, speaking their minds, degrading themselves (and their men) through more overt pursuit of sexual satisfaction. Commenting on the variety of writings from which early moderns could learn about the truth of womanhood, Lisa Jardine reflects on the mixture of messages. Is this a paradox? How good was Elizabethan England for its uncrowned women?

> If we confine our attention to texts of the former kind we shall come to the conclusion that the early modern period was indeed a "paradise for women." If we confine our attention to texts of the latter kind we shall conclude that women were more oppressed during this period than at any time before or since. Neither view is accurate, although each has its firm following amongst contemporary historians.[70]

In the age of Elizabeth, something was different in the relation of the sexes. Callous denunciation of the lewd and "froward" manners of women, such as had amused many medieval and early modern consumers of antifeminist writings and ballads,[71] was no more acceptable at the court of a female prince than would have been assertions of the natural passionlessness of women, such as our Victorian ancestors appreciated. But the Catholic reverence for asexual sanctity could not long survive Henry VIII's attack on the monasteries; under Elizabeth as under her Stuart successors, the preaching of the national church attended with respect to at least some of the proconjugal propaganda coming from the continent. The code of sixteenth-century sexual honor did not condemn men or women inflamed by the fire of love. Married love, after all, was the goal Protestants had prescribed for all, even those who served God in the special calling of the priesthood. Circe and Calypso might lure heroes off the track, distracting them from public service and courageous action; but at home virtuous Penelopes would be waiting, and the polity had reason to be pleased. A Puritan like Daniel Rogers, writing in 1642 when memories of the queen's evasion of marriage were receding, hails "Matrimoniall Honour":

> Marriage is the Preservative of Chastity, the Seminary of the Commonwealth, the seed-plot of the Church, pillar (under God) of the world, right-hand of providence, supporter of laws, states, orders, offices, gifts and services: the glory of peace, the sinews of warre, the maintenance of policy, the life of the dead, the solace of the living, the ambition of virginity, the foundation of Countries, Cities, Universities, succession of Families, Crownes, and Kingdomes; Yea (besides the being of these) it's the wellbeing of them being made, and whatsoever is excellent in them, or any other thing, the very furniture of heaven (in a kinde) depending thereupon.[72]

This was the world the Reformers predicted. Marriage could be, for the fortunate and the blessed, the very furniture of heaven, the "right-hand of providence." The unmarried Elizabeth saw "the ambition of virginity" in different terms. Was it really inevitable that the best of virgins had no higher goal than to become the best of wives? Was virginity special because it was something to be preserved and dutifully delivered over to this matrimonial "solace of the living" and "seed-plot" of church and state? Had Protestant zeal for the sanctity of marriage overlooked something important? We might recall the vestals, lifelong priestesses, whose intact bodies held the honor of Rome secure. The queen and her image makers did not forget them. Painted as an allegory of virtue and as modern vestal virgin, posed in court finery as a royal sister of the Roman Tuccia, Elizabeth holds a sieve in two major portraits of 1579 and 1580 and in a number of lesser copies. Tuccia, a nobly born priestess of the Temple of Vesta, was accused of breaking her vow of chastity. To refute the vile calumnies, she picked up a sieve, carried it to the Tiber river, and brought it back full of water to show the goddess that her commitment was intact and her continence unimpeachable.[73] Virgins notoriously attracted skeptics. If pagan paragons such as Tuccia or Lucretia had to go to great lengths to prove their virtue, the fascination virgins on trial inspired was, if anything, magnified in Christendom: virgins including Agnes, Agatha, Lucy, and Margaret fight off pagan tyrants, risking rape, welcoming martyrdom, in order that their saintly continence continues to awe and inspire.[74] But not everyone was persuaded. The years 1558–1603 were the last epoch in which a broad public was invited to admire the glories of chastity, without its splendor being obscured by criticism and disbelief, marred (in my view, fatally) by prurience and condescension. In the Britain of the seventeenth and eighteenth centuries, sexual purity continued to be preached at women and expected of the unmarried. But its meanings would be changed, in line with the tilt toward a different social, class, and economic landscape, a different estimation of the significance of the private sphere.[75] Chastity's public presence and operations were, under the watchful eye of the Protestant bourgeoisie, relocated into a more narrowly domestic sphere. The future of female chastity was in the hands of a domestic ideology, and an increase in the surveillance of female behavior was its predictable partner. As many historians claim, one of the side-effects of the decline of the aristocracy was the rise of a specifically gendered conception of virtue.[76] Honor was for a feudal culture based on bloodlines, status, and genealogy. In a society where mounted knights carrying swords were no longer a typical sight, honor had a different look. For middle-class women, "honor" was chastity understood as "negative continence," surely a demeaning privilege, as the seventeenth-century writer Samuel Butler complained:

> Virtue, as it is commonly understood in woman, signify's nothing else but Chastity, and Honor only not being Whores: As if that Sex were capable of no other morality, but a mere Negative Continence.[77]

Michael McKeon clarifies the transition:

> By the end of the eighteenth century, the centrality of the feminine gender to modern conceptions of inner virtue had become so evident that its neglect makes questions of virtue unaskable.... In associating female virtue with chastity, the eighteenth century is commonly thought to mark a low point of careless patriarchal cynicism. But it may be more accurate to see that association in the context of the progressive critique of patrilineal honor, a critique in which women, besieged by discredited aristocratic honor, come to embody the locus and refuge of honor as virtue.[78]

The Reformation's campaign against wonders, idols, relics, and mysticism, against sacramental machinery and salvific intercession, was explicitly connected to a wider social disenchantment with chastity. Such a revulsion pours out of the writings of John Calvin, Martin Luther, and others.[79] It was one of the pillars of the Reformed dispensation. This is not a question of the conservative versus the progressive, nor the feminist versus the misogynist. Both celibacy and marriage appealed to conservatives, and women could be as easily dismissed by a matrimonial idealism as by an ascetic one. Protestantism helped relocate virtue onto a this-worldly foundation and facilitate the compromise between material flourishing and spiritual perfectibility. Some would see this as progress, others as a cynical resignation to a human nature whose conversion to the life of the angels would require interventions of an order different from the monastic disciplining of the soul. The new church would restore the priesthood of all believers, in loyalty to its idea of the early Christian community. It would also strengthen the institution of marriage and rethink the role of sexuality within it. In her important study of *Sexuality, State, and Civil Society in Germany, 1700–1815*, Isabel V. Hull emphasizes the place of marriage as the keystone of the Protestant social edifice:

> Marriage, far from being a necessary evil, or at most a limited good for loving individuals, was redefined as the most appropriate conduit for one's relation to God and, finally, the original link in the chain of analogues jus-

> tifying the sociopolitical hierarchy. Marriage was God-given; it was the natural condition for all humans, lay and clerical.... Marriage ... was not merely a social institution; it was also a sexual union. The Reformation consequently marks another upward revaluation of sexual behavior. As in the twelfth century, the process of revaluation was channelled exclusively into marriage and consequently changed that institution, while also altering the hierarchy of sexual delicts outside it. Reformers were unanimous about two points. First, they accepted sexual desire as a universal human appetite that could only very rarely be stifled. Encouraging celibacy was fruitless and promoted hypocrisy, or worse.... Further, neither virginity nor celibacy were holy attributes.[80]

Marriage might have its problems. But its renunciation had created too many openings for very unholy "abominations," as Protestants were quick to complain. Christianity (like Judaism) acknowledged that sexual desire was natural and innate, at least since the expulsion from Eden. To deny nature was to license perversion.[81] Breed an angel and you will provide all the more room for the demon to hide under his clothes. The ideal known for its abuses had trouble promoting itself as ideal. Monasticism and its prize ornament, celibacy, were key points for Protestant-Catholic conflict, and the supernatural pretensions of sexual renunciation were easy targets. Austere Protestant critics complained that stories of the bizarre miracles of virgin saints and their hair-raising escapes from torture and worse were just for the gullible. The naïve may imagine pure and sexually abstinent saints as having intercessory power.[82] But how could such power translate to the believer whose achievement of asexual perfection was, in the main, a failure? Surely there were better ways of improving one's chances at salvation. If celibacy was, as the Roman Catholic Church claimed, crucial to the life of perfection, then why did it do such a bad job of convincing its own clergy to keep themselves well away from all carnality?

The skeptics had reasons for their doubts, and there was truth behind the popular medieval mockery of the lecherous monk and the predatory priest. Despite pressure and outcries from their superiors, priests continued to practice concubinage: sons of priests frequently followed their unmarried fathers into the priesthood, and "by the fifteenth century Church authorities had largely abandoned attempts to penalize women who became sexually involved with clerics."[83] While orthodox Christianity claimed to follow its founder in accepting the fact of marriage and the necessity of procreation, its patristic inheritance led it to look at even marital sex with suspicion: sex within marriage was tolerable, but sexual pleasure was wicked and so should be minimized, in line with the preferences of experts like Augustine and Jerome.[84] This inconsistency inspired choleric rants from the sixteenth-century Reformers, who welcomed conjugal pleasure as a sign of the strength of the bond and even saw it as a legitimate human goal.[85] According to Calvin, the Catholic Church did more to degrade marriage than any number of brothels; it was, he writes in the *Institutes of the Christian Religion* (4.12.27–28), "an astonishing shamelessness on their part to peddle this ornament of chastity as something necessary ... [and thus] the too superstitious admiration of celibacy became prevalent. After this came those frequent and unrestrained rhapsodic praises of virginity, so that scarcely any other virtue was commonly believed to compare with it."[86] Celibacy, far from being the original ideal for the Christian priesthood, was a late development, a "superstition" that weakened marriage without bringing dignity to the clergy. Calvin reminds his audience of the apostolic freedom of priests and bishops to be married (*Institutes,* 4.12.27), a freedom destroyed when the church opted for a "new tyranny" and "with immoderate affection for virginity began to discriminate against marriage."[87]

To Calvin's mind, there are two ways of being virgin. One option is "sincere" or what I would call radical virginity: the choice of the committed celibate; abstinence on principle and for life. The other, the second sort of virginity, is the chaste love of married partners. Calvin has no doubt that what was falsely called "monastic perfection" is the less perfect. Vows are a poor substitute for the quality of a life led with effort and devotion, a life in holy matrimony.[88] And Puritans in England gratefully accepted Calvin's lead: "The Puritans, like other Protestants, had to satisfy themselves first of all that Paul's commendation of chastity was of special not general application and implied no rule of celibacy or disapproval of marriage."[89] Chastity no longer had to fight off the appeal of the conjugal life: it could now migrate into the very space it had fled. But at what cost? What price matrimonial chastity?

There are few moments in the history of the chastity plot that are as influential as this one, or (to my mind) as peculiar. In the conversion of chastity and the loss of its magical powers, Calvin is a pivotal figure. He saw himself as demystifying an ideal, saving a Pauline principle from the abuses and distortions of the papists. But I prefer to see the effects of the Reformation on the ideal of chastity as a decline rather than a demystification. Chastity was officially kept alive, but what the Reformed churches put in its place was a weak and accommodating surrogate, chastity disenchanted. Protestants were well aware that Paul encouraged a life of sexual renunciation, for those strong enough to embrace it. It could have posed a dilemma. How to elevate marriage from this grudging acceptance, at the very core of Christian thinking about faith and the sexual? How to save the concept of chastity while denying everything that made it difficult, complex, heroic? One way of stressing this erosion is to distinguish between a liberal and a radical notion of sexual purity, as John Rogers does in his remarkable article on "The Enclosure of Virginity."[90] "Marital chastity," writes Rogers, "was becoming in seventeenth-century England the normative affirmation of temperate conjugal sexual behavior." Recommended by the Reformers, and later championed by Puritans, this doctrine of a moderate, tempered, conjugal chastity offered little that was challenging. While it may have freed the pious from a nagging sense of inadequacy if they could not live up to standards of sustained sexual abstinence, it was remarkably lacking in "apocalyptic energies."[91] Where, in this capacious new world of wedded virtue and continent marriage, were the mystical powers of the virginal body?

Throughout the twists and turns of the eunuch's plot, the virgin had been a paradox, a contradiction to a society that needed and valued the custom of marriage and that repeatedly legislated for it. Paul had spoken with admiration of the unmarried woman, who can please God rather than an earthly husband. Many husbands were not so sure that this was a good deal. Those who argued for the greater blessings delivered by the wife's resignation to her "Lord at home" missed the urgency of Paul's praise. For why did the Pauline virgin preserve her bodily integrity? Was it because her purity proved the intrinsic value of her personality? Was it because her chastity registered her spiritual self-possession, as later doctrines of liberal individualism suggested, and as my plot's final heroine, Clarissa Harlowe, wanted to believe? Nothing in the eschatological expectations of early Christianity would support such a view of the virgin's value. The virgin about whom Paul is thinking does not spend her time worrying about her personality or reflecting on the special beauty of her sexual innocence. She is in a hurry for the end of time to arrive. This is not what the bourgeois Miss is about. Maidenly and delicate, she is keeping herself for marriage. Chastity is praised in both instances. But it is hard to recognize it as the same virtue. The "struggle for the proper form of chastity," as Rogers nicely puts it, is "a contest between the competing alternatives of chaste marriage and sustained virginity."[92] The ideal of "chaste conjugality" assumed that the pious would put aside the call for sexual abstinence. This, as Rogers observed, abandons the "sacred vehemence" that connects the ascetic to the revolutionary, that renders the position of the powerful virgin "ecstatic and uncontainable." After the Reformation, marriage itself was different. The act of marriage was officially no longer a sacrament but a civil contract, a "temporal, worldly thing," in Luther's words.[93] Yet in becoming civil and, in a sense, secularized, marriage did not lose its value. Indeed, many believers in the Protestant camp were convinced that these changes enhanced the status of marriage. The newer discourse stressed the positive good of mutual companionship and care as much as the other traditional uses of marriage for procreation and as a remedy against fornication. Chastity, to be sure, did not sink unnoticed into the appendices of cultural history. It continued to be promoted. Insistence on premarital virginity (at least for females) and fidelity within marriage upheld the cultural values of sexual regulation and restraint. But the stakes had changed.

In the old war of spirit against flesh, transcendence against carnality, the institution of marriage had served as a curious compromise. It was affirmed. The marriage bed is pure, Paul admitted. "A bond ordered by God," John Chrysostom wrote in his Twelfth Homily on Colossians, and the judgment was canonical. Yet there was always a nagging sense that, for those fully initiated into the Christian program, marriage was dispensable. Most admirable were the lifelong virgins, the eunuchs for the kingdom of heaven. In their lives, eros could be converted from earth to heaven, lustful appetites overcome. For the less strong, as Paul explained, marriage was a useful remedy against fornication, a *pharmakon*. "Until comparatively recent times," John Bugge writes in the first sentence of his *Virginitas: An Essay in the History of a Medieval Ideal*, virginity was "the single most essential prerequisite for a life of perfection in Christianity."[94] Virginity was a shield, a spear against concupiscence, and the armor the Christian can take on as a protection against corruption. Physical integrity, on the Christian view, stands for something profound in the world of the spirit. Of course not everyone can embrace it. It takes a gift, or *charisma*, granted to some by the grace of God. The virginity of the celibate monks and nuns in their retreat from the pollution of the world is, Bugge continues, "a visible sign of membership in the group of the elect."[95] What the nonelect did was important as well. They were expected to guard their bodies with fear and trembling, to be restrained in their nuptial embraces, to give no occasion for shame, and to refrain from tempting others. If they could not triumph over their sexual being, they could at least curb it. That was the advice most Christians took (or at least acknowledged) as they went on with their conjugal duties and debts, falling in love at times, conceiving children for the church, forming pious families. It might make sense to speak as the Greeks and Romans did, about the sexual decorum of married people as chastity as well as associating chastity with the requisite avoidance of sex by the unmarried. But to call married love itself *chastity* as Luther, Calvin, Spenser, and a long Puritan tradition begins to do? That was odd.

The new world of middle-class virtue was one unfriendly to the high-wire act of principled virginity, to the risks as well as the ambitions of a life outside the walls of the family household, whether in the desert, in the cloister, or in some Amazonian dream of women warriors and martyred heroines. In this world women were to behave. This was not a rule Elizabeth recognized, nor was middle-class culture a pill she had to swallow. An ideal like chastity that went through its youthful schooling under the church fathers, that absorbed much of a repressed or secret Gnostic tradition, made a splash in secular circles when it moved into courtly romance and medieval pastoral. Virginity, the glory of the Mother of God and subject of triumphant portrayals in Romanesque and Gothic religious art, was the ideal governing the lives of female religious in convents and cloisters.[96] Transferred from cloister to castle, sexual purity tells us less about moral perfectionism than about aristocratic attempts to distinguish between noble and base, refined and common. Renaissance writers at the time of Elizabeth had inherited a set of conventions about sublimated eros and its power to ennoble the soul from Italian imitators of Petrarch and from a loose combination of Neoplatonic influences, most prominently the commentary of Marsilio Ficino (1433–1499) on Plato's *Symposium* and the romances of Lodovico Ariosto (1474–1553). This was a heritage the queen did not mind acknowledging; it was also, not by coincidence, the literary heritage adapted by the greatest of her poetic celebrants, Edmund Spenser, the poet whose epic romance about wandering knights in Faeryland is probably the last and most notable showcase for chastity as a heroic ideal. This was an ideal suitable for a queen who flaunted her power and autonomy, recognizing no authority over her own. But it was a difficult model for anyone else, and a confusing clue to what female sexual virtue was meant to look like. Elizabethan chastity may have helped overcome the contradiction of a social world incoherently torn between norms and deviations, desires and frustrations. But it could not establish a precedent. Just as Hippolytus discovered when he sought to emulate the purity of his beloved Artemis, heroic chastity may be only for the gods.

✷ 7 ✷
The Virgin's Fall

May I never survive one moment that fatal one
in which I shall forfeit my innocence.

Pamela Andrews, heroine of SAMUEL RICHARDSON'S
Pamela, or Virtue Rewarded (1740)

Marriage versus Virginity: Elizabeth and the Faerie Queene

Queen Elizabeth I of England is the last of history's powerful virgins. Her radiance was, as she asserted, not that of the phoenix destined to reappear but the final blaze of a special magic. Never again in the Protestant world would virginity be at home with the power of the sacred and the ecstatic; no one in the reigns of the Stuarts and their successors proved able to use effectively the scenario of absolute sovereignty that the Virgin Queen was able to adapt to her own ends. Elizabeth understood that sharing her throne with a consort could only limit her authority. For her, celibacy was the best choice. Politically as well as personally, the queen thrived on the contradictions of her myth, adopting an Amazonian persona when she wanted to appear the warrior-empress; acting out tender maidenly motherhood when she wanted to discourage foreign policies she considered risky; playing the unattainable goddess while toying with the idea that someday she would satisfy the wishes of her subjects and turn her virginity to more practical uses.

Jakob Burckhardt titled one of the sections of his influential *The Civilization of the Renaissance in Italy* (1860) "The State as a Work of Art." In few places was this aestheticizing as obvious as it was in Elizabeth's England. A poetic imagination and a keen sense of theatricality supplemented what in some cases was luck, some good management, and some sheer bravado. Together these served to cover over a number of cracks in the system, to obscure points of danger or vulnerability in each of the three most important battlegrounds of the Elizabethan settlement: the religious, the political, and the legal.[1] As Stephen Greenblatt wrote in 1984,

> Queen Elizabeth [was] a ruler without a standing army, without a highly developed bureaucracy, without an extensive police force, a ruler whose power is constituted in theatrical celebrations of royal glory and theatrical violence visited upon the enemies of that glory. Power that relies upon a massive police apparatus, a strong, middle-class nuclear family, an elaborate school system, a power that dreams of a panopticon in which the most intimate secrets are open to the view of an invisible authority, such power will have as its appropriate aesthetic form the realist novel; Elizabethan power, by contrast, depends on its privileged visibility. As in a theatre, the audience must be powerfully engaged by this visible presence while at the same time held at a certain respectful distance from it.[2]

The unmarried queen survived numerous assassination attempts, a Catholic rebellion in 1569, and papal excommunication a year later. Her legitimacy was contested, and her gender was often viewed as a disqualification. Yet she held power, inviting the fantasy of intimacy—the audience powerfully engaged—while at the same time enforcing awe, remaining at a certain respectful distance. The queen's virginity was, in my terms, one of her canniest choices. Even some of her contemporaries agreed. A Scots diplomat named James Melville described her situation in the early 1560s. "By taking a husband," he told her, "you would be merely a queen, but while remaining celibate you are both queen and king together, and you have too great a heart to imagine giving yourself a master."[3] Refusing marriage, the queen stood outside the social economy to which all other laypersons were subject.[4] This was Elizabeth's grand fiction. Her celibate privilege—her unique and sovereign autonomy—was as precious a gift to her nation as to herself. At the helm of the state was an intact and incorruptible maiden, her body a guarantor of the nation's integrity. If the motives of history's other defiant virgins could be looked at with skepticism, no such suspicions should proliferate around the person of the queen.

Elizabethan virginity belongs to the history of European politics and to the complicated story of how England reinvented itself as a Protestant realm, a reinvention that was far from complete when Elizabeth ascended to the throne. Yet if her unusual choice of celibacy for herself belongs to that history, it also fails to belong. It marks not so much a transition, a new possibility or form of social experience, as an incongruity. No other events in the history of women, the history of the monarchy, or the history of Protestant institutional practice followed from this one. The death of the queen marked the end. On or around March 24, 1603, the phoenix rose from this terrestrial orb, presumably to join the divine triumvirate of Juno, Minerva, and Venus whose impressive pedigree the queen more than matched, according to royal panegyrists. In a famous painting of 1569 by Hans Emworth, *The Judgment of Paris,* it is undecided which beauty deserves the award of the golden apple. On the entrance of Eliza, the question is clearly settled. Juno, who rules over marriage, and Venus, who champions unchaste love, compete for her favor; Minerva, the armored virgin, looks to her in sisterhood. But it is the moon goddess Diana who wins the queen's allegiance. To construct the work of art that was the queen's body politic, a great deal of collaboration was required. If her personal authority required confirmation, so did her anomalous situation as a celibate Protestant woman ruler in a Europe full of Catholic enemies and rivals. Associating with mythological celebrities helped place this exception to the customary law of gender hierarchy. If she failed to secure her kingdom by giving her people a successor, she could at least be a legend. The choice of classical pastoral and deities well in the background of current theological reality was strategic: ambiguous, yet imparting a certain air of mystery.

The queen's many symbolic personae allowed for equivocation: what was she *really*? The poet Edmund Spenser decided to split the difference in his *Faerie Queene*: If she was Gloriana, a most royal "Empresse" destined to marry and rule jointly with her consort Arthur, she was also Belphoebe, a version of Diana, and she was also Una, Britomart, Mercilla, and Cynthia, chaste paragons all. Spenser's Elizabeth would contain multitudes. In her various personifications, she thrived in the forests and meadows, and she dazzled in the court and on the battlefield; she was the elusive genius of the hunt, the "Lady of May," and a fierce warrior, girded with her chastity.[5] Spenser, it could be argued, was diplomatic. Or canny. He put into play all these "mirrors" of her majesty in order to compliment her sovereignty while eliding the question: Was her celibacy actually good for the realm? That is to say, did the rhetoric of chastity strengthen her political position or simply distract from it?

Both during her reign and after, the queen's unusual sexual status was at once glaringly obvious and without explicit ideological consequences. Her divine counterparts Minerva and Diana had claimed the independence of the virginal state but denied it to mortal women. Elizabeth too: she was special—and not inclined to allow anyone else to be special in the same way. The royal virginity could have been an embarrassment. The queen's celibacy was equivocal. It stood at once for continuity and for change. It evoked the old spiritual tradition captivated by the sacrificial excellence of renunciation, and yet it performed on the new post-Reformation stage from which the eunuch had been banished. For generations of church fathers, priests, monks, nuns, and their admirers, and even the ordinary lay public, the eunuch's plot had condensed a number of ideas about the fortifying effects of sexual abstinence and caution. Clerical celibacy, the most visible of the plot's social and institutional ramifications, was a straightforward way to separate the elite from the rank and file. The opportunity of sainthood for virgin martyrs or ascetic athletes kept a place in Christian culture for the highflyer and daredevil. That place was vacated with the anticelibacy campaign of Martin Luther and John Calvin. Temperate marriage, not vowed abstinence, was the way humans could please their Creator. A sexual virtue tested in the social arena, and proven through its labors of constancy, righteousness, and love, would purify the passions and educate the soul. "Matrimonial Honour," wrote the Puritan divine Daniel Rogers in 1642, is the true jewel of continence. Married love may be hard work, but it is also grace and glory.[6] We are a long way from the eunuch's solitary splendor.

Spenser wanted to worship at the altar of married love, an ideal he and the Reformers struggled to identify with chastity in its new dispensation. Even in the generous terms he allowed himself in his epic *Faerie Queene*, the program was unwieldy. To fashion his poetic self-image, Spenser had divergent materials to combine: the looser morals of pastoral eroticism, absorbed from his Italian models; the Christian and Platonic asceticism that he considered crucial to any heroic lifestyle; the competition with Virgil to become the national poet for a modern age; the pleasures of myth, fable, allegory, and fairy tale. The package would be large by the standards of the most ambitious of bards: I think it proved too much for Spenser. He could not turn Diana and Venus, Mary and Eve, the Amazon and the blushing maiden, into one unified and compelling archetype. This was not his fault. Chastity, in its long history, was a challenge to any effort to make the moral life accommodating, relaxed, and reassuring. To mark out the excellence of the athlete of God, chastity has to maintain a certain standard. It needs to be strenuous, not consoling; unworldly, not sociable and companionable; rapturous, not comfortable.

In *The Faerie Queene* Spenser did something untoward when he made his "champion" and "flower of chastity" a young woman with a crush who is destined to marry and found a race of kings. Her name was Britomart, and the fate of Britain lay in her womb. Britomart represents the power of chastity in a new sense, one that Jerome or Methodius would not have recognized. She is a woman who can perform like a male. She puts on male clothes, covers her beauty with helmet and armor, and competes as a knight in every arena from which her sex is excluded. In every combat she enters, she is the victor. This is a dangerous role for a woman. Unlike the British nemesis Joan of Arc or Radigund, the powerful Spenserian Amazon Britomart defeats and kills, Britomart's transvestism is permissible. Authorized by God for a noble purpose, her androgyny (which she will give up in marriage) means that the fragile virtue in her person is armed with unshakable conviction.[7] Hers is a feminine purity protected by masculine strength.

Britomart's chastity is simple. No temptation can unsettle her; no brute rapist can succeed against her. But it is a virtue that needs maturation, and her quest is meant to provide that. If her purity is steadfast, it is weakened by the thinness of her experience and the naïveté of her judgment. From the moment she appears in the poem, she shows that she can defend sexual virtue because she has the toughness to fight back against aggressive male sexuality, a force which, however, she does not entirely understand. Her confusion in the face of male sexuality is important for the kind of education Spenser believes she needs. While she wears the arms and armor of an Amazon, Britomart has no talent for the autonomous life: neither the cloister or the martyr's crown are in her future. Hers is not the exemption from the normal female condition which the poem allows to such followers of Diana as the huntress Belphoebe, immune to most human emotions and quick to resent any attempt at courtship. Ultimately Britomart will do her duty: she will lay down her arms and concede the superiority of men—indeed, will welcome male sexuality with all its privileges, rights, and brutalities. It is male sexual attraction, after all, that has first fired Britomart into action and caused her to adopt the role of Amazon warrior. Britomart fights for chastity and wins, every time. She dismembers rapists and disembowels rival Amazons when their embrace of active sexual desire is too patent. She walks through a diabolical trap in the castle of Busirane, assailed by every sort of perverse and insidious form of erotic suggestion, and emerges almost entirely unscathed. She even unhorses the man she loves, proving that she chooses the terrain and sets the rules in the game of their courtship. But she is the champion of chastity because hers is the love that will not be satisfied with anything less than virtuous wedlock and mutual love.

No one should disdain Britomart's goal. The marriage plot is popular for good reasons. Her objective—to carry on her quest in the face of danger after danger until she discovers the man she is meant to marry—is nonetheless a goal that has left behind most of what is valuable about chastity. What attracts us to happy marriages is not what attracts us to sexual renunciation. They belong in different discourses, offer different challenges, promise different rewards. Marriage, at the very least, involves accommodation, adjustment, and settling. One who is married acknowledges the existence of an other, admits that person's stake in her life, signs on for their shared understandings and misunderstandings, or if not, risks the failure of that marriage. Eunuchs find their fulfillment elsewhere. The celibate, vowed to renunciation of married love and sexual sharing, can retain a claim on the unconditional. The absolutism of chastity disdains the mixed goods of marriage. But it is that absolutism, depicted as the highest and most honored life, the otherworldly vocation of sacrifice and unyielding self-possession, which the Protestant revaluation of marriage questions.

The Maid Britomart and the Maid Belphoebe: Edmund Spenser Tries to Have It Both Ways

> The one social formulation that is insistently promulgated in the [*Fairie Queene*] is marriage. It is the fulfillment, the great destiny, the natural duty of the major characters. Indeed, throughout his career as England's Protestant poet, Spenser presents marriage as the ideal human bond.
>
> ANN BAYNES CORTO[8]

Born of a family from the "middling" classes, Edmund Spenser acquired property and wealth as a colonial servant in Ireland, lost everything, and died in poverty in London.[9] Glory was his—intermittently. A secure place proved more elusive. Spenser is best known as author of *The Faerie Queene,* a sprawling, digressive, episodic epic dedicated to Elizabeth, a poem Spenser worked on for more than fifteen years and left unfinished, publishing three books in 1590 and three more in 1596. In his grand design, Spenser intended to bring together England and Faeryland, the rule of the "royall virgin" (*FQ*, 3.3.49) and the legendary landscape of chivalry, magic, and romance. The English nation, he proposes, has a high destiny, in line with the historical and cosmic plan devised by divine Providence and glimpsed by the reader in the heroic adventures of Britomart and Artegall, Arthur and Guyon, Redcrosse and Una, Amoret and Scudamour, and Belphoebe and Timias. What that plan is remains largely unknown to the figures Spenser places somewhere between Britain and Faeryland, who wander in an enchanted landscape, challenging each other to armed combat, rescuing maidens and young men in distress, combating the beauty and poison of witchcraft, all in the name of their moral education as Spenser conceived it.

Not everything is obscure about Spenser's plan. There is to be a reward for such moral education, painful as it is. Every steadfast lover, tried in blood and suffering, can hope for marital peace; the blessings of Venus will be sanctioned by the stern guidance of Diana. Love directed by virtue is a complex thing, which does not reveal its nature cheaply. It would be nice to imagine that fiction, at least, could provide a space for a passion as careless as it is benign: simple, spontaneous, an artless upsurge of breathless excitement, accompanied by the usual single-minded intensity of the lover, and even by its usual habit of fading as other intensities intervene. But that would not be the love Spenser considers worthy, nor the fiction he sets out to write. True love must prove itself by testing itself against two compelling rivals: absolute and dedicated virginity, abjuring all amorous attachment, and wanton love, which allures with images of ease, luxury, and abandon and can switch as readily from sensuous languor to perversity. The challenge to true love takes shape in the poem through a number of characters the chaste Britomart must confront and vanquish: Marinell (books 3–5) the "reluctant bachelor," who disdains love and distrusts women; Malecasta (book 3, canto 1), the giddy chatelaine of Castle Joyous who makes a pass at her, believing she is a man; the Amazon queen Radigund (book 5), Britomart's "parodic anti-type," the objectionable version of female power who has imprisoned Britomart's object of desire and subjected him to a humiliating emasculation; Scudamour (books 3–5), the jealous and too-ardent betrothed; Busirane (book 3, canto 9), the malevolent seducer for whom sexual love is degradation and power play; Artegall, her beloved, whom she defeats in battle more than once (books 4–5); and even Guyon (books 4–5), the Elfin knight of Temperance who knows only how to overcome passion with reason, not love.[10]

Only Britomart is given the major quest: to seek and learn the anatomy of love, to discover the redefinition of chastity as constancy, to save love from the excesses of courtesy and courtliness, pastoral whimsy and Catholic repression.[11] Britomart uses violence to combat the wrongful violence of sexual love and social oppression. In her remarkable transvestite shape, the temptation of virginity as the ideal destination of feminine virtue is addressed and dismissed. This exemplary lady has spots of vulnerability. She is susceptible to the charms of the male sex, or rather to one instance of that sex, the Briton Artegall, her prophesied husband and the half brother of Prince Arthur, projected to become the father of Britomart's children and the ancestor of the Tudor line: that will happen, Spenser reveals, when the poem moves out of legend and into history, as it were. Britomart is the knight who tests the steel of true love and prevails, even if her promised marriage never happens in the poem. A flight from marriage into the pure precincts of chaste celibacy is not her plan, nor is it ever presented as a worthwhile alternative. Was Spenser giving his queen a lesson?

The promised end of the *Faerie Queene* is deferred and ultimately unreachable, much like the promised end of the Christian Apocalypse. But readers can glimpse what it would look like. Virtue and glory, private desires and public achievement, will sit down together at the marriage feast that must eventually be celebrated at the court of the queen of Faeryland. Civic duty and poetic play will lend each other their blessings and modulate with grace the excesses each might entail. Such is the metaphorical magic of a narrative device like marriage, converting discord and contestation into harmony, pacifying the war between the sexes, and establishing continuity for the social order, especially when that social order depends on the marital success of its monarchs.

The golden age was long past when Elizabeth came to the throne, her admiring poet Edmund Spenser wrote in the proem to book 5. Justice, despairing of humanity, had fled to the distant skies; truth and virtue were unknown or despised. But then a "dread Souerayne Goddesse" was bestowed by Providence upon a needy people. A sacred empire would be entrusted to a sacred imperial virgin, the earthly representative of a divine order and the close simulacrum of the Roman virgin goddess, Astraea, guardian of justice.[12] It was certainly odd to have an unmarried woman exercising sovereign power. English kings, like biblical patriarchs and Roman emperors before them, conformed to a model so familiar as to seem inevitable: males were the head of the body politic, fathers were responsible for the health and strength of their families, virility was a blessing, and the spectacle of royal cradles that were continually refilled assured the realm's future and happiness. Yet what had been the profile of monarchy in the hands of its male princes for the last 250 years, at least since Edward II? Neither the dynastic nor the political history of pre-Elizabethan Britain offered much in the way of confidence. Some kings neglected their manly or spousal responsibilities in favor of less conventional loves. Edward II preferred Piers Galveston to his wife Isabella, the "She Wolf of France"; Henry VI, mad and deposed, found little assistance from his wife, Margaret of Anjou; Henry VIII and a number of his predecessors scattered "natural" children among their mistresses. If stability at the center of power should symbolically be backed up by sexual and marital stability, England (like most kingdoms) failed to live up to the standard. A virgin's open and well-publicized defiance of heteronormative expectations offered an interesting novelty. But, as we shall see, only if that virgin was a queen.

As virgin and as sovereign, Elizabeth possessed a sacred body. What the law acknowledged as her body politic was eternal or, as the doctrine had it, perpetual, remaining dedicated to the mystical well-being of the realm and surviving as it survived. "Created out of a combination of faith, ingenuity and practical expediency," Marie Axton explains, the royal body in its political incarnation was "held to be unerring and immortal." But as natural body, the queen was a woman among women, "subject to infancy, infirmity, error and old age."[13] As such, shouldn't she do what women are "meant" to do?

The moment of *The Faerie Queene* is late in the career of Elizabeth. Spenser, in offering his services and his counsel to his queen, almost puts himself on her level. He presents her with his admiration but also his advice. Elizabeth disliked advice. On the other hand, she liked admiration, especially when it arrived in such a sophisticated and lofty package. Spenser's gambit did not work, or at least not as fully as he had hoped. The queen did not welcome Spenser into her inner circle. He was, after all, barely middle-class, a gentleman by education rather than birth. Elizabeth did not give him all the offices and pensions he solicited, perhaps because her closest adviser Lord Burghley (Sir William Cecil) was not a fan of Spenser's. But she did not rebuff him, either. There was something in the offering of Spenser's romance of chastity from which she could take pleasure. Beginning book 3, "The Legend of Britomartis, or Of Chastity," Spenser speaks to her directly:

> It falls me here to write of Chastity,
> The fayrest vertue, far above the rest.

Yes, I could look for examples of chastity from the world of Faery and paint its portrait with the imaginary colors of magic and enchantment. But why should I do so, when the quintessential and most perfect form of it already exists "shrined in my Soueraine's brest"? (*FQ*, proem to book 1, cantos 3–5). Chastity (the virtue to which book 3 is dedicated) exceeds the virtues already covered in books 1 and 2, holiness and temperance, virtues equally moral and supernatural but whose heroic stature is best represented by males, in this case by the knights Redcrosse and Guyon. To portray chastity, the poet explains with elaborate deference and singular modesty, is beyond his skills. Compared with the queen's presence, in which chastity is rendered glorious, all literary copies are mere shadows, inadequate and partial. Yet there is a chance these "shadows" can achieve something, and the two from whom much is expected are offered as tributes to the lady they resemble. Gloriana the queen of Faeryland is the figure who represents Elizabeth's rule and majesty: it is from her court that all the knights' quests begin and it is to her favor and the foot of her throne all seek to return. Gloriana is alluded to in the poem but she is never seen in person. More active is Elizabeth's other shadow, the angelic huntress Belphoebe (another name for Cynthia, the lunar goddess of chastity). She is identified as the foster daughter of Diana and twin to Amoret. Belphoebe is "upbrought in perfect Maydenhead" (*FQ*, 3.6.28); she haunts the woods and like other magical virgins, has special skills of healing (*FQ*, 3.5.43–50). Belphoebe, Spenser explained to Ralegh, represents the queen in her "private person." She is a "fair flower" of chastity and virginal virtue, forever spotless and unyielding to masculine desire, standing firm "on the highest stayre of th'honorable stage of womanhead" and an example to all women of what they may aspire to—if they remain single and pure (*FQ*, 3.5.52–55):

> Her berth was of the wombe of Morning dew,
> And her conception of the ioyous Prime,
> And all her whole creation did shew
> Pure and unspotted from all loathly crime,
> That is ingenerate in fleshly slime. (*FQ*, 3.6.3)

Belphoebe is unlike all the other idealized women in the poem in that, kind and courteous as she is, she repudiates love and marriage. She has no specific Christian associations, and her excellence is that of nature in its pristine and even wild character. She does, nonetheless, resemble in many respects her theological and mystical sisters in those medieval traditions the Reformation had contemplated skeptically. Compared by the poet to a fountain that arises from the earth immaculately, without the intervention of men or art, Belphoebe stands for a kind of generativity: complete, full, and possessed in itself. She needs no mate, no complement. Raised with Diana and her nymphs, at home with the wilderness, Belphoebe may suggest the allure of paradise. But hers is a paradise with no room for others. When in the poem she and others are threatened by the monster Lust (book 4, canto 7), Belphoebe has more than enough power to attack and kill that persistent threat. Friendship and love, however, are closed books to her, and she fails to feel compassion for the faithful and wounded squire Timias, who adores her. Here we may suspect veiled criticism on Spenser's part. If Sir Walter Ralegh, on whom Timias was supposed to be based, ventured too far when he portrayed Elizabeth as the mutable and fickle moon goddess Cynthia and bore the sting of the queen's disapproval, Spenser takes similar chances: he has chosen to make one of the queen's avatars a figure notable for her self-absorption.[14] When Spenser asked the queen to recognize her sisterhood to the cool Belphoebe, he gave up being the perfect courtier.

Come, recognize yourself in my "mirrors more than one," Spenser invites the queen. Be Gloriana: and then you will reign with a devoted consort at your side. Or be Belphoebe, and claim the "heavenly" lamp of ideal womanhood's "four lamps of beauty":

> But either Gloriana let her chuse,
> Or in Belphoebe fashioned to bee:
> In th'one her rule, in th'other her rare chastitee.
> (*FQ*, proem to book 3, canto 5)

Spenser's expansive, digressive poem was planned as a gift to an idealized sovereign. It is also a work of political propaganda, a literary mirror in which the "dearest dred" Lady is invited to see herself and learn. In the proem to book 1, Spenser calls Elizabeth "O Goddesse heavenly bright, / Mirrour of grace and Majestie diuine, / Great Lady of the greatest Isle." A "celebration and extension of the queen's political mythology," the epic of knights, elves, maidens in distress, cross-dressing and sexual perversion, enchantment and deception, love and loss, claims to offer praise to a British sovereign, just as Spenser's master, Virgil, offered his to a Roman emperor, Augustus Caesar.[15] *The Faerie Queene* has a dynastic program. Even more central to its intentions, it has a moral program, educational and explanatory, one wrapped in the form of quest romance, chivalric adventure, and pastoral allegory. Its plan was to announce and glorify the consummation of all virtues in one display of perfection, but a display which has three intersecting faces: that of a queen, a royal marriage, and a court. For each virtue, there could be a story, including a hero and the hero's quest. But all the virtues together fuse in the vision of a reign of justice, divinely sanctioned, Protestant and classical in one.

Spenser's was a difficult and confusing task, made more confusing by the poet's failure to bring any of the heroic quests to a resolution. The plan is certainly there, set out in Spenser's dedicatory letters and sonnets: the epic will tell the story of the founding of a realm through its natural and supernatural ancestry. Gloriana, fairy queen of Cleopolis, will marry Arthur, the legendary descendant of Briton kings, brought up by the wizard Merlin (*FQ*, 2.9.68). In conception and scope, *The Faerie Queene* will do for Britain what the *Aeneid* did for Rome. In the *Aeneid*, Aeneas (son of a goddess) brought the line of the Trojan royal family to a second Troy, and from there the royal line continued to the Rome founded (according to legend) by his descendants. The Tudor line, like that of the Julio-Claudian masters of the world before it, is legitimate by the grace of the gods, secured by the feats of heroes, by sacrifice and ordeal, made exemplary in the struggles of virtue with vice.

And here Spenser's story diverges, in interesting ways. Virtue, in the British case, takes the unusual form of female heroism in a number of its key incidents. Military virtue—power and honor in their traditional forms—is incomplete, even flawed, if not balanced by sexual virtue, by the discipline of chastity, the form of honor best represented by glorious women, although also (in Virgil) by the exemplary self-restraint of Aeneas's renunciation of the love of Dido. Spenser's homage is, however, tempered by what may seem like criticism, criticism of the queen and her celibate policies. Are these, he wonders, the right way to honor the virtue with which she has been identified? What about virtuous marriage, that popular and inescapable social bond? A duty most humans must accept, whether their destinies are noble or base. They too can be chaste within marriage, their new Protestant guides told them. The austere path of the eunuch is neither necessary nor desirable.

Chastity, Spenser is sure, is the "fayrest virtue, far above the rest." And yet, what is chastity in this poem? A manifold and proliferating ideal, it includes the chastity of Belphoebe, the athletic and pure follower of Diana; the chastity of the noble lovers Amoret and Scudamour; the chastity of Britomart the lovestruck cross-dressing knight; the chastity of Florimell, who loves Marinell, who resists her; and the chastity of Mercilla the just queen who reigns alone. Only Belphoebe is dedicated to an ascetic life, to the virginal avoidance of love and marriage. All the others experience the passion of love and pursue the consummations through which they hope to find happy union. The unmarried queen may well recognize herself in Belphoebe's staunch resistance and celibacy. But it is Britomart who is appointed "knight of chastity." And Britomart's quest has nothing to do with the preservation of virginal purity. Her goal is to find the man whose face she has fallen in love with in a vision, to fight and defeat him in battle, to save him from the base servitude to an Amazon giant, and in some yet unwritten future, to marry him and establish a line of kings, last of whom will be the Elizabeth to whom the poem is addressed. To be chaste, Spenser suggests, does not amount to a refusal of love. Quite the opposite. It is in and as chaste, faithful marriage that love is fully realized. Spenser is a Protestant. He writes at the end of a century which saw Luther and Calvin attack with great bitterness the abuses of clerical celibacy, promote the holiness of marriage, and recommend that all good Christians find pious companionship in the matrimonial bed. If Elizabeth is being hailed as patron of chastity, she may well have been puzzled by the depiction of it she is being asked to contemplate. Has her refusal of marriage been, in fact, a victory for chastity or a misunderstanding of it?

Shakespeare; or, The Negation of Chastity

> Virginity, like an old courtier, wears her cap out of fashion, richly attired, but unsuitable, just like the brooch and the toothpick, which wear not now.... Get thee a good husband, and use him as he uses thee. So, farewell.
>
> Parolles to Helena, *All's Well That Ends Well* (1.1.152–55, 209–11)[16]

"Give up your virginity," the cynical and cowardly soldier Parolles advises young Helena in Shakespeare's difficult comedy *All's Well That Ends Well.* Helena is determined, by any ruse and any means necessary, to get herself married to the man of her choice. And, by most standards, her plan is the right one. Virginity is against the rule of nature, Parolles continues; it "breeds mites, much like a cheese, consumes itself to the very paring, and so dies with feeding its own stomach." It is "peevish, proud, idle, made of self-love, which is the most inhibited in the canon" (*AW*, 1.1.140–44). Helena has nothing against the idea of shedding her virgin "livery." She just wants to lose it "to her own liking." Getting a good husband is her intention, as it was Britomart's. Like the Briton maid, Helena already knows whom she wants. The trouble is, he doesn't want her. Although Count Bertram, the man who disdains her love, is a snob, a cad, and a sorry excuse for a nobleman, she is undeterred. She must force him into marriage, pretend to be dead, and if she wants to get him to acknowledge the marriage, she must trade places in bed with a young woman he prefers (appropriately named Diana). It is more than most girls would do, no matter how ardent their passion. And, by her lights, it works out.

In comedy's moral universe it is marital accord, rather than chaste sublimity, that is worth fighting for; sexual innocence is means rather than end. Comedy loves the marriage plot, even if it also loves frustrating it, exposing its absurdities. Helena's maiden integrity helps her assert the moral authority she needs. Her virtue, pluck, and skill with medicines do the rest, winning her the support of those in power. Virginity is only one of the excellences she will bring to the marriage, although she loses it not in a solemn and joyous honeymoon night but in a lowlife bed trick. After he finds himself bound to the deflowered Helena through a night of passion he thought he was having with someone else, the wretched Bertram finally confesses himself defeated. Here a *maiden's plot* furnishes all the ingredients for a *marriage plot,* as most modern spectators and readers have learned to expect. Bertram, chastened and educated, will be Helena's loyal husband at last, and, as summed up by their ruling king in the epilogue, "All is well ended."

Helena's positive estimation of the goods of marriage is widely accepted by a number of Shakespeare's readers as the orthodox doctrine of the romantic comedies. Germaine Greer, in *The Female Eunuch,* accepts the orthodoxy. She is not afraid to provoke her feminist readers by praising the "unromantic" conception of happy monogamy in that unpopular play *The Taming of the Shrew,* cleared as it is of "the detritus of romance, ritual, perversity and obsession." Shakespeare, Greer argues, was "one of the most significant apologists of marriage as a way of life and a road to salvation." She adds, "The new ideology of marriage needed its mythology, and Shakespeare supplied it."[17] The rival mythology, the romance enthralled with the wild and headstrong virgin with her too-hasty pride and her nagging hunger for independence, strikes Greer as overly adolescent. The religious glorification of the celibate is defeatist rather than radical; it proposes to bring about "total annihilation in a generation or two."[18] Our real world doesn't need goddesses or martyrs. Marriage, however much a compromise, is the most honest of our options. In it, convention trumps dissidence, and desires are tailored into a properly socialized shape. That is what marriage means.

Consulting Parolles for advice on how to lose her virginity on her own terms (having it taken by force or fraud is a prospect Helena's self-respect does not countenance), the heroine shows no need to dissemble or affect a simpering, maidenly modesty. Sex has no horrors for her. So what good is her virginity? It is merely an obstacle standing in the way of her happiness: she would do better to "like him" who dislikes virginity—that is, to admit her enthusiasm for the "enemy to virginity," the deflowerer who will "undermine" and "blow it up" (*AW,* 1.1.111–21). Virginity, Parolles suggests, is wrong just to the extent it impedes such a happy (if explosive) conclusion. Extending the syllogism, the Shakespearean logic mockingly equates virginity, adultery, and fornication: they are all objectionable because of the obstructions they pose to the concord of the married. If there is a worthwhile chastity, or "honesty," as the language of the period has it (*AW,* 1.3.91, 3.5.12–13), it is warm, not cold; giving, not withholding. In Helena's passionate confession that her love is like a "religion" or "idolatry," she explains that the sacred climax of her worship is nothing less than the moment when "Dian was both herself and Love" (*AW,* 1.3.208–9). Chaste married love is Helena's ideal, as she explains to the king she has miraculously restored to health:

> Now, Dian, from thy altar do I fly,
> And to imperial Love, that god most high,
> Do my sighs stream. (*AW*, 2.3.75–77)

And there is no way to achieve that idea, no way to fly to Love's side, except by surrendering the maidenhood Helena is eager to lose. Neither desert nor cloister have any attractions to her, or to Shakespeare's other well-spoken and enterprising maiden heroines. Chastity matters for the sake of a woman's honor, and the honor of her family (*AW*, 4.2.47–50), but it is the chastity of a woman true to her marriage vows that is the jewel to be saved. Faced with men who assail or doubt their virtue, well-behaved and forthright young women in the comedies stay resolutely within the conventional. Their world is not the dazzling, magical landscape of wandering Spenserian beauties, but a populated, social, historical world where people argue and negotiate, adapt and persuade, cheat and cajole. Spenserian virgins, we recall, stake all on their metaphysical integrity and very little on their ability to reason, speak, discuss, and exchange. Amoret and Florimell, virgins who always seem to be running away from something worse than death (well signposted in the poem as rape, sexual perversion, and violation), may recognize with terror that they are lost, entrapped, deceived. But only magical and spiritual forces can save their maidenhood from such horrors. Fortitude and moral fiber required allegorical personification rather than good arguments if they were to triumph in Faeryland.

This is not how it looks for maidens on a Shakespearean stage. Shakespearean virgins know that their virtue is a social and a moral asset, and they are pleased when it is acknowledged; Helena's virtues are praised by everyone in the play except the man of her dreams. But Shakespearean virgins don't believe their sexual purity elevates them over change, mutability, nature, or fortune. They are, as Camille Paglia suggests, more Dionysians than Apollonians, more mobile and improvisational than static and sublime:

> Rosalind is Shakespeare's answer to Spenser's Belphoebe and Britomart, whom he spins into verbal and psychological motion. Rosalind is kinetic rather than iconistic. She too is a virgin. Indeed, her exhilarating freshness depends on that virginity. But Shakespeare removes Amazonian virginity from its holy self-sequestration and puts it into social engagement. Rosalind, unlike the high-minded Belphoebe and Britomart, has fun. She inhabits newly reclaimed secular space.[19]

Wit and strategy will do more for these maidens than timeless, immobile innocence. If happiness is to be their lot, they will need to establish its conditions. And they do. Spenserian chastity fluctuated between enchantment and escape, sanctuary and violent exposure, unicorns and lascivious maniacs. Shakespearean chastity is more device than metaphysics. Smart girls, who don't want to be exploited, learn through their own arts and courage how to protect their sexual integrity. Even sentimental heroines, almost too ethereal to be believed, can work out a strategy without the help of mystical allegories or supernatural mediation. Prospero's naïve daughter Miranda, threatened by her father with rejection and shame if she misplaces her virtue, just needs to be told and she modestly obliges. Magic and divine intervention are superfluous in her case. The fairies on her island have other work to do.

In this disenchanted comic space, what has happened to the old religion of the asexual absolute? Shakespeare has no time for it, not even in his romances. Ambiguity and metamorphosis reign in the dream or fairy worlds. Reality may be elusive, even misleading. But there is no escape hatch, no bridge to a domain of the unconditional. In this spirit I propose Shakespeare as the messenger of chastity's eclipse. He is the skeptic in a changed sexual climate. His view of female and male sexuality is, I believe, modern in a fashion inaccessible to Spenser and the theological-philosophical tradition that lies behind chastity's long-lived romance with perfection. After Shakespeare, the future of virginity "inhabits ... secular space" (as Paglia rightly puts it). And this will be, of necessity, where society has superseded nature as chastity's lodging. Modern romances have left heaven for earth.

In the old metaphysical regime, paradise was always the reference point, and its loss was something that could be repaired, if the conditions were right. The task was one sacred virginity took seriously. According to the conventions observed by the romance of chastity, virgins are a special dispensation left by an absent God to compensate for the disappointments of reality, which far too often favors the immoral over the moral, the tyrannical over the just. Virgins have redemptive power. They keep alive the obscured image of holiness, the primal trace of God's image in human flesh, at least according to Christianity's high-flown hypothesis. Theirs is a special kind of magic; their purity enables them to heal, inspire, and solace; their integrity can act as a kind of fortress, as the official portraits of Elizabeth showed, shielding the vulnerable from invasion and defining the boundaries. Corruption may have the power to spoil and disfigure everything mortal and human. But virginal nature is a kind of counter-corruption, weeding out the contaminants, distinguishing the additive from the primordial and true, identifying the thing itself at times when copies and simulacra have clouded the perception of those who have lost the original condition. So the virgin state of olive oil exposes and shames the secondary mixtures, the derivative wannabes. So society, if it is tempted by the relativism of values or the sinfulness of vice, can look with relief to the innocent figure of the virgin, the child, the primitive: somewhere there is a condition we haven't spoiled, an understanding so intuitive that reasoning and sophistry have no purchase on it. At its full weight the theme and condition of virginity deserved awe, not Parolles's mockery. Northrop Frye in *The Secular Scripture* has articulated the most ambitious of virginity's traditional defenses, a defense I have had occasion to introduce before: "What is symbolized as a virgin is actually a human conviction, however expressed, that there is something at the core of one's infinitely fragile being which is not only immortal but has discovered the secret of invulnerability that eludes the tragic hero."[20]

Does anyone still believe in the secret of invulnerability? No character in Shakespeare is allowed to entertain that fantasy for long. No one is invulnerable, no identity is clear and unequivocal. Crowned heads, world-storming heroes, patriarchs or Amazons, proud maidens or devious villains, they are one and all subject to contingency and contestation. No integrity escapes the world and its annihilating ironies. All may aspire, but the clay in their feet will show up. What the Renaissance offered the uncertain and the wondering was a type of wisdom and worldliness informed by the ironies of Michel de Montaigne and the mockery of François Rabelais. This was a profane and disenchanted wisdom Spenser tried to look away from, until he was obliged to break off his grand design with his *Mutabilitie Cantos*. But if Spenser ends with mutability, Shakespeare begins there. Reality may be a matter of mechanics, of strength and counterstrength, of chance and opportunity. Nature is a riddle, not an answer. Gone from the Shakespearean landscape are the unchanging celestial spheres, revolving calmly around the earth; gone are the fixed stars, the cosmos as Ptolemy saw it. Gone too are moral certainties, intimations of immortality, victories for the virtuous and conversion for the corrupt. It is in this connection that I think it fair to identify Shakespeare's indifference to chastity: there are many characters in his plays who worry about it, who persecute and misjudge and destroy because of their doubts about it. There are some identified as the pure and the virginal—for example, Marina in *Pericles* or Perdita in *The Winter's Tale*—who bring solace and closure where there was chaos and malice. But the metaphysical power of chastity is dead for him.

In a number of the myths of chastity I have been studying, it is clear that the idea of sexual purity allowed something to be imagined that was still, safe, and self-enclosed. A comparable vision of stillness and imperturbability influenced Stoic and monastic traditions. The ascetic perfectionist argued that such a fortress could exist in the soul, that tempest and uncertainty could have no dominion over a mind steeled in discipline, a will purified by concentration. No Shakespearean hero could agree. In Shakespeare's world, static invulnerability is a phantom and a joke. No king, no matter how magnificent his authority, is exempt from ruin, no lover secure in a transcendent idyll. Where is stasis to be found? In death, if at all.

Maddened by sexual jealousy, Othello can employ only the most brutal violence to crush the chaos he believes has come to him through the woman he loves. Her purity, he was sure, would bring him peace and plenitude. But even the sanctioned sexual union that is marriage cannot save him from anxiety, from his "bloody thoughts" (*Othello,* 3.3.460). His bloody thoughts, like those of those other sexual pessimists Hamlet and Leontes, obsessively turn around that image of unknowable mobility which is a woman's sexuality. For all these tortured misogynists, it is not just the menace of infidelity that darkens their minds but sex itself: it refuses to allow the stillness, the security, the fixed world they think they need. Only death—or the stony imprisonment of a statue, a frozen ideal—can convert a living woman into a fetish of perfection. Ophelia, that careful virgin, is harried by the admonishments of her father, her brother, and her suitor, that she guard above all her "chaste treasure" (*Hamlet,* 1.3.31): though she promises to keep the memory of their warnings "lock'd" (1.3.85–86), her discretion is not enough to banish the doubt. As long as she lives, she is a woman and represents the same "rank" lusts that, Hamlet believes, are the cause of his mother's treachery and his father's murder. Even Laertes may prefer the dead virginal Ophelia to a live and mobile one: Now she can be worshipped with "virgin rites" (5.1.226) as a "ministering" angel and a saint: "Lay her i' th' earth, / And from her fair and unpolluted flesh / May violets spring!" (*Hamlet,* 5.1.233–35). This is the dire truth. That female body from which all human life springs, that can be warmth, fertility, and erotic movement, is dangerous. Plenitude and prodigality are separated by only the thinnest of threads. Virtue promises to make the provocative woman into a contained, legible, unsurprising being, but what a phantasm is virtue! Distrusted as a futile attempt to keep sexual energy contained, chastity gets scant respect from Shakespeare. The only good woman is a dead woman: that would be the conclusion toward which the inexorable logic of their sexual skepticism drives Hamlet, Othello, Posthumus, Leontes, and Claudio, Shakespeare's paranoid heroes. As the Renaissance scholar Valerie Traub explains, "For women in Shakespearean drama, 'chastity' requires being still, cold, and closed; to be 'unchaste' is to be mobile, hot, open."[21] And mobility can be reckless, warmth unfixed; what is open can be contaminated, and what is alive can shift on you. The grave is safe, "a consummation," Hamlet reflects, "devoutly to be wish'd" (*Hamlet* 3.1.64–65). Any other consummation is probably a trap.

The reality for Elizabethans as for us is that continual "circulation of social energy" so memorably described by Stephen Greenblatt, a field with no "single master discourse," no central, stable locus of meaning: "There is no escape from shared contingency." All is exchange, subtle and elusive, a "network of trades and trade-offs," with no originary moment or pure act.[22] And with the eclipse of originary purity, the fetish of virginity loses its meaning, at least its metaphysical meaning and its mythological form. It is rare to find Shakespearean homage to virgin goddesses. Sex, on the other hand, is pervasive. And sexual cynicism, one could even say sexual pessimism, is never far away. Sonnet 129 speaks from a postlapsarian knowledge:

> Th'expense of spirit in a waste of shame
> Is lust in action, and till action, lust
> Is perjur'd, murd'rous, bloody, full of blame,
> Savage, extreme, rude, cruel, not to trust,
> Enjoy'd no sooner but despised straight,
> Past reason hunted, and no sooner had,
> Past reason hated as a swallowed bait
> On purpose laid to make the taker mad:
> Mad in pursuit and in possession so,
> Had, having, and in quest to have, extreme,
> A bliss in proof, and prov'd, [a] very woe,
> Before, a joy propos'd, behind, a dream.
> All this the world well knows, yet none knows well
> To shun the heaven that leads men to this hell.[23]

A hell, a waste, a dream that warps the mind and embitters the heart: even in situations where sexual consummation is expected, and approved, such as the situation in which Othello finds himself when alone with his new bride Desdemona, the very fact of sex can horrify and disgust.[24] Is human sexual desire the sign of our imperfection, as Augustine believed? Mani taught this, and his message stuck with Augustine even after he turned to orthodoxy. So did Marcion and any number of Gnostics, Shakers, and confused minds of all kinds. "Dualism at its most inveterate," writes John Bugge in *Virginitas,* has "sporadically" resurfaced, among the Cathars in twelfth- and thirteenth-century France, among various "pietistic and millenarian sects" setting up utopian and celibate settlements in the New World, the Shakers, the Rappites, the Koreshans, and the Sanctificationists, from New Lebanon, New York, to Sabbathday Lake, Maine, from Maryland to Florida and Ohio.[25] All lived in ways that early Gnostic communities would have recognized: most denied any significant distinction between women and men, and many believed that spiritual rebirth requires the abandonment of physical reproduction. Shakespeare may be a sexual pessimist. He is no Gnostic. The ropes of nature that tie humans to their carnal selves are permanent; we will not remake our creation by emptying out the toxins of desire from our lecherous bodies or freezing our appetites through a diet of chastity. But the very necessity that makes us return again and again to that expenditure of spirit pushes us again and again to revulsion, boredom, and shame. Enjoyment and disgust are swallowed in one draft.[26] Such is the case for all, noble and base alike.

Measure for Measure is an instructive case for the sexual pessimist. Its theme is the bait that, once swallowed, makes the drinker mad. Written for King James's second Christmas after inheriting the throne from Elizabeth, it represents a world where chastity incites lust and the state's sickness is understood solely through its failure to distinguish sexual virtue from sexual crime. Authority is not transcendent and infallible. It is abdicating, elusive, corrupted, and unclear. Liberty—that central moral value—is misunderstood as license. And all justice is collapsed into one form: repression of sex. Viennese government is governance via shame. The pimps and whores of Vienna make money out of human immoderation; the righteous elite conceal their lusts under a mask of cold continence. As in Plato's *Republic,* the measure of a polity's flourishing rests on its sexual practices. Social justice is read through the oblique glass of sexuality. What syphilis is to the body, injustice and misrule are to the state. Yet it would be absurd to expect that strict laws and prohibitions will repair the world thus contaminated. Claudio, a young and wellborn Viennese, is condemned to death for impregnating his betrothed. The bawds and procurers who keep the brothels full continue to operate. The infection of sex spreads through the city, tumbling the deputy ruler, Angelo, from his sanctimonious height, threatening the dedication to virginity of the young novice Isabella. Claudio contemplates the scene with bitterness. Far from restraint being our prudent procedure in matters of sex, the only restraint on the sexual liberty we indulge is death:

As surfeit is the father of much fast,
So every scope, by the immoderate use,
Turns to restraint. Our natures do pursue,
Like rats that raven down their proper bane,
A thirsty evil, and when we drink, we die.
(*MM*, 1.2.117–23)

In such society, the eunuch's plot fails to summon up the respect it might have hoped for. Yet the marriage plot, the alternative proposed by the Protestant Reformers, cannot so easily cure everything in this blighted garden. Social rituals and moral contracts do not go far enough in dispelling a skepticism toward sexual desire and the carnal body that Shakespeare's "diseased" husbands like Leontes and Othello are too quick to feel. Greenblatt mentions "the primal male nausea at the thought of the female body," which is "most fully articulated" by the mad king Lear:[27]

But to the girdle do the gods inherit,
Beneath is all the fiends': there's hell, there's darkness,
There is the sulphurous pit, burning, scalding,
Stench, consumption. Fie, fie, fie! Pah, pah!
Give me an ounce of civet, good apothecary,
Sweeten my imagination. (*King Lear*, 4.5.126–31)

Lear's view of female humanity from the waist down is shared, at least at moments, by those who feel themselves betrayed, by a Troilus or an Othello. The cynical Thersites in *Troilus and Cressida*, perhaps the most savage play among Shakespeare's investigations of love and honor, sums up the world of the heroes around Troy: "Lechery, lechery, still wars and lechery, nothing else holds fashion. . . . Yet in a sort lechery eats itself" (*Troilus and Cressida*, 5.2.197–98, 5.4.34). Angelic chastity may be an illusion, and Troilus's faith in his Cressida is misplaced, but the lascivious produce nothing else but disgust, as the community recoils. Discord in the city is frequently represented by the free running of sexual underworlds and dysfunction at the top by sexual distrust and violence. The very thought of infidelity is enough to drive the great ones like Othello, Posthumus, or Leontes mad; the "ocular proof" of it in Cressida causes Troilus's "madness of discourse" (*Troilus and Cressida*, 5.2.145). There seems little virginity can do to remedy the situation.

In Shakespeare, the question of lawful and unlawful sexuality is everywhere, pressuring the comedies and the tragedies, the sonnets and the long poems like *Venus and Adonis*, *The Rape of Lucrece*, and *The Phoenix and Turtle*. Before it does anything else, Shakespearean sex raises a question of judgment. How can we distinguish the good of sex from the bad, legitimacy from crime, fidelity from faithfulness? Some would say that the answer is ready at hand and the ambiguities exaggerated. Society has sanctioned marriage. The community is invited to celebrate this single, lawful bond, one that snatches sex from the hands of anarchy and ushers reproductive energies into their appropriate, fruitful channels. But can a contract do that much? Hamlet famously did not believe that. If women are monsters of lust and vanity, and men are just as whorish, how could marriage turn a sow's ear into a silk purse?

> I have heard of your paintings, too, well enough. God hath given you one face, and you make yourself another. You jig, you amble, and you lisp, and nickname God's creatures, and make your wantonness your ignorance. Go to, I'll no more on't: it hath made me mad. I say, we will have no more marriages. (*Hamlet*, 3.1.145–50)

Can marriage turn disorder to order, shut out the demons of appetite and will, contain the trickery of the female, erase taboo, and banish obsession? Can the institution of marriage silence the doubts about carnality which every puritan has reinvented, every doubting husband suffered from, every policeman of desire rediscovered? Is there any sexual morality powerful enough to cure the "intemperate surfeit" that comes with the erotic disease (*The Two Noble Kinsmen*, 4.3.67)? Once the serpent has awakened Eve and Adam from their childlike slumbers, what could bring peace to the garden again?

The church's flight toward consecrated virginity was one response to the problem posed by sex. Marriage, more popular and more traditional, was another. Stanley Cavell, who has studied Shakespearean marriage with great care, notes that "Shakespeare's investigation of marriage has no end."[28] The comedies turn on marriages thought about, pursued, evaded, and celebrated, on couples who mistake one another and, with luck, get it right. The tragedies are even more comprehensively stirred by the problems of marriage, jealousy, doubt, or obsession. When the comic temper reigns, marriage is allowed to be a resolution, and absurdity or confusion dissolve, as do dreams, onto thin air. There may be real danger within the precincts of authority and normalcy. Usurpation and treachery may threaten legitimate rule and sanctioned inheritance, as they do in *The Tempest* or *As You Like It*, when brother displaces brother and theft displaces established ownership. And then there arises, as if by magic, a counterforce to the malicious intentions that bring disorder to the state and enmity to the family. This is comedy's credo: love between the sexes, no matter how breathlessly or frivolously inspired, can put nature back on its feet and break the spell of discord. As long as Shakespeare chooses to indulge this bit of hocus-pocus, his comedies can succeed in convincing us that sex is not the enemy, that Aphrodite can be tamed.

But a tame Aphrodite makes a wild Artemis less important. Shakespeare's poetry has little room for the marvels of the celibate life. What future in his world for the converts to continence, the otherworldly eunuchs, those studying a map to the angelic life? *Measure for Measure* reflects on the sanctified virtue of chastity, and its conclusions are discouraging. A puritan like Angelo, "a man of stricture and firm abstinence" (*MM*, 1.3.12), "whose blood is very snow-broth," and who "never feels the wanton stings and motions of the sense" (*MM*, 1.4.56–58) is invited to have his ascetic virtue tested by being given the jurisdiction of the sexually intemperate city of Vienna. Imposing an impossibly rigid rule against all laxity, deviance, and unrestrained sexuality, Angelo is undone by his own hypocrisy.[29] Aroused by the very purity his rule is supposed to protect, Angelo tries to force the chaste Isabella to serve his lusts. If the legitimacy of authority rests on the preservation of virtue, as the play starts off by asserting, then the city is in poor hands. The problem for Vienna, it appears, is not "liberty" but weak and evasive rulers, inspired to displace their failures onto a demonized sexual underclass and a population that can be cowed into guilt and shame. Good government needs better resources. But those resources will not be religious ones.

What is the place, finally, of the saint in the city? Shakespeare is grudging. Those who claim to opt for abstinence—for example, the noblemen in *Love's Labour's Lost* or Isabella in *Measure for Measure* here—find their aspirations frustrated. And Vincentio, the duke who abdicates in favor of the disastrous deputy Angelo, is playing a dubious game with other people's lives when he chooses withdrawal and noninvolvement, claiming to love "the life removed" and to be free from any "dribbling dart of love" (*MM*, 1.3.7–8, 1.3.1–3). Pretending to be a friar, the duke can fix the mess he has created only by turning into a master manipulator and pushing his pawns through their paces. Nor is Isabella any better placed to improve the condition of the community. Renouncing the world and marriage, aspiring to the nun's spiritual union with a heavenly lover, she is pushed into returning to the city on the last day before she finally takes the veil.

By all rights Isabella should exercise a compelling moral authority. Lucio, an inveterate abuser of women, confesses himself unable to play with her as he would normally "play with all virgins so," because she is in his eyes "a thing enskied, and sainted," by "her renouncement an immortal spirit" (*MM*, 1.4.33–36). If the laws of romance applied, Isabella's purity would be a knockdown argument, softening the hearts of the strictest of judges, compelling sympathy when she makes the case to Angelo to spare her brother's life. Her brother is optimistic: "Bid her make friends with the strict deputy," he asks his friend Lucio. "In her youth there is a prone and speechless dialect such as move men" (*MM*, 1.2.168–71). Isabella herself acknowledges a confidence in the power of her holiness: I will bribe you, she boasts to Angelo, with gifts from heaven, prayers from "fasting maids, whose minds are dedicate to nothing temporal" (*MM*, 2.2.158–59).

Her resolute virtue, as it happens, has the opposite effect. Angelo is a tough case. Unusual for a male in Vienna, he is immune to the easy pleasures of the whorehouse, and he is enough of a brute to reject a suitable wife for the absence of a dowry. His vulnerabilities lie elsewhere, as he discovers from the arousing presence of this "saint." What could be more attractive, Angelo finds, than the opportunity to "raze the sanctuary, and pitch our evils there?" This fall into lust is unexpected and cannot be the fault of such a strict and "precise" character. Surely it is the devil, baiting his hook with saints "to catch a saint" (*MM*, 2.2.175–86), as it is Isabella's holy innocence rather than ordinary female sensuality that so maddens Angelo.

Spenser would have drawn quite a different moral from Angelo's dilemma. In the world of the *Faerie Queene*, the lecherous are thwarted by the heroic chastity of Britomart or Belphoebe; they are blocked from succeeding with the rapes and violations they dream of. But Shakespeare's eloquent and pious novice pushes provocation too far. The more she resists, the more dishonorable are the plots Angelo devises. Even while admitting his own forbidden lust, he fails to retract his condemnation of Claudio. The saint's intervention, if anything, made things worse. In the end, bloodshed is averted, and the sexual assault the play permits is stripped of its horror, but only by a heavy-handed exercise of authority, whereby the returned duke steps in to defeat Angelo and, by a series of implausible tricks, to restore Claudio. So what was achieved by Isabella's famous virginity? And what sort of comment was her creator making about his former sovereign?

The Elizabethan writer who appears immune to the Virgin Queen's cult of chastity is the only one whose fame eclipses hers. Indeed if Elizabeth had depended on Shakespeare for servicing her mysteries, her temple would have fared no better than did Diana's Temple at Ephesus at the mercy of the iconoclastic attentions of Saint Paul and his followers. Proud and austere chastity does not get good press in Shakespeare. The other face of sexual virtue—the desire to shine and be approved in the eyes of others—is something he is much more willing to place before our eyes. Playing the paragon comes with risks. As many who seek honor and stature discover, these are capricious commodities. Reputation is a prize too fickle to be held securely even by the most adept of players. There is plenty to be said about how the "part" of virtue is played, how it bewitches and cheats those who want its rewards. A reputation for chastity, the prize for which "good" women must compete, is the most treacherous of all these lures. You can be as spotless as a Desdemona or an Imogen; yet the "proof" that you require is constantly being devalued, debased, forged, and denied. Heroes can slide and still come back, their glory only temporarily in shadow. (Hercules and Achilles survived a period in dresses, sewing with the other ladies.) Saints climb even higher on the ladder of grace if they dig themselves out of the pit of degradation and despair. Such second acts are unavailable to women. Once doubted, the chastity of a woman is almost impossible to restore.[30] How can the proud claim of the virgin survive this world of whispers and shadows, corruption and innuendo?

To gamble on the reputation of the virtuous is a game only for the reckless in Shakespeare. Yet the possibility of such vindication—the end for which Lucrece had to die, the vindication which Hermione only just receives, and Hero wins only by feigning her own death—is the primal fantasy of all too many chastity plots. If the pure virgin is to matter, her body must be as good as her word. She claims to stand for truth in a world of ambiguity and equivocation. And that improbable desire for epistemic certitude, for a knockdown answer to the question posed by the chastity test, is connected to the extravagant ambition which most other practices of virtue, even the most perfectionist, only gesture at. That is the quest to make truth speak in the body, to manifest the sacred through the flesh, to display a pristine sign of the spirit in the shape of matter itself. That, finally, is the desire the chastity plot never wants to give up. In a world of relativity and approximation, the chastity plot contends that there is something that is purely and entirely itself.

It is not hard to see why such an ambition would appeal to a sovereign, especially one with the particular strengths and weakness of Elizabeth. All princes need to summon up the mysteries of kingship, the smoke and mirrors that allow authority to dazzle those who are willing to be dazzled: Elizabeth's dependence on such smoke and mirrors was simply larger than most. Inheriting the mantle of the pure and inviolable maid, Elizabeth found a way to defy convention and to keep criticism (almost) under wraps. She would be the impossible heroine of her own courtly romance. Her laureate Spenser understood clearly what was required. Absolute in her self-possession, militant in her repudiation of the claims of love and dependence, here was a virgin paragon in the romance tradition. In the long-running play she wrote (with a lot of expert help), Elizabeth could provide a noble and heroic spectacle, stunning mere men into submission and embarrassing mere women by the comparison. The subject, as Spenser saw, was an enchanting one, even if the reality had a few rough spots. Offering his epic as a political tool for his royal mistress, Spenser revived the ideals of the romance tradition in a Protestant climate. He obliged his poetry to live with the contradictions, hoping that the oxymoron of married chastity would save both romance and realism, eternity and mutability. Shakespeare, his near contemporary, was more skeptical.

Sexual purity, like any moral absolute, promises more than it can deliver. With Shakespeare, we fall into an imperfect world, and that is where we belong. Radical autonomy would leave us on an island, talking only to ourselves. And even the cloister hears about the upheaval outside its walls. Once we leave Eden, once we have stopped being children in a fantasy pastoral or "green world," there is no protected space, no life that is not exposed to others, no body that succeeds in remaining intact. To act is to be acted upon: hence the rightness of Hegel's scorn—innocence is for the inhabitants of zoos. Dismantling the argument for purity is not Shakespeare's main objective, and he is happy enough to borrow platitudes about the magical reconciliations performed for romance by maidens such as Marina, Miranda, Perdita, or Helena. But neither history nor drama can depend on these fragile beings. Virginity does not redeem. Unlucky are those who expect the world to be saved by chastity.

The Rape of Clarissa: The Maiden's Plot Expires

For those who care about literature, the cruelest blow to chastity's fond dream can be dated precisely. The injury happened in the middle of the eighteenth century, and in a novel. During the night of June 12, after six months of the heroine's harassment, confinement, and resistance, Robert Lovelace raped Clarissa Harlowe. She was unconscious at the time, drugged by her persecutor and his accomplices. On September 21 of the same year, she died. Both Clarissa and Lovelace are characters in Samuel Richardson's epistolary novel of 1747–1748. Their deadly but fictional combat is the most important event in the history of modern chastity. Chastity could not save Clarissa; it could not abash her tormentor; it could not convince a skeptical world that this exemplary and scrupulous young lady was not, in fact, a corrupted and devious manipulator. The secret of the romance of "virgin-baiting," as Northrop Frye expressed it—the serious message within its sometimes implausible or melodramatic situations, all the ruses and stratagems that entrap the naïve and pit them against their demonic antagonists—is that integrity needs to be imagined, even if it can never establish itself in any personal form.[31] Integrity is what Clarissa values above all. Too bad that she has to subject herself to rape and will herself into an early grave to prove it, to triumph over all, "by virtue only of her innocence." The story of Clarissa is told in skeleton form by her antagonist, the man who hounds and torments her and in his perverse way loves her:

> But here is Miss Harlowe, virtuous, noble, wise, pious, unhappily insnared by the vows and oaths of a vile Rake, whom she believes to be a man of honour: And, being ill used by her friends for his sake, is in a manner forced to throw herself upon his protection; who, in order to obtain her confidence, never scruples the deepest and most solemn protestations of honour. After a series of plots and contrivances, all baffled by her virtue and vigilance, he basely has recourse to the vilest of arts, and, to rob her of her honour, is forced first to rob her of her senses. Unable to bring her, notwithstanding, to his ungenerous views of cohabitation, she awes him in the very entrance of a fresh act of premeditated guilt, in presence of the most abandoned of women, assembled to assist his cursed purpose; triumphs over them all, by virtue only of her innocence; and escapes from the vile hands he had put her into: Nobly, not franticly, resents: Refuses to see, or to marry the wretch; who, repenting his usage of so divine a creature, would fain move her to forgive his baseness, and make him her husband.[32]

Clarissa is devout, self-monitoring, and upright. She is proof against the gallantry of a well-spoken and well-presented seducer. In this she matches the heroism of the tradition's virgin martyrs and female warriors of virtue. Although she is, as Lovelace puts it, "insnared," her soul never consents to his designs. She could, at a stretch, be compared to Thecla and Agnes, and all the martyrs who gave their inviolate bodies to death in the cause of sanctity. Not a Catholic but a devout Anglican whose everyday reading matter includes devotional tracts and who as a girl corresponded with Anglican divines, Clarissa had little option except to await the fulfillment of her social role by being married off to a suitor acceptable to her family.[33] There was no Paul to entice her into a life of ascetic adventure. Clarissa was raised in a culture where feminine modesty and bodily integrity were valued for secular rather than religious reasons. The palm of martyrdom and the crown of virginity are anachronistic ideals she is supposed to read about and then forget. Her role in life as in the history of the novel should have been to launch—at a higher level—the career of the sentimental virgin. Clarissa is the "pure woman" without the simpering, the stupidity, and the "blankness of innocence" that so often are taken to be the necessary signifiers (and shields) of that feminine purity.[34] As we shall see, the cult of propriety that idealized the ladylike virtues of modesty, delicacy, and tractability saw itself as fashioning a remarkable moral authority for the good and faithful woman—but only if her desires were so firmly in check as to be nonexistent. To the indignant eye of Mary Wollstonecraft, well aware of the uses to which an erotic exemplar like Clarissa had been put, the cult of femininity pretends to respect women while it in fact despises them. Admiring them only for "artificial graces," passivity, and self-doubt, it makes impossible their pursuit of a virtuous life, not to speak of the sort of active and effective life desired by a woman as intelligent as Clarissa. The pure woman of sentimental fiction and the conduct books' recommendation exists only to inspire male desire.[35] Denied liberty, rationality and education, what can she be but an empty mirror containing nothing of itself, a "cipher" as Clarissa discovers with pain?[36]

Because she is raped and dies, insisting that the sanctity of her body be respected in the grave as it hadn't been on earth (she forbids the dissection of her corpse), Clarissa provides a model of the pure woman and the "Proper Lady" who cannot readily be satirized. She exists between two worlds. On the one hand, she belongs to the spiritual world and there (as her creator believed) she should blaze forth as a saint, even if an exceptionally attractive and well-dressed one. On the other hand, she belongs to the secular or temporal one, the world of virgins on the marriage market, where Samuel Johnson's assurances about chastity, property, and inheritance as the conditions of woman's value are unquestionable, at least for the immediate future. Her tragedy, her anachronistic "opacity," as Terry Castle puts it, is that she is explicable in neither.[37] In *Clarissa,* the chastity plot finds neither vindication nor supersession. It is prolonged, teased out, and its pleasures and pains exhaustively cataloged, but its logic has been fatally shaken. The maiden's plot would continue and flourish in Clarissa's century and the next. But her history is greater than it—and more ambivalent. *Clarissa,* writes Corrinne Harol, "is not a novel of triumphant or defeated female virtue; nor is it the hagiography of a saint, who is martyred for her virginity. . . . It is a novel about the conflict of those narratives . . . the interaction of these plots makes *Clarissa* anachronistic to the eighteenth century on two levels."[38]

Just as the age of the maiden's plot was beginning its most vigorous and ideologically influential moment, Clarissa appeared to spread a doubt no thoughtful observer could ignore. What good is female virtue—what good, indeed, is that purity and chastity without which no respectable woman could hope to be admired, even tolerated? Everyone demanded it, yet the virgin's perfection can be as poisonous to herself as it is confusing to others. The cultural work of refining and legitimating the middle class's still relatively recent seizure of ideological authority was supposed to be assigned to her. But the very sexual probity for which she was honored, even worshipped, was the object of skepticism, mockery, and assault. As Clarissa discovers, nothing in her inner soul can verify an integrity invisible to the public world, scorned and disbelieved by her own family, and yet essential to her very being. She may know, even after her rape, that she has not succumbed to sexual corruption. But that is not something she, or anyone else, can prove.

At the start of her story, before Lovelace's "plots and contrivances" have done their work of deceiving, entrapping, and abasing her, Clarissa is widely acknowledged to be a paragon, a model and pattern for all young ladies. Clarissa aspires to excellence and has every reason to pride herself on her achievement. Chastity is just one of her virtues. Good household management, learning and discretion, charity and piety, all these are also what distinguish her.

For all her exceptional qualities, Clarissa fails to save herself from being drugged and raped while she is her tormentor's prisoner in a London brothel. Yet, as Lovelace admits and all her detractors end by acknowledging, Clarissa is perfect, an angel in a world of mere women, her purity brutally tested and equal to the test, if not sufficient to keep her alive. The plots around Clarissa are multiple. Her value as heiress, paragon of virtue, and beauty provides her envious relatives with enough reason to plot against her happiness and conspire to crush her spirit. Clarissa comes from a rich and social-climbing family. They want to increase their wealth by marrying Clarissa to a repulsive suitor who promises to bring new estates into the Harlowe grasp, a plot that will have the additional advantage for this unaccountably mean-spirited family of undermining their exceptional relative's dignity and pride. Their opponent, a notorious libertine, better born and connected than the Harlowes, is fixated on a rival plot. Robert Lovelace wants to make Clarissa one of his conquests, a prize all the more desirable because of her virtue, modesty, and fame. Plotting is the rake's genius and his favored occupation: plots, intrigues, contrivances, stratagems, expedients and inventions are his reason for living, his art and his study. If he gives them up, he worries, he will be but a "common man." The bourgeois family plots only reactively. Lovelace desires a more diabolical outcome: to reduce her to a "woman," someone under his power, made of common clay rather than noble virtue. Clarissa believes she does not plot at all. She enjoys the admiration she inspires for the quality of her character and person, and although her mortal self is destroyed by the rapist's relentless persecution, her will remains inviolate, her right to admiration finally affirmed. But enjoying admiration is a dangerous pleasure for one like Clarissa, whose value is her chastity and whose glory is her modesty. How can such a recessive quality be made available to public knowledge? Wouldn't its very presence, as something on display, contradict its nature? What can make a manifestation of something that thrives on refusing manifestation?

Chastity in the Christian tradition is a virtue of the soul. In the secular tradition it is the honor of the female sex, precious to their families and spouses as much as to themselves: hence its worth is social and exists on the borderline between private and public, asserted and concealed. Some scholars who have thought about the problem here suggest that there are two chastities: one religious, one political. It may be that it was one of Richardson's first readers who introduced the distinction, as Michael McKeon suggests. The English kinship system, he writes in *The Origins of the English Novel, 1600–1740*, stresses "the injunction of female chastity," an injunction that was "overdetermined":

> Patrilineal culture required chastity so as to ensure the direct transmission of the inheritance; Christian culture required it not only as a moral virtue but also to encourage, over all competing kinship ties, the "spiritual" kinship of the Church. . . . As a contemporary critic of Samuel Richardson put it, there are two species of chastity, "political" and "religious." The influence of the first derives from the fact that "in all societies there are families, inheritances, and distinctions of ranks and orders. To keep these separate and distinct, to prevent them from falling into confusion . . . the chastity and continence of women are absolutely and indispensably necessary." Religious chastity was first "recommended and enforced" by Jesus Christ and his disciples. But the institutional consequences of strict continence "were pernicious to the publick good, they discouraged marriage, and established that ecclesiastical tyranny, under which all Europe groaned before the reformation and the resurrection of letters."[39]

Clarissa was Samuel Richardson's second attempt at a chastity plot. The author had been stung by the reaction to his novel *Pamela, or Virtue Rewarded* (1740), the story of a maidservant's success in reforming and marrying her libertine master. Pamela Andrews fought to preserve her virginity and won. Her virtue was generously rewarded. The gentry could do no more than surrender in the face of the working-class maiden's moral stamina. Mr. B, a study in arrogance and single-minded lust, gratefully recognizes Pamela's superiority in character and mind. To the lower-middle-class Richardson, such an acknowledgment proved the necessity and validity of a cultural correction. The dubious morals of literature and the aristocracy required a major cleanup, a conversion achieved through the sexual courage of the pretty Pamela, assisted by no one and nothing except her own prudence, self-possession, and cunning. The intact body of an insignificant young woman from the upright lower classes was proof of a moral revolution. But readers, who loved the novel, still mocked its message.

In *Pamela* Richardson depicted a war between the classes. In their uncomfortable relations, ruled by inequalities of money, respect, and education, the powerful and the powerless had little in common. Richardson noticed that sex was one thing they shared. But they differed greatly in the dangers to which sex exposed them. A servant had little hope of resisting the sexual overtures of her "betters." Yet she could only be ruined by her surrender, while the predator—shielded by class privilege—risked nothing. Richardson was determined to challenge this situation. Could chastity be the route by which a subordinate class reversed a system designed to keep them in thrall? That, crudely speaking, was Richardson's gamble. Sexual virtue was a commodity whose value depended on its scarcity. However, when he designed the scenario that would justify the moral reversal he so tenderly wished to perform, his aspirations met an obstacle he found most uncomfortable. Skeptical readers saw another plot in Pamela's struggle against co-option. The fifteen-year-old domestic servant, protected by no one, understood that her only negotiating power was the sexual opportunity she could hold back or deliver. She was not a principled martyr but a rational calculator. And marrying the man who had tried again and again to rape her sent an ambiguous message to the advocates of female purity. Or so Richardson's readers noted. Their reaction threatened to debase the virtue the novelist wanted the world to admire.

In returning in *Clarissa* to the problem he had made for himself, Richardson decided that his next exemplary heroine would neither succeed in preserving her virginity nor find happiness in the love of those who sought to corrupt it. Clarissa was also a paragon. Unlike Pamela, she was an heiress, much admired, exquisitely dressed, learned and full of maxims, famous for her virtue and good sense. Richardson's revised champion of chastity would be the ornament of a rich family, a goddess and a saint, whose superiority was beyond doubt. Why, then, must she be tortured and humiliated?

Clarissa is a painful book to read, and not just because of its extreme length. The narrative, told in letters between Lovelace and his friend Belford, Clarissa and her friend Anna Howe, and a few others, covers less than a year: January 10 to December 18. The locations are few: Clarissa's family estate in the country, where she is subjected to a claustrophobic and humiliating restraint; the various London houses Lovelace hides her in, including a brothel; her final refuge in a poor family's rooms in Covent Garden. The heroine's situation is harrowing. She is imprisoned, trapped, deceived, and raped. Refusing to marry Lovelace, who is the man who has disgraced her, and himself, she flees into an early death. She can hope for no mercy from her mercenary family who are jealous of her independent wealth, nor from her supposed suitor. The rake Lovelace is an aristocrat in love with plots. Intrigue is his way of playing with those he considers his inferiors. And everyone in the world is his inferior, in his view, until he meets the principled Clarissa. Because she is difficult to win, she is the one he wants: her innocence is his stimulus, her pride in her chastity the provocation he cannot resist. The chastity plot presented by *Clarissa* is one of the most familiar in literature's supply: sexual purity attracts violation; if it enhances social and cultural value, it also invites defilement and suspicion. Virgins may be beloved by heaven. On earth they are prey. It is not only master manipulators like Lovelace who admit to feeling keen pleasure less from the sexual act than from the thrill of robbing the unwilling and putting the morally upright to shame. Rakes love virgins, Lovelace repeats on many occasions, just as wolves love little lambs. Their fascination with outraged modesty and their steady commitment to ruining reputations are proof of their interest. And if there should be that anomaly, the attractive woman who never wavers and holds out through all assaults and temptations, she may not be a woman at all.

If Elizabeth was the last of her line, so was Clarissa. "Clarissa," writes Corrinne Harol in her study of *Enlightened Virginity in Eighteenth-Century Literature*, "is, quite literally, the end of her line … unique and inimitable.… On the one hand, *Clarissa* looks far backward, to a patriarchy based in authority and obedience and to a religious model of virginity based in transcendence. On the other hand, it looks forward to feminist critiques of eighteenth-century ideas about female sexuality and its importance to property and inheritance."[40]

Chastity enjoyed a long career. Exalted in some contexts, compromised in others, its history overlapped with the West's thinking about women. Civilizations rose and fell; cities grew, fought, and festered; needs created opportunities, and scarcity created profit; markets chased consumers, and producers chased products. In all this the contribution of women remained essential. For how else were societies to reproduce themselves except through the bodies of women? Sexual appetites can be satisfied in a number of ways, not all dependent on the participation of females and not all dependent on the participation of human beings. But family names and family identities relied on this singular property, the guarantee of legitimacy through the chastity of women. And this same elusive virtue—female honor, female purity, the deliverance of an unsullied body to the marital bed—was intricately confused with another, more substantial virtue: the eunuch's proud renunciation of sensual weakness and family entanglements, a virtue obviously not restricted to one gender.

With the death of Clarissa, the maiden's plot lost its last chance to absorb the strange sublimity of the eunuch's plot. The eunuch's sacrifice was sanctioned by an institutional setting and also by a grand narrative of Fall and salvation, corruption and recovery. As long as the community of Christians saw themselves as pilgrims on this earth, tethered to a higher calling, destined to escape their bodily confines and, if possible, join the angels, the ideal of chastity could symbolize a kind of moral integrity that tempted the best and the boldest, or at least chastened the repentant followers of the flesh. Augustine looked to chastity for a release from his nagging sensual appetites; Paul believed those in a hurry for the next world would be happy to be bothered no longer with the demands of marriage and sexual cohabitation; Gregory of Nyssa believed consecrated virginity could repair the defacement of the divine image originally intended as our own, and Methodius agreed. But with the European Reformation, the prestige of chastity suffered a blow, and Clarissa's melancholy vindication—she dies acclaimed as a saint and heroine—failed to convince her eighteenth-century readers, many of whom were sorry she didn't get to marry her rapist.

Two types of integrity have figured so far in this study; at various times each dominated the ways societies from Rome to London imagined sexual ethics. The religious version of excellence, the cloistered or otherworldly ideal, declined in tandem with changes in Christian practice and belief. Its decline was hastened by a more full-blooded embrace of the secular as competent to generate its own code of values. In Protestant countries, concern for sexual respectability continued to wield its own authority. The honorable and discreet woman fulfilled her duties in a spirit of piety and obedience; those duties included sexual ones. Men who wanted to be known for their integrity avoided profligacy, debauchery, and shame. The ideal was a good life on earth, a life where conduct and conscience agreed, and such a life could be presented openly to the public and the Lord. Expectation of an eschatological reversal of earthly norms and values did not need to figure in the imagining of sexual morality. With holiness transferred from the otherworldly to the this-worldly, the eunuch ceased to play an inspiring role, and even virginity was important mainly as an indicator of careful behavior to come, in the "holy household." But even in the post-Tridentine Catholic world, it was hard to get excited about the idea of the committed celibate as a paragon of heroic achievement, sacrificial and sublime.

I began this book with two portraits, Thecla and Pamela, saint and maiden. One indignantly rebuffs all offers of sexual love, honorable and dishonorable; the other uses her sexual fastidiousness as a tease and a pedagogical device, coaxing her libertine master into middle-class respectability. Both are paragons of virtue—to their fans, at any rate. Their popularity raises questions I continue to find interesting: What is the value of virtue? How does virtue save the world? How did women's chastity manage to fascinate, annoy, and trouble so many people? Is it truly a "profoundly interesting subject" for a female scholar, as Virginia Woolf proposed in *A Room of One's Own*?[41] Woolf, I believe, was not expecting a serious answer. For her we must look to the makeup of men, not women, if we are to understand the history of chastity's "immense power" and the "social stigma exerted on its behalf." Male desire to own a woman's mind and body, to reserve it for private and personal use, is one explanation Woolf considers; male anxiety about the limits of knowledge overall could be another motive. The toxic doubt about female fidelity which Shakespeare gives to Othello, Leontes, Posthumus, and, to stretch a point, Hamlet and Lear, is a version of the epistemological anxiety that has rattled skeptics and idealists as long as philosophers have wondered whether the appearances we see are any indication of the truth we do not see. This is a point the American philosopher Stanley Cavell has made, and its relevance to the chastity plot is, I hope, clear. Blaise Pascal also noticed the problem: man is neither angel nor beast, and the misfortune is that he who would act the angel acts the beast.[42]

"Perfectionism" is one name of a disease for which "misanthropy" is another name. Both have a history of attracting misogynists. The angelic vocation I have tried to track in the writings and images of Christian thinkers from Paul to the Renaissance haunts the discourse of sexual virtue and, by extension, the reputation and opportunities of women. Yet female chastity, while clearly an obsessive concern for most who have held forth about sexual virtue, is not the whole picture. Christianity's identification of spiritual aspiration and sexual renunciation was a remarkable experiment in changing the template of human possibility. And that experiment was, from the start, indifferent to gender distinctions; indeed, one of its objectives was to suggest to the Creator that the difference between the sexes was an accident and a mistake, one that he must have added in an absentminded moment, much like the establishment of the British Empire. The radical passion for renunciation would have ended in a world without procreation or increase, one with neither male nor female.

That did not happen. The eunuch's plot was, all things considered, unrealistic. Thecla is radiant; her single-minded purity turns wild beasts into friends and detractors into disciples. Yet her power works best in isolated acts of defiance and resistance. Sublime chastity finds its proper home in a cave. Today people who would have been saints in the past can find themselves shunned as hysterics. Secular society did better with the maiden's plot: it was effective in brokering compromises between idealism and accommodation. Sentimental conceptions of marriage, when they arrived, continued the work: making marriage into a romance was one way courtly attempts to sublimate the erotic could survive in a more pragmatic climate. Treating marriage as a moral discipline, as the Puritans did, was another fruitful spin on the marriage plot, one that transferred some of the intensity of the chapel into the private spaces of the family home.

My position is less accommodating. I believe that the two genres—chastity plots and marriage plots—can only unhappily be forced to cohabit. Clarissa Harlowe's readers wanted to see her married to her dashing persecutor, her virtue and integrity vindicated by the surrender of insolence at the feet of humility, deception cowed by sincerity. Clarissa had no such illusions. With her the plot comes to an end. If sexual ethics have any purchase in the age of #MeToo, we will need other ideals than that of chastity and other models for sexual flourishing than the idea of marriage. It is time for another plot.

The city had no place for the saint. This was Clarissa's sad discovery. Given the nonarrival of the millennium, moral perfectionism and human flourishing remained separate, locked in their mutual shunning (although political utopians in the socialist movements of the nineteenth century hoped otherwise). The chastity plot in its Christian and triumphalist mode aspired to win on the plane of the earth what heaven prefigures. For the eunuch, reality as we know it can be changed—returned to the prelapsarian script—if we give back the sexual permission our Fall necessitated. The social order could be turned upside down, added the radicals of the Middle Ages inflamed by millenarian prophecies: all on earth would be brothers and sisters, holding everything in common, equal in a shared struggle against the hosts of the Antichrist.[43] The eunuch's idea of what sexual ethics requires, we have to admit, was not widely shared by the moralists whose opinion about social and sexual matters played a major role in shaping the marriage plots of the eighteenth and nineteenth centuries. Christian virtue was sufficiently exercised by the duties and trials of everyday life. Marriage, not celibacy, took over as the testing ground of moral and social worth.

What glory, then, for the virgin? If she survives the ordeals of courtship, the modern virgin is folded into a plot that claims to respect her at the price of marginalizing her. While Clarissa suffers, Pamela triumphs. What she has learned from her successful resistance to sexual disgrace and to any union with Mr. B short of a proper, legitimate, and publicly sanctioned marriage is that her moral education will continue after the ceremony is over. It is as a wife that she enjoys whatever power she has to awaken the spiritual lives of others, and that power is wholly dependent on her husband's pleasure. Her piety, constancy, prudence, and sheer energy will be redirected into the domestic sphere where her "soulful interiority" has the chance to shine, no longer (as before) confined to the written word.[44] Yet after all, what is she, the socially climbing Mrs. B? An ornament to a man whose morals horrified her, a token of toleration in a snobbish little community that can't wait for her feet of clay to show. Richardson's first attempt at glorifying sexual virtue backfired—the virgin marries and begins to bore us—but his second would make no such mistake. A purity proof against any and all violation, resistant to calumny and suspicion, this is not a quality available to women in the world, no matter how carefully monitored or self-controlled. Social seclusion is no guarantee, as many bawdy tales of medieval nuns assumed or pretended. Even if pregnancy might be admitted as a reliable testimony to the loss of feminine honor, what form of evidence can certify a virgin's status? Legends about the skeptical Salomé's testing of the virginity of Mary, just after the young woman betrothed to the elderly Joseph had given birth to the Son of God, make a point of revealing that even parturition cannot be taken as knockdown ratification of a woman's fall. The search for truth in the body of a female virgin, together with the strange set of myths that have grown up around the idea of a membrane that closes and secures the inner vessel that is a woman's purity, was doomed to fail. But something else replaced the theory of the hymen as the physical sign of a mystery within. That "something else" was the cult of pure womanhood.

The Cult of Pure Womanhood

> Purity of mind, or that genuine delicacy, which is the only virtuous support of chastity, is near akin to that refinement of humanity, which never resides in any but cultivated minds. It is something nobler than

> innocence, it is the delicacy of reflection, and not the coyness of ignorance. The reserve of reason, which, like habitual cleanliness, is seldom seen in any great degree, unless the soul is active, may easily be distinguished from rustic shyness or wanton skittishness: and, so far from being incompatible with knowledge, it is its fairest fruit.
>
> MARY WOLLSTONECRAFT[45]

The nineteenth century produced a variation on the chastity plot with a genius all its own. What this variation was has been the topic of much debate among historians of sex and gender, and few have made as much of a splash about it as did Thomas Laqueur when he suggested, in his 1990 volume *Making Sex: Body and Gender from the Greeks to Freud*, that "sometime in the eighteenth century, sex as we know it was invented."[46] It had arrived, a two-sexed world, males and females as contrasted as if they came from different species, or different planets. This was not, Laqueur insists, the fruit of science's careful self-correcting or the result of painstaking observation. It was politics, and it was culture. A social relation—that of woman to man—was redefined, he argues, as a differential relation of bodies: reproductive bodies, physiologically complicated and mysterious bodies, bodies that bore more meaning than they had ever done before.

Biology jumped into the space theology and mythology used to occupy. And biology, together with anatomy and a curious kind of chemistry that eventually became identified with hormones, was newly entrusted with the power to define women. In this "grand effort to discover the anatomical and physiological characteristics that distinguished men from women," Nancy Cott observes, experts both moral and medical came to a conclusion that would have surprised Ovid: "women were passionless," by nature rather than by education or coercion.[47] Laqueur paraphrases in his book the new knowledge about the special qualities of women: "They possessed to an extraordinary degree, far more than men, the capacity to control the bestial, irrational and potentially destructive fury of sexual pleasure."[48] Havelock Ellis, doctor and social reformer, investigating "the psychology of sex" for his book of 1897, was less persuaded than his contemporaries. Ellis saw no reason to believe that sexual feelings were any less active in women than in men. The supposed "sexual anaesthesia" of women was in fact only present in a small minority suffering from some disorder of sexual or general health. Women did indeed choose, according to their readiness for sex, to defer or delay the approaches of the male, but that apparent modesty, or coquetry, does not arise from passionlessness but is a function of the periodicity of sexual desire. Why, then, the fuss over female chastity? Ellis is sure its origin is the jealousy of men who consider themselves owners of those women and who believe their property rights threatened by the imagined or real interest of other men: "If a woman's chastity is the property of another person, it is essential that a woman be modest in order that men may not be tempted to incur the penalties involved by the infringement of property rights."[49]

Modesty in women, on the other hand, was something Ellis looked on with rather more appreciation. It comes out of a fear or inhibition associated with sexual bodily parts and actions, he asserted, and as such is highly attractive to modern men, who find themselves unable to feel attracted to women who lack all trace of this appealing characteristic.[50] If females are responsible for saying no or "wait," these impulses to conceal and retire are necessary tools in the organization of sexuality—both to keep it alive and to keep it from disintegrating into some shapeless free-for-all. Further, in a development only partly acknowledged by the moralists and pundits who argued for feminine asexuality, the characterization of women as passionless served the long-term interest of their greater share in education and professional life: if they were indeed less carnal, more moral, more self-controlled, all the more reason for them to be allowed into those significant public arenas that had been closed off to them on the grounds of their inferiority.[51] A modest and chaste woman, as Mary Wollstonecraft insisted, is also a rational woman. Anatomy, in this special case, served the needs of culture. Society had to be defended from the unrestrained lusts of men, who (exempt from the danger of pregnancy) had no natural reasons to curb their urgent desires. Fortunately for all (though perhaps not for women), a number of experts concluded, women are not "troubled with sexual feeling of any kind. What men are habitually, women are only exceptionally," as William Acton memorably phrased it in *The Functions and Disorders of the Reproductive Organs* (1863).[52] "Before the 1800s," Lucy Bland explains in *Banishing the Beast*, her 1995 study of feminism, sex, and morality in the nineteenth century, "women were assumed to be as sexual as men, indeed more sexual; after the 1800s, this began to change to a view of women as lacking sexual carnal desire."[53] Obstetricians were consulted for their newfound knowledge about women, their sensitivities, and their capacity for pleasure, and they concurred that "woman was a reproductive creature who was, by nature, socially dependent on man but somehow morally superior to him."[54]

Mary Wollstonecraft, despite her passionate denunciation of this female social dependence, acknowledged that, when it came to modesty and chastity, women have the advantage. Only those poor women who have been debauched in the service of men's demands are exempt: they have gone too far to be moved by society's expectation of their propriety.

Yet Wollstonecraft resists the smug conclusion. Parting company from the experts' opinions, Wollstonecraft insisted that it is not nature but good sense, rationality, and respect for virtue that truly make women modest and chaste: those are the same reasons that should encourage a male embrace of modesty. If the moral teams are, as they seem to be, unequally divided, the trouble is with lack of enlightenment, not some whimsical result of biology's determinism.[55]

Nothing in the age of the martyr, the cloister, and the chastity test had defined women's role in contradistinction from men's in quite the way that the guardians of commonsense defined it in the generations after Wollstonecraft. In her time and for the next century or so, an entire industry devoted to advising, chastising, and extolling women was busy producing tracts, sermons, conduct books, and even light literature: the message was, yes, women were not men, and they should not presume to their stature or privileges. What God was unable to enforce, biology had accomplished. And what biology could not do, middle-class morality would, Cott points out: "The middle-class moralists made female chastity the archetype for human morality."[56] And this swerve toward the feminization of morality was already well under way before Queen Victoria's day. Women, Jean-Jacques Rousseau explained in 1762, were "charged by nature" not just with bearing children but maintaining the honor of the family and the happiness of their husbands. Unfaithful men are, it is true, "barbarous" and "unjust." But their faults are nothing compared to the wreckage done by the unchaste woman: "The strictness of the relative duties of the two sexes is not and cannot be the same. When woman complains on this score about unjust man-made inequality, she is wrong. This inequality is not a human institution—or, at least, it is the work not of prejudice but of reason." Seeming to anticipate the very arguments Wollstonecraft would use against him, Rousseau proceeds to put the Platonic presumption in its place. How can women serve as "guardians"? How can they push aside the effects of their sexual and reproductive constitution? What else are they for? Rousseau's answer: "There is no parity between the two sexes in regard to the consequences of sex. The male is male only at certain moments. The female is female her whole life or at least during her whole youth. Everything constantly recalls her sex to her; and, to fulfil its functions well, she needs a constitution which corresponds to it."[57]

Women, of course, had always been different from men: more carnal, less attentive to the claims of reason, a temptation and a reminder of humanity's curse. That at least was the view of the antifeminist camp, best represented in *The Canterbury Tales* by the Wife of Bath's fifth husband, Janekin the "clerk of Oxenforde," who plagued her with his "Book of

Wicked Wives," full of the misogynistic rants of Jerome, Tertullian, Walter Map, and the like, and all sorts of tales of lascivious and violent women, from Pasiphaë and Clytemnestra on. The wife Allison, comfortable with the warmth of her appetites and the solidity of her property, is unimpressed: she smacks him to the floor; he responds in kind until, alarmed by his own violence, the young clerk repents, hands over the mastery of the household to Allison, and together they burn the offensive book.[58] Janekins did not disappear, and there were other voices, equally strident. Yet proponents of the carnal theory of essential femininity were outnumbered in Victorian times by those prepared to find nobility in the figure of the caring, patient woman, or to be charmed by a combination of sexual appeal and natural timidity. Laqueur is particularly intrigued by the coexistence of these incompatible sentiments, recognizing that it is the nature of ideology to be contradictory: "In the enormously enlarged public sphere of the eighteenth and particularly the postrevolutionary nineteenth centuries," battles over sexual difference were fought, and "no one account of sexual difference triumphed."[59]

What was the moral status of the female sex? It was a puzzle that set a great many minds into action. The possibility that women represented not a lesser but a greater degree of moral excellence was a remarkable development. An unexpected second act for Eve, who could now reverse the hated double standard that followed on her dereliction. The human race was corrupt, undeniably, but more of that baseness could be traced to males: women had the chance to bring humanity into a new era, an era of reform. Puritans in New England, evangelicals and sentimentalists in England, and their fellow travelers on the Continent took the "question of woman" into a new direction, borrowing something from religion and something from changed economic conditions, which encouraged a fixation on the domestic household as women's proper setting and sanctuary. A close companion to this view of the domestic woman, keeping self-control, discipline, and virtue as the guiding principles of the household, was the myth of the child-woman, pure and for all intents and purposes sexless. "A curious feature of the Victorianising of women," writes Gordon Rattray Taylor in his 1958 book *The Angel Makers*, "was the attempt to depict them as ethereal beings, lacking human desires and appetites"; women before the eighteenth century may have been able to keep up with their male counterparts in sensuality, drink, gambling, and idle chat: now the ideal woman raised suspicion when she so much as ate a biscuit.[60] Caring, sweet, and unenlightened, the pure woman could be a vessel of spiritual refinement; pale and prone to illness and fatigue, her mind, when not occupied with pleasing a man or caring for a child, tended to revert to piety and prayer. If she was titillating, she was also off-limits. She was white beyond whiteness, barely attached to a body, vulnerable, helpless, and oblivious to any hint or suggestion of eroticism. In a book with the simple title *White*, Richard Dyer points to the entwinement of Christianity, with its fantasy of disembodiment and transcendence, and the "cultural register of whiteness," noting that "*Christianity* (and the particular inflection it gives to Western dualist thought) is founded on the idea—paradoxical, unfathomable, profoundly mysterious—of incarnation, of being that is in the body yet not of it."[61]

The "white ideal," Dyer argues, is marked deeply by Christianity (and Christianity, despite its global reach and Near East origins, is marked by it). And the white ideal is where the notion of purity goes to collect its ideological tools. From the examples of Christ and the Virgin Mary, who mysteriously mix something of the divine with something of the human, Christians inherit the challenge of turning a mortal, fleshly, and creaturely being into something that strives to be more than it can be. According to Dyer, "Such striving (which in woman must also be passive) is registered in suffering, self-denial and self-control, and also material achievement, if it can be construed as the temporary and partial triumph of mind over matter. These constitute something of a thumbnail sketch of the white ideal."[62]

Imperialist discourse applied this familiar metaphysic to its own racist project. The white colonist could be sure that the rights of dominion were justified, since whiteness denotes moral as well as aesthetic superiority. Mind is more white than matter. And, an addition with dire consequences, woman is more "white" than man. Women are, or must be, purity incarnate, and white women are the purest of the pure.[63] To become civilized, something that can indeed be distributed to the other parts of the globe, non-Europeans will need to become more "white."[64] And this has implications for gender ideology. Indeed, racialist anxieties are visibly entangled within the eighteenth- and nineteenth-century Protestant reconstruction of the chastity plot, a plot that now is overwhelmingly addressed toward women. In line with a long tradition of desexualizing some women in order to oversexualize others, the white woman was situated in the place of mind rather than matter. Imperialist ideology trumped the old cynicism about female lasciviousness, as well as the traditional philosophical theory that women's inferior powers of reasoning justify their subjection to the moral guidance of men. In the new mythology, women were just more moral by nature. Compared to the "native" woman, the delicate body and modest conduct of the white woman is fragile and perhaps untouchable. The mystery of bodilessness which Dyer identified with the miraculous nature of the Virgin Mother can now be transferred onto a terrain where the Roman Catholic Church has almost no purchase. Yet without a cloister or an official role for the celibate exception—the mysteriously and admirably bodiless—the discourse of sexual chastity runs into what could be a fatal contradiction. Dyer relates it to the impossible costs of racial idealism, which ultimately writes its own death notice: "To ensure the survival of the race they (i.e., whites) have to have sex—but having sex, and sexual desire, are not themselves very white."[65]

Imperial discourse is a discourse about whiteness, a "white mythology." Few scholars would deny that. That it is also a discourse about chastity is a point Dyer and other postcolonial critics want to emphasize. The contact between Europe and its colonies was a sexual contact as well as a racial one. Sexually, the other promised more excitement, less inhibition, a dangerous sexuality. The dark were sensual. But that raised some old ascetic ideas. What if that sensuality was a cover for a disturbing lack of innocence? Maybe this would be the revenge of the colonized: that erotic relations with them could pollute and dirty all that is most precious about the white race.[66] Here was a new and disturbing role for the Christian ambivalence about sex. Purity, cleanliness, virginity were the property of one race, the race intended to rule.[67] Its women were different from women in general. They were innocent, immaculate, impeccable. Did that mean they were sexless?

The first half of the nineteenth century is critical to this last part of my argument for a number of reasons. At the very moment when demands for reform in the relations between the sexes were becoming hard to ignore, when feminists and socialists were bringing sex, its pleasures, and its abuses into public consciousness, a rearguard action ensured that the virgin would be around for a while. Today's "Power Virgins" (to borrow Elizabeth Abbott's term for the youth wing of the Christian Right) are the heirs of this curious development.[68] And, despite the fundamentalist leadership of this recent movement and its dependence on church organizations, its dominant character is secular, not religious. Why premarital sexual continence matters to the new virginity-positive cultural push has very little to do with the reasons chastity mattered to Paul, or Thecla, or Gregory of Nyssa: perhaps we have to consult Pamela Andrews if we want to understand what has been going on.

8

Losing the Plot

THE POLITICS AND POETRY OF MODERN VIRGINITY

I think that words like purity, morality, and decency are very nice words.
I wish that the women's movement would reclaim those words.

SUSAN BROWNMILLER

Disassembling the Chastity Plot

Even after the death of Clarissa, the world was not finished with virgins. Victorians were avid readers of Samuel Richardson's novels and of the many sentimental and thrilling stories about young women finding their way through the trials of courtship. Such readers knew that marriage was the reward for the virtuous and the resistant; they knew also that marriage was the sole "trade" for women, the definition of their life, and the reason they were put on the earth.[1] Being a bachelor could be enviable, for those with the money and the class advantages to smooth the way; a spinster was an identity only the brave could embrace.[2] Clarissa, in her desperate moments, wished Protestant convents existed to shelter single women estranged from their families and unwilling to put themselves into the power of men; the formidable Mary Astell had proposed an idea for a secular and rational nunnery in 1695, and hers was one of several seventeenth- and eighteenth-century schemes for female communities, whose residents could there find education as well as freedom from the obligations of both spiritual dedication and marriage.[3]

The moment was, however, too soon—or perhaps too late. The nineteenth century would see fresh attempts by reformers to unshackle women from marriage and the grip of patriarchal ideals. Socialist feminists joined forces with Godwinians, Owenites, or Fourierists to see what it was like to live communally without the institutions sanctioned by state or church.[4] Free or irregular unions were one possibility if public disdain and accusations of immorality weren't too much of a deterrent. But separatist lifestyles, in small group households or under the mantle of spinsterhood, also appealed to "new women." Chastity, chosen out of a commitment to radical principles, might be a way of resisting what a later critic of the "compulsory" heterosexual/marriage system called the "disorder" of the social relations between the sexes.[5]

Kate Mills, a reforming feminist and social worker in London in the late nineteenth century, expressed a sentiment shared by others dissatisfied with gender inequities and ill at ease with the artificial virtues that were meant to ornament the life of the "Perfect Woman."[6] Marriage, Mills was sure, was the culprit. If women were not expected to find in this oddly persistent institution everything that made their lives livable and valuable—financial support, social recognition, moral deference, and practical utility—then they might be free to imagine a new social plot. Mills could have enrolled in the Outsiders' Society, the imaginary community Virginia Woolf proposes in *Three Guineas* (1938) which would set itself up outside in every sense. It would be pacifist, egalitarian, separatist, cosmopolitan.[7] And it would be a place for women on their own. "I believe celibacy to be infinitely higher than any existing form of marriage," Kate Mills declared in 1889.[8] The single life, if combined with sexual self-control, represented a profession less compromised than that of the married woman, the mother, and the prostitute. As a political identity, it had a deep connection with the culture of reform in nineteenth-century Britain and the United States.

Chosen as a political identity and self-definition, celibacy can sustain some of the radical potential that earlier feminists saw in it; in 2001, David Jay founded the Asexual Visibility and Education Network to support just such an oppositional status outside, as Benjamin Kahan argues, the hetero/homosexual binary and the cultural imperative "You Must Have Sex."[9] Yet even to asexuality's advocates, the resistance to compulsory sexuality and to sexual exploitation does not include a nostalgia for purity.[10] Second, third, and fourth waves of feminism and contemporary LGBTQ+ politics have avoided appeals to moral purity and did so even in the 1980s and 1990s "sex wars," the intense and polarizing squabbles over pornography that shook up the world of Western feminism and forced a rethinking of sexual ethics—a project to which I hope to be contributing. It is partly because of the discomfort around demands to censor pornographic representation that contemporary campaigns for sexual justice and gender rights often target puritanism and "sex negativity." Feminists have been opposing the pure womanhood gospel too long to risk reviving it under the cover of a new celibacy. At the same time, as the present campaigns against sexual harassment show, uncritical embraces of erotic liberationism have done little to achieve sexual and gender justice.

Can *purity* be a word that is ever used without a cringe? Protecting the purity of the American people (and the delicate sensibilities of women) has far too often been an alibi for homophobia, as we saw in the disgraceful political response to the AIDS crisis. But Victorian feminism told a different story.[11] A history of moral regulation in the period from the 1830s to the 1920s emphasizes both the liberal and the radical support for "purity campaigns," as Alan Hunt observes: "Although not all suffragists agreed with the slogan, the intimate connection between sexual purity and suffrage is enshrined in Christabel Pankhurst's famous slogan: 'Votes for Women, Chastity for Men' (1913)."[12] Many of the leaders of the suffrage movement took vows of celibacy, Susan B. Anthony and Margaret Fuller among the most celebrated.[13] Until the passage of several versions of the Married Women's Property Act (in the United States in 1848; in the United Kingdom in 1870 and 1882), marriage precluded property ownership for women; voluntary celibacy addressed this objection and allowed women to demand a political voice. Given the scarcity of options, spinsterhood looked pretty good.

It was, however, only the "advanced" who took up the challenge or even entertained its possibility. Conventional femininity stayed well within the conventions. And the convention was marriage. Women "who wanted to be women" were not ready to examine the costs of the gendered regime and its effects on their inner as well as their outer lives. Clarissa's fans knew that Mary Astell's "Serious Proposal to the Ladies" was only a distraction. Chastity meant the good behavior of those destined for marriage or firmly placed within its moral confines. Nuns had not been banished in the age of Henry VIII only to come back as bluestockings and feminists. The prizes (such as they were) would belong to the chaste and virtuous Protestant wife. The "celibacy plot" (Benjamin Kahan's phrase) was no competition for the marriage and the courtship plot.

In the various twists added to the chastity plot between the age of Clarissa and the "born-again virgins" of evangelical America, one of the most popular narratives involved the testing of an eligible bride through the ordeals of courtship. Medieval chastity tests included ordeals performed as public spectacles, aimed at locating the evidence of impurity in physical signs—usually bodily ones (Did the urine run "clear and sparkling"? Was there blood emitted during the marital act?). Often the signs considered revealing were significantly removed from the relevant organs of the female body: a chaste woman can drink from a special ivory drinking horn without spilling a drop; when forced to grasp a hot iron or walk across a burning grate, the innocent are unharmed, or their injuries heal quickly.[14] Such wonders are frankly too histrionic for modern tastes.[15] Of course it is important to verify the character of a candidate for the crown of "true womanhood," but testing purity in the way contemporary Christians prefer involves a scrutiny of the heart, at best, or of the clothing, gait, and public presentation. The modest heroine beloved by eighteenth- and nineteenth-century Americans and Europeans can be recognized by her blushes, her cast-down gaze, her delicacy, and, it has to be said, her prudishness.[16] The format of the examination is a formula for feminine excellence; it is also a tried-and-true recipe for narrative titillation. Could a heroine silence her own desires? Could she preserve her unmarred innocence under the scrutiny of a skeptical public? Could she fight off the advances of a rake or the financial temptations offered as sweetener in exchange for an illicit liaison? Then she deserved the social sanction of marriage. If not, her fate could be grim.

Readers who understood the rules of the game mourned the crushing of female paragons of virtue in the cruel battle of the sexes. They continued to expect purity from their heroines of fiction. And they continued to enjoy the lecherous plots of the rakes bent on those virgins' dishonor. Sophisticated readers shared with mass audiences the same recognition that pure maidens were the proper object of pleasurable if condescending concern, and they welcomed ever-new variations on the maidens' plots in forms as popular as the melodrama, the gothic romance, and the early motion picture.

Whether sexual behavior, and gender expectations, conformed perfectly to the models such fictions provided is another question. Chastity plots are good at telling us about meanings; for a historical reckoning with social practices, we would need to defer to the sociologists. After Richardson's *Pamela*, did more people assume that advantageous marriages could be won through a valiant defense of one's maidenhead? Did thoughtful men and women worry about the incoherence of sexual morality after reading about the rape of Clarissa? Clarissa's example could have told her admirers that an intelligent and self-respecting woman needs something more than vigilance in her dealings with men. Even an exemplary inner life will not give the heroine the rewards her virtue deserves. She needs a society where authoritarian fathers have lost their credibility and women have been granted rights over their own property, persons, and marital histories.

That society was not Clarissa's, nor was it her readers'. Middle-class women in the two centuries after Richardson were finding ways to drill holes in the fences of privacy and domesticity, pursuing work outside parenting and housekeeping as their working-class sisters had been doing for a long time, without the benefits of an ideology of self-fulfillment. It is, admittedly, the history of the middle-class woman that makes the fate of the chastity plot a necessary object of inquiry. The middle-class woman is the one targeted by the conduct books and their ideals; in the life and limitations of the middle-class European and American woman, the stigma of gender continued throughout the nineteenth and much of the twentieth century to determine moral and sexual reality.[17] Women could demand an education; they could even demand the vote; increasingly they wore clothes that allowed them to move, exercise, be at ease in their environments. But the same women who got on bicycles and fought for gender and racial emancipation would continue to worry that revealing their sexual desires could make them no longer respected. They would continue to be told by preachers, novels, and conduct books that modesty, bashfulness, delicacy, and ignorance were precious ingredients in the construction of the truly feminine ideal.

In Tom Perrota's 2007 novel, the eponymous abstinence teacher—the ideal whose example the grumpy heroine is asked to follow—is named JoAnn Marlow, and she is introduced in this way:

> The guest speaker wasn't just blond and pretty; she was *hot*, and she knew it. You could see it in the way she moved towards the podium—like a movie star accepting an award—that consciousness she had of being watched, the pleasure she took in the attention. She wore a tailored navy blue suit with a knee-length skirt, an outfit whose modesty somehow provoked curiosity rather than stifling it.

Announcing herself to an audience of public-school adolescents, JoAnn shows that she is cool: she likes the right music; she loves long rides on her boyfriend's Harley; she is expert at competitive sports; and she is a virgin. If they feel sorry for her, they have it backwards. Her boyfriend is happy about it. The unenlightened may think she is a prude. But she is confident, indeed gloating, that she has won out over her more sexually permissive contemporaries, who now have STDs, unwanted children, and regrets. They don't like themselves. She, on the other hand, likes herself all too much. "I'm a strong, self-sufficient individual, and I can look myself in the mirror and honestly say that my mind and my body are one hundred percent mine. They're mine and mine alone, and I'm proud of that," she boasts. This Christian apostle of chastity speaks the language of popular feminism—empowerment; you go, girl—and she also speaks the language of hypersexuality: her boyfriend, whose semidressed photo she shows her audience, is "superhot," and saying no to him is not easy, she admits. She adds, "But when it gets hard, I just remind myself of my wedding night, and how amazing it's going to be when I give myself to my husband with a pure heart, a clear conscience, and a perfectly intact body. Because that's going to be my reward, and mark my words, people—it is going to be so good, oh my God, better than anything you can even imagine."[18]

It is a markedly different way of imagining the reward of chastity. Like Pamela, JoAnn and the young people she inducts into the purity campaign will be more than compensated for their restraint by what they enjoy after the wedding, when they give their blameless and clean body to their spouse.[19] (Some "abstinence teachers," such as the best-selling Josh Harris, went further: God doesn't want the unmarried to run the risk of temptation, so infatuation, dating, and reading romance novels all should be avoided.)

In chapter 7, the chastity plot took us from the exemplary careers of those virtuous paragons Clarissa and Pamela through a long line of modest heroines and pure maidens to come out, in our time, at an interesting moment. As I noted in the introduction, conservative Christians in the United States have been busy running purity campaigns, appealing to a fear of sex and a perhaps stronger fear of feminism, liberalism, ethnic diversity, and moral uncertainty. "Say no to sex" is the motto, and abstinence education for all, with government support, is the strategy. Congress first showed its interest in the abstinence campaign during the Reagan years, with the 1981 passage of the Adolescent Family Life Act; intensified its investment when it overhauled the nation's welfare system in 1996; and pumped more money into abstinence-only education curricula under George W. Bush in the first decade of the twentieth century.[20] Yet is abstinence the motto around which the religious right wants to unite? The first twenty years of the twenty-first century have made the intentions of the morality crusade even more unreadable—a crusade that operates under the flag of "family values" and has never pursued its connections with the radical ascetic program that bequeathed Christianity its love for chastity and renunciation. While I have been researching this book, the moral purity campaign of the Christian Right has been concentrating its energies on legal and political battles against abortion and reproductive rights, rather than the glories of chastity, something not obviously valued by Republican leaders in the United States today.

In the period from the death of Clarissa to the last, limping stages of the evangelical abstinence campaigns in the United States, it is the maiden, not the eunuch, who dominates the chastity plot. I would like to be able to say that her days are numbered. A flurry of Hollywood movies and mainstream television series from the 1980s through the 2010s made virginity and its loss a plot point. *Little Darlings* (1980), *Fast Times at Ridgemont High* (1982), *Sixteen Candles* (1984), and *Beverly Hills 90210* (1990–2000) courted their young audiences with debates about whether sexual purity mattered, whether virginity was a stigma or something to be proud of. Horror movies found a great resource in the generic convention Carol Clover famously called "The Final Girl Narrative." In the slasher films that sought to match the success of John Carpenter's *Halloween* (1978), the one character who survives to confront and (at times) defeat the killer is a virginal young woman:

> She is the Girl Scout, the bookworm, the mechanic. Unlike her girlfriends (and Marion Crane [from *Psycho*]) she is not sexually active.... The Final Girl is boyish.... Her smartness, gravity, competence in mechanical and other practical matters, and sexual reluctance set her apart from the other girls and ally her, ironically, with the very boys she fears or rejects, not to speak of the killer himself.[21]

Less conventional treatments of chastity and its modern meanings have addressed sophisticated viewers: the telenovela-style TV series *Jane the Virgin* (2014–2019, developed by Jennie Snyder Ullman and starring Gina Rodriguez) began with the premise that the modern American virgin is exceptional, even freakish. Conceiving immaculately because her gynecologist mistakenly administers artificial insemination, Jane Gloriana Villanueva is a principled, ambitious, and sexy Latina of advanced views and an energetic social conscience. She has no need of abstinence campaigners to tell her she is a worthwhile human being. While she makes it clear to her boyfriends that erotic play (highly desirable and initiated just as often by her) cannot go as far as intercourse, she is no prude. She does aspire to be a moral paragon and, for the most part, she succeeds. But her conception of morality would not offend even the most politicized feminist. The one hundred episodes of *Jane the Virgin* occupy a special region on the ideological map of the modern United States, a map we know is fought over by feminists and their enemies, by racists and antiracists, by advocates of immigration and ethnic diversity and those who dream (often violently) of an old, white, nativist America, where fathers rule and families are not blended. Jane's vow to keep her virginity and her warm, if intermittent, Catholicism would, on the face of it, be a problem for a progressive and a feminist. Jane is both. She considers abortion without indignation (though she ultimately rejects that option); she is untroubled by divorce, illegitimacy, and the casual promiscuity of her social circle.

Yet in almost every way that matters, Jane is morally upright, eschewing lies and unkindness, battling for social justice and gender equality. Indeed, her moral exemplarity is visibly annoying to those who care for her. If Pamela was created to teach her social superiors what virtue is, Jane's variation on the strong virgin type seems designed to poke gentle fun at the messes created by the good. The narrative takes great pleasure in showing that a paragon can err, and that she can shift gears, rethinking her principles with the benefit of editing. It is no accident that she is a writer and a compulsive list-maker. The program is dedicated to bringing Latina characters and references to a wider public; it is unusual in its readiness to look affectionately if teasingly at traditional religion. Jane's immaculate conception is neither the end nor the beginning of her sexual script. A mother before she loses her virginity (which she is, for complicated reasons, unable to do until some months after her wedding), Jane proves that modern female virtue can be complicated but triumphant.

Even more interesting is the recent British dramatic series *Fleabag* (2016, 2019), developed by Phoebe Waller-Bridge from her successful one-woman show at the Edinburgh Fringe Festival in 2013. The character Fleabag, played by Waller-Bridge, is funny, depressed, self-hating, and reckless; she is also sexually alive and a feminist. In the second season she meets her match in the person of a handsome Catholic priest, called simply "The Priest," played by Andrew Scott. The Priest is "hot," as no one can resist remarking. He is also honorable, committed to his vows of celibacy, which he does not view as an anachronistic nuisance but as a way to devote his passions—and his moral energies—to the love and care of others. Renouncing amorous attachments and keeping himself apart from the demands of family life, the Priest astonishes his contemporary fans because he believes sincerely in the relevance of chastity to the love of God and to the perfectionism of the spiritual life. As a priest in the world, he is no monk and no ascetic. The Priest puts his Christianity to practical work. He is a counselor on call for any distressed soul who needs him. He does not condemn; he does not appear to judge or to chastise. Not for him are the rewards of otherworldly detachment or the narcissistic rush that human "angels" may experience as a result of their tangible superiority to all us lesser and fleshly types. But indeed, he is a man who feels passion, and he cannot disguise his attraction when Fleabag lays siege to him. Her seduction of him, first rebuffed gently, then succumbed to, is something he takes very seriously indeed. But he resolves that it must not recur. Openly susceptible to desire, he explains that if he has sex, he will be in love. And he is. But committed to his religious vow, he must sacrifice Fleabag. The repercussions of this interesting event are extraordinary—not in terms of their effects on Fleabag, who shows she can understand despite her pain, but on the viewers. The disappointment, the call to change the ending and allow the union of the lovers, provoked a response not much short of hysterical. What is more remarkable is the ability of popular culture to entertain the possibility of a celibate character who is neither corrupt nor corrupting, neither sanctimonious nor hypocritical. Has chastity become hot again?

In their 1968 album *The Kinks Are the Village Green Preservation Society*, the British rock band the Kinks knew that virginity was quaint. God might want to save "little shops, china cups, and virginity." Beyond the village green and the fantasy of a white, empire-loving, churchgoing, cricket-playing, and xenophobic "little England," no one else cared. Sexual morality between the 1880s and the Second World War had been shifting in the European and Anglo-American world, clumsily, fitfully, if sometimes dramatically, as "new women" cut their hair, removed their corsets, and got onto bikes. With the influence of the feminist movement and, in England at any rate, a vigorous journalistic debate about moral reform among progressives and their opponents, the question of the double standard found its way into public attention. Women who went out to work in offices and shops in the early twentieth century were just as vulnerable as was Pamela to the sexual overtures of their bosses and colleagues. But their chances of marrying respectably were not going to be destroyed if the word got around that their record was less than spotless. By the time Albert Kinsey finished his mammoth studies of *Sexual Responses in the Human Female* (published in 1953), more than 66 percent of women who married between the ages of twenty-six and thirty were not virgins when they married.

Why, in the face of these changes, the admiration for the virgin's version of sexual morality persisted as long as it did is a question I would like to keep open. According to some writers who have thought about the subject, the traditional reputation of virginal virtue had been easy enough to explain: on the jacket of Anke Bernau's 2007 book *Virgins: A Cultural History*, we can read the traditional association affirmed, "If God in heaven preferred virgins, so did the marriage market." Patriarchy, as Samuel Johnson believed, needed virgins. Catholic, Protestant, and Jewish traditions were clear that commendable women were sexually reliable women and that the sanctity of households depended on the purity of women who courted the blessings of heaven by keeping any rumor or hint of impropriety far from the door. For most of Western history, virgins were considered a good thing, and female virgins were the recommended version. Since the rise of the feminist movement, drawing public attention to women's demands for equal education, equal work, and equal rights to sexual pleasure, things have gotten more ambivalent, yet Bernau argues that we would be wrong to think that today the virginity question is dead.[22] Virginity can be sexy, and indeed defloration belongs among the persistent fantasy items in the pornographic repertory. Jean-Jacques Rousseau, unpredictable as usual, breaks out of the mold by scorning the virgin as an object of desire. It is only the old, the ugly, and the insecure who would fetishize defloration, he contends:

> Why this barbarous avidity to corrupt innocence, to make a victim of a young person who ought to have been protected, and who by this first step is inevitably dragged into an abyss of miseries from which she will emerge only at death? . . . The pleasure [in sleeping with a virgin] does not come from nature; it comes from opinion, and from the vilest opinion, since it is connected with self-contempt. He who feels himself to be the basest of men fears comparison with all others and wants to be the first to get there in order to be less odious. . . . An old satyr—worn out by debauchery, without charm, without respect, without consideration, without any kind of decency, incapable and unworthy of pleasing any woman who knows anything about lovable people—believes he can make up for all that with a young innocent by taking advantage of her inexperience and stirring her senses for the first time.[23]

The chance to "pollute the pure," to claim dominion over a sexual partner no one else has managed to win, or—at ever more sordid levels—to force sexual knowledge onto the young, the unknowing, and the unwilling, is enough to keep interest high on a number of websites. It was no different in the eighteenth century, when novelist John Cleland's protagonist Fanny Hill could sell her virginity several times over to the patrons in her brothel. Virginity can attract the fetishist because of its scarcity (no one has more than one maidenhead) and because—in heterosexual situations—the man who spoils the virgin believes he makes the child into a woman and thus proves himself master over that mysterious "continent" Sigmund Freud identified with female sexuality.[24] But even some fetishists hold back: Edward Cullen, the glamorous vampire in the *Twilight* movie series (2008–2012), scrupulously restrains his sexual desire for the human Bella and, honoring her virginity beyond the point where she wishes to give it up, insists they abstain until marriage.[25] Vampire eroticism will never be the same.

As recently as November 2019, the social media sphere buzzed with indignation at the rapper T.I.'s boast that he takes his eighteen-year-old daughter Deyjah Harris for an annual virginity test to oversee the state of her hymen. "The worst dad in the world," complained the Twittersphere.[26] "Abusing," "controlling," "disgusting" were other comments, as well as "beyond possessive."[27] The quickest responses came from gynecologists who denounced the scientific status of virginity testing, while others were reminded that the United Nations and the World Health Organization had called for a ban on virginity testing in October 2018.[28] Jennifer Gunter, OB/GYN ("Twitter's resident gynecologist"), who writes columns for the *New York Times* and has authored a book called *The Vagina Bible*, passionately insisted that "hymen tests were not a thing": they are medically unnecessary and unable to prove sexual experience or the lack of it.[29] Jill Filipovic of the *Guardian* goes further: "First things first: virginity doesn't exist and there's no way to test it.... The entire concept of virginity is misogynistic: men aren't valued for their sexual inexperience, there's no male virginity test, and male sexual desire and experience are considered both normal and appropriate.... There is no good reason for the concept of 'virginity' to persist. Not one. Virginity, whatever it means, has no bearing on morality, goodness or innocence.... Yes, let's do away with abusive, invasive, misogynistic virginity tests. But if we want to fight misogyny, we need to reject virginity itself, too."[30]

If doing away with the concept of virginity is indeed a necessary step for feminists and anyone who wants to fight misogyny, there could be a solution. Mina Loy, the avant-garde poet and futurist author of the 1915 *Feminist Manifesto*, has the right idea. Her ingenious if drastic solution was for all women to "sacrifice their virtue" with a vengeance. As it stands, Loy argued, the choice for women is simple, and dreadful: you can choose between "Parasitism, & Prostitution—or Negation." If women expect help from the avant-garde in their rebellion, they will be bitterly disappointed, she warned. The macho futurists such as Filippo Tommaso Marinetti declaimed their scorn for traditional femininity but believed that women would just go on within the "closed circle" of their sex—obliged to be women and wives or carnal, amoral lovers, slaves to and inferior to men.[31] The feminist movement as constituted in her time is hopeless, Loy insists, and cannot break itself away from "the rubbish heap of tradition." Feminist reformers are deluded if they trust in economic legislation, social change, or access to education and the vote. All that is just "glossing over reality."[32]

In the spirit of her futurist friends, Loy calls for women to reject the fetish of their own femininity. For the sake of their self-respect, women must wipe out in themselves—and in others—the notion that there is anything impure about sex. Modesty, the "anaemic" virtue of women's "subjugated adolescence," imprisons them in "a white muslin girl's school" ("The Black Virginity") or in "Transparent nightdresses made all of lace"; the guardians of their purity lock the doors with chains, doors that keep inside and behind the curtains those "virgins who / Might scratch" ("Virgins Plus Curtains Minus Dots"). Squeaking, giggling, fluttering, virgins are for sale, but if you go too close you realize that they are just dolls, with eyes of glass ("Three Moments in Paris").[33] Loy asserts that women, in rejecting the morality of "virtue" and the shame associated with sex, will deliver an immense boon. They will detach from sex all the cloying and demeaning elements, all the "honour, grief, sentimentality, pride & consequently jealousy." To effect this revolution, all it takes is a small sacrifice. The female population, at puberty, needs to take the crucial step, "the unconditional surgical destruction of virginity." If no woman is a virgin, there will be no way to distinguish between the slut and the angel, the mistress and the wife. Forget "Reform, the only method is Absolute Demolition."[34]

Conclusion

According to Friedrich Nietzsche, the ascetic's imagination has no shortage of ways to keep boredom at bay. Fighting sensuality delivers pleasures and sensations not far short of the pleasures and sensations the sensualist values so highly. Some people may think them even more exciting. The struggle against the self is "the last *pleasure the ancient world invented.*"[35] What has it accomplished, this ascetic ideal? he asks at the end of his *Genealogy of Morals*. What does it all mean, this "hatred of humanity, of animality, of inert matter: this loathing of the senses, of reason even; this fear of beauty and happiness; this longing to escape from illusion, change, becoming, death, and from longing itself"?[36] Maybe a will to nothingness; maybe a strange beauty, as nature is twisted into a new form and the mind learns to love the stimulating effects of denial.

Nietzsche's recognition of the ascetic will to power has guided me in my reading of chastity. I have found things to admire in the saint, the eunuch, and those who aspire to the condition of the angels. And I have found things to criticize. I have found a persistent ambivalence in the moral tradition that identified the good woman with the sexless and undesiring woman. Christianity celebrated the elite vocation to the single, celibate life, yet it feared and suppressed the bid for independence and moral authority such a vocation can represent, for men as well as women. It will hardly have come as a surprise that our most oppressive ideologies of gender demand a sexual self-control from women that they do not demand from men, or that female sexual purity is supposed, in many societies, to serve as a symbol of social purity, an exclusive category that works to ensure the integrity of a society, a family, or a class.[37]

Chastity's war against sexual norms and sensual pleasures is certainly hyperbolic; some might say unhealthy. That it also involves a long (and unwinnable) war against marriage is a fact not as well recognized as it should be. Here we could recall the philosopher Stanley Cavell's argument that "some image of human intimacy," which we could call "marriage, or domestication," could be understood as "the fictional equivalent of what the philosophers of ordinary language understand as the ordinary," and that fiction's "favorite threats to forms of marriage" are usually forms of "melodrama" or "tragedy."[38] Philosophy has rarely welcomed the marriage plot with Cavell's grace. Nietzsche, who knew the advantages of the ascetic life for the intellectual and the scholar, also knew how celibacy protects "that repulsive and gloomy caterpillar form in which alone the philosopher could live and creep about."[39] He asks, "What great philosopher hitherto has been married? Heraclitus, Plato, Descartes, Spinoza, Leibniz, Kant, Schopenhauer—they were not; more, one cannot even imagine them married."[40] Cavell knows this legacy, and he resists it. In Cavell's view, at its best, marriage represents the coming together of the personal and the public, the pedestrian and the romantic. Marriage as an ideal (the marriage plot in its fantasy form) promises that the tension between the sexes will be resolved into conversation and acknowledgment that the delight of Adam and Eve is still available, even after the Fall.[41]

But too often marriage does not live up to this ideal, and it can bring madness, alienation, and the loss of self-knowledge. In such cases it is necessary to reject marriage, as does Nora in Henrik Ibsen's *A Doll's House*. Even if Nora does not know immediately where to take herself when she leaves her husband at the end of the play, she knows it will not be in marriage, not for any reason. Rejection of the domestic is one way of understanding what happens in the genre of melodrama, in Cavell's view. Through other forms, tragic and melodramatic, Cavell suggests, it is possible to discern an "alternative route to integrity and possibility,"[42] admittedly a hyperbolic and sometimes violent one, a route taken by some of the extraordinary and independent women he celebrates in classical Hollywood melodramas, women whose nonconforming—usually in their rejection of marriage and heteronormativity—often leaves them solitary, unintelligible to others, and certainly on the far side of happiness as generally, ordinarily understood.[43] The chastity plot, although not one of Cavell's genres, is also an alternative to the marriage plot. For some of the characters I study in this book, it was the chastity plot that provided "an alternative route to integrity and possibility." That their hopes were disappointed as often as the hopes of the married is not in doubt. But they shouldn't be dismissed without at least considering what they were looking for and why.

In this study, I have tried to brush the forms of chastity against the grain, to dislodge them from some of the more obvious associations they have acquired in their long career. I don't mean for this to become whitewashing: chastity's demerits must not be dismissed. The Amazonian tradition of Artemis and her wild girls has not dominated the field, and the imperious attitudes of Elizabeth did not transfer easily to other virgins. All too often, chastity comes off as fussy and timid, hostile to life, love, and the whole messy, glorious spectacle that is the human body and libido in all its neediness and spontaneity. The demand for chastity, especially the chastity of women and girls, has crushed and terrorized. It insinuated a disdain for physical longing and sexual vitality. It came with a turn against important curiosities and pleasures, with a refusal to take seriously human vulnerability and a call to distrust those experiences and intensities people continue to expect from sex and continue to miss out on.

All these things are true and more. Yet they are not the only things that can be said about my strange virtue. Denial can be productive, as Nietzsche's genealogies of morality make clear. The eunuch's no was also a yes. Most important to my story of the chastity plot was Christianity's radical notion, its claim that forgoing sex and generation would hasten the kingdom of heaven and introduce a new kind of creaturely being to this world. Ascetic renunciation was one way of imagining transformation. That transformation could be natural, interfering with the biological destiny of males and females. And that transformation could be unnatural, which is to say spiritual or metaphysical. But it was first of all social. Through Christ's call to live outside the family and to leave the worry about future generations to others, certain personal, social, and spiritual freedoms became available, briefly, for those women willing to embrace celibacy. Certain possibilities of invention, certain alternative deployments, came into view. For one, the bracing call to live in the body without succumbing to its demands for pleasure and gratification gave the ascetic a way to remake the conditions of selfhood, even to reimagine the conditions of nature, matter, and history. For another, the exceptional position claimed by the radically abstinent in a Christian world offered women (and others) a life apart from the family and motherhood and a way of thinking about themselves less constrained by social obligations, expectations, and definitions.

Christian chastity did not bring paradise back. Nor did it even win the allegiance of the faithful en masse. Most Christians, like everyone else, opted for marriage. Then they tried to prove that marriage could be the same as chastity. This was the most peculiar of all the awkward alliances in the history of the chastity plot. Could you do your duty to society and your family while living under the shadow of the eunuch? Can you make a credible accommodation between ascetic barrenness and conjugal fecundity? An honest appraisal of chastity's implications suggests otherwise. For the radicals drawn to the eunuch's swerve against normalcy, the romance of renunciation was a watershed, a parting of the ways. Jesus throws down the challenge in Luke 14:26: "If any *man* come to me, and hate not his father, and mother, and wife, and children, and brethren, and sisters, yea, and his own life also, he cannot be my disciple." Here was a chance to step beyond social assumptions, to make real the evangelical liberty of Christ's preaching. That hope did not evaporate, even as the concessions to marriage and generation continued to be made. Chaste liberation—as, for instance, the Shakers understood it—involved a powerful attack on the institution of marriage and gender division. As it happens, this route remains relatively unexplored, even by feminist opponents of the patriarchal social order. Feminists in the revolutionary movements of the early twentieth century, like their predecessors among the utopian socialists of the nineteenth, demanded sweeping changes to social and sexual arrangements, called for an end to the slavery of marriage and the demeaning characterization of women—but not men—through their biological attributes. Better a life alone, and better a life with other women, than absorption into the doll's house.

If the feminist critique of the cult of pure womanhood has been successful—and I think there are reasons to hail some of its successes in the last two hundred years—the same cannot be said for the feminist critique of marriage. I do believe that the possibility of a life outside compulsory heterosexuality, outside the conjugal imperative, is something the chastity plot, in at least some of its incarnations, was getting at. The chastity plot is, or was, an alternative to the marriage plot. Yet in almost every instance, it has been folded back and entwined into the marriage plot. What is chastity for, ask the moral experts advising women and their guardians? Why cultivate the virtues of modesty, delicacy, and feminine docility, as the conduct books require? Why sympathize with the heroines who must navigate the tests of courtship and assess both their own behavior and the suitability of the men proposing themselves as partners? Because the marriage plots—and what Davida Pines calls "the cultural imperative to marry"—are by far the most popular of the social scripts tailored for women.[44] And because the traditional marriage plot is designed around the figure of a virtuous if often troubled maiden whose passage into the state of matrimony is the goal, the desideratum, and the reward for all her efforts at sexual self-control. What else, after all, can a woman do? What other trade does she have?

The uncritical celebration of marriage and its swallowing up of all alternatives amount to a serious flaw in our imaginings of happiness, one which a number of my chastity stories try to expose. All too often, a heroine who aspires to or identifies with her chastity is a heroine ultimately cut down to size, tamed or converted by the heteronormative imperative. What Turandot desires, and cannot have, is what Thecla and Diana believed they could demand. Elizabeth could have it as the Virgin Queen, but Tracy Lord would be a cold, unfeeling statue unless she learns she has "feet of clay"—and a vulnerable body, even vulnerable to rape. Fear of the virgin is an interesting social symptom or, as Freud would argue, a psychological one: no wonder that priests and brutality and blood are often part of the picture, and not just symbolically. There is something intimidating about her. The virgin is sovereign, self-owning: that is why she is an exception to the gender binary and, in some cultures, imagined as a third sex.[45] Most narratives, and most societies, acknowledge her only to turn away as quickly as possible. An angry patriarch in Shakespeare's *A Midsummer Night's Dream* threatens his daughter with ostracism, or worse, if she tries to thwart his will by fleeing into the cloistered life. Yet if her enthusiasm for courtship were to lead her too far into sexual activity, she would be just as much a pariah. That chastity plots work by sustaining such double binds should not be a surprise by now. But the extent of their incoherence is worth remarking on. The fact that the injured and oppressed Clarissa could be expected to redeem the wounds to her virtue by marrying her rapist shows how poorly the Christian-secular moral world deals with the problems it creates.

To turn back to the uglier sides of the chastity plot, I think the most remarkable is the bond between misogyny and sexual purity, a contract as intimate as it is pervasive. Misogyny, or women hating, is difficult to analyze but easy to recognize. It is also remarkably flexible, adapting to any number of social conditions, ideological positions, and religious doctrines. It shows itself at just about every moment when there is a question of how to define women. If women are stupid, men should watch out; but if they are intelligent, it is just as bad. If the weaker sex is made without strong sexual feelings, they are castrating bitches; if they are innately libidinous, it's just what you would expect. Idolizing women removes them from human agency and will; demonizing them turns them into clever pieces of machinery or narcissistic animals immune to conscience and honor. As Mary Douglas famously explained, wherever there are distinctions (and the boundaries between the sexes are paradigmatic here), there is a problem about ambiguity, and it almost always seems to be women—especially virgins—who are held responsible. Anxieties about purity emerge, Douglas argues, from the possible permeability of boundaries, and this is true whether the boundaries are conceptual (Is a virgin not a woman? Is a whore not a woman? What distinguishes men from women?) or social and material (What belongs in the house? What doesn't? Which children must I raise? What freedoms can I permit to my wife, or to myself?).[46] Misogyny is not the inevitable accompaniment of every problem of boundary fixing, but it is a quick escape from complexity.

Recent explosions of misogyny into the public sphere have shocked even those long accustomed to the battles around sexual and gender justice. Many of these attacks are protected by online anonymity; others choose the most conspicuous sites of power. Liberal commentators compete with each other to defend similar diagnoses of what we might as well call the "misogyny nation." The hate, the fear, the pathos, and the violence seem to be reactions against a social and sexual world that has, for some people, become too complex to navigate. What has happened to white male supremacy, to the God-given right of males to solicit sex from women? The more feminism questioned the fixity of gender boundaries, the more intense the agitation from those who find their intellectual dexterity as challenged as their moral discrimination.

We have become used to the expression "toxic masculinity" and, even more recently, to the expanding web of denunciation and suspicion that holds together the manosphere. Every day new psychological and political alliances pop up, lumping together white supremacists, weapon fetishists, and the surprising number of Western males who feel themselves displaced, disrespected, and sexually deprived. It is here that questions of chastity have recently resurfaced, if in a perverse manner. On a number of blogs, websites, Reddit pages, and the like, the self-pitying and the left behind complain about women—or more precisely, they complain about women's sexual withholding and power to say no. The most notorious at the time of this writing is the online subculture of unhappy and angry males who self-identify as "Incels" and who believe that their failure to compete in the contemporary sexual marketplace is both a matter of involuntary celibacy and—obviously—not their fault. It is women who are to blame, only now it is not the proper young ladies holding out for a wedding ring who are the problem but the impure, highly sexed, and highly privileged "Staceys"—confident, alluring, self-flaunting, and rejecting. Incels are, by their own admission, attracted to violence and to the aggrieved entitlement of the alt-right; they feed each other rants full of rage, ressentiment, and despair, and their targets—the enemies who need putting down—are the traditional ones: Jews, women, those who are enjoying life.[47] The cult of the Incel has so far been associated with an ever-growing number of massacres in the United States and Canada, the one defining the movement being the massacre at Isla Vista, California, by the twenty-two-year-old college dropout Elliot Rodger on May 23, 2014, followed by similar murderous attacks near Roseburg, Oregon, on October 1, 2015, by Chris Harper-Mercer; in Parkland, Florida, on February 14, 2018, by Nikolas Cruz; and in Toronto, Ontario, on April 23, 2018, by Alek Minassian. Jia Tolentino quotes a diatribe on Incels.me: "Women are the ultimate cause of our suffering. They are the ones who have UNJUSTLY made our lives a living hell. We need to focus more on our hatred of women. Hatred is power."[48]

Just as there is a toxic masculinity—and, not as acknowledged as it should be, a toxic femininity—there is a toxic chastity. At its most monstrous this is the chastity that obsesses the old Count Tolstoy in the 1880s and 1890s. Initially a believer in the possibility of happy marriage, Leo Tolstoy depicted at least one, the Levins in *Anna Karenina* (1875–1878), in which love is not corrupted by sensuality and virtue is shared by men and women. Then his demons took over. Tolstoy could neither give up sexual relations nor come to terms with them. Sex, he became convinced, makes human life hell. Society deceives us all, pretending that sexual desire is natural, healthy, and susceptible to prudent domestication. Sex is nothing of the sort. It is "loathsome, ignominious, painful."[49] God and our moral conscience are clear on this point: the only good is to abstain. And yet everything in society conspires against that aspiration toward chastity, in particular the "domination by women" whose greatest pleasure is to degrade men, exhibiting themselves like whores and preying on male's lustful weakness.[50] In full Incel mode, Tolstoy puts into the mouth of his most misogynistic spokesmen the indictment of the female sex, who are men's enemies because they keep him ensnared to this "filthy abomination." Yet in all fairness, Tolstoy does not descend to the stupidity of our modern-day contemporaries. He turns the question on members of his own sex and their historic privileges. Who has turned women into these serpentine coquettes? It is men who have educated them to be so, and it is society that compliments young men on their successful debauchery and bribes innocent women into violating their purity, all for the sake of some financial support and a place in the respectable world of the married.

The document of Tolstoy's rebellion against what he considered the tyranny of the sexual is his story "The Kreutzer Sonata" (1889). Marriage is just copulation, insists his character Pozdnyshev, who has murdered his wife out of a (probably unfounded) belief in her infidelity. In Pozdnyshev's view, we pretend there is a distinction between licit and illicit sex, between love, conjugal affection, sentiment, on the one hand, and brutal lust, on the other. But that is a lie, he contends. Women have been corrupted by men's lusts, and have, in a twisted fashion, come to dominate men, just as the humiliated Jews dominate the gentiles who oppress them by using their financial power. Enslaved socially, women avenge themselves:

> The way things are at present, the woman is deprived of the rights possessed by the man. And, in order to compensate for this, she acts on the man's sensuality, forces him into subjection by means of sensuality, so that he's only formally the one who chooses—in actual fact it's she who does the choosing. And once she has mastered this technique, she abuses it and acquires a terrible power over men.[51]

Yes, Pozdnyshev concedes, it is common to believe that sexual love is approved because it contributes to the preservation of the human race. "The world must be peopled," Shakespeare's Benedick says to himself as he turns his thoughts away from bachelorhood to a union with Beatrice, much to the approval of the audience of *Much Ado about Nothing*. But should we approve? Why should the human race continue? Because, according to Pozdnyshev, "Of all the passions, it is sexual, carnal love that is the strongest, the most malignant and the most unyielding. It follows that if the passions are eliminated, and together with them this ultimate, strongest passion, carnal love, the goal of mankind will be attained and there will be no reason for it to live any longer."[52]

Tolstoy did not go out and shoot young college girls. He did make a hell out of his own marriage and, while pressuring his wife Sofya Andreyevna to adopt his utopian and minimalist ideals—including celibacy—he continued to force sexual relations on her, much to his shame. His recommendation, that modern society stop its insipid and contradictory idealization of erotic love, was joined to a political and thoughtful critique of the sexual double standard. In "The Kreutzer Sonata" and in other writings, he denounces the way middle- and upper-class women are brought up to be trivial playthings, obsessed with their own appearance, blind to their own physical, moral, and intellectual strengths. Chastity, he concludes, can never be a law or a precept. But it can be an ideal, a prefiguration of a world made peaceful, simple, and just. Infuriated by his own failure to live up to this ideal (Tolstoy would not have lasted a week in a Shaker community), he left us this most bitter of all the chastity plots. It was promptly banned, although Sofya managed to talk the tsar into rescinding the ban. That she knew the story was aimed against her was clear: "I am a buzzing fly entangled in this web, sucked of its blood by this spider," she wrote in her diary.[53] But she faithfully copied it out, line by line. And then she wrote her own riposte, a different version of "The Kreutzer Sonata," with the mistreated wife the innocent victim of her fanatical husband's jealousy and sexual pessimism.

Is that the last word on chastity, Tolstoy's impossible accusation of the slavery of sexual passion and the cry for the human race to terminate itself rather than fail to live up to its ideals? The Incels do not accept his challenge, nor do they seem to be aware of it. As I noted in my introduction, there has always been a tension between the major plot of the eunuch's renunciation and the minor plot, which praises the maiden's modesty and advocates continence within marriage. The most recent iteration of the *Catechism of the Catholic Church* tries to swing both ways: "Both the sacrament of Matrimony and virginity for the Kingdom of God come from the Lord himself.... Esteem of virginity for the sake of the kingdom and the Christian understanding of marriage are inseparable, and they reinforce each other." It quotes John Chrysostom: "Whoever denigrates marriage also diminishes the glory of virginity. Whoever praises it makes virginity more admirable and resplendent. What seems good only in comparison with evil would not be truly good. The most excellent good is sometimes even better than what is admitted to be good. (*De virg.* 10.1)."[54]

At its peak, from the fourth century to the High Middle Ages, the eunuch's ideal associated asexuality—that is, a sexless state of existence—not only with humans' original and unmarred condition but with mystical rapture. To reject the material world, as the vowed celibate is meant to do, is not merely a diffident or prissy attitude. It does not fit comfortably with the moral self-satisfaction of the believer who thinks sin is something other people do. It is a passion. For those who try to practice such an ethic—perhaps best described as the attempt to turn human being into a condition of impersonality, self-dissolution, or absence, what Simone Weil called "decreation"—integration with the social world and its values can prove almost impossible. The eunuch's plot still appeals to the Catholic Church as the "more excellent good." Consecrated virginity is the resplendent virtue, the one for perfectionists. Tolstoy wonders why the world has tried so hard to deny the superiority of this ideal, given the horrors of marriage, the lies of society, and the humiliations of sex. The story told in Genesis thinks otherwise. Adam and Eve chose the complexities of knowledge over the charms of innocence. Tradition calls this choice the "felix culpa," the fortunate fall. Those who fell in love with radical chastity hoped to reverse it, to become unsullied through disembodiment, and to turn the mess of history into the peace of the desert. Their chastity plot failed, but the way we imagine sex and its problems has been permanently affected by their failure and its meanings. There is no going back to a state of nature or an erotic pastoral, to a condition before the complexities of plots, the wounds of repression, and the disappointments of idealism. To do justice to the messy world of sex and gender, to fight misogyny and think more carefully about sexual ethics, it is not enough just to criticize the old. If we are to do justice to the messy world of sex and gender, to work toward a sexual ethic adequate to the demands of the present, it is necessary to understand the history of those concepts that are available to us. The task of a genealogy is to provide such an understanding. Its promise, perhaps its hope, is that thinking through the presence of the past opens up an intellectual space for less shopworn words, bolder images, more capacious and unpredictable plots.

Notes

Introduction

Epigraph: Virginia Woolf, *A Room of One's Own* (New York: Harcourt, 2005), 62–63.

1. Woolf, *Room of One's Own*, 49.

2. On the curious alliances between social purity feminists, middle-class evangelicals, and working-class radicals, see Lucy Bland, *Banishing the Beast: Feminism, Sex and Morality* (London: I. B. Tauris, 1995), 95–115; and Alan Hunt, *Governing Morals: A Social History of Moral Regulation* (Cambridge: Cambridge University Press, 1999). This attraction of women activists to moral reform movements is strikingly unlike the socialist feminism described by Barbara Taylor in *Eve and the New Jerusalem: Socialism and Feminism in the Nineteenth Century* as a "revolutionary humanism which challenged hierarchies at all levels of social existence" (London: Virago, 1983), 275. Sexual radicalism, with its clear mandate to undo the inequities of marriage and bring down the double standard in sexual behavior, dissuaded some middle-class feminists: temperance, abolition of slavery, equal rights for women, and support for prostitutes were principles that could unite a broad spectrum of the "buttoned-up" and the sexually heterodox. But the fear of offending against chastity did not vanish.

3. Linda Dillow and Lorraine Pintus, *Gift-Wrapped by God: Sweet Answers to the Question "Why Wait"?* (Colorado Springs, CO: WaterBrook Press, 2002); Joshua Harris, *I Kissed Dating Goodbye* (Colorado Springs, CO: Multnomah Books, 1997).

4. Breanne Fahs, "Daddy's Little Girls: On the Perils of Chastity Clubs, Purity Balls, and Ritualized Abstinence," *Frontiers: A Journal of Women Studies* 31, no. 3 (2010): 116–42, quotation at 120.

5. Wendy Shalit, *A Return to Modesty: Discovering the Lost Virtue* (New York: Free Press, 1999), 91, xxxix–xxx, 2–5, 160–67.

6. Saba Mahmood, *Politics of Piety: The Islamic Revival and the Feminist Subject* (Princeton, NJ: Princeton University Press, 2005), esp. 99–113 and 174–99.

7. According to Jennifer Wright Knaust, such "biblical marriages" have little backing in the Bible itself. See Jennifer Wright Knaust, *Unprotected Texts: The Bible's Surprising Contradictions about Sex and Desire* (New York: HarperCollins, 2011).

8. The position defended by Shalit and attacked by feminist blogger and journalist Jessica Valenti; see Jessica Valenti, *The Purity Myth: How America's Obsession with Virginity is Hurting Young Women* (Berkeley, CA: Seal Press, 2010), esp. 37–72.

9. Modern experts on sexual difference reverse the opinions of their medieval counterparts: "Whereas in Roman law it was assumed that men were the sexual aggressors and women their victims, canon lawyers, again under the influence of the

church fathers, stressed the sexually predatory nature of women. They found support for their views in contemporary medical opinion, which depicted women as sexually insatiable by nature; some medical authorities believed, for example, that without regular moisturizing with male semen, the uterus would dry up—hence women's constant need for sex." Steven Ozment, *When Fathers Ruled: Family Life in Reformation Europe* (Cambridge, MA: Harvard University Press, 1983), 11. I return to the Victorian fantasy of the sexless woman in chapters 7 and 8.

10. Callie Beusman, "'Slut-Shaming' Has Been Tossed Around So Much, It's Lost All Meaning," *Jezebel* (blog), December 12, 2013, https://jezebel.com/slut-shaming-has-been-tossed-around-so-much-its-los-1478093672.

11. Charles Taylor, *A Secular Age* (Cambridge, MA: Belknap Press of Harvard University Press, 2008), 495.

12. Valenti quotes Wendy Shalit, *Girls Gone Mild: Young Women Reclaim Self-Respect and Find It's Not Bad to Be Good* (New York Random House, 2007), 10, in Valenti, *Purity Myth*, 51.

13. Christine J. Gardner, *Making Chastity Sexy: The Rhetoric of Evangelical Abstinence Campaigns* (Berkeley: University of California Press, 2011).

14. See Anke Bernau, *Virgins: A Cultural History* (London: Granta Books, 2007), 171–86, where Bernau adds the view from Britain in the 1990s and the first decade of the twenty-first century to her fine account of the "new virginity" movements; despite the different flavor of Protestant evangelicism in the United States and the United Kingdom, there are many similarities.

15. C. Taylor, *Secular Age*, 26, 1–2.

16. C. Gardner, *Making Chastity Sexy*, 86.

17. Fahs, "Daddy's Little Girls," 117. Peter S. Bearman and Hannah Bruckner are sociologists who have been tracking the effects of abstinence education over twenty years, and their conclusion is that the virginity pledges do contribute to a "delay" of first intercourse among young and religious Americans, but only if they are "embedded in an identity movement." See Bearman and Bruckner, "Promising the Future: Virginity Pledges and First Intercourse," *American Journal of Sociology* 106, no. 4 (January 2001): 839–912, quotations at 859, 891.

18. See Laura M. Carpenter, *Virginity Lost: An Intimate Portrait of First Sexual Experiences* (New York: New York University Press, 2005), 5.

19. Linda Kay Klein, *Pure: Inside the Evangelical Movement That Shamed a Generation of Young Women and How I Broke Free* (New York: Touchstone, 2018).

20. See Carpenter, *Virginity Lost*, 3.

21. Bearman and Bruckner concluded in 2005 that those who took the pledge were six times more likely to have oral and anal sex than the nonpledgers, and that 88 percent of pledgers had in fact backslid, not only having sex before marriage but avoiding contraception or safe-sex practices. The increase in vulnerability to sexually transmitted diseases (STDs) was disturbing, to say the least. See Peter S. Bearman and Hannah Bruckner, "After the Promise: The STD Consequences of Adolescent Virginity Pledges," *Journal of Adolescent Health* 36, no. 4 (April 2005): 271–78. Their results were widely reported—and contested by conservatives.

22. Sherry Ortner, *Making Gender: The Politics and Erotics of Culture* (Boston: Beacon Press, 1996), 43.

23. Ortner, *Making Gender*, 56.

24. Ortner, *Making Gender*, 57.

25. As persuasively argued in Kathleen Coyne Kelly and Marina Leslie, eds., *Menacing Virgins: Representing Virginity in the Middle Ages and Renaissance* (Newark: University of Delaware Press, 1999), where the editors, with a number of the contributors, pay tribute to the "contradictory" and "ambivalent" meanings of virginity/chastity. The militant or "menacing" virgin is, like the "willful maiden Hermia" in Shakespeare's *A Midsummer Night's Dream*, a threat to husbandly and fatherly control. Spiritual integrity—a quality of the soul—is not always present in those who can claim physical intactness. But even the secular idealization of bodily "innocence" coexists uneasily with the commendation of marriage, the state for which the model virgin would seem to be intended. "An object of anxious fascination, and the focus of an enduring cultural obsession," as the editors aptly remark (21), virginity's instability and contradictions do not make it less significant as an ideal. Quite the contrary. I share the authors' belief in the combination of "menace" and conformity in this paradoxical virtue and have tried to give both eunuch and maiden a say in the "chastity plot."

26. All biblical quotations are from New Revised Standard Version (RSV), specifically *The New Oxford Annotated Bible*, 4th ed., ed. Michael D. Coogan (Oxford: Oxford University Press, 2010).

27. See Norman Cohn, *The Pursuit of the Millennium: Revolutionary Millenarians and Mystical Anarchists of the Middle Ages* (1957; repr., London: Pimlico, 2004).

28. John Bugge, *Virginitas: An Essay in the History of a Medieval Ideal* (The Hague: Martinus Nijhoff, 1975), on the sponsa Christi (58–79).

29. George R. R. Martin, *A Song of Ice and Fire: A Game of Thrones, Book 1* (New York: Bantam Books, 1996), 435–36.

30. Immanuel Kant, *Observations on the Feeling of the Beautiful and the Sublime*, ed. Patrick Frierson and Paul Guyer (Cambridge: Cambridge University Press, 2011), 22; Immanuel Kant, *Lectures on Ethics*, ed. Peter Heath and J. B. Schneewind, trans. Peter Heath (Cambridge: Cambridge University Press, 1992), 152.

31. Michel Foucault, *Les aveux de la chair*, vol. 4 of *Histoire de la sexualité* (Paris: Gallimard, 2018), 149–205.

32. Michael Frassetto, ed., *Medieval Purity and Piety: Essays on Medieval Clerical Celibacy and Religious Reform* (New York: Garland, 1998), vii.

33. See Peter Brown, *The Body and Society: Men, Women and Sexual Renunciation in Early Christianity* (New York: Columbia University Press, 1988), 40–42.

34. Glenn Holland, "Celibacy in the Early Christian Church," in *Celibacy and Religious Traditions*, ed. Carl Olson (Oxford: Oxford University Press, 2008), 65–83.

35. Michel Foucault, "Technologies of the Self," in *Technologies of the Self: A Seminar with Michel Foucault*, ed. L. H. Martin, H. Gutman, and P. H. Hutton (London: Tavistock, 1988), 16–49.

36. "Chastity and virginity are moral categories denoting a relation between the will and the flesh; they are not categories of sexuality": this decided judgment appears in an article by Arnold I. Davidson, "Sex and the Emergence of Sexuality," *Critical Inquiry* 14, no. 1 (Autumn 1987): 16–48. I would normally prefer to agree with Davidson, but I believe the demarcation is too clean. Early Christians, their medieval descendants, and their Puritan or Calvinist heirs did understand the combats of will and flesh as sexual combats, and the inner life was thus forced into sharp relief as a place rife with sexuality. The point of the radical celibate is to become free of that sexual mess. If achieved, this form of perfection stands at an oblique angle to sexuality; it does not exist in a field where sexuality has no purchase at all. That is why I have promoted the

idea that chastity is as much a metaphysical and an aesthetic construction as a fact about sexuality, even a deviant fact about sexuality. But, as Eve Sedgwick, Theodora Jankowsi, and others have been arguing, the asexual and the celibate could belong in a longer, more random list of sexual and queer possibilities. Just as early modern opponents of Catholicism liked to call abstinence and celibacy "perverse" positions, so the chaste might, in company with Monique Wittig's lesbian, escape normal categories of sex and gender.

37. See, for one among many descriptions, Friedrich Nietzsche, *Human, All Too Human: A Book for Free Spirits*, trans. Marion Faber, with Stephen Lehmann (Lincoln: University of Nebraska Press, 1984), 97–102.

Chapter One

Epigraphs: Michel Foucault, "Nietzsche, Genealogy, History," in *Language, Counter-Memory, Practice*, trans. Donald F. Bouchard and Sherry Simon (Ithaca, NY: Cornell University Press, 1997); John Milton, *Milton's Selected Poetry and Prose*, ed. Jason P. Rosenblatt (New York: W. W. Norton, 2011), lines 737–42, p. 60.

1. J. K. Elliot, *The Apocryphal New Testament: A Collection of Apocryphal Christian Literature in English Translation* (Oxford: Oxford University Press, 1993), 364.

2. Paul seems less than enthusiastic about Thecla's ardor for the ascetic life. According to Virginia Burrus, women's choice of sexual continence, while officially celebrated, encountered a regular pattern of male diffidence and outright impediment in the early church because female sexual asceticism represents "resistance to male control." See Virginia Burrus, "Word and Flesh: The Bodies and Sexuality of Ascetic Women in Christian Antiquity," *Journal of Feminist Studies in Religion* 10, no. 1 (Spring 1994): 27–51, esp. 46–48. See also Virginia Burrus, *Chastity as Autonomy: Women in the Stories of Apocryphal Acts* (Lewiston, NY: Edwin Mellen Press, 1987).

3. Ian Watt, *The Rise of the Novel: Studies in Defoe, Richardson and Fielding* (Harmondsworth, UK: Penguin, 1972), 196.

4. Woolf, *Room of One's Own*, 62–63.

5. Woolf, *Room of One's Own*, 49–50.

6. Virginia Woolf, *Three Guineas* (London: Hogarth Press, 1986), note 38, pp. 166–67.

7. Mary Wollstonecraft, *A Vindication of the Rights of Men, with A Vindication of the Rights of Women and Hints*, ed. Sylvana Tomaselli (Cambridge: Cambridge University Press, 1995), 76, 78, 116.

8. Wollstonecraft, *Vindication*, 68.

9. Wollstonecraft, *Vindication*, 171.

10. Wollstonecraft, *Vindication*, 217.

11. As argued elegantly by Mary Poovey, *The Proper Lady and the Woman Writer: Ideology as Style in the Works of Mary Wollstonecraft, Mary Shelley, and Jane Austen* (Chicago: University of Chicago Press, 1984).

12. Wollstonecraft, *Vindication*, 93–106, where her target is also Dr. John Gregory (1724–1773), author of *A Father's Legacy to His Daughters*, one of the period's most influential books on female education.

13. *Boswell's Journal of a Tour to the Hebrides with Samuel Johnson* (New York: Viking Press, 1936), 168.

14. Henry Fielding, *The History of Joseph Andrews and His Friend Mr. Abraham Adams* (New York: Signet, 1960), 20.

15. Kyle Harper, *From Shame to Sin: The Christian Transformation of Sexual Morality in Late Antiquity* (Cambridge, MA: Harvard University Press, 2013), 165; Asterius of Amasea, *Homily 5*, "On Divorce," transcribed by Roger Pearce, accessed March 30, 2018, http://www.tertullian.org/fathers/asterius_05_sermon5.htm.

16. Friedrich Nietzsche, *On the Genealogy of Morals*, in *"On the Genealogy of Morals" and "Ecce Homo,"* trans. Walter Kauffman and R. J. Hollingdale (New York: Vintage, 1989), Essay III.

17. Maud Burnett McInerney, *Eloquent Virgins from Thecla to Joan of Arc* (New York: Palgrave Macmillan, 2003), 34; Brown, *Body and Society*, 78–79.

18. Brown, *Body and Society*, 158–59.

19. Samuel Richardson, *Pamela, or Virtue Rewarded* (London: Penguin, 1985), 63 (Letter 15).

20. Northrop Frye, *The Secular Scripture: A Study of the Structure of Romance* (Cambridge, MA: Harvard University Press, 1976), 86.

21. Max Weber, *From Max Weber: Essays in Sociology*, ed. and trans. H. H. Gerth and C. Wright Mills (London: Routledge and Kegan Paul, 1948), 276–81.

22. Mieke Bal, *Death and Dissymmetry: The Politics of Coherence in the Book of Judges* (Chicago: University of Chicago Press, 1988), 41–50.

23. Although Jephthah does talk of a "burnt offering" or "holocaust" as a thank-you to God for giving him the victory over his enemies, it is possible that his daughter's fate was not death but a life of virginity: both daughter and father bemoan the unhappy fate his rash vow entailed, but the penalty of lifelong celibacy may have been as distressing as the possibility of a sacrificial killing, something Jews had been prohibited to do since Abraham.

24. Bal, *Death and Dissymmetry*, 41.

25. Bal, *Death and Dissymmetry*, 46, 66–67.

26. Corrinne Harol, *Enlightened Virginity in Eighteenth-Century Literature* (New York: Palgrave Macmillan, 2006), 131–45.

27. Northrop Frye introduces the "mythos of summer" in *Anatomy of Criticism: Four Essays* (Princeton, NJ: Princeton University Press, 1971), 186–203.

28. For these and other pastoral conventions, see N. Frye, *Secular Scripture*, 48–124. See also Teresa Shaw, *The Burden of the Flesh: Fasting and Sexuality in Early Christianity* (Minneapolis: Fortress Press, 1998), in which she connects Christian asceticism, virginity, and the pagan myths of the golden age (161–219). I have learned much from her account.

29. Arthur Heiserman reminds us that the romance plot used in the Greek and Roman "novels" of Chariton, Longus, Achilles Tatius, and Apuleius are stories of erotic suffering and that perhaps the most enchanting of them, Chariton's *Chareas and Callirhoe* (approx. 50 CE) defends the idea that "we can have it both ways—the pleasures of Aphrodite and the pleasures of chastity." Arthur Heiserman, *The Novel Before the Novel: Essays and Discussions about the Beginnings of Prose Fiction in the West* (Chicago: University of Chicago Press, 1977), 84. Edmund Spenser, as I will argue in chapter 7, was very taken with this idea.

30. Stephanie Coontz, *Marriage, A History: From Obedience to Intimacy, or How Love Conquered Marriage* (New York: Viking, 2007), 14.

31. Coontz, *Marriage*, 34–49.

32. For Hume, see David Hume, *Enquiries Concerning Human Understanding and Concerning the Principles of Morals*, ed. L. A. Selby-Bigge (Oxford: Oxford University Press, 1975), 270. For Luther, see Martin Luther, "Commentaries on I Corinthians 7 and I Corinthians 15, Lectures on I Timothy," in *Luther's Works*, vol. 28, ed. Hilton C. Oswald (St. Louis, MO: Concordia Publishing, 1973), 312–13. Hume's rejection of the "train of monkish virtues" consigns celibacy and humility to history's leftovers, things that "harden the heart, obscure the fancy, and sour the temper" (*Enquiries*, 270). Here he moves close enough to the camp of Luther and the Puritans, who wanted regeneration of the whole being, body and soul, to be an event in the world, not in some empty region of pure renunciation. See Charles Taylor, *Sources of the Self: The Making of the Modern Identity* (Cambridge: Cambridge University Press, 1989), 222.

33. Friedrich Nietzsche, *"The Antichrist," "Ecce Homo," "Twilight of the Idols," and Other Writings*, trans. Aaron Ridley and Judith Norman (Cambridge: Cambridge University Press, 2007), 173.

34. Benjamin Kahan, *Celibacies: American Modernism and Sexual Life* (Durham, NC: Duke University Press, 2013).

35. Valerie Traub, *The Renaissance of Lesbianism in Early Modern England* (Cambridge: Cambridge University Press, 2002).

36. Philip Rieff, *Freud: The Mind of the Moralist*, 3rd ed. (Chicago: University of Chicago Press, 1979), 148.

37. Sigmund Freud, *Civilization and its Discontents*, trans. James Strachey (New York: W. W. Norton, 2005), 42–43.

38. "When something you desire is actually an obstacle to your flourishing," Lauren Berlant writes, then a "relation of cruel optimism exists." Lauren Berlant, *Cruel Optimism* (Durham, NC: Duke University Press, 2011), 1. Attachment to projects of social improvement, structural transformation, emancipatory politics, moral perfectionism, providential justification, or romantic satisfaction are, she says, "optimistic" and also "cruel": cruel because "the object that draws your attachment actively impedes the aim that brought you to it initially" (1). Attachment to the civilizing process is "cruelly optimistic," at least in Freud's diagnosis. The cruelty in the case of ascetic aspirations is literal: illness and pain are victories in the fight against the flesh; frustration is a proof of achievement.

39. Friedrich Nietzsche, *On the Genealogy of Morals*, Essay III, §9 (hereafter cited in text as *GM* III). On Nietzsche and asceticism, see Richard Schacht, ed., *Nietzsche, Genealogy, Morality: Essays on Nietzsche's "On the Genealogy of Morals"* (Berkeley: University of California Press, 1994); Georg Simmel, *Schopenhauer and Nietzsche*, trans. Helmut Loiskandl, Deena Weinstein, and Michael Weinstein (Urbana: University of Illinois Press, 1991); Christopher Janaway, *Beyond Selflessness: Reading Nietzsche's Genealogy* (Oxford: Oxford University Press, 2007); Gilles Deleuze, "Active and Reactive," in *The New Nietzsche: Contemporary Styles of Interpretation*, ed. David B. Allison (New York: Delia, 1977); Alenka Zupancic, *The Shortest Shadow: Nietzsche's Philosophy of the Two* (Cambridge, MA: MIT Press, 2002); and Bernard Reginster, *Nietzsche on Overcoming Nihilism* (Cambridge, MA: Harvard University Press, 2006). Discussion of asceticism in the scholarly world is lively; see Gavin Flood, *The Ascetic Self: Subjectivity, Memory and Tradition* (Cambridge: Cambridge University Press, 2004); Oliver Freiberger, ed., *Asceticism and its Critics* (Oxford: Oxford University Press, 2006); Vincent Winbush and Richard Valantasis, eds., *Asceticism* (Oxford:

Oxford University Press, 1995); and the wonderful work of Vladimir Jankélévitch, *Le pur et l'impur* (Paris: Flammarion, 1960).

40. A forceful case for refusing art's offer to compensate us for a disappointing reality is made by the critic Leo Bersani in *The Culture of Redemption* (Cambridge, MA: Harvard University Press, 1990).

41. Geoffrey Galt Harpham, *The Ascetic Imperative in Culture and Criticism* (Chicago: University of Chicago Press, 1987), xi–xiii, 203–19.

42. Foucault, "Nietzsche, Genealogy, History," 161.

43. Michel Foucault, *The Archaeology of Knowledge*, trans. A. M. Sheridan Smith (London: Tavistock, 1972), 4.

44. Foucault, "Nietzsche, Genealogy, History," 144.

45. Foucault, "Nietzsche, Genealogy, History," 142.

46. Max Weber, *The Protestant Ethic and the Spirit of Capitalism*, trans. Talcott Parsons (New York: Scribners, 1959), 119. On religious asceticism, see also "The Social Psychology of the World Religions," and "Religious Rejections of the World and their Directions," in Weber, *From Max Weber*, 267–359.

47. I borrow this formulation from Chiara Bottici's impressive *A Philosophy of Political Myth* (Cambridge: Cambridge University Press, 2007).

48. Judith Butler, *The Psychic Life of Power: Theories in Subjection* (Stanford, CA: Stanford University Press, 1997), esp. 1–30.

49. Peter Brooks, *Reading for the Plot: Design and Intention in Narrative* (Cambridge, MA: Harvard University Press, 1992), 99. My account of plot is heavily indebted to Brooks's rich psychoanalytic theory, as will become obvious. Also indispensable to me: Leo Bersani, *A Future for Astyanax: Character and Desire in Literature* (New York: Columbia University Press, 1984).

50. Paul Ricoeur, "Narrative Time," in *On Narrative*, ed. W. J. T. Mitchell (Chicago: University of Chicago Press, 1981), 165–86, at 167; see also Brooks, *Reading for the Plot*, 14.

51. Watt, *Rise of the Novel*, 153–54.

52. Richardson, *Pamela, or Virtue Rewarded*, Letter 15, 63.

53. Laura Mulvey, "Visual Pleasure and Narrative Cinema," in *Visual and Other Pleasures* (Bloomington: Indiana University Press, 1989), 22.

54. I will be speaking more fully about the "marriage plot" in the next sections, but let me here mention some highlights from the enormous literature on this theme: Joseph Allen Boone, *Tradition Counter-Tradition: Love and the Forms of Fiction* (Chicago: University of Chicago Press, 1987); Davida Pines, *The Marriage Paradox: Modernist Novels and the Cultural Imperative to Marry* (Gainesville: University Press of Florida, 2006); Rachel Blau DuPlessis, *Writing beyond the Ending: Narrative Strategies of Twentieth-Century Women Writers* (Bloomington: Indiana University Press, 1985); Rachel Brownstein, *Becoming a Heroine: Reading about Women in Novels* (Harmondsworth, UK: Penguin, 1982); Nancy K. Miller, *The Heroine's Text: Readings in the French and English Novel, 1722–1782* (New York: Columbia University Press, 1980); Jean H. Hagstrum, *Sex and Sensibility: Ideal and Erotic Love from Milton to Mozart* (Chicago: University of Chicago Press, 1980); Michael McKeon, *The Origins of the English Novel, 1600–1740* (Baltimore: Johns Hopkins University Press, 1987); Lawrence Stone, *The Family, Sex and Marriage in England 1500–1800* (New York: Harper and Row, 1977); Stanley Cavell, *Pursuits of Happiness: The Hollywood Comedy of Remarriage* (Cambridge, MA: Harvard University Press, 1981); Northrop Frye, *Anat-*

omy of Criticism (Princeton, NJ: Princeton University Press, 1957); Joseph A. Boone, "Modernist Maneuverings in the Marriage Plot: Breaking Ideologues of Gender and Genre in James's *The Golden Bowl*," *PMLA* 101, no. 3 (May 1986): 374–88; Evelyn J. Hinz, "Hierogamy versus Wedlock: Marriage Plots and their Relationship to Genres of Prose Fiction," *PMLA* 91, no. 5 (October 1976): 900–913; Lisa O'Connell, "Vicars and Squires: Religion and the Rise of the English Marriage Plot," *Eighteenth Century* 52, no. 3/4 (Fall/Winter 2011): 383–402; and now Lisa O'Connell, *The Origins of the English Marriage Plot: Literature, Politics and Religion in the Eighteenth Century* (Cambridge: Cambridge University Press, 2019), who clarifies: "The term 'marriage plot,' of course, is ambiguous. At one level it means any narrative that ends, or almost ends, in a marriage or marriages and that is largely concerned throughout with courtship" (5). O'Connell wants to put pressure on that common understanding, believing it too loose and historically evasive to describe the new genre of fiction developed in England—by Richardson, in fact. For my purposes, however, I need both that conventional conception of the marriage plot and the socialist-feminist evaluation of marriage as, indeed, a plot against women, their labor, and their significance.

55. See Foucault, *Les aveux de la chair.*

56. The Eastern churches, both Orthodox and Eastern Catholic, require celibacy from bishops but not from lower orders.

57. Boone, *Tradition Counter-Tradition*, 2.

58. Samuel Richardson, *The History of Sir Charles Grandison*, Letter 38, Miss Byron to Miss Selby, in *The Novels of Samuel Richardson*, vol. 2, ed. William Lyon Phelps (London: Croscup and Sterling, 1902), 282.

59. "The whole duty of man" is mentioned in the Bible, in the book of Ecclesiastes 12:13, Authorized (King James) Version; the expression is familiar from the title of the devotional book by Richard Allestree, *The Whole Duty of Man* (London: W. Norton, 1701), first published 1658; "esteem enlivened by desire" is from the title of a book by Jean Hagstrum, *Esteem Enlivened by Desire: The Couple from Homer to Shakespeare* (Chicago: University of Chicago Press, 1991), and the line appears in Thomson's poem "The Seasons"; see James Thomson, *The Complete Poems* (Oxford: Clarendon Press, 1981).

60. Sigmund Freud, *Beyond the Pleasure Principle: The Standard Edition of the Complete Psychological Works of Sigmund Freud*, ed. James Strachey and Anna Freud (London: Hogarth Press, 1955), is the classical locus for the hypothesis of the Freudian "death drive." Although Freud doesn't use the expression "death-in-life," it is an apt description for that ensemble of self-destructive impulses he associates with inertia, the repetition compulsion, and the general revulsion from the energy and tension life demands.

61. Brooks, *Reading for the Plot*, 51, 52.

62. Harol, *Enlightened Virginity*, 2.

63. Harol is persuasive about the "logical incompatibilities" of a number of models that purport to explain "why patriarchy loves a virgin." The most popular one at present, she writes, is the patrilinear legitimacy model, which is sometimes treated as if it were "trans-historical," a mistake in her view. Not that the association of virginity with property and legitimacy is wrong; but the tendency to generalize it to cover all cultural valuations and investments in virginity/chastity needs correction, or at least greater specification. "There is no necessary relationship between virginity and chastity": premarital sexual inexperience is no guarantee of fidelity to the marital bed—

that is, no guarantee of "wedded chastity," as English Protestants liked to call it. Modern feminists (Harol names Gerda Lerner, Sherry Ortner, and Carole Pateman, but Simone de Beauvoir could be added as well as many socialist feminists) argue that "patriarchy reproduces itself via control over female sexuality. Enforced standards of virginity and chastity are disciplinary devices used to motivate women into servicing patriarchal mandates." Yet "virginity seems an unlikely foundation for the source of male authority over women." As she sees it, virginity in the eighteenth century "becomes gradually disembodied, as it becomes a figure for virtue," in response to pressures from religio-political conflict and "the new scientific methods" (Harol, *Enlightened Virginity*, 5). Virginity, she concludes, is best understood as a myth, performing a number of tasks in a number of symbolic systems.

64. For "tragedies of seduction," see Boone, *Tradition Counter-Tradition*, 102; see also Tony Tanner, *Adultery and the Novel: Contract and Transgression* (Baltimore: Johns Hopkins University Press, 1979).

65. N. Frye, *Secular Scripture*, 86.

66. N. Frye, *Secular Scripture*, 86.

Chapter Two

Epigraphs: René Girard, *Violence and the Sacred* (Baltimore: Johns Hopkins University Press, 1979), 118; Friedrich Nietzsche, *Daybreak: Thoughts on the Prejudices of Morality*, trans. R. J. Hollingdale (Cambridge: Cambridge University Press, 1997), bk. 1, sec. 76, p. 45.

1. Gilbert Murray, *Euripides and His Age* (New York: Henry Holt, 1913), 86.

2. See W. S. Barrett's commentary in Euripides, *Euripides Hippolytos*, ed. and with commentary by W. S. Barrett (Oxford: Clarendon Press, 1964), 154.

3. Euripides, *Hippolytus*, trans. David Kovacs, Loeb Classical Library (Cambridge, MA: Harvard University Press, 1995), 59, 113 (hereafter cited parenthetically in text as *Hipp.* with line number).

4. Saint Jerome, for one, was unafraid of the arrogance of the pure. In 384 he wrote a letter to the upper-class adolescent Eustochium, who had declared herself ready for a life of perpetual virginity and found herself an exception among the young ladies of her class in Rome. They think they are pious and chaste Christians, but they are all whores and fakes, Jerome assures her. You are too good to mix with them, so watch out, Jerome cautions, or their envy will plague you: "Learn from me a holy arrogance: Know that you are better than all of them." Letter 22, §16, in *Jerome: Letters*, in *Library of Ancient Christian Writers*, vol. 33 (New York: Paulist Press, 1963), 163.

5. "An asyndeton . . . in the grammar of life," observes Froma I. Zeitlin, *Playing the Other: Gender and Society in Classical Greek Literature* (Chicago: University of Chicago Press, 1996), 229.

6. Dale Launderville, *Celibacy in the Ancient World: Its Ideal and Practice in Pre-Hellenistic Israel, Mesopotamia, and Greece* (Collegeville, MN: Liturgical Press, 2010), 286.

7. Zeitlin, *Playing the Other*, 222.

8. The Greeks invented the notion of "hysteria" and associated it with the disturbance caused by a "wandering womb," therefore, we may assume, a female problem. If your womb is not functioning properly, you are highly vulnerable to a range of dramatic symptoms; see Jane Rowlandson, *Women and Society in Greek and Roman Egypt*

(Cambridge: Cambridge University Press, 1998), 340. Because menstruation exhibits these "disequilibria" of the female body, to be subject to it disqualifies women from the rights and duties of participating in public assemblies and the serious business of the city.

9. I have also consulted Euripides, *Hippolytos*, trans. Anne Carson, in *Grief Lessons: Four Plays by Euripides* (New York: New York Review of Books, 2006); W. S. Barrett's Greek edition with commentary, Euripides, *Euripides Hippolytos*; and two other modern translations: Euripides, *Hippolytus*, ed. and trans. Michael R. Halleran (Newburyport, MA: Focus Classical Library, 2001); Euripides, *Hippolytos*, trans. Robert Bagg (New York: Oxford University Press, 1973).

10. That the play's use of the two to destroy each other is not a trivial indictment of conventionality should be obvious. Froma I. Zeitlin brings out its more troubling concern with the antagonistic powers of eros: eros is the snare and the disease, binding those who resist being bound to one another, denying the autonomy of the self and the illusions of identity. See Zeitlin, *Playing the Other*, esp. 222–34.

11. The fullest discussion of sophrosyne is Helen North, *Sophrosyne: Self-Knowledge and Self-Restraint in Greek Literature* (Ithaca, NY: Cornell University Press, 1964). The first reference in classical poetry to feminine sophrosyne in the "limited significance" of chastity (in archaic literature it appears as early as the seventh century BCE) is made by Aeschylus's character King Danaus in *The Suppliants*; See North, *Sophrosyne*, 36–38. I will discuss this paradox in chapter 3. See also Helen North, *From Myth to Icon: Reflections of Greek Ethical Doctrine in Literature and Art* (Ithaca, NY: Cornell University Press, 1979), esp. chapter 1, "The Mythology of Sophrosyne," in which she states, "The first and most widespread myth of masculine sophrosyne—found all over the world, not just in Greece—is that of the chaste young man who repels the amorous advances of an older, married woman" (33).

12. Bernard Williams, *Shame and Necessity* (Berkeley: University of California Press, 1993), 78, 89, 92–93.

13. Aristotle, *Nicomachean Ethics*, trans. W. D. Ross, revised by J. O. Ursom (Oxford: Oxford University Press, 1954), 3.1118b, pp. 28–34.

14. "*Aidos* ('shame') is a vast word in Greek. Its lexical equivalents include 'awe, reverence, respect, self-respect, shamefastness, sense of honour, sobriety, moderation, regard for others, regard for the helpless, compassion, shyness, coyness, scandal, dignity, majesty, Majesty.' Shame vibrates with honour and also with disgrace, with what is chaste and with what is erotic, with coldness and also with blushing. Shame is felt before the eyes of others and also in facing oneself." Anne Carson, preface to Euripides, *Hippolytos*, in *Grief Lessons*, 163–64.

15. See Brooke Holmes, *The Symptom and the Subject: The Emergence of the Physical Body in Ancient Greece* (Princeton, NJ: Princeton University Press, 2010), 253–59.

16. It is closely allied to Artemis, who is named "Aidos" on a red-figured vase described by Walter F. Otto, *The Homeric Gods: The Spiritual Significance of Greek Religion*, trans. Moses Hadas (London: Thames and Hudson, 1979), 293n11.

17. Barbara Cassin, Vinciana Despret, and Marcos Mateos Diaz, "Vergüenza," in *Dictionary of Untranslatables: A Philosophical Lexicon*, ed. Barbara Cassin, translation edited by Emily Apter, Jacques Lezra, and Michael Wood (Princeton, NJ: Princeton University Press, 2014), 1195–98, at 1196.

18. Hesiod, *Theogony, Works and Days, Testimonies*, trans. Glenn W. Most (Cambridge, MA: Harvard University Press, 2007), 363. Lucian appropriates Phaedra's

point, with the same references to Hesiod, in the *Amores*, his mocking dialogue comparing the merits of pederastic and conjugal love. The immediate source may well be Achilles Tatius's *Leucippe and Clitophon*, which has a lively and amusing rhetorical contest on the same subject. Hippolytus's authority is invoked by the pederast in *Amores* to promote the idea of acquiring children by buying them at shrines and temples. This would be a much more rational alternative to the present necessity of intercourse, so humiliating and "unbeautiful." The Loeb translation of the relevant passage in *Amores* is this: "For Shame too is a twofold goddess with both a beneficial and a harmful role." Lucian, *Works*, vol. 8, trans. M. D. MacLeod (Cambridge, MA: Harvard University Press, 1967), 153.

19. A highly appropriate death (unlike Racine's poisoning), since Artemis is associated with hanging and strangulation, by a curious set of equivalences, alluded to in the epithet *Artemis Apankhoumene* and a story Pausanias tells about the goddess's worship at Kaphyae in Arkadia. Helen King argues that suicide by hanging is what one chooses to avoid the bloodshed of rape or unwanted defloration, hence it is what the daughters of Danaus threaten when they seek to escape their aggressive cousins. Artemis herself does not bleed; she who resists the transition to womanhood will be similarly hostile to the onset of menarche, with all its implications that she is "ripe" for marriage, defloration, and childbirth; also that her womb, her lower "mouth," is open, to be closed ideally in pregnancy. Phaedra may regret the whole business. Should she have died before things got to this point? Hanging herself, King argues, is her fantasy of inverting the process. See Helen King, "Bound to Bleed: Artemis and Greek Women," in *Images of Women in Antiquity*, ed. Averil Cameron and Annélie Kuhrt (London: Croom Helm, 1987), 109–27. See also Helen King, *Hippocrates' Woman: Reading the Female Body in Ancient Greece* (London: Routledge, 1998), 21–98, for fascinating discussions of menstruation and other "women matters" in antiquity. Nicole Loraux began the discussion in 1981 with her paper on sexual difference and tragedy "Le lit, la guerre," where she describes the suicides by hanging of the womanly women (Phaedra, Jocasta) as conforming to a certain "orthodoxy" of gender. Nicole Loraux, "Le lit, la guerre," *L'Homme* 21, no. 1 (January–March 1981): 37–67, at 65. Loraux continues the argument in a later study, "to the effect that hanging was associated with marriage—or rather, with an excessive valuation of the status of bride (*nymphe*)—while a suicide that shed blood was associated with maternity." Nicole Loraux, *Tragic Ways of Killing a Woman*, trans. Anthony Forster (Cambridge, MA: Harvard University Press, 1987), 15.

20. If, as we might have expected from such a plot, Aphrodite's aim was to punish Hippolytus for refusing to honor her, why not affect *him* with an ungovernable passion—ideally a transgressive or ridiculous one, as Zeitlin suggests? Aphrodite operates in a circuitous way. Phaedra is used as a stand-in for Hippolytus. His destruction is worked, cruelly, through her, in order that the duality of both concepts—eros and sophrosyne—be more acutely observed. Greek civic ideology, in the sixth and fifth centuries BCE, was committed to the notion that the virtues could cooperate, hence that the crucial practice of sophrosyne could not exclude any other good equally valued, like, in this instance, love. But that faith was delusional. Sophrosyne fails, in Euripides, because it kills the very momentum of eros—which is to say, its drive to loosen, extend, combine, and confuse.

21. The two goddesses are set up in parallel, indeed mirroring, positions. To overlook one is to overlook the other, at least according to Justina Gregory: "The two god-

desses have more in common than Hippolytus imagines. The poet repeatedly links them through imagery: the bee that traverses Artemis' meadow at 77 reappears as Aphrodite's emblem at 563–64, and the poet associates both goddesses with the sky, with destructive shafts, with cool water. He makes them speak the same language, and by the end of the play it will have become clear that the two goddesses share the same goals and methods." Justina Gregory, *Euripides and the Instruction of the Athenians* (Ann Arbor: University of Michigan Press, 1997), 58–59. But Artemis remains unsubdued, immune to the power of the love goddess; see *Homeric Hymn to Aphrodite*, hymn 5, lines 16–20. Just as Aphrodite and Artemis frame each other, neither sufficient to themselves or free of everything they denounce in the other, so Phaedra and Hippolytus will turn out to be the mirroring parts of a mixed-up whole (the "uneasy harmony," or *dustropos harmonia*, of which the Chorus speaks at *Hipp.*, 161–62); see also Zeitlin, *Playing the Other*, 238–39.

22. Zeitlin, *Playing the Other*, 238.

23. Girls who are no longer children but not yet women have posed a problem to many societies. The liminal status of the virgin in Israel, Greece, and Rome goes well beyond the ideal Artemis may be thought to represent and gives many headaches to fathers and those entrusted with the guarding of virgins. Tertullian, advocating the practice of veiling virgins in the Christian communities of the second and third centuries CE, captures the ambiguity of the virginal state for women and their families. A virgin, he writes, does not need to be veiled in early childhood but "from the time she begins to be self-conscious, and to awake to the sense of her own nature, and to emerge from the *virgin's* sense, and to experience that novel (sensation) which belongs to the succeeding age ... a virgin ceases to be a virgin from the time that it becomes possible for her *not* to be one." Tertullian, *On the Veiling of Virgins*, chap. 11, in *Ante-Nicene Fathers*, vol. 4, *Tertullian, Part Fourth; Minucius Felix; Commodian; Origen Parts First and Second*, ed. Alexander Roberts and James Donaldson, revised by A. Cleveland Coxe (Peabody, MA: Hendrickson Publishers, 1999). See also Mary F. Foskett, *A Virgin Conceived: Mary and Classical Representation of Virginity* (Bloomington: Indiana University Press, 2002), 51; Bal, *Death and Dissymmetry*, 42.

24. Jean-Pierre Vernant, *Mortals and Immortals: Collected Essays*, ed. and trans. Froma I. Zeitlin (Princeton, NJ: Princeton University Press, 1991), 197.

25. In Homer, she receives that title too: see Homer, *Iliad* 21.470. Some consider her barbaric, not Greek, or at least some of her avatars seem to be "foreign," as Pausanias says of Laphirian Artemis, whose festivities involve huge burnt offerings of live game birds, bears, wolves, boars, and fruit, plus a procession headed by the most beautiful virgin in a chariot drawn by yoked deer. Pausanias, *Guide to Greece*, vols. 1 and 2, trans. Peter Levi (London: Penguin, 1979), vol. 2, 7.18.7.

26. See Otto, *Homeric Gods*, 80–90.

27. *The Homeric Hymn to Aphrodite*, 5.17–19, as cited in Homer, *The Homeric Hymns*, trans. Jules Cashford, with an introduction and notes by Nicholas Richardson (London: Penguin, 2003), 86.

28. Otto, *Homeric Gods*, 88, citing Pausanias, *Guide to Greece*, vol. 2, 6.23.8. Hippolytus is an idealist destined for disappointment because the image he has of the world and the self is based on an impossibility: there is no simple and untroubled integrity, no such thing as a state or identity without division and mixture. The play, like Greek tragedy in general, agrees with the callow male adolescent that women represent this

"ill-fitted composition" to an inordinate degree, their bodies and their moral senses being more porous and inconsistent than men's. But shouldn't that vulnerability increase the value of lifelong virginity for them, given that virginity symbolizes a self-containment and unbrokenness of composition that eros's entanglements can only blur? Christianity certainly thought so: the process by which the original ideal of perfect chastity, preached to the moral elite of both sexes, becomes a feminine specialty will be described in the following chapters.

29. Vernant, *Mortals and Immortals*, 198.

30. In J. G. Frazer, *The Golden Bough: A Study in Magic and Religion*, abridged ed., vol. 1 (New York: Macmillan, 1922), 1–8.

31. *Miasma*, or defilement, can pollute the unprepared just as it pollutes and makes a pariah out of those who commit murder, step unknowingly into sacred precincts, or suffer from a divinely sent mania.

32. Søren Kierkegaard's Johannes the Seducer writes on one of the last pages of his "Diary": "I could not really fall in love with Diana, but I do not deny that I would give much for a conversation with her. She must be well versed in various kinds of tricks." Søren Kierkegaard, *Either/Or*, vol. 1, trans. David F. Swenson and Lilian Marvin Swenson, revised by Howard A. Johnson (Princeton, NJ: Princeton University Press, 1971), 431.

33. Debates about the existence of such feminine "rites of passage" or initiations into puberty must always acknowledge the guiding spirit of the great classicist Jane Ellen Harrison, who "loved bears in all forms" and wrote with passion about Brauron and its cult. See the appealing portrayal of Harrison in Francesca Wade, *Square Haunting: Five Writers in London between the Wars* (New York: Tim Duggan Books, 2020), 143–93, quotation at 183. That an adolescent girl would need first to become a wild animal before she can accept and fulfill her adult place in the household, as guardian and agent of reproduction, wife and mother, does not seem too extraordinary. It is important that the girl becoming a woman both know what it is like to be wild—in the state of nature—and tamed, and for this knowledge the transitional period of virginal "playing the bear" provides an education, an exposure to the excitements of danger (life outside human life and the city) and the inevitability of civil integration. Potentially a danger to the man who would like to take her into his home and bed, the girl, as so often said, is in need of taming. J. E. Robson cites Mary Douglas: "Danger lies in transitional states, simply because transition is neither one state nor the next, it is undefinable. The person who must pass from one state to the next is himself in danger, and emanates danger to others." (See Mary Douglas, *Purity and Danger: An Analysis of the Concepts of Pollution and Taboo* [London: Routledge, 1966], 97.) Robson comments, "But what makes her young wildness dangerous, in particular, is what happens when she begins to menstruate: she can, of course, now conceive a child, 'outside wedlock,' that is with no respect for the *mores* of civilized society. Such a wild union would be appropriate for animals, but not for civilized human beings.... Marriage is not only cognate with, but may be perceived as, the final state of the taming process begun by female puberty rites. At marriage, the girl rids herself of her animality and is now a δαμορ wife or 'tamed one,' since she has submitted to Aphrodite's yoke." J. E. Robson, "Bestiality and Bestial Rape in Greek Myth," in *Rape in Antiquity: Sexual Violence in the Greek and Roman Worlds*, ed. Susan Deacy and Karen F. Pierce (London: Duckworth, 1997), 65–96, quotation at 70–73. Robson's interpretation, which aligns with some of the arguments I want to make in this chapter and the next, solves

many of the problems that have confused other commentators on the Brauron rite and female initiation in Greece. For a contemporary reference to these rites, see Aristophanes *Lysistrata,* 639–46. I am indebted to Christiane Sourvinou-Inwood's careful discussions in her *Studies in Girls Transitions* (Athens: Kardamitsa, 1988), 21–61. See also Pierre Vidal-Naquet, *The Black Hunter: Forms of Thought and Forms of Society in the Greek World,* trans. Andrew Szegedy-Maszak (Baltimore: Johns Hopkins University Press, 1986), 129–56, esp. 145–46. The rites at Brauron are the only ones Vidal-Naquet thinks parallel the initiation rites Greeks expected of boys entering the ephebia. Since girls don't become citizens, what need do they have to pass through status transition? Well, because the change from virginity to marriage is a change in status and in identity. Vidal-Naquet develops the argument also found in Walter Burkert, *Greek Religion,* trans. John Raffan (Cambridge, MA: Harvard University Press, 1985), that "hunting cultures" conceived of virgin sacrifice as a sometimes necessary substitute for the body of the wild bear or buffalo; hunting "steals" a life from the wild, and those divinities who protect the wild—Artemis above all—can take vengeance on the hunter for their crime; only a comparable sacrifice, as Agamemnon's of his virgin daughter, can satisfy them. Scholars had been puzzled for a long time about what was meant by "playing the bear" at Brauron. "The myth," Vidal-Naquet continues, is not difficult to explain: in exchange for the very advance of culture implied by the killing of wild animals, an advance for which men are responsible, the girls are obliged before marriage—indeed, before puberty—to undergo a period of ritual "wildness"(Vidal-Naquet, *Black Hunter,* 146).

34. Burkert, *Greek Religion,* 151–52.

35. Victoria Wohl, *Intimate Commerce: Exchange, Gender and Subjectivity in Greek Tragedy* (Austin: University of Texas Press, 1998), 72. Pausanias's description of the sanctuary and rites at Troizen, in Corinth, was written sometime in the late second century CE. "I have seen Hippolytos's house," he reports; one envies him. He saw also Hippolytos's stadium, and "above it is the shrine of Peeping Aphrodite: whenever Hippolytos was exercising, Phaidra would watch him from up here and lust for him. Here as I said before, the myrtle still grows with perforated leaves. When Phaidra was in despair of any way to ease love she wantonly ruined the leaves of the myrtle." The account of the Trozenian ritual is one of many, but Pausanias's has its own unreliable charm: "The Trozenians have a priest of Hippolytos consecrated for his whole lifetime, and a tradition of annual sacrifices, and there is another thing they do: every virgin girl cuts off a lock of hair for him before their marriage and brings it to the shrine to dedicate it. They will not hear of his death dragged behind the horses, nor show his grave although they know it; they believe that the Charioteer in heaven is their own Hippolytos, and that the gods have given him this honour." Pasusanias, *Guide to Greece,* vol. 1, 2. 13.1–3.

36. Burkert, *Greek Religion,* 261.

37. See Simon Goldhill, *Foucault's Virginity: Ancient Erotic Fiction and the History of Sexuality* (Cambridge: Cambridge University Press, 1995), 4–35; John. J. Winkler, *The Constraints of Desire: The Anthropology of Sex and Gender in Ancient Greece* (New York: Routledge, 1990), 101–25.

38. Goldhill, *Foucault's Virginity,* 36.

39. In a memorable passage in *Beyond the Pleasure Principle,* Freud speaks of the injury to self-love caused by loss of love and failure leaving a narcissistic scar. Freud, *Beyond the Pleasure Principle,* 20.

40. Jean-Pierre Vernant, *Myth and Society in Ancient Greece*, trans. Janet Lloyd (New York: Zone, 1990), 33; Elaine Fantham et al., "Women in Classical Athens: Heroines and Housewives," in *Women in the Classical World* (New York: Oxford University Press, 1994), 85. I discuss the conflation between sacrificial maidenhood and the bloodletting of the hunt in a later section of this chapter, see also Vidal-Naquet, *Black Hunter*. 14.

41. Zeitlin, *Playing the Other*, 276.

42. H. King, *Hippocrates' Woman*, 75–83.

43. Sophocles, *Antigone* 791. I am citing Martha Nussbaum's translation of the line, in Martha Nussbaum, *The Sleep of Reason: Erotic Experience and Sexual Ethics in Ancient Greece and Rome* (Chicago: University of Chicago Press, 2013), 88.

44. See Giulia Sissa, *Sex and Sensuality in the Ancient World*, trans. George Staunton (New Haven, CT: Yale University Press, 2008), 60–61, for the passage from Aristotle's *Problems* 4.15.

45. Diogenes Laertius, *Lives of Eminent Philosophers*, vol. 2, trans. Robert Drew Hicks, Loeb Classical Library185 (Cambridge, MA: Harvard University Press, 1925); for Epicurus, see 10.1.127–28, 10.1.6–7; for Diogenes, see 6.2.69.

46. Robert Parker, *Miasma: Pollution and Purification in Early Greek Religion* (Oxford: Clarendon Press, 1983), 74–103.

47. Sissa, *Sex and Sensuality*, 37.

48. Giulia Sissa draws attention to the way "the traditional image of desire caused by a divine agent" is "overturned" or at least challenged by Medea's claim to be the agent of her own emotions. Was it here, in this fifth-century tragedy, that "love became secularised and ceased to be represented as a form of bewitchment?" Sissa, *Sex and Sensuality*, 17.

49. See Ovid, *The Art of Love and Other Poems*, trans. J. Mozley, translation revised by G. P. Goold, Loeb Classical Library 232 (Cambridge, MA: Harvard University Press, 1979).

50. Aeschylus, *Eumenides*, 737–38. I cite the translation offered by Zeitlin, *Playing the Other*, 117. Alan Sommerstein's translation for the Loeb Library *Oresteia* gives it as, "I commend the male in all respects (except for joining in marriage)." Aeschylus, *Oresteia: Agamemnon, Libation-Bearers, Eumenides*, ed. and trans. Alan H. Sommerstein, Loeb Classical Library 146 (Cambridge, MA: Harvard University Press, 2008), 449.

51. See the interesting discussion in Daniel Mendelsohn, *Gender and the City in Euripides' Political Plays* (Oxford: Oxford University Press, 2002), 52–55, and 137–223, on Demeter, marriage, fertility, violence, and violation.

52. Ken Dowden calls this "Bremmer's Principle," with reference to J. N. Bremmer, "Effigies Dei in Ancient Greece: Poseidon" in *Effigies Dei: Essays on the History of Religion*, ed. Dirk van der Plas (Leiden, Neth.: Brill, 1987), cited in Ken Dowden, *Death and the Maiden: Girls' Initiation Rites in Greek Mythology*, (London: Routledge, 1989), 37.

53. Vernant, *Myth and Society*, 34–35.

54. Zeitlin emphasizes the exchange of roles between Hippolytus and Phaedra, "his secret double"; "his initiation into the world" resembles "the experience of the female body" (*Playing the Other*, 234–35). In his mixture of masculinity and femininity, Hippolytus resembles another rebel, Cainis, a Lapith girl who responded to her rape by Poseidon by demanding to be turned into a man and became one of the toughest,

fearsome in battle, worshipping, it is said, only the sword, not the disreputable gods with their predatory designs on woman. In an essay on rape, Zeitlin writes of Caineus, as he became, "Who, one the one hand, might better defend women against rape than one who owes his present identity to the revulsion inspired by the forcible penetration of his once female body? Yet this hybrid/hybristes whose figure is a response to the exaggerated outrage of the obdurate virgin incarnates a hypermasculinity on the side of a warrior violence." In this, Zeitlin continues, he is not unlike "those warrior women, the Amazons, who mix masculine with feminine traits and express in fullest form some of the most persistent anxieties on both sides about sexuality and the trauma it represents as the initiation into adulthood." Froma I. Zeitlin, "Configurations of Rape in Greek Myth," in *Rape: An Historical and Social Enquiry*, ed. Sylvana Tomaselli and Roy Porter (Oxford: Blackwell, 1986), 122–51, at 134.

55. The Amazons appear in art and myth as the polar opposites of the Greeks, like the giants and centaurs and other rude monsters. But exotic as they are, they are also close. Considered barbarians, they are still taken as wives or concubines; warriors, they defy the image of femaleness as docile and subordinate. Athenian myth, Zeitlin writes, "brings them into the very heart of Attica by having Theseus abduct their queen and transfer her to his territory. When he puts her aside in favour of a second wife, Phaedra, her Amazon sisters, in order to avenge her, leave their usual ground to invade Athens itself, meeting defeat finally on the sacred hill of the Areopagus by the Acropolis" (Zeitlin, *Playing the Other*, 135).

56. Aristophanes has women attacking Euripides as a misogynist (*Lysistrata* 368–69 and *Thesmophoriazusae* 81–85), but acknowledges elsewhere how Euripides understands the constraints and troubles of their lives in Athens (*Frogs* 1049–53).

57. See Apollodorus, *The Library*, vol. 2, trans. James G. Frazer (Cambridge, MA: Harvard University Press, 1921): "In consequence of the wrath of Aphrodite, for she did not honor the goddess, this Smyrna conceived a passion for her father, and with the complicity of her nurse she shared her father's bed without his knowledge for twelve nights. But when he was aware of it, he drew his sword and pursued her, and being overtaken she prayed to the gods that she might be invisible; so the gods in compassion turned her into the tree which they call *smyrna* (myrrh). Ten months afterwards the tree burst and Adonis, as he is called, was born, whom for the sake of his beauty, while he was still an infant, Aphrodite hid in a chest unknown to the gods and entrusted to Persephone. But when Persephone beheld him, she would not give him back. The case being tried before Zeus, the year was divided into three parts, and the god ordained that Adonis should stay by himself for one part of the year, with Persephone for one part, and with Aphrodite for the remainder. However, Adonis made over to Aphrodite his own share in addition; but afterwards in hunting he was gored and killed by a boar" (3.14.4). On the story of Adonis and the erotic festivals celebrated by Greek women in his honor, see the fascinating work by Marcel Detienne, *The Gardens of Adonis: Spices in Greek Mythology*, trans. Janet Lloyd (Princeton, NJ: Princeton University Press, 1994).

58. Zeitlin, *Playing the Other*, 220. The *Homeric Hymn to Aphrodite* puts the case clearly: "No one else (with the exception of Artemis, Athena, Hestia) none of the blessed gods or human beings, can ever escape Aphrodite." (in Homer, *Homeric Hymns*, 34–35).

59. That Hippolytus is noble and heroic, not an abnormality destined to be rejected by his society, is a point made forcefully by David Kovacs, *The Heroic Muse: Studies*

in the "Hippolytus" and "Hecuba" of Euripides (Baltimore: Johns Hopkins University Press, 1987), 29–31. That the particular intensity of his "nobility" belongs to a reactionary and nostalgic strand in 4th century Athenian society, sympathetic to the oligarchy, is one of the ways Justina Gregory interprets the tensions within the central virtue of sophrosyne, at the time of the play a word with "unmistakable conservative overtones" (62). Rosselli disagrees: it is the hoplite virtue. In a democratic society, Burkert argues, "men who behave as *semnoi*" (as Hippolytus does, to the servant's dismay) "risk being considered pompous and ridiculous" (*Greek Religion*, 273).

60. Gregory, *Euripides and the Instruction of the Athenians*, 56. See also the 1929 essay by E. R. Dodds, "Euripides the Irrationalist," in *The Ancient Concept of Progress and Other Essays on Greek Literature and Belief* (Oxford: Clarendon Press, 1973), 87.

61. If I accept that the state of sexual innocence is something I cannot keep, I have assented to life's mutability, and to the inevitable push of aging and maturity. Immortals don't need such an acknowledgment. But it is fundamental to our knowledge of what it is to be human. The gods can steer us wrong here, as Apollo does when he tempts Admetus with the possibility of cheating death.

62. Jean-Pierre Vernant, introduction to Detienne, *Gardens of Adonis*, xxxix.

63. "Normal 5th-century practice required, certainly, that the man who entered a sacred place or took part in a sacred ritual should be ἁγνῶς (*hagnos*), but ἁγνεία was a purely formal affair of observing taboos (of avoiding, or purging, pollution caused by such things as physical uncleanness or contact with some aspect of birth, sex, or death. Hippolytus's requirement of *moral* purity is alien to the ordinary Greek cult until Hellenistic times; his insistence that the purity must be innate would be extraordinary even then." William S. Barrett, commentary in Euripides, *Euripides Hippolytos*, 172. Hippolytus identifies himself with a way of being and acting that belongs to a special but traditional form of religious practice.

This was not only a Greek preference. Not only in fifth-century Athens but in Palestine, Egypt, and Babylon, anyone taking part in a sacred ritual was expected to be "pure" and undefiled. As generally understood, this referred to the requirements of cleanliness, purgation through baths or abstinence from food, absence of contact with birth or death or sex, with blood or violence. Many ritual functions could only be performed by young boys or maidens who because of their age were necessarily pure. Any contact with the dead, and certainly any shedding of blood in violence, war, or sacrifice, excluded the violators from sacred things and made their accidental presence fatal to the successful outcome of all rites, religious or civic. But cultic purity and moral purity are not the same thing. See Burkert, *Greek Religion*, 269–72; Jean Rudhardt, *Notions fondamentales de la pensée religieuse et actes constitutifs du culte dans la Grèce classique* (Paris: Picard, 1992), 28–32; Mary Douglas, *Purity and Danger*, 42–58. Elsewhere Douglas nicely understates, "One of the great puzzles in comparative studies of religion has been the reconciliation of the concept of pollution, or defilement, with that of holiness." Mary Douglas, *Implicit Meanings: Essays in Anthropology* (London: Routledge, 1975), 47.

64. Burkert, *Greek Religion*, 74–84, quotation at 76.

65. Parker, *Miasma*, 3–12.

66. Yet religiously consecrated areas—*hiera*—are not off-limits to the people: indeed, they are much in demand as safe places to keep money and the civic treasury, as meeting places for assemblies, sanctuaries in times of fever or invasion. Some could only be used toward the business of the cult, those at Delphi and Eleusis requiring

exceptionally high degrees of respect. Cf. Rudhardt, *Notions fondamentales de la pensée religieuses*, 24–26.

67. Parker, *Miasma*, 19, citing Hippocrates, *Morb. Sacr.* 148.55 ff. J., I.46 G ("On the Sacred Disease"); see also Rudhardt, *Notions fondamentales de la pensée religieuses*, 28, explaining that those who are excluded from sanctuaries come from several categories: murderers and those polluted by crimes, men who willingly prostituted themselves, women caught in adultery, and anyone who has just had sex without washing themselves.

68. Brown, *Body and Society*, 8–9: the best book that has been and will ever be written on this topic.

69. Robert Parker, *On Greek Religion* (Ithaca, NY: Cornell University Press, 2011), 40–63.

70. Zeitlin, *Playing the Other*, 247.

71. Although it was sent by Poseidon, the bull is also a manifestation of Dionysus, who "leaps" into the pure temple. Cf. Marcel Detienne, *Dionysos at Large*, trans. Arthur Goldhammer (Cambridge, MA: Harvard University Press, 1989), 55.

72. Mark Kuefler, *The Manly Eunuch: Masculinity, Gender Ambiguity, and Christian Ideology in Late Antiquity* (Chicago: University of Chicago Press, 2001), 248.

73. Good and succinct descriptions of these lives can be found in Richard Finn, *Asceticism in the Greco-Roman World* (Cambridge: Cambridge University Press, 2009), esp. chap. 5, "Caveman, Cenobites, and Clerics," 131–55.

74. An excellent scholarly introduction to these cultural opportunities, and their theoretical formulation by the church fathers, is Joyce Salisbury, *Church Fathers, Independent Virgins* (London: Verso, 1991).

75. The Third Ecumenical Council, held at Ephesus in 431 CE, met to address a bitter controversy between the bishop of Constantinople, Nestorius, who was supported by the Antiochians, and the supporters of Cyril of Alexandria, who had Rome on their side. The issue was the interpretation of the humanity of Christ. When he took form in Mary's womb, was he still divine? In what sense can a mortal woman be said to give birth to the Godhead? Nestorius believed it was better to call Mary the *Anthropotokos*, or "mother of man," for to call her "the mother of God" sounded heretical. How could God have a mother? After the Council sided with Cyril, Marian devotees in Constantinople took it as a sign in favor of the increased dignity and prestige of the Virgin Mary, in whom "God the Word was enfleshed and became man." That this traditional assurance was a rather loose and opportunistic interpretation of the council, which made no dogmatic decisions and did not produce the definition of Mary as *Theotokos*, is argued by Richard Price, "Theotokos: The Title and its Significance in Doctrine and Devotion," in *Mary: The Complete Resource*, ed. Sarah Jane Boss (Oxford: Oxford University Press, 2007), 56–73. See also Miri Rubin, *Mother of God: A History of the Virgin Mary* (New Haven, CT: Yale University Press, 2009), 41–49.

76. Leslie Fiedler, *Love and Death in the American Novel* (London: Paladin, 1970).

Chapter Three

Epigraph: D. H. Lawrence, *Women in Love* (Oxford: Oxford University Press, 1998), 5.

1. Mendelsohn, *Gender and the City*, 4.

2. Campbell Bonner, "A Study of the Danaid Myth," *Harvard Studies in Classical Philology* 13 (1902): 129–78, at 137.

3. Cavell, *Pursuits of Happiness*, 53.

4. Cavell, *Pursuits of Happiness*, 53. Cavell further reiterates, "I have said before that the idea of innocence, indispensable to classical romance as a preoccupation with virginity, remains at issue in the genre of remarriage, where the status of literal or physical virginity is presumably no longer a question" (148–49). I will return to Cavell and *The Philadelphia Story*'s "unique" and blatant preoccupation with literal virginity, with "purity as chastity" in the last section of this chapter.

5. Not a controversial claim. For brilliant treatments of these issues, see Frances Ferguson, "Rape and the Rise of the Novel," in *Misogyny, Misandry, and Misanthropy*, ed. R. Howard Bloch and Frances Ferguson (Berkeley: University of California Press, 1989), 88–112; Watt, *The Rise of the Novel*; Nancy Armstrong, *Desire and Domestic Fiction: A Political History of the Novel* (New York: Oxford University Press, 1987). On the "two great instances of categorial instability that are central to the rise of the novel"—generic and social, questions of truth and questions of virtue—see Michael McKeon, "Generic Transformation and Social Change: Rethinking the Rise of the Novel," in *The Theory of the Novel: A Historical Approach*, ed. Michael McKeon (Baltimore: Johns Hopkins University Press, 2000), 382–99.

6. G. W. F. Hegel, *Elements of the Philosophy of Right*, trans. H. B. Nisbet (Cambridge: Cambridge University Press, 1991), §§161 and 163.

7. Marianne Moore, the "blameless bachelor" as she called herself, is representative of the modernist aesthetic I associate with the "ascetic avant-garde," in which company should be included Paul Valéry, Simone Weil, Stéphane Mallarmé, John Cage, and many others. (Their stories will be told more fully in a project that will follow this one.) I owe the reference to Moore's poem and my understanding of chastity in her work and life to Ellen Levy, *Criminal Ingenuity: Moore, Cornell, Ashbery, and the Struggle between the Arts* (Oxford: Oxford University Press, 2011).

8. Levy, *Criminal Ingenuity*, xxii–xxiii.

9. On the Amazons, I rely on Page duBois, *Centaurs and Amazons: Women and the Pre-History of the Great Chain of Being* (Ann Arbor: University of Michigan Press, 1991); and Kathryn Schwartz, *Tough Love: Amazon Encounters in the English Renaissance* (Durham, NC: Duke University Press, 2000). King Pelasgus, taken aback by his conversations with the defiant Danaid maidens, mutters that he would have guessed them to be the unwed and "flesh-eating" Amazons (*Suppliants* 286–87).

10. Though the modern horror film, with the innovation of the "Final Girl," has come up with virgins even bloodier than mine. See Carol Clover, *Men, Women, and Chain Saws: Gender in the Modern Horror Film* (Princeton, NJ: Princeton University Press, 1992), which I discuss in chapter 8.

11. A. H. Sommerstein, ed. and trans., *Aeschylus I: Persians, Seven Against Thebes, Suppliants, Prometheus Bound*, Loeb Classical Library 145 (Cambridge, MA: Harvard University Press, 2009). Further citations from this edition will be indicated parenthetically in text, with line numbers.

12. Giacomo Puccini, *Turandot: Lyric Drama in Three Acts and Five Scenes*, libretto by Giuseppe Adami and Renato Simoni, trans. K. H. B. de Jaffa (Milan: Ricordi, 1926), 55. The libretto for the opera has as a distant source the play by Carlo Gozzi, in *Five Tales for the Theater*, ed. and trans. Albert Bermel and Ted Emery (Chicago: University of Chicago Press, 1989).

13. I quote from Apollodorus and Hyginus, *Apollodorus' "Library" and Hyginus' "Fabulae": Two Handbooks of Greek Mythology*, trans. and with an introduction by

R. Scott Smith and Stephen M. Trzaskoma (Indianapolis: Hackett, 2007), 153. On Pausanias's remark, see R. P. Winnington-Ingram, "The Danaid Trilogy of Aeschylus," *Journal of Hellenic Studies* 81 (1961): 141.

14. A. F. Garvie, *Aeschylus' "Supplices": Play and Trilogy* (Cambridge: Cambridge University Press, 1969), 172–77.

15. See duBois, *Centaurs and Amazons*, esp. 83–86.

16. Anne Pippin Burnett, *Catastrophe Survived: Euripides' Plays of Mixed Reversal* (Oxford: Oxford University Press, 1971), 1.

17. Friedrich Engels, *The Origin of the Family, Private Property and the State in the Light of the Researches of Lewis H. Morgan*, in *The Marx-Engels Reader*, 2nd ed., ed. Robert C. Tucker (London: W. W. Norton, 1978), 734–59, at 739.

18. Cavell, *Pursuits of Happiness*, 87.

19. Milton, *Milton's Selected Poetry and Prose*, 249.

20. That such a possibility existed may be surprising to most students of marriage in the ancient world. But see Jean Pierre-Vernant: "We have evidence of another custom which also testifies to the existence of a state of crisis in the normal processes of matrimonial exchange. It is what the anthropologists refer to as *svayamvara*; the selection of a husband is left up to the free choice of the daughter. Here again historical evidence and legendary tradition overlap and are mutually illuminating. Herodotus tells us the story of Kallias, victor at the Olympic and Pythian games and renowned for his sumptuous extravagance. However, the historian adds, he is chiefly admired for the way he behaved toward his three daughters. He settled very rich dowries on each of them and 'gave each one to the man she elected to choose as a husband.' To leave the choice of a husband to the daughter herself, who has full powers to select the man she wants, is in some ways similar to the typically noble procedure of marriage by competition. The two themes are often presented as doublets, or are associated, in legend." Vernant, *Myth and Society*, 71.

21. Marcel Detienne, *The Writing of Orpheus: Greek Myth in Cultural Context*, trans. Janet Lloyd (Baltimore: Johns Hopkins University Press, 2003), 37–49.

22. Detienne, *Writing of Orpheus*, 47.

23. Detienne, *Writing of Orpheus*, 48–49.

24. Detienne, *Writing of Orpheus*, 49.

25. Detienne, *Writing of Orpheus*. All quotations are from the first paragraph on page 38.

26. Detienne, *Writing of Orpheus*, 38–39.

27. See Bal, *Death and Dissymmetry*, 41–93.

28. Claude Calame, *Choruses of Young Women in Ancient Greece: Their Morphology, Religious Role, and Social Functions*, rev. ed., trans. Derek Collins and Janice Orion (Lanham, MD: Rowman and Littlefield, 2001), 145.

29. An encouraging exception: Charles Mee's reimagining of the play as *Big Love*, first produced in 2000 in Louisville, Kentucky, and then in 2015 in New York, where audiences are said to have found the themes eerily relevant.

30. The reliable popularity of my local cinema's summer festival of "Pre-Code Movies" demonstrates just how tenacious and attractive, in popular culture anyway, is the figure of the woman in protest against marriage. What distinguishes these sexy, sophisticated heroines of Hollywood glamour in the movies of 1931–1933 from their immediate successors is precisely this: they want to have careers and they want to have fun, and they fail to see how marriage and domestic virtue are essential to their hap-

piness and fulfillment as women. In a number of the movies—Ruth Chatterton in *Female* (1933) is the genre's epitome—the heroines follow the same course I describe in this chapter, from assertive or brittle independence to conversion and reconciliation/resignation. Alison Drake, Chatterton's character, is a rich and promiscuous free spirit who runs a car company and refuses all proposals of marriage or even steady companionship until her principles are worn down by her ideal mate, the engineer Jim Thorne: Alison finally agrees to tie the knot, hands the business over to Jim, and has nine children.

31. Kathleen Coyne Kelly talks about the renewed interest in "the paradox of bodily and spiritual integrity." Kathleen Coyne Kelly, *Performing Virginity and Testing Chastity in the Middle Ages* (London: Routledge, 2000), 1–16, 119–41. See also Kahan, *Celibacies*, which "traces the emergence of celibacy as a crucial social identity in the 1840s and charts the evolution of this social identity into a sexual identity, narrating the transformation of chastity from a traditional gender assignment to a sexual practice that is visibly the site of modernist innovation." (8).

32. Hesiod, *Theogony*, 1008.

33. Ernest Crawley, *The Mystic Rose: A Study of Primitive Marriage* (London: Macmillan, 1902), 320.

34. Crawley, *Mystic Rose*, 347–49.

35. "If for a boy the significance of the rites of passage was to mark his accession to the condition of a warrior, for the girl who took part alongside him in these same rites, and who was also often subjected to a period of seclusion, the initiatory trials had the force of a preparation for marriage." Vernant, *Myth and Society*, 34; see also Helene P. Foley, *Ritual Irony: Poetry and Sacrifice in Euripides* (Ithaca, NY: Cornell University Press, 1985), 22.

36. Louise Bruit Zaidman and Pauline Schmitt Pantel, *Religion in the Ancient Greek City*, trans. Paul Cartledge (Cambridge: Cambridge University Press, 1993), 29; Foley, *Ritual Irony*, 39. For the precise and "logical" details (only for those with strong stomachs), see Albert Henrichs, "Human Sacrifice in Greek Religion: Three Case Studies," in *Le sacrifice dans l'antiquité: Huit exposés suivis de discussions* (Geneva: Fondation Hardt, 1981), 195–235; and Jean-Louis Durand, "Greek Animals: Toward a Topology of Edible Bodies," in *The Cuisine of Sacrifice among the Greeks*, ed. Marcel Detienne and Jean-Pierre Vernant, trans. Paula Wissing (Chicago: University of Chicago Press, 1989), 87–105.

37. Marcel Detienne, "Culinary Practices and the Spirit of Sacrifice," in Detienne and Vernant, *Cuisine of Sacrifice*, 9. The "consent" could be registered by the animal "bowing its head, *hekousion kataneuei*," according to Walter Burkert, *Savage Energies: Lessons of Myth and Ritual in Ancient Greece*, trans. Peter Bing (Chicago: University of Chicago Press, 2001), 11.

38. Derek Hughes, *Culture and Sacrifice: Ritual Death in Literature and Opera* (Cambridge: Cambridge University Press, 2007), 13.

39. Hughes, *Culture and Sacrifice*, 13–14: "Neither archaeology nor history suggest that Greek myths of human sacrifice preserve any trace of actual sacrificial practices ... There are reports of Greek human sacrifice in the classical period. Archaeology has not provided any confirmation of this belief."

40. Loraux, *Tragic Ways of Killing a Woman*, 32.

41. Loraux, *Tragic Ways of Killing a Woman*, 33.

42. See Foley, *Ritual Irony*, chap. 1, "Drama and Sacrifice."

43. Loraux, *Tragic Ways of Killing a Woman*, 37.

44. Loraux, *Tragic Ways of Killing a Woman*, 38.

45. Sigmund Freud, "The Taboo of Virginity," in *On Sexuality*, vol. 7 of *The Pelican Freud Library*, ed. and trans. James Strachey and Angela Richards (Harmondsworth, UK: Penguin, 1977), 265–83 (279).

46. Freud, "Taboo of Virginity," 279, citing a discussion later included in Ferenczi's *Thalassa: A Theory of Genitality* (1924).

47. Freud, "Taboo of Virginity," 265–66.

48. Freud, "Taboo of Virginity," 270.

49. Freud, "Taboo of Virginity," 265.

50. See Freud's compatible conclusions from an earlier (1912) essay in Sigmund Freud, "On the Universal Tendency to Debasement in the Sphere of Love," in Freud, *On Sexuality*, 247–60.

51. Claude Lévi-Strauss, *Language and the Analysis of Social Laws*, in *Structural Anthropology*, trans. Claire Jacobson and Brooke Grundfest Schoepf (London: Penguin, 1968), 61.

52. Engels, *Origin of the Family*, 739, italics in the original.

53. Engels, *Origin of the Family*, 739.

54. Hesiod, *Theogony*, 593–16.

55. Engels, *Origin of the Family*, 739.

56. See Aline Rousselle, "Body Politics in Ancient Rome," in *From Ancient Goddesses to Christian Saints*, vol. 1 of *A History of Women in the West*, ed. Georges Duby, Michelle Perrot, and Pauline Schmitt Pantel, trans. Arthur Goldhammer (Cambridge, MA: Belknap Press of Harvard University Press, 1992), 302.

57. Jean-Pierre Vernant, *Myth and Society*, 55.

58. François Lissarrague, "Regards sur le mariage grec," in *Silence et fureur: La femme et le marriage en Grèce; Les antiquités grecques du Musée Calvet*, ed. Odile Cavalier (Avignon: Fondation du Musée Calvet, 1996), 415–33.

59. Lissarrague, "Regards sur le mariage grec," 416

60. Lissarrague, "Regards sur le mariage grec," 416–17, citing Aristotle and a text by one Pollux from the time of the emperor Commodus: classical and Hellenistic seem to be on the same page in the marriage practice manual.

61. Claudine Leduc, "Marriage in Ancient Greece," in Duby, Perrot, and Pantel, *From Ancient Goddesses to Christian Saints*, 235–97, at 240.

62. Leduc, "Marriage in Ancient Greece," 242–47, 265, 272–82, 285.

63. Vernant, *Myth and Society*, 34.

64. Catherine Clément, *Opera, or the Undoing of Women*, trans. Betsy Wing (London: Virago, 1989), 100.

65. Catherine Clément, *L'opéra ou la défaite des femmes* (Paris: Bernard Grasset, 1979), 185–227. Clément's chapter on *Turandot* is called "Furies and Gods, or Wanings of the Moon" (in the English translation, Clément, *Opera*, 96–117). Turandot, she explains, has a special reference to menstruation and to fears of blood, both flowing and blocked, and to a story told by Lévi-Strauss, a Cashinawa legend; see Claude Lévi-Strauss, "The Origin of the Moon," trans. John and Doreen Weightman, in *The Origin of Table Manners*, vol. 3 of *Mythologiques* (Chicago: University of Chicago Press, 1990), 97: Because a girl refused to get married, her mother chopped off her head and set it in the stars; from that time on, women have bled once a month. In another variation, a myth from another American tribe, the young woman rejects her suitor because he

is her brother: it is his head, rolling around nomadically and energetically, that turns into the moon and inflicts the curse of menstruation on the sister who rejected him (Lévi-Strauss, "Origin of the Moon," 94). Although all the operas read by Clément have the prolixity of hysteric fantasies, this one has a remarkably extravagant menu: lunar death and fantasies of cannibalism, the dangerous virgin tamed in a pastiche of initiation mysteries, Greek paganism, human sacrifice and menstrual origins; Orientalist sadism; and colonialist anxieties. The mythic abundance would make Frazer proud. Even a superficial glance at the opera catches some allusions Clément was too busy to bother with (the cruel virgin is invoked as having withdrawn from the earth, leaving it covered with endless snow, a blight that will not be relieved until the royal maiden reappears and April can return). Most important of all the symbolic associations is the linkage between virginity and a murderous power latent in nonhuman nature. The first time we see Princess Turandot, Clément remarks, she appears elusively at her window, silent, inaccessible, beautiful and terrible. Turandot the Pure, "white as jade, cold as the sword." Only when the moon rises does she make herself visible to the public, who are shouting for the taste of blood. "O severed head! O bloodless one! Come! Appear! Show yourself in the sky!" "O pale lover of the dead!" (Clément, *Opera*, 99). One small gesture; off with his head. This cool lady has murder on her mind. And all her victims are in love with her.

66. Gozzi, *Five Tales for the Theater*, 182–83.

67. Carlo Gozzi, *Five Tales for the Theater*, 163.

68. "The very idea of being subject to this man is enough to destroy me," Turandot cries out in horror. Friedrich Schiller, *Turandot, Prinzessin von China: Ein tragikomisches Märrchen nach Gozzi*, in *Sämlichte Werke*, vol. 3 (Munich: Carl Hanser Verlag, 2004), 858.

69. For two versions of this plot, compare Alfred, Lord Tennyson, *The Princess* (1847), wherein high-minded maidens forswear the company of men, and Shakespeare, *Love's Labour's Lost* (1598), where the high-minded shunning is done by pure, noble young men.

70. "From Gozzi's text to Schiller's the shift of tone is striking. Gone is the local Venetian color: the dialect of the masks, the third enigma 'il leone d'Adria,' and various touches of satire directed at the audience in the Teatro San Samuele. Schiller replaced the local folk texture of Gozzi with a decorous smoothness of undeniable charm, but a charm very different from that produced by Gozzi's quirky shifts of level." William Ashbrook and Harold Powers, *Puccini's "Turandot": The End of the Great Tradition* (Princeton, NJ: Princeton University Press, 1991), 51.

71. Giacomo Puccini, *Turandot*, 46.

72. Puccini, *Turandot*, 54.

73. Alexis de Tocqueville, traveling in early nineteenth-century America, was struck by the freedom and frankness of young unmarried girls and by the fact that their confidence in the public sphere evaporated once they became wives. French women had the opposite experience: expected to be silent and naïve until marriage, they stepped into a wide sphere of possibility after marriage. See Alexis de Tocqueville, *Democracy in America*, ed. Isaac Kramnick, trans. Gerald Bevan (London: Penguin, 2003).

74. On the mixed-up modernist notions of sex, degeneration, utopia, and dystopia, see Bram Dijkstra, *Idols of Perversity: Fantasies of Feminine Evil in Fin-de-Siècle Culture* (Oxford: Oxford University Press, 1988), a connection forcefully stated on page 187.

That Darwinism helped pull women off the pedestal of household sainthood but also served to feed cultural fears of female sexuality is something Dijkstra is right to stress. The "coming of the new Darwinian creed" did not abolish male chivalry. But it could turn it toward odd configurations, heightening the supposed distinction between the sexes and creating a new cult of feminine "specificity," identified with the spiritual, the intuitive, the childlike, and the "little."

75. Giacomo Puccini, *Turandot*, trans. William Weaver (London: Alma Books, 2011), 108.

76. The three "masks"—the comic characters of Ping, Pang, and Pong—are appropriately made the mouthpiece of a prurience everyone else can pretend to overlook: "What is she? A female with a crown on her head! And a cloak with fringe! But if you strip her naked . . . she's flesh! She's raw flesh! It's inedible!" Sure, Turandot is grandiose. But a woman is a woman. "We can't wait to see that Tigress, that 'She-Marshall of Heaven,' surrender in the soft cushions of her bed: Glory to the beautiful, unclad body which now knows the mystery it was ignorant of!" (Clément, *Opera*, 100).

77. Jules Michelet, *La sorcière* (Paris: Flammarion, 1966), 31.

78. See Theodor Adorno and Max Horkheimer, "Odysseus, or Myth and Enlightenment," in *The Dialectic of Enlightenment*, trans. Edmund Jephcott (Stanford, CA: Stanford University Press, 2007).

79. Lévi-Strauss, *Origin of Table Manners*, 97.

80. Freud, *Taboo of Virginity*, 265.

81. I am drawing on Frye's theories of the mythos of romance, in N. Frye, *Anatomy of Criticism*, 186–206, and Northrop Frye, *A Natural Perspective* (New York: Columbia University Press, 1995), esp. 72–117.

82. "If the genre [of romantic comedy, LD] is as definitive of sound comedy as I take it to be, then this phase of the history of cinema is bound up with a phase in the history of the consciousness of women." Cavell, *Pursuits of Happiness*, 16.

83. Cavell, *Pursuits of Happiness*, 54.

84. Zeitlin, *Playing the Other*, 284.

85. N. Frye, *Anatomy of Criticism*, 163–64.

86. Cavell, *Pursuits of Happiness*, 4–5.

87. N. Frye, *Secular Scripture*, 102–15.

88. Cavell, *Pursuits of Happiness*, 54.

89. N. Frye, *Natural Perspective*, 65.

90. Cavell, *Pursuits of Happiness*, 142.

91. Among many discussions, I can mention those of Thomas Laqueur, *Making Sex: Body and Gender from the Greeks to Freud* (Cambridge: Harvard University Press, 1990); Anke Bernau, *Virgins: A Cultural History* (London: Granta Books, 2007); Marie H. Loughlin, *Hymeneutics: Interpreting Virginity on the Early Modern Stage* (Lewisburg, PA: Bucknell University Press, 1997); Ottakar Nemecek, *Virginity: Pre-Nuptial Rites and Rituals* (New York: Philosophical Library, 1958); Giulia Sissa, *Greek Virginity*, trans. Arthur Goldhammer (Cambridge, MA: Harvard University Press, 1990); Kathryn Schwarz, "The Wrong Question: Thinking through Virginity," *differences* 13, no. 2 (Summer 2002): 1–34.

92. Cavell, *Pursuits of Happiness*, 141.

93. Cavell, *Pursuits of Happiness*, 8.

94. Stanley Cavell, *Conditions Handsome and Unhandsome: The Constitution of Emersonian Perfectionism* (Chicago: University of Chicago Press, 1990), 125; Stanley

Cavell, *Contesting Tears: The Hollywood Melodrama of the Unknown Woman* (Chicago: University of Chicago Press, 1996), 44-45.

95. See also the essential developments of Cavell's themes in Stanley Cavell, *Disowning Knowledge in Six Plays of Shakespeare* (Cambridge: Cambridge University Press, 1997).

96. Freud, "On the Universal Tendency to Debasement," 259.

Chapter Four

1. Eric Robertson Dodds, *Pagan and Christian in an Age of Anxiety: Some Aspects of Religious Experience from Marcus Aurelius to Constantine* (Cambridge: Cambridge University Press, 1965), 34.

2. Elaine Pagels writes that it was "a revolution in sexual attitudes and practices." I think that is right, and my argument supports hers. But even revolutions grow on ground already prepared. See Elaine Pagels, *Adam, Eve, and the Serpent* (New York: Random House, 1988), xviii.

3. Brown, *Body and Society*, 111.

4. David G. Hunter, *Marriage, Celibacy, and Heresy in Ancient Christianity: The Jovinianist Controversy* (Oxford: Oxford University Press, 2007), 111.

5. Foucault uses the expression "technologies of the self" throughout his later work. His seminar "Technologies of the Self" is easily accessible in the collection *Technologies of the Self: A Seminar with Michel Foucault*, ed. Luther H. Martin, Huck Gutman and Patrick H. Hutton (London: Tavistock, 1988), 16–49.

6. On the Gregorian Reforms, see the revelatory discussion in Suzanne Verderber, *The Medieval Fold: Power, Repression, and the Emergence of the Individual* (New York: Palgrave Macmillan, 2013).

7. Shaw, *Burden of the Flesh*, 180–87.

8. Peter Brown, "The Notion of Virginity in the Early Church," in *Christian Spirituality: Origins to the Twelfth Century*, ed. Bernard McGinn, John Meyendorff, and Jean Leclercq (New York: Crossroad, 1985), 427–43, quotations at 429, 433. See also Hannah Arendt, *The Human Condition*, 2nd ed. (Chicago: University of Chicago Press, 1998), 12–60.

9. Brown, "Notion of Virginity," 435–38.

10. McInerney, *Eloquent Virgins*, 30–31.

11. Lucian of Samosata, *Lucian: Selected Dialogues*, ed. and trans. C. D. N. Costa (Oxford: Oxford University Press, 2005), 74–87, quotations at 76, 77.

12. Celsus, *On the True Doctrine: A Discourse against the Christians*, trans. R. Joseph Hoffmann (New York: Oxford University Press, 1987), 25, 73.

13. From Origen, *Contra Celsum*, trans. Owen Chadwick (1953; repr., with corrections, Cambridge: Cambridge University Press, 1965), cited in Ramsay MacMullen, *Christianizing the Roman Empire (A.D. 100–400)* (New Haven, CT: Yale University Press, 1984), 37.

14. Strabo, *Geography* 7.3.4, cited in Ross Shepard Kraemer, *Her Share of the Blessings: Women's Religions among Pagans, Jews, and Christians in the Greco-Roman World* (Oxford: Oxford University Press, 1992), 3; Kramer also notes the emphasis on women's religiosity in 2 Timothy 3:6–7, Jerome, *Against Vigilantius*, and Juvenal's *Sixth Satire*.

15. Friedrich Engels in Karl Marx and Friedrich Engels, *Marx and Engels on Reli-*

gion, ed. Reinhold Niebuhr (New York: Schocken Press, 1967), 316. See also John G. Gager, *Kingdom and Community: The Social World of Early Christianity* (Englewood Cliffs, NJ: Prentice-Hall, 1975).

16. Wayne Meeks, *The First Urban Christians: The Social World of the Apostle Paul* (New Haven, CT: Yale University Press, 1983), 52–55, 72–73.

17. A survey of such "female attraction" to Christianity over a number of centuries can be found in Monique Alexandre, "Early Christian Women," in Duby, Perrot, and Pantel, *From Ancient Goddesses to Christian Saints*, 409–44.

18. Madeleine Scopello, "Jewish and Greek Heroines in the Nag Hammadi Library," in *Images of the Feminine in Gnosticism*, ed. Karen L. King (Philadelphia: Fortress Press, 1988), 70–90.

19. In *The Nag Hammadi Library in English*, ed. James M. Robinson (New York: HarperCollins, 1990), 141–60.

20. A wide sampling of such material is discussed in K. King, *Images of the Feminine*.

21. K. King, *Images of the Feminine*, 239–75.

22. Wilhelm Schneemelcher, ed., *New Testament Apocrypha*, vol. 2, *Writings Relating to the Apostles, Apocalypses and Related Subjects*, trans. R. McL. Wilson (Louisville: Westminster John Knox Press, 2003), 228.

23. Ross Shepard Kraemer, the feminist historian of religion, cautions: "Yet material that seems on its face to point to the significant presence of women, such as stories in the canonical gospels, may in fact be deceptive" (Kraemer, *Her Share of the Blessings*, 128, also 130–39).

24. Alexandre, "Early Christian Women," 431–35.

25. Ramsay MacMullen, *Christianity and Paganism in the Fourth to Eighth Centuries* (New Haven, CT: Yale University Press, 1997), 8.

26. Peter Brown, *The Cult of the Saints: Its Rise and Function in Late Christianity* (Chicago: University of Chicago, 1981), 46. Disagreement with the "common supposition" that Christianity was attractively open "to two large categories of persons for whom paganism, in all its varieties, nowhere had much room: women and slaves along with the vulgar masses," is registered by MacMullen, *Christianity and Paganism*, 7, esp. 7n13.

27. Gillian Cloke, *This Female Man of God: Women and Spiritual Power in the Patristic Age, AD 350–450* (New York: Routledge, 1995), 4.

28. Possidius, in his life of Augustine, mentions the sister and her order of consecrated virgins at Hippo; a letter Augustine writes clarifying the "Rule" governing the cloistered life of this group of nuns does not speak of her specifically; see Allan D. Fitzgerald, ed., *Augustine through the Ages: An Encyclopedia* (Grand Rapids, MI: Wm. B. Eerdmans, 2009), 68, 309. See also Peter Brown, *Augustine of Hippo: A Biography*, new ed. (Berkeley: University of California Press, 2000), 17: "Yet we only know from passing references in the *Confessions* and from other works, that Augustine had at least one brother, Navigius, perhaps two sisters." (and Brown describes—briefly—the household led by Augustine's sister on pp. 199 and 411).

29. This remarkable theme in theology as well as pastoral practice is covered thoroughly by Elizabeth A. Clark, "The Celibate Bridegroom and His Virginal Bride: Metaphor and the Marriage of Jesus in Early Christian Ascetic Exegesis," *Church History* 77, no. 1 (March 2008): 1–25.

30. See Ambrose, *Epistle* 63; K. Kelly, *Performing Virginity*, 42.

31. Peter Brown, "East and West: The New Marital Morality," in *A History of Pri-*

vate Life, vol. 1, *From Pagan Rome to Byzantium*, ed. Paul Veyne (Cambridge, MA: Harvard University Press, 1987), 297.

32. David Flusser, *The Sage from Galilee: Rediscovering Jesus' Genius*, with R. Steven Notley (Grand Rapids, MI: Wm. B. Eerdmans, 2007), 76–96.

33. Its spread was not wholly the result of missionary activity, as Ramsay MacMullen argues in *Christianizing the Roman Empire*, 34.

34. See, among many others, R. Joseph Hoffmann, introduction to *Porphyry's Against the Christians*, by Porphyry, ed. and trans. R. Joseph Hoffmann (Amherst, NY: Prometheus Books, 1994), 8.

35. Gerd Theissen, *The Social Setting of Pauline Christianity: Essays on Corinth*, trans. John H. Schütz (Philadelphia: Fortress Press, 1982), 69–143; Stephen J. Patterson, "*Askesis* and the Early Jesus Tradition," in *Asceticism and the New Testament*, ed. Leif E. Vaage and Vincent L. Winbush (New York: Routledge, 1999), 49–69.

36. Elizabeth A. Castelli, "Disciplines of Difference: Asceticism and History in Paul," in *Asceticism in the New Testament* (New York: Routledge, 1999), 171–85, at 178.

37. But cf. Bugge, *Virginitas*, 56–57: "It is interesting to note that the first Christians saw *ascesis*—essentially a pagan idea—as something quite different from virginity, which they considered not a matter of resolve at all but a *charisma*, a free gift of God.... Still, the agonistic function of individual asceticism was more obviously retained within monasticism, where virginity as a necessary condition for combat against the personified forces of evil remained a literary theme well into the Middle Ages."

38. John Chrysostom, *John Chrysostom, On Virginity*, trans. Sally Rieger Shore (New York: Edwin Mellen, 1983), 15.

39. Brown, *Body and Society*, 139.

40. The phrase is from a thirteenth-century manuscript by Peter the Chanter, from a text often attributed to Augustine in the Middle Ages. See Pierre J. Payer, *The Bridling of Desire: Vies of Sex in the Later Middle Ages* (Toronto: University of Toronto Press, 1993), 9.

41. Elizabeth A. Clark, *Reading Renunciation: Asceticism and Scripture in Early Christianity* (Princeton, NJ: Princeton University Press, 1999), 3.

42. Harper, *From Shame to Sin*, 135. This is a brilliant, witty and persuasive book, from which I have learned enormously.

43. "As long as there are philosophers on earth, and wherever there have been philosophers (from India to England, to take the antithetical poles of philosophical endowment), there unquestionably exists a peculiar philosophers' irritation at and rancor against sensuality: Schopenhauer is merely its most eloquent and, if one has ears for this, most ravishing and delightful expression. There also exists a peculiar philosophers' prejudice and affection in favor of the whole ascetic ideal; one should not overlook that." Nietzsche, *Genealogy of Morals*, Essay III, §7, p. 106.

44. *The Genealogy of Morals* of 1887 is the most important, but Nietzsche is mining this terrain from 1881 (*Daybreak*) to 1888 (*Twilight of the Idols*), and the case against the ascetic pathology appears also in *The Gay Science* (1882), *Thus Spake Zarathustra* (1883–85), and *Beyond Good and Evil* (1886).

45. Nietzsche, *On the Genealogy of Morals*, Essay III, §11, p. 117.

46. Nietzsche, *On the Genealogy of Morals*, Essay I, §8, p. 34 (translation modified).

47. I am paraphrasing the argument of Nietzsche, *On the Genealogy of Morals*, Essays II and III, pp. 57–96, 136–61.

48. For Nietzsche's objections to the "natural man" of Rousseau, see Friedrich Nietzsche, *Untimely Mediations*, ed. Daniel Breazeale, trans. R. J. Hollingdale (Cambridge: Cambridge University Press, 1983), 151; and Keith Ansell-Pearson, *Nietzsche contra Rousseau: A Study of Nietzsche's Moral and Political Thought* (Cambridge: Cambridge University Press, 1997). A culture oblivious of the strange mutations of the ascetic is not a paradise Nietzsche prefers to imagine. Nor does he hail a modernity that has broken its ties with asceticism. All honor to the ascetic ideal insofar as it is honest! (*Genealogy of Morals*, Essay III, §26, p. 158). But the self-intoxicated free spirits of today, Nietzsche objects, merely maintain the ascetic ideal under a mask and fool themselves that they are liberated. They are joined in this by their brothers in modernity, the "abstinent, heroic" minds devoted to "objective" science, the courageous truth-seekers on their unconditional crusade against the illusions and ideals of the past (pp. 148–161). Faith in the ascetic ideal rages on, providing new treatments for new illnesses, all of which it has created itself.

49. See Paul Veyne's decided treatment of the moral life of the Roman Empire in Veyne, *From Pagan Rome to Byzantium*, 1–233; Paul Veyne, *Sexe et pouvoir à Rome* (Paris: Tallandier, 2005).

50. Bugge, *Virginitas*, 19: "We have seen, then, that as there is unanimity over the original sexual state of man among these Christian thinkers, there is also a certain like-mindedness about the nature of the original transgression and its tragic effects for the race. In a word, man's first sin was somehow equivalent to sexual intercourse; its principal effects were death and sexuality itself. The idea is not found stated explicitly; rather, it remains recessive, something subscribed to which will not bear outright expression. Nevertheless, the proposition that "the original sin was sex" is a premise implicit in, and logically necessary to, the arguments these Fathers make over the nature of the first things. It takes the shape of a sustained intuition about the character of Christian perfection, and, as such, continues to exert an influence upon subsequent thought far beyond the point at which it would have been unacceptable as explicit doctrine." See also James A. Brundage, *Law, Sex, and Christian Society in Medieval Europe* (Chicago: University of Chicago Press, 1987), 6–8, 62–65.

51. K. J. Dover, "Classical Greek Attitudes to Sexual Behaviour," in *Women in the Ancient World: The Arethusa Papers*, ed. John Peradotto and J. P. Sullivan (Albany: State University of New York Press, 1994), 143–57. For a spirited defense of the value of passionate erotic attachment, see Martha Nussbaum's portrayal of "The Therapy of Desire" in its multiple Greek and Roman forms. Nussbaum acknowledges a long-lasting philosophical debate about pleasure and the appetites, and she rightly insists that for many thinkers, for Aristotle as well as the Stoics, the trouble with the passions is not that they are irresistible and mindless impulses. Passions are also judgments, introducing their own evaluative register into the complexities of human life. And far too often, the way they judge is wrong. Hence virtue has (generally) to take arms against them. If the wise Greeks and Romans could be corrected, Nussbaum seems to say, then we moderns could learn from their deep understanding of emotions like love but find different solutions than that of extirpating the passions. I summarize the arguments of Martha Nussbaum, *The Therapy of Desire: Theory and Practice in Hellenistic Ethics* (Princeton, NJ: Princeton University Press, 1994), but Nussbaum's thoughts on this subject can be found in many other places, and a fuller treatment of the difference between classical and Christian sexual ethics would need to engage with her more than I can do here.

52. The first translators of it, D. Armand and M.-Ch. Moons, dated it prior to the Council of Nicaea in 325. See Susanna Elm, *Virgins of God: the Making of Asceticism in Late Antiquity* (Oxford: Clarendon Press, 1994), 34. I am quoting in this paragraph from the translation by Teresa M. Shaw in Vincent Winbush, ed., *Ascetic Behavior in Greco-Roman Antiquity: A Sourcebook* (Minneapolis: Fortress Press, 1990), 9–44.

53. John Chrysostom, *On Virginity*, 8.

54. John Chrysostom, *On Virginity*, 37.

55. Pseudo-Athanasius, *On Virginity*, trans. David Brakke, in *Corpus Scriptorum Christianorum Orientalium*, vol. 593 (Louvain: Editions Peeters, 2002), 6.

56. On these matters, see Clark, *Reading Renunciation*, 204–32.

57. Elizabeth Castelli, "Virginity and Its Meaning for Women's Sexuality in Early Christianity," *Journal of Feminist Studies in Religion* 2, no. 1 (Spring 1986): 61–88, asks the hard questions: "Did women use the Christian categories to try to break the severely limiting conventions of the social order? Was such a rupture possible, given the shared notion of patriarchal dualism which created the material and ideological realities of both late antiquity in general and early Christianity in particular?" (65) On the enthusiasm of women for Christian asceticism (we know nothing about what Greek or Roman women might have felt had they been given opportunities to study pagan philosophical asceticism), the official answer is that they were motivated by love of Christ, by proper humility, by the desire to perfect themselves. Yet advocates for virginity did freely expound the indignities of marriage (John Chrysostom is most eloquent; see *On Virginity*, 51–72), the pains of childbirth, the sorrows of raising children, even the shame of being a sex object who all too soon loses youthful beauty and the attention it inspires: all in efforts to rouse virginal recruitment.

58. Cited in Jo Ann McNamara, *A New Song: Celibate Women in the First Three Christian Centuries* (New York: Harrington Park Press, 1985), 96.

59. Pseudo-Athanasius, *On Virginity*, 2.

60. Pseudo-Athanasius, *On Virginity*, 28.

61. From the anonymous "Homily on Virginity," in Winbush, *Ascetic Behavior in Greco-Roman Antiquity*, 35.

62. *The Acts of Andrew*, in Schneemelcher, *Apocrypha*, vol. 2, *Writings Relating to the Apostles*, 101–51, at 129–30.

63. Saint Gregory of Nyssa, "The Life of Saint Macrina," in *Ascetical Works*, trans. Virginia Woods Callahan, vol. 58 of *The Fathers of the Church* (Washington: Catholic University of America Press, 1967), 164.

64. Giulia Sfameni Gasparro, "Asceticism and Anthropology: *Enkrateia* and 'Double Creation' in Early Christianity," in Winbush and Valantasis, *Asceticism*, 127–46, at 141. See also Elm, *Virgins of God*, 47–59; Dyan Elliot, *Spiritual Marriage: Sexual Abstinence in Medieval Wedlock* (Princeton, NJ: Princeton University Press, 1993).

65. Aline Rouselle, *Porneia: Desire and the Body in Antiquity*, trans. Felicia Pheasant (Oxford: Basil Blackwell, 1988), 145.

66. On the "touring" movement, see Wayne A Meeks, *First Urban Christians*, 82. On participation by widows and young women of an age to be married, see McNamara, *New Song*, 31–34.

67. Gillian Clark, "Women and Asceticism in Late Antiquity: The Refusal of Status and Gender," in Winbush and Valantasis, *Asceticism*, 33–48, at 37.

68. Rouselle, *Porneia*, 132.

69. Kathryn Gravdal, *Ravishing Maidens: Writing Rape in Medieval French Literature* (Philadelphia: University of Pennsylvania Press, 1991), 21–22.

70. Michel Foucault's list is even fuller. See Foucault, *Les aveux de la chair*, 149.

71. Elm, *Virgins of God*, 48. The homily "On Virginity" was formerly credited to Pseudo-Basil.

72. Elm, *Virgins of God*, 106–12; Castelli, "Virginity and its Meaning," 75–76. See also Stephen J. Davis, *The Cult of St. Thecla: A Tradition of Women's Piety in Late Antiquity* (Oxford: Oxford University Press, 2001), on Thecla's transvestism: "In the context of an ancient society that held fast to misogynistic assumptions about women's weakness, the act of dressing 'like a man' would have signified a radical break from customary assumptions about women's identity in society. While it may indeed have been a way of enacting the 'no longer male and female' of the Galatians baptism formula, it also was 'a symbol of the ambiguities, tensions, and hostilities' in early Christian attitudes toward women."

73. Elm, *Virgins of God*, 113–20.

74. Porphyry, *Letter to Marcella*, 33, cited in Rouselle, *Porneia*, 187; italics mine.

75. Bugge, *Virginitas*, 57.

76. See Stefan Heid, *Celibacy in the Early Church: The Beginnings of a Discipline of Obligatory Continence for Clerics in East and West*, trans. Michael J. Miller (San Francisco: Ignatius Press, 2000), for a view that clerical continence was recognized as an obligation for all higher clerics from the days of the earliest churches, even before the Council of Nicaea in 325. Heid argues that even the tradition for married priests in the Orthodox Church is not based on "ancient" practice, since in the east also the "prevailing trend was strongly in favor of exclusively unmarried or else widowed clerics" (179). His view is inconsistent with those of most church historians, as he admits, and his arguments do not go very far, sometimes claiming as little as that "sexuality in antiquity is far removed from sexuality in our times" (321–22).

77. Session XXIV, 11 Nov. 1563, *Doctrina de sacramento matrimonii*, can.10, cited in Hunter, *Marriage, Celibacy, and Heresy*, 7n9.

78. Brundage, *Law, Sex, and Christian Society*, 5.

79. Hunter, *Marriage, Celibacy, and Heresy*, 87–170.

80. Kate Cooper, *The Virgin and the Bride: Idealized Womanhood in Late Antiquity* (Cambridge, MA: Harvard University Press, 1996), ix.

81. The Apocryphal Acts appeared in the second and third centuries. They have a fair share of gnostic ideas and images, and are said to reflect popular piety of the age, especially of the less educated. Telling of the journeys and adventures of Peter and Paul, Thomas, Andrew, John, and many others, they are full of shipwrecks and miraculous rescues, reports of sorcery (some ascribed to Paul himself), last-minute escapes, exotic locales, improbable coincidences, sudden conversions, and the like. Stories of wives converted by the apostles and rushing to keep their husbands out of their beds (even resorting to the old chestnut, the bed-trick) are particularly popular. See the edition prepared by J. K. Elliott, based on the 1924 translation of M. R. James: Elliott, *Apocryphal New Testament*.

82. Brown, *Body and Society*, 326–27: those Brown describes as "uncanny" and "strange" seemed free from the profane corruptions their worldly colleagues faced every day.

83. Daniel Boyarin, *Carnal Israel: Reading Sex in Talmudic Culture* (Berkeley: University of California Press, 1993), 5–60.

84. See Finn, *Asceticism in the Greco-Roman World*, ch. 2.

85. Brown, *Body and Society*, 158–59.

86. Foucault, *Les aveux de la chair*, 189–90. Pierre Payer writes that later medieval theologians all accepted the divine intention that humans should have sexual intercourse; certainly by the thirteenth century in the West this was the accepted teaching (Payer, *Bridling of Desire*, 22).

87. Payer, *Bridling of Desire*, 21, citing Gregory of Nyssa, *On the Making of Man*, 16–17.

88. Shaw, *Burden of the Flesh*, 188–89.

89. Robin Lane Fox, *Pagans and Christians* (New York: HarperCollins, 1986), 336.

90. Brown, *Body and Society*, 56.

91. Lane Fox, *Pagans and Christians*, 335.

92. This last possibility, devoutly seized on by the practitioners of "spiritual marriage," or *syneisaktism*, vigorously denounced by, among others, John Chrysostom, and Jerome in his letter 20:14, to Eustochium: "They often occupy the same bed, and yet they call us suspicious if we fancy anything amiss." For Chrysostom's "refutation" and attack on this practice, see the text and introduction in Elizabeth A. Clark, *Jerome, Chrysostom and Friends: Essays and Translations* (New York: Edwin Mellen Press, 1979), 158–205. The Council of Ancyra tried to ban the practice: "We prohibit those who live together with men as if they were their sisters from doing so." And ten years later a similar canon was issued by the Council of Nicaea. See Elm, *Virgins of God*, 48–51; Brown, *Body and Society*, 267. The reemergence of the idea in a new and more subtle form came in the Middle Ages with Hugh of St. Victor, according to John Bugge, who sees it as a revival of encratic sympathies (Bugge, *Virginitas*, 84–87).

93. Clement of Alexandria, "On Marriage," *Miscellanies, Book III*, in *Alexandrian Christianity*, vol. 2, *Selected Translations of Clement and Origen with Introductions and Notes by John Ernest Leonard Oulton, D.D. and Henry Chadwick* (Philadelphia: Westminster Press, 1954), pp. 40–92. Subsequent in-text citations are to this edition, with chapter and page number.

94. Brown, *Body and Society*, 133.

95. *Ad uxorem* (To His Wife), *Monogamia* (Monogamy), and *De exhortatione castitatis* (An Exhortation to Chastity) are cited from Tertullian, *Tertullian: Treatises on Marriage and Remarriage*, trans. William P. Le Saint (New York: Newman Press, 1951).

96. John Chrysostom, *St. John Chrysostom on Marriage and Family Life*, trans. Catharine P. Roth and David Anderson (Crestwood, NY: St. Vladimir's Seminary Press, 2002), 75–76, at 79.

97. In his Montanist period, his attitude hardened: "To an unmarried man every women is 'another woman' as long as he is not married to her, and the selfsame action which makes one woman a wife makes another an adulteress. Marriage and fornication are different only because laws appear to make them so; they are not intrinsically different, but only in the degree of their illegitimacy. For what is it that all men and women do in both marriage and fornication (*stuprum*)? They have sexual relations, of course, and the very desire to do this, our Lord says, is the same thing as fornication." Tertullian, *De exhortation castitatis*, in *Treatises on Marriage and Remarriage*, pp. 56–57.

98. Tertullian, *Monogamy*, in *Treatises on Marriage and Remarriage*, pp.70, 104.

99. Gary Anderson, "Celibacy or Consummation in the Garden? Reflections on Early Jewish and Christian Interpretations of the Garden of Eden," *Harvard Theological Review* 82, no. 2 (April 1989): 121–48, at 121.

100. Brown, *Body and Society*, 138–39.

101. Brown, *Body and Society*, 138.

102. MacMullen, *Christianizing the Roman Empire*, 74.

103. With the extravagant poetics of medieval romance and courtliness, romantic passion is rehabilitated—or, as many critics argue, "invented." Provençal lyricists protested to anyone listening: my love is chaste and blameworthy just because it is so single-minded, excessive, self-sacrificing, and absorbing. Passion itself purifies. Innocence can return in the shape of *amour fou* (mad love), to the true lover who does not count the costs. Love is a religion. I am paraphrasing a commonplace view of love and courtliness which critics today generally treat with caution, if not wholehearted repudiation. It is, however, a catchy one.

104. Foucault, *Les aveux de la chair*, 206–15, at 209.

105. Karen A. Winstead, in the introduction to her *Chaste Passions: Medieval English Virgin Martyr Legends* (Ithaca, NY: Cornell University Press, 2000), writes of her girlhood fascination with the arresting stories of martyred and saintly young women, "suffering excruciating tortures to safeguard their 'purity'" (2). Nietzsche would understand. Other recent work on the virgin martyrs is almost always presented by feminist scholars, at least in North America; see also Maud Burnett McInerney, "Rhetoric, Power, and Integrity in the Passion of the Virgin Martyr," in K. Kelly and Leslie, *Menacing Virgins*, 50–70; on Christian women's hunger for suffering, taken as a way to exult and transfigure, not to abase and repress, see Caroline Walker Bynum, *Holy Feast and Holy Fast: The Religious Significance of Food to Medieval Women* (Berkeley: University of California Press, 1987), 165–86.

106. See, among much remarkable work by recent feminist scholars on "the autonomous women virgins of the Encratite/Syrian churches whose power was equal to that of male virgins," the arguments in Theodora A. Jankowski, *Pure Resistance: Queer Virginity in Early Modern English Drama* (Philadelphia: University of Pennsylvania Press, 2000), esp. 33–53. The pushback against the power virginity might lend to Christian women was strong, and Jankowski covers the usual suspects, torn between their desire to welcome women into the ascetic life and their fear of the "works of women," the never-subsiding sexual heat and seductiveness of Eve's daughters. See also Elaine Pagels, *The Gnostic Gospels* (New York: Random House, 1979), 10–14; Brown, *Body and Society*, 89–96.

Chapter Five

For the epigraphs, I have used the following editions: Porphyry, *On Abstinence from Killing Animals*, trans. Gillian Clark (Ithaca, NY: Cornell University Press, 2000); Plotinus, *The Enneads*, 4th ed., trans. Stephen MacKenna (New York: Larson Publications, 2000); John Calvin, *Institutes of the Christian Religion*, ed. John McNeill, trans. Ford Lewis Battles (Philadelphia: Westminster Press, 1960).

1. Meeks, *First Urban Christians*, 85. In cultivating such separation, Christians were simply following their Jewish ancestors, whose religious scruples and distrust of assimilation kept them apart. Christianity, as the church historian Franz Overbeck complained in the nineteenth century, made its peace with "the world." Judaism did not. Diaspora was for Judaism not a temporary state but an identity.

2. Heid, *Celibacy in the Early Church*, 21.

3. Meeks, *First Urban Christians*, 74–80.

4. Novatian, *In Praise of Purity*, in *The Trinity; The Spectacles; Jewish Foods; In Praise of Purity; Letters*, vol. 67 of *The Fathers of the Church*, ed. and trans. Russell DeSimone (Washington, DC: Catholic University of America Press, 1972), 170.

5. Novatian, *In Praise of Purity*, 167.

6. Weber, *From Max Weber*, 323–28; Immanuel Kant, *Observations*, 57.

7. See Wayne Meeks, *The Origins of Christian Morality: The First Two Centuries* (New Haven, CT: Yale University Press, 1993), esp. chap. 2, "Turning: Moral Consequences of Conversion."

8. Justin Martyr, *1. Apology 14*), in *Ante-Nicene Fathers*, vol. 1, *The Apostolic Fathers, Justine Martyr and Irenaeus*, ed. A Cleveland Coke, Alexander Roberts and James Donaldson (Peabody, MA: Hendrickson, 1885), 167. Justine uses the term *sophrosyne*, which different translators render as "continence," "chastity," or "temperance": see Meeks, *Origins of Christian Morality*, 35.

9. Max Weber, "Religious Rejections of the World and their Directions," in *From Max Weber*, 350.

10. Max Weber, *Economy and Society: A Outline of Interpretive Sociology*, vol. 2, ed. Guenther Roth and Claus Wittich, trans. Ephraim Fischoff et al. (Berkeley: University of California Press, 1978), 1166.

11. Weber, "Religious Rejections," 326–27.

12. Weber, "Religious Rejections," 328.

13. Thomas Browne, *Religio Medici, Second Part*, §9, 80, in *The Prose of Sir Thomas Browne*, ed. Norman J. Endicott (Garden City, NY: Doubleday Anchor Books, 1967).

14. John Rogers, "The Enclosure of Virginity: The Poetics of Sexual Abstinence in the English Revolution," in *Enclosure Acts: Sexuality, Property and Culture in Early Modern England*, ed. Richard Burt and John Michael Archer (Ithaca, NY: Cornell University Press, 1994), 229–50, at 241.

15. Brown, *Body and Society*, 268.

16. Douglas, *Purity and Danger*, 159.

17. Many scholars believe that concupiscence was discovered by Augustine, who did not have far to look. See Peter Brown's review of Sarah Ruden's new translation of Augustine's *Confessions* (New York: Modern Library, 2017), in *New York Review of Books* 64, no. 16 (October 26, 2017): 45–46. It is, of course, not true that Augustine was first on the scene: as early as Paul and the Gnostics, concupiscence was identified as the enemy, and radicals such as Tatian and Julian Cassianus believed marriage was basically a laboratory for the nurturing and growth of concupiscence. Julian Cassianus is the most outspoken in his love for "Eunuchry." Only those who give up marriage and sex entirely will be saved. It is a view with the virtue of simplicity. See John T. Noonan, *Contraception: A History of its Treatment by the Catholic Theologians and Canonists*, enlarged ed. (Cambridge, MA: Harvard University Press, 1986), 56–106.

18. Dale Martin sets Paul's *Letter to the Corinthians* in the context of contemporary beliefs about disease and pollution: "The ideology of the body presupposed by most early Christian literature, though not by any means all, reflects the invasion etiology of disease. . . . Early Christians seem generally to have believed that disease was caused by the invasion of hostile, cosmic, personal agents." Dale B. Martin, *The Corinthian Body* (New Haven, CT: Yale University Press, 1995), 163–64. That the Adamic "myth" as interpreted by Augustine breaks away from the "pre-ethical" beliefs about sexual defilement or the defilement caused by crimes of violence or blasphemy is claimed by Paul Ricoeur, *The Symbolism of Evil*, trans. Emerson Buchanan (Boston: Beacon Press, 1967), 25–99.

19. Vladimir Jankélévitch, *L'Innocence et la Méchanceté, Traité des vertues*, vol. 3 (Paris: Flammarion, 1986), 187.

20. Jankélévitch, *L'Innocence*, 175–84.

21. As Hegel put it, "History is not the soil on which happiness grows. The periods of happiness in it are the blank pages of history." See G. W. F. Hegel, *Lectures on the Philosophy of World History*, trans. H. B. Nisbet (New York: Cambridge University Press, 1975), 79.

22. But for a contrasting view on the relation of late Roman and early Christian women to the Virgin as "female icon of religious authority," see Karen Cooper, "The Virgin Mary and Female Authority," in *Virginity Revisited: Configurations of the Unpossessed Body*, ed. Bonnie MacLachlan and Judith Fletcher (Toronto: University of Toronto Press, 2007), 100–115.

23. Nicholas Tucker, "Philip Pullman: I'm Quite Against a Sentimental Vision of Childhood; In Conversation with the Author of His Dark Materials," Literary Hub, October 19, 2017, https://lithub.com/philip-pullman-im-quite-against-a-sentimental-vision-of-childhood/.

24. Wallace Stevens, "Evening without Angels," in *The Collected Poems of Wallace Stevens*, 2nd ed., ed. Chris Beyers and John M. Serio (New York: Vintage Books, 2015), 145.

25. G. W. F. Hegel, *Phenomenology of Spirit*, trans. A. V. Miller (Oxford: Oxford University Press, 1977), 82; G. W. F. Hegel, *Phänomenologie des Geistes*, Theorie Werkausgabe (Frankfurt: Suhrkamp, 1970), 46.

26. René Ragrid, *Eclogues cum Dissertatione de Carmine*, trans. Thomas Creech (Oxford, 1684), cited by Paul Alpers, *What Is Pastoral?* (Chicago: University of Chicago Press, 1997), 16–18.

27. See Annabel Patterson, *Pastoral and Ideology: Virgil to Valéry* (Berkeley: University of California Press, 1987).

28. Ernst Robert Curtius, *European Literature and the Latin Middle Ages*, trans. Willard R. Trask (Princeton, NJ: Princeton University Press, 1990), 184–202.

29. Curtius, *European Literature*, 186–87.

30. Hegel, *Phenomenology*, 467.

31. Hegel, *Phenomenology*, 492.

32. Hegel, *Phenomenology*, 389.

33. Hegel, *Phenomenology*, 399–400; Hegel, *Phänomenologie*, 483–84.

34. Hegel, *Phenomenology*, 126; Hegel, *Phänomenologie*, 163.

35. *Angelism*: the desire for an extreme purity and for an escape from carnality.

36. Jacques Maritain, *The Dream of Descartes*, trans. Mabelle L. Andison (New York: F. Hubner, 1944), 28.

37. René Descartes, *Discourse on Method*, Part II, in *The Philosophical Works of Descartes*, vol. 1, ed. John Cottingham, Robert Stoothof, and Dugald Murdoch (Cambridge: Cambridge University Press, 1985), 116.

38. Percy Bysshe Shelley, "Adonais: An Elegy on the Death of John Keats," in David Perkins, ed., *English Romantic Writers* (New York: Harcourt, Brace, and World, 1967), stanza 50, lines 462–63, p. 1053.

39. Blaise Pascal, *Pensées*, ed. and trans. Roger Ariew (Indianapolis, IN: Hackett, 2005), 36; Blaise Pascal, *Œuvres Complètes*, ed. Louis Lafuma (Paris: Seuil, 1963), 515.

40. Allen Tate, "The Angelic Imagination," in *The Man of Letters in the Modern World: Selected Essays, 1928–1955* (London: Thames and Hudson, 1955), 113–32.

41. See John M. Rist, "Plotinus on Matter and Evil," *Phronesis* 6, no. 2 (1961): 154–66.

42. Brown, *Body and Society*, 178–89, at 178.

43. I rely here on the fascinating chapter on Porphyry in Robert Louis Wilken, *The Christians as the Romans Saw Them*, 2nd ed. (New Haven, CT: Yale University Press, 2003), 126–63.

44. I paraphrase here the account of the Christian "arts" and "practices" of subjectivity for which the late work of Michel Foucault is known, and which his posthumous volume, *Les aveux de la chair* (2018) elaborates in terms of the same preoccupations with chastity, virginity, and continence I have been trying to explain.

45. This is the aspect of Christianity that so annoys the author of the *His Dark Materials* and *The Book of Dust* trilogies (1995–2019), as any of Philip Pullman's readers knows. In Pullman's novels, the Magisterium and its branch, the General Oblation Board, representatives of a religious power with many similarities to the Christian church, devise a fiendish plan to undo the Fall into knowledge and sexuality. Their warped conception of "innocence" is Pullman's constant target.

46. Augustine, *Confessions*, trans. Ruden, 175.

47. Augustine, *Confessions*, 176.

48. Augustine, *Against Julian*, trans. Matthew A. Schumacher (New York: Fathers of the Church, 1957).

49. See Iain Gardner and Samuel N. C. Lieu, eds., *Manichaean Texts from the Roman Empire* (New York: Cambridge University Press, 2004), 11.

50. Brown, *Augustine of Hippo*, 45.

51. I. Gardner and Lieu, *Manichaean Texts*, 186.

52. Brown, *Augustine of Hippo*, 31.

53. Brown, *Augustine of Hippo*, 35–49.

54. Henry Chadwick, *Augustine* (New York: Oxford University Press, 1986), 11–13.

55. Brown, *Augustine of Hippo*, 36.

56. C. S. Lewis, *The Allegory of Love: A Study in Medieval Tradition* (Oxford: Oxford University Press, 1936), 14.

57. Lewis describes Hugh of St. Victor's clarification of Augustine's mature position: "If we had stayed in the state of innocence we should have generated *sine carnis incentivo*" (*Allegory of Love*, 15–16). And Albertus Magnus qualifies: the desire for intercourse is not a sin. Rather it is an evil, a punishment for the Fall. Later thinkers, including the great Thomas Aquinas, agreed that it is the danger to reason which makes carnal passion a menace. "Innocent" sexuality, for Thomas, would be thoughtful, deliberate, free from urge and impulse. It doesn't sound like much fun.

58. On the "Paradise-myth," see James Grantham Turner, *One Flesh: Paradisal Marriage and Sexual Relations in the Age of Milton* (Oxford University Press, 1994), v.

59. John Chrysostom, *Homily 13 on Romans 1*, cited in Noonan, *Contraception*, 132.

60. Methodius, *Symposium: A Treatise on Chastity*, trans. Herbert Musurillo, Ancient Christian Writers 27 (Westminster, MD: Newman Press, 1958), Logos 4.2.

61. Renato Poggioli, *The Oaten Flute: Essays on Pastoral Poetry and the Pastoral Ideal* (Cambridge, MA: Harvard University Press, 1975), 105.

62. H. King, *Hippocrates' Woman*, 86–88.

63. Musurillo's introduction speculates that the hymn as well as the dialogue was produced for Methodius's patron, "the Lady from Termessus" (Methodius, *Symposium*, 11).

64. Martha C. Nussbaum, *The Fragility of Goodness: Luck and Ethics in Greek Tragedy and Philosophy*, rev. ed. (Chicago: University of Chicago Press, 2001), 179–83.

65. Cited in John D. Zizioulas, "The Early Christian Community," in McGinn, Meyendorff, and Leclercq, *Christian Spirituality*, 23–43, at 38.

66. Bernard of Clairvaux, *Sermon on the Song of Songs* 20:6–7, in Bernard of Clairvaux, *The Works of Bernard of Clairvaux*, 2 vols., trans. Killian Walsh (Kalamazoo, MI: Cistercian Publications, 1971), 2:152.

67. Etienne Gilson, *The Mystical Theology of St. Bernard*, trans. A. H. C. Downes (Kalamazoo, MI: Cistercian Publications, 1990), 93, glossing Bernard of Clairvaux, *Sermon on the Song of Songs* 31:3–4.

68. Methodius, *Symposium*, Logos 8:2.

69. Methodius, *Symposium*, Logos 10:5.

70. Methodius, *Symposium*, Logos 10:6.

71. Methodius, *Symposium*, Logos 1:2.

72. Brown, *Body and Society*, 166.

73. On Origen in comparison to other understandings of ascetic transformation see David Brakke, *Athanasius and Asceticism* (Baltimore: Johns Hopkins University Press, 1995), 145–49.

74. On the Gnostics' uses of mythic imagery, see Brown, *Body and Society*, 107.

75. Brown, *Body and Society*, 185. Simon Goldhill, even less impressed, calls it a "didactic tract" overly interested in regulation, and unlike the Platonic pastoral of the *Phaedrus*, too clumsy to handle graceful erotics or the transformations of innocence into sophistication (*Foucault's Virginity*, 3). But Maud McInerney disagrees: it is a "jeu d'esprit" in homage to Plato and "more sophisticated than has generally been acknowledged." (*Eloquent Virgins*, 53).

76. Foucault, *Les aveux de la chair*, 161–76.

77. On the medieval imagination as "antifeminist," see R. Howard Bloch, *Medieval Misogyny and the Invention of Western Romantic Love* (Chicago: University of Chicago Press, 1991), 164.

78. Bloch, *Medieval Misogyny*, 112.

79. Roger Boase, *The Origin and Meaning of Courtly Love: A Study of European Scholarship* (Manchester, UK: Manchester University Press, 1977), 101; 83.

80. This is the theme of Sarah Kay's important work: "Contradiction is central to the makeup of courtly literature, to the intellectual environment, and to its critical reception today." Sarah Kay, *Courtly Contradictions: The Emergence of the Literary Object in the Twelfth Century* (Stanford, CA: Stanford University Press, 2001), 2.

81. A vast literature. In addition to Kay's *Courtly Contradictions*, Lewis's *Allegory of Love*, and Boase's *Origin and Meaning of Courtly Love*, I have consulted Bernard O'Donoghue, *The Courtly Love Tradition* (Manchester, UK: Manchester University Press, 1982); Joan M. Ferrante and George D. Economou, *In Pursuit of Perfection: Courtly Love in Medieval Literature* (Port Washington, NY: Kenikat Press, 1975); L. T. Topsfield, *Troubadours and Love* (Cambridge: Cambridge University Press, 1975); C. Stephen Jaeger, *The Origins of Courtliness: Civilizing Trends and the Formation of Courtly Ideals, 939–1210* (Philadelphia: University of Pennsylvania Press, 1985); Jean-Charles Huchet, *L'Amour Discourtois: Les "Fin'Amors" chez les premiers troubadours* (Toulouse: Privat, 1987); and René Nelli, *Troubadours et trouvères* (Paris: Hachette, 1979).

82. Lewis, *Allegory of Love*, 1–43.

83. Lewis, *Allegory of Love*, 2.

84. C. Stephen Jaeger, *Ennobling Love: In Search of a Lost Sensibility* (Philadelphia: University of Pennsylvania Press, 1999), 6.

85. Jaeger, *Ennobling Love,* 6.

86. Lewis, *Allegory of Love,* 20.

87. Bloch, *Medieval Misogyny,* 151, 3.

88. Bernart de Ventadour, "Lancan ve la folha" ("When I see the leaves"), in *Lyrics of the Troubadours and Trouveres,* ed. and trans. Frederick Goldin (New York: Anchor Books, 1973), no. 27, pp. 148–55, lines 50–51.

89. Jaeger, *Ennobling Love,* 134.

90. On the roaming noble youths and their unstable prospects—find an heiress, seek adventure, die young, play the game of courtly love—see Georges Duby, *The Chivalrous Society,* trans. Cynthia Postan (Berkeley: University of California Press, 1977): to avoid fragmenting inheritances, "most of the young men were kept in a state of celibacy and danger" (120–22); see also Georges Duby, *The Knight, the Lady and the Priest: The Making of Marriage in Medieval France,* trans. Barbara Bray (Chicago: University of Chicago Press, 1983), 216–26.

91. Bernard of Clairvaux, *Sermons on the Song of Songs*4:3, in Bernard of Clairvaux, *Works,* 1:4.

92. Bernard of Clairvaux, *Sermons on the Song of Songs* 20:6–7, in Bernard of Clairvaux, *Works,* 2:152.

93. See Curtius, *European Literature,* 122.

94. Marina Warner, *Alone of All Her Sex: The Myth and the Cult of the Virgin Mary* (New York: Vintage, 1976), 129.

95. Warner, *Alone of All Her Sex,* 130–33.

96. See René Nelli, *L'érotique des troubadours,* vol. 2 (Toulouse: Union générales des Editions, 1974), 289–314. Nelli speculates that courtly society would have practiced sodomy to avoid the crude and carnal fact of procreation (140).

97. Denis de Rougemont, *Love in the Western World,* rev. ed., trans. Montgomery Belgion (Princeton, NJ: Princeton University Press, 1983), 60. De Rougemont's work was, as Roger Boase remarks with some acidity, widely read and widely sneered at by critics; the claims about Cathar influence are impossible to verify, and the myth of a foundational Western love-ideal that shuns marriage for a chaste adulterous passion is, in Boase's view, a mix of "bad history and bad psychology" (*Origin and Meaning of Courtly Love,* 81).

98. Nelli, *L'érotique des troubadours,* 33–74.

99. That courtly love exists on a "plane of immanence" is asserted by Gilles Deleuze and Félix Guattari, *A Thousand Plateaus: Capitalism and Schizophrenia,* trans. Brian Massumi (Minneapolis: University of Minnesota Press, 1987), 156: "It would be an error to interpret courtly love in terms of a law of lack or an ideal of transcendence." The field of immanence is not internal to the self.

Chapter Six

Second epigraph: Roger Ascham describing Elizabeth, his sixteen-year-old pupil, in a letter of April 4, 1550; see Roger Ascham, *The Whole Works of Roger Ascham,* vol. 1, part 1, ed. J. A. Giles (London: J. R. Smith, 1864), lxiii. Her mind has, he comments with pride, "no womanly weakness."

1. Brown, *Body and Society,* 278.

2. *Carmina Burana* 25, quoted in O'Donoghue, in *Courtly Love Tradition,* 57.

3. Hilda Graef, *Mary: A History of Doctrine and Devotion* (1963; repr., Notre Dame, IN: Christian Classics, 2009). See also Luigi Gambero, *Mary and the Fathers of the Church: The Blessed Virgin Mary in Patristic Thought*, trans. Thomas Biffer (San Francisco: Ignatius Press, 1999); Bertrand Buby, *Mary of Galilee*, 3 vols. (New York: Alba House, 1997).

4. Rubin, *Mother of God*, 44.

5. I borrow the translation and the reference from Rubin, *Mother of God*, 44.

6. See Foskett, *A Virgin Conceived*, 1–74.

7. John Milton, *Complete Poems and Major Prose*, ed. Merritt Y. Hughes (New York: Odyssey Press, 1957), 42–50.

8. See Elkin Calhoun Wilson, *England's Eliza* (New York: Octagon Press, 1966), 200, 204–29. Helen Hackett has trenchantly identified "some of the problems" associated with the theory of the "cult of a second Virgin," meaning that Elizabeth was meant to substitute as a Protestant replacement for the Virgin Mary; see Helen Hackett, *Virgin Mother, Maiden Queen: Elizabeth I and the Cult of the Virgin Mary* (London: Macmillan, 1995), 6–12. That they are continuities Hackett is the first to admit. That the iconography bridges both female figures of power and chastity is evident. But that a "cult" of a religious type was created to fill the "gap" left by the demotion of Mary the Mother of God seems to Hackett an exaggeration. I will return to this set of issues in chapter 7.

9. John Jewel, "An Apology for the Church of England" (1564), cited in Frances A. Yates, *Astraea: The Imperial Theme in the Sixteenth Century* (London: Penguin, 1977), 78. See also John. N. King, *Tudor Royal Iconography: Literature and Art in an Age of Religious Crisis* (Princeton, NJ: Princeton University Press, 1989), 182–201; Hackett, *Virgin Mother, Maiden Queen*, 50–52, 77–78; Louis Montrose, *The Subject of Elizabeth: Authority, Gender, and Representation* (Chicago: University of Chicago Press, 2006), 86.

10. Yates, *Astraea*, 51–59 and figures 6b–9c; Roy Strong, *Splendour at Court: Renaissance Spectacle and the Theater of Power* (Boston: Houghton Mifflin, 1973), 113–19.

11. Roy Strong, *Gloriana: The Portraits of Queen Elizabeth* (New York: Thames and Hudson, 1987), 112–15. Sir Arthegall, the Knight of Justice in Spenser's *Faerie Queene* and intended spouse of the Tudor ancestor Britomart the Knight of Chastity, carries a shield bearing an ermine (bk. 3, canto 2, st. 25), see Edmund Spenser, *Spenser: The Faerie Queene*, ed. A. C. Hamilton (New York: Routledge, 2001).

12. George Peele, *Works*, vol. 1, ed. A. A. Bullen (London, 1888), 363, as quoted in Yates, *Astraea*, 60.

13. Peele, *Works*, vol. 1, 364, quoted in Yates, *Astraea*, 61.

14. For all of Spenser's poetry except *The Faerie Queene* I use the Norton Critical Edition: Edmund Spenser, *Edmund Spenser's Poetry*, ed. Anne Lake Prescott and Andrew Hadfield, 4th ed. (New York: W. W. Norton, 2013).

15. Even more delighted were the people. Wilson, in *England's Eliza*, 5–6, describes a ballad called *A Songe between the Quene's Majestic and Englande* in which "England" sings a joyful welcome to "Bessy": "Oh, swete virgin pure! Longe may ye endure, to reigne over us in this lande: For your workes do accord, Ye are the handmaid of the Lord, for he hath blessed you with his hand." Elizabeth shared this providential theory of her accession to the throne.

16. The phrase is Sir Francis Walsingham's, as quoted by Christopher Haigh, *Elizabeth I* (London: Longman, 1988), 12.

17. A copy of her speech is in Elizabeth I, *Elizabeth I: Collected Works*, ed. Leah S. Marcus, Janel Mueller, and Mary Beth Rose (Chicago: University of Chicago Press, 2000), 58.

18. Francis Bacon, "In Felicem Memoriam Elizabethae," trans. James Spedding, in *The Works of Francis Bacon*, vol. 6 (London: Longman, 1858), 312.

19. Sir John Harington, *Nugae Antiquae*, ed. Henry Harington, with Thomas Park, vol. 1 (London: Vernor and Hood, 1804), 358.

20. On this point, the literature is extensive. Most helpful is Susan Doran, *Monarchy and Matrimony: The Courtships of Elizabeth I* (London: Routledge, 1996).

21. J. E. Neale, *Queen Elizabeth I* (London: Cape, 1934; repr. Chicago: Academy Chicago Publishers, 2001), 74: "Her virgin state, which Elizabeth ascribed to a godly vocation, might with more conviction be ascribed to politics." Citation refers to the reprint edition.

22. Doran, *Monarchy and Matrimony*, 5; Carole Levin, *The Heart and Stomach of a King: Elizabeth I and the Politics of Sex and Power* (Philadelphia: University of Pennsylvania Press, 1994), 6–7.

23. Here the quality and quantity of the scholarship leave little to be desired. I am guided by such experts as Louis Adrian Montrose, who explains his intention to write "about the projection of power and contestation of authority, as these were manifested in the production, circulation, and appropriation of the royal image," and as oriented not so much toward the "person" of the queen as "about the field of cultural meanings that were personified in her" (*Subject of Elizabeth*, 1) It is important to remember that the scope of Elizabeth's complex exercise of power and seduction doesn't always relate to the experience or opportunities available to others in that culture: "cultural meanings" personified in her could be said to be of a singular species. The queen could combine the identities of woman, virgin, Petrarchan beloved, mother, goddess, nurse, and warrior. She could unite in her person the male and the female sex, the patriarchal privilege she inherited from her father and the maidenly modesty she represented as an exemplary product of the best humanist education for women. Little of that potent mix was available for general circulation. Elizabeth was, in fact, an exception, an anomaly, and recognized as such, with either enthusiasm or distaste. What in other women would be an "either-or" is in Elizabeth a right to be contradictory. This makes her career as jealous guardian of chastity a singular instance, one that reflects some of the contemporary cultural "meanings" of purity but introduces many that had no other site or embodiment. I will treat her as her own genre. To this extent, I am concerned with her "person" and not only with what symbolic purposes it is used to serve.

24. Harington, *Nugae Antiquae*, 360.

25. In Bacon, "In Felicem Memoriam Elizabethae," 305.

26. Bacon, "In Felicem Memoriam Elizabethae," 310. Mary Tudor, Elizabeth's half sister, might also have enjoyed an exemption from marriage with the freedom to rule on her own. No one, neither her father nor her brother, had bothered to see her united with an appropriate prince, and Mary chose her husband (disastrously, as it turned out) for herself at the age of thirty-eight, a year after her accession. Maureen Quilligan argues that "the situation of the two Tudor queens demonstrates in Renaissance history what incest narratives demonstrate in theory: the potential for active female agency. When she remains unmarried, for whatever reason, a woman is freer to choose her own desire actively." Maureen Quilligan, *Incest and Agency in Elizabeth's England* (Philadelphia: University of Pennsylvania Press, 2005), 36–37.

27. See Richard Helgerson, *Self-Crowned Laureates: Spenser, Jonson, Milton and the Literary System* (Berkeley: University of California Press, 1983).

28. Francis Bacon, "In Felicem Memoriam Elizabethae," 317 (Latin, 302).

29. Claude Lévi-Strauss, "The Structural Study of Myth," in *Structural Anthropology*, trans. Claire Jacobson and Brooke Grundfest Schoepf (New York: Basic Books, 1963), 229.

30. Thomas Dekker, *Old Fortunatus*, ed. Oliphant Smeaton (London: J. M. Dent, 1904), 4.

31. Elizabeth's first speech to Parliament, in response to the Commons' petition about her marrying, exists in several versions. In one copy, called the "Landsdowne MS," she speaks of her preference for the single "estate" and her hopes that God will allow her to remain in it, although committing herself to do what is best for the realm. Her last words are the famous: "And in the end this shall be for me sufficient: that a marble stone shall declare that a queen, having reigned such a time, lived and died a virgin." See Elizabeth I, *Elizabeth I: Collected Works*, 58. William Camden's Latin translation of the speech is, as the editors of *Elizabeth I: Collected Works* Leah S. Marcus, Janel Mueller, and Mary Beth Rose say, "the version in which the speech has been best known to later ages, but it freely embroiders and condenses the speech as we have it from the early sources" (58n1). They point out that Camden's version adds, "To conclude, I am already bound unto a husband, which is the kingdom of England, and that may suffice you," plus the description of the queen stretching out her hand to show the members of Parliament the ring she put on at her coronation, signifying her marriage to the kingdom (59).

Louis Montrose, *The Purpose of Playing: Shakespeare and the Cultural Poetics of the Elizabethan Theatre* (Chicago: University of Chicago Press, 1996), 152, quotes both the speech of February 10, 1559, and the later one of January 28, 1563. But did Elizabeth always intend to remain unmarried? Susan Doran doubts that: "Certainly there is very little evidence to support the view, which appears in so many biographies, that from the very beginning of her reign the queen had made a conscious decision to remain unwed either because of her implacable hostility to matrimony or her decision to rule alone. It is not generally recognised that the story of Elizabeth swearing an oath to follow a life of virginity soon after her accession is little more than a myth." See Susan Doran, *Monarchy and Matrimony: The Courtships of Elizabeth I* (London: Routledge, 1996), 1. As John N. King reports, the "myth" was set into motion by the *Annales* produced in 1615 by William Camden, who reported the speech in which she explained her preferred "choice of life" and her hope to see the following inscription on her tomb: "Here lyes interr'd ELIZABETH, A virgin pure until her Death." Camden, however, "falsified the contemporary record of the queen's speech." See John N. King, "Queen Elizabeth I: Representations of the Virgin Queen," *Renaissance Quarterly* 43, no. 1 (Spring 1990): 30–74, quotations at 35–36, 69–72. Unmarried the queen certainly remained, and there is no reason to doubt her enshrinement as "pure." What needs correction is the idea that Elizabeth's relation to virginity—her way of "fashioning" the mantle of purity to her own political and symbolic purposes—remained singular and constant. King, writing in 1990, divides her realm into two parts: the first "reign," until 1581, existed under the sign of the nubile, marriageable virgin; the second, from 1581 until her death in 1603, under that of the stellar crown of perpetual virginity. The citation from Elizabeth's speech asserting her commitment to the celibate life has, accordingly, to be taken with a bit of caution, because of the varying emphases, as do the other important ones relevant to my argument about the queen's celibate strategy. The copy of the manuscript letter in Elizabeth's hand held by the National Archives gives a slightly different phrasing to the one cited by Montrose: "And as I assure yow that after my death yow will have many stepdames, yet shall you never have any more mother, then I meane to be to you all." Elizabeth I, speech delivered to the Speaker Thomas Williams, 28 January 1563, SP 12/27, f. 143r–144v, accessed August 23, 2017, http://www.nationalarchives.gov.uk/education/resources/elizabeth-monarchy/answer-of-the-queen/.

32. Thomas Norton, *To the queenes maiesties poore deceived subiectes of the northe contreye* (London: L. Harrison, 1569), cited in Susan Frye, *Elizabeth I: The Competition for Representation* (Oxford: Oxford University Press, 1993), 55. Maureen Quilligan is intrigued by the queen's use of "all the problematic family relationships of her own life—mother, stepmothers, father, brother, sister" in her fashioning of the metaphors to express the attachment of governor and governed: that she is spouse and mother of the realm reworks the role of the church, Christ's bride as well as mother of all believers. See Quilligan, *Incest and Agency*, 73.

33. S. Frye, *Elizabeth I*, 6.

34. J. King, "Queen Elizabeth I: Representations," 36–44.

35. Cited in Wilson, *England's Eliza*, 218.

36. David Lee Miller, *The Poem's Two Bodies: The Poetics of the 1590 "Faerie Queene"* (Princeton, NJ: Princeton University Press, 1988), 3.

37. S. Frye, *Elizabeth I*, 16–21.

38. Louis A. Montrose, "*A Midsummer Night's Dream* and the Shaping Fantasies of Elizabethan Culture; Gender, Power, Form," in *Rewriting the Renaissance: The Discourses of Sexual Difference in Early Modern Europe*, ed. Margaret W. Ferguson, Maureen Quilligan, and Nancy J. Vickers (Chicago: University of Chicago Press, 1986), 65–87, at 86.

39. Stephen J. Greenblatt, *Sir Walter Ralegh: The Renaissance Man and His Roles* (New Haven, CT: Yale University Press, 1973), 52–53; the passage reappears, shortened, in Stephen Greenblatt, *Renaissance Self-Fashioning: From More to Shakespeare* (Chicago: University of Chicago Press, 1980), 167.

40. Yates, *Astraea*, 109.

41. John Lyly, *Euphues and His England*, in *John Lyly, Euphues: The Anatomy of Wit; Euphues and His England*, ed. Morris William Croll and Harry Clemens (London: Routledge, 1916), 432, 448.

42. Lyly, *Euphues and His England*, 439.

43. Lyly, *Euphues and His England*, 440.

44. Lyly, *Euphues and His England*, 438–39. See also Wilson, *England's Eliza*, 231–38.

45. See Bloch, *Medieval Misogyny*, 155–56.

46. Ralegh's first prefatory sonnet on "this conceipt of the Faery Queene," was printed as one of the "commendatory verses" with the 1590 edition of the *Faerie Queene*, bks. 1–3, and now appears in the Hamilton-edited Spenser, *Spenser: The Faerie Queene*, 721.

47. Ralegh's "Commendatory Verses I" was printed as an appendix at the end of Spenser's epic rather than before it, as one might expect. See *Spenser: The Faerie Queene* (Hamilton ed.), 721.

48. Walter Ralegh to Robert Cecil, Letter 25, July 1592, in Edward Edwards, *The Life of Sir Walter Ralegh, Together with His Letters*, vol. 3 (London: Macmillan, 1868), 51. Also cited in Greenblatt, *Sir Walter Ralegh*, 23–24.

49. Lewis, *Allegory of Love*, 145.

50. On the sacred triangle, see Ernst H. Kantorowicz, *The King's Two Bodies: A Study in Medieval Political Theology* (Princeton, NJ: Princeton University Press, 1957), 101n4.

51. As Frances Yates puts it in her seminal article "Queen Elizabeth as Astraea," *Journal of the Warburg and Courtauld Institutes* 10 (1947): 27–82, reprinted in Yates, *Astraea*, 39.

52. Linda Gregerson, "Sexual Politics," in *The Cambridge Companion to Spenser*, ed. Andrew Hadfield (Cambridge: Cambridge University Press, 2001), 180–199, at 190.

53. See Wilson, *England's Eliza*, chap. 6, "Laura, or Idea." See also Gregerson, "Sexual Politics," on the essential "absence" of the Petrarchan beloved: "The lady refuses, the lady sickens or dies, the lady's remoteness makes her a perfect site for erotic and poetic ambition" (182).

54. Yates, *Astraea*, 81, 103, 109.

55. I am drawing on Frank Kermode's exemplary studies of Spenser and historical allegory reprinted in Frank Kermode, *Renaissance Essays* (London: Fontana, 1973): "Spenser and the Allegorists" (12–32) and "'The Faerie Queene': I and V" (33–59).

56. My interpretation here relies on the careful discriminations of Cinzia Arruzza, *A Wolf in the City: Tyranny and the Tyrant in Plato's Republic* (New York: Oxford University Press, 2018), 160–62, 175, 183–86.

57. Greenblatt, *Sir Walter Ralegh*, 54.

58. A. N. McLaren, *Political Culture in the Reign of Elizabeth I: Queen and Commonwealth 1558–1585* (Cambridge: Cambridge University Press, 1999), 9, citing John Guy, "Tudor Monarchy and its Critiques," in *The Tudor Monarchy*, ed. John Guy (Oxford: Oxford University Press, 1997).

59. On the complex requirements of these Tudor "feats of incorporation," see McLaren, *Political Culture*, 73–104.

60. Wilson, *England's Eliza*, 213.

61. Louis Montrose, "Spenser and the Elizabethan Political Imaginary," *ELH* 69, no. 4 (Winter 2002): 907–46, at 916, 926.

62. *The Famous History of the Life of Henry VIII*, known to its first audiences as *All Is True* (1613), is cited from William Shakespeare, *William Shakespeare: The Complete Works*, ed. Gary Taylor et al., with introduction by Stanley Wells (Oxford: Clarendon Press, 1988), 1193–1224. The scene of Elizabeth's birth is probably not by Shakespeare. Too bad. Helen Hackett compares *Henry VIII* to a more blatantly hagiographic play about the dead queen from the early days of James's reign, Thomas Heywood, *If you know not me, you know no bodie, or the troubles of Queene Elizabeth* (1604). Heywood portrays Elizabeth's life before she became queen, with special interest in the famous "persecution" of the Protestant daughter of Anne Boleyn by her Catholic sister, a period also beloved by John Foxe in his *Book of Martyrs*. The young Elizabeth, imprisoned in the Tower, is attacked by wicked Catholic priests but saved by angels, who recognize in her fortitude and patience the makings of a saint and seem already to know about her eventual retention of virginity, something Elizabeth accepts when she faces her tormenters expecting to die: "A Virgin and a Martyr both I die." In part 2 of the play (probably performed in 1606), Heywood depicts the reign itself and the vic-

tory over the Spanish Armada, here singling out the queen's Amazonian tendency to put on arms, or at least get her public to believe she would do so. See Hackett, *Virgin Mother, Maiden Queen*, 227–29.

63. Yates, *Astraea*, 78.

64. See Richard Mulcaster, *The Quenes maiesties passage through the citie of London to westminster the daye before her coronacion*, facsimile ed. (New Haven, CT: Yale Elizabethan Club, 1957); Neale, *Queen Elizabeth I*, 59–63; Wilson, *England's Eliza*, 62–66; S. Frye, *Elizabeth I*, 30–40; Yates, *Astraea*, 29–111; and, on similar symbolism in later pageants and displays, see Roy Strong, *The Cult of Elizabeth: Elizabethan Portraiture and Pageantry* (London: Pimlico, 1977).

65. Bacon, "In Felicem Memoriam Elizabethae," 305.

66. See Marie Axton, *The Queen's Two Bodies: Drama and the Elizabethan Succession* (London: Royal Historical Society, 1977), 12–13.

67. McLaren, *Political Culture*, 102.

68. Elizabeth I, *Elizabeth I: Collected Works*, 51–52. See also Kantorowicz, *King's Two Bodies*, 7–14; Axton, *Queen's Two Bodies*; D. Miller, *Poem's Two Bodies*, 108–9; Greenblatt, *Renaissance Self-Fashioning*, 166–67; Katherine Eggert, *Showing Like a Queen: Female Authority and Literary Experiment in Spenser, Shakespeare, and Milton* (Philadelphia: University of Pennsylvania Press, 2000), 4–6.

69. Stone, *Family, Sex and Marriage*, 152.

70. Lisa Jardine, *Still Harping on Daughters: Women and Drama in the Age of Shakespeare* (New York: Columbia University Press, 1983), 39.

71. Mark Rose, *Heroic Love: Studies in Sidney and Spenser* (Cambridge, MA: Harvard University Press, 1968), 7–8.

72. Daniel Rogers, *Matrimoniall Honour, or a Treatise of Matrimony* (London: Peter Nevil, 1642), 7.

73. The story was told by Pliny, Valerius Maximus, and Petrarch, and everyone knows it is true. See Marina Warner, *Monuments and Maidens: The Allegories of the Female Form* (London: Picador, 1985), 242–44; K. Kelly, *Performing Virginity* 1, 63. For the story in reference to Elizabeth, see Yates, *Astraea*, 113120; Strong, *Gloriana*, 94–107.

74. See the excellent studies by K. Kelly, *Performing Virginity*, the essays in K. Kelly and Leslie, *Menacing Virgins*, and the account of Greek virginity tests in Giulia Sissa, "Maidenhood without Maidenhead," in *Before Sexuality: The Construction of Erotic Experience in the Ancient Greek World*, ed. David M. Halperin, John J. Winkler, and Froma I. Zeitlin ((Princeton, NJ: Princeton University Press, 1990), 339–64.

75. My arguments here are greatly indebted to the work of McKeon, *Origins of the English Novel*; Watt, *Rise of the Novel*; and Jürgen Habermas, *Strukturwandel der Öffentichkeit: Untersuchungen zu einer Kategorie der bürgerlichen Gesellschaft* (Neuwied, Ger.: Luchterhand, 1975).

76. This change is still in the future during the period I am examining, but by the end of the seventeenth century, conduct books in England represented women as needing less, not more, redemption than men. Nancy Armstrong, whose history of the "domestic ideology" and gender representations is indispensable, notes in her essay on "The Rise of the Domestic Women" that the educator Timothy Rogers insisted in 1697 that women "are generally more serious than men," more cultivated in those passive virtues of modesty, humility, and honesty that are crucial to a postaristocratic society. Frugal and practical capacities are more valuable in a woman than

talent for lavish display. Rather than an "ornamental body," better to have a reticent character, a reputation for vigilance and domestic economy. Why a human female is more desirable in such a context than a robot is unclear. See Nancy Armstrong and Leonard Tennenhouse, eds., *The Ideology of Conduct: Essays in Literature and the History of Sexuality* (New York: Methuen, 1987), 96–141, quotation at 104. And see also in this volume, on the earlier period, Ann Rosalind Jones, "Nets and Bridles: Early Modern Conduct Books and Sixteenth-Century Women's Lyrics," 39–72, esp. 55–60: "Moral virtue is defined as the property of lower ranks," and the appreciation of "feminine duty" is deliberately aimed against the old and new aristocracy: vain, worldly, and glittering.

77. Samuel Butler, *Prose Observations*, cited in McKeon, *Origins of the English Novel*, 158.

78. McKeon, *Origins of the English Novel*, xxv, 158.

79. Merry E. Wiesner, *Women and Gender in Early Modern Europe* (Cambridge: Cambridge University Press, 1993), is to the point: "One of the key ideas of the Protestant Reformation was the denial of the value of celibacy and the championing of married life as a spiritually preferable state" (58).

80. Isabel V. Hull, *Sexuality, State and Civil Society in Germany, 1700–1815* (Ithaca, NY: Cornell University Press, 1996), 18–20.

81. Harol, *Enlightened Virginity*, 17–38.

82. Eamon Duffy, *The Stripping of the Altars: Traditional Religion in England 1400–1580* (New Haven, CT: Yale University Press, 1992), 173–77.

83. Brundage, *Law, Sex, and Christian Society*, 536–39.

84. Although there were theologians in the thirteenth century and earlier who viewed sexual pleasure in marriage as only a venial sin, as long as its aim was the approved encouragement of conception. Compare Brundage, *Law, Sex, and Christian Society*, 447–5

85. Brundage, *Law, Sex, and Christian Society*, 90–92, 549.

86. John Calvin, *Institutes of the Christian Religion*, 2 vols., ed. John T. McNeill, trans. Ford Lewis Battles, Library of Christian Classics (Philadelphia: Westminster, 1960), 2:1252–53.

87. Calvin, *Institutes of the Christian Religion*, 2:1253.

88. Calvin, *Institutes of the Christian Religion*, 2:1248–54.

89. William Haller and Malleville Haller, "The Puritan Art of Love," *Huntington Library Quarterly* 5, no. 2 (January 1942): 235–72, at 244.

90. Rogers, "Enclosure of Virginity," 229–50.

91. J. Rogers, "Enclosure of Virginity," 232.

92. J. Rogers, "Enclosure of Virginity," 246.

93. Martin Luther, "On Marriage Matters," in *Luther's Works*, vol. 46, *The Christian in Society III*, ed. Helmut T. Lehmann and Robert C. Schultz (Philadelphia: Fortress Press, 1967), 265; Alan Macfarlane, *Marriage and Love in England: Modes of Reproduction 1300–1840* (Oxford: Basil Blackwell, 1986), 151.

94. Bugge, *Virginitas*, 1.

95. Bugge, *Virginitas*, 56–58.

96. See the rich and nuanced discussion of the religious "image" of virginity and the mixed messages it sent to secular medieval women as well as to their sisters in the monastic orders, in Penny Schine Gold, *The Lady and the Virgin: Image, Attitude, and Experience in Twelfth-Century France* (Chicago: University of Chicago Press, 1985).

The best account of the meanings of the church's cult of virginity is that of Bugge, *Virginitas*. Bugge discusses the "sexualization of virginity unwittingly spawned by Bernardine mysticism" (137), another intriguing development of this complex virtue.

Chapter Seven

1. The royal virginity, in fact, helped make better sense of that peculiarly local idea, the sovereign as not simply "queen" but "queen-in-parliament," an idea reinforced by the habit monarchs indulged in, of taking themselves as "married to their realm." In Elizabeth's case, things were uncertain: which was the wife (the subordinate), which the husband (the head)? Her unusual sexual status allowed the issue to be skirted. I follow here the thorough discussion in McLaren, *Political Culture*, 99–102.

2. Stephen Greenblatt, "Invisible Bullets: Renaissance Authority and Its Subversion, *Henry IV* and *Henry V*," in *Political Shakespeare: Essays in Cultural Materialism*, 2nd ed., ed. Jonathan Dollimore and Alan Sinfield (Manchester, UK: Manchester University Press, 1994), 18–47, at 44.

3. Quoted in William Monter, *The Rise of Female Kings in Europe, 1300–1800* (New Haven, CT: Yale University Press, 2012), 123, 139. I have already mentioned Bacon's appreciation: "The reigns of women are commonly obscured by marriage . . . whereas those that continue unmarried have their glory entire and proper to themselves" ("In Felicem Memoriam Elizabethae," 310).

4. See Jankowski, *Pure Resistance*, 136–98.

5. See Helen Hackett, "A New Image of Elizabeth I: The Three Goddesses Theme in Art and Literature," *Huntington Library Quarterly* 77, no. 3 (2014): 241–47.

6. D. Rogers, *Matrimoniall Honour*, as cited in Edmund Leites, *The Puritan Conscience and Modern Sexuality* (New Haven, CT: Yale University Press, 1986), 12. On Puritan discipline, see Christopher Hill, *Society and Puritanism in Pre-Revolutionary England* (New York: St. Martin's Press, 1997). On marriage and discipline in Germany, see Lyndal Roper, *The Holy Household: Women and Morals in Reformation Augsburg* (Oxford: Oxford University Press, 1989).

7. Spenser, *Spenser: The Faerie Queene*, bk. 4, canto 6, st. 17 (hereafter cited in text as *FQ*). Subsequent text citations with book, canto, and stanza numbers refer to this edition.

8. Ann Baynes Corto, "'A Ball of Strife': Caroline Poetry and Royal Marriage," in *A Royal Image: Representations of Charles I*, ed. Thomas N. Corns (Cambridge: Cambridge University Press, 1999), 26–36, at 27.

9. For Spenser's biography, see Andrew Hadfield, *Edmund Spenser: A Life* (Oxford: Oxford University Press, 2012).

10. On Marinell as "reluctant bachelor," see Thomas P. Roche Jr., *The Kindly Flame: A Study of the Third and Fourth Books of Spenser's "Faerie Queene"* (Princeton, NJ: Princeton University Press, 1964), 185. On Radigund as Britomart's "parodic antitype," see A. C. Hamilton, ed., *The Spenser Encyclopedia* (Toronto: University of Toronto Press, 1997), 115.

11. On Britomart's quest to seek and learn the anatomy of love, see Lauren Silberman, *Transforming Desire: Erotic Knowledge in Books III and IV of "The Faerie Queene"* (Berkeley: University of California Press, 1995), esp. chap. 6.

12. I am summarizing the famous arguments of Yates, *Astraea*, esp. 68–71.

13. Axton, *Queen's Two Bodies*, 28, 12.

14. See Philippa Berry, *Of Chastity and Power: Elizabethan Literature and the Unmarried Queen* (London: Routledge, 1989), 148–53.

15. On *The Faerie Queene* as "celebration and extension of the queen's political mythology," see Susan L. Wofford, "*The Faerie Queene*, Books I-III," in Hadfield, *Cambridge Companion to Spenser*, 106–23, at 106.

16. William Shakespeare, *All's Well That Ends Well*, in *William Shakespeare: The Complete Works* (hereafter cited in text as *AW*, with act, scene, and line numbers). All Shakespearean citations are from this 1988 compact Oxford Shakespeare volume.

17. Germaine Greer, *The Female Eunuch* (1970; repr., New York: Harper Perennial, 2006), 232, 234.

18. Greer, *Female Eunuch*, 262.

19. Camille Paglia, *Sexual Personae: Art and Decadence from Nefertiti to Emily Dickinson* (New York: Vintage, 1991), 200, and see also 170–212.

20. N. Frye, *Secular Scripture*, 86.

21. Valerie Traub, *Desire and Anxiety: Circulations of Sexuality in Shakespearean Drama* (New York: Routledge, 1992), 28, 41. My arguments in this paragraph owe much to Traub's interpretation of defensive sexuality in Shakespeare, a fine bringing together of cultural materialist and feminist ideas. I regret I only discovered the book in the last two weeks of writing this one.

22. Stephen Greenblatt, *Shakespearean Negotiations: The Circulation of Social Energy in Renaissance England* (Berkeley: University of California Press, 1988), 3–7.

23. William Shakespeare, Sonnet 129, in *William Shakespeare: The Complete Works*, 767.

24. Cavell, *Disowning Knowledge*, 135–37.

25. Bugge, *Virginitas*, 138–39. On the American sects, see Sally L. Kitch, *Chaste Liberation: Celibacy and Female Cultural Status* (Urbana: University of Illinois Press, 1989).

26. Something very familiar to readers of John Donne's poetry, as Christopher Ricks observes: "The expense of spirit in a waste of shame is *love* in action." The sexual pessimism is corrosive; it is also ungenerous, even ungrateful. Christopher Ricks, "Donne after Love," in *Literature and the Body: Essays on Populations and Persons*, ed. Elaine Scarry (Baltimore: Johns Hopkins University Press, 1988), 33–69.

27. Greenblatt, *Shakespearean Negotiations*, 132.

28. Cavell, *Disowning Knowledge*, 217.

29. On these issues, see the excellent reading of *Measure for Measure* by Jonathan Dollimore, "Transgression and Surveillance in *Measure for Measure*," in *Measure for Measure: A Norton Critical Edition*, ed. Grace Ioppolo (New York: W. W. Norton, 2010), 175–89.

30. See also Maureen Quilligan, "Staging Gender: William Shakespeare and Elizabeth Cary," in *Sexuality and Gender in Early Modern Europe: Institutions, Texts, Images*, ed. James Grantham Turner (Cambridge: Cambridge University Press, 1993), 208–32.

31. N. Frye, *Secular Scripture*, 86.

32. Samuel Richardson, *Clarissa, Or the History of a Young Lady*, ed. Angus Ross (London: Penguin, 1985), 1206, Letter 413, Lovelace to Belford (Tuesday, August 15).

33. On Clarissa's correspondence with Anglican divines, see Jacob Sider, "The Beatified Clarissa," in *Prose Immortality, 1711–1819* (Charlottesville: University of Virginia Press, 2015), 78–96, at 79.

34. See the exceptional study by Poovey, *Proper Lady and Woman Writer*, esp. 3–81.

35. I am summarizing the arguments of Mary Wollstonecraft, *A Vindication of the Rights of Women* (1792), in Wollstonecraft, *Vindication*, 65–294.

36. "And I am but a *cipher*, to give him significance, and *myself* pain?" Richardson, *Clarissa*, 567, Letter 175, Clarissa to Anna Howe (Sunday, May 7); see also the illuminating volume by Terry Castle, *Clarissa Ciphers: Meaning and Disruption in Richardson's "Clarissa"* (Ithaca, NY: Cornell University Press, 1982).

37. Castle, *Clarissa's Ciphers*, 20.

38. Harol, *Enlightened Virginity*, 169.

39. McKeon, *Origins of the English Novel*, 157, citing *Critical Remarks on Sir Charles Grandison, Clarissa, and Pamela* (1754), intro. Alan D. McKillop, Augustan Reprint Society, no. 21, ser. 4, no. 3 (1950), 29–30, 32–33.

40. Harol, *Enlightened Virginity*, 167, 169.

41. Woolf, *Room of One's Own*, 62–63.

42. Pascal, *Pensées*, §329.

43. See Cohn, *Pursuit of the Millennium*.

44. O'Connell, *Origins of the English Marriage Plot*, 95–99.

45. Wollstonecraft, *Vindication*, 208–9.

46. Laqueur, *Making Sex*, 149.

47. The celebrated study of the nineteenth century's reversal of the traditional view of female carnality—at least the prevalence of such a reversal in Anglo-American definitions of women—is that of Nancy F. Cott, "Passionlessness: An Interpretation of Victorian Sexual Ideology, 1790–1850," *Signs* 4, no. 2 (Winter 1978): 219–36.

48. Laqueur, *Making Sex*, 150.

49. Havelock Ellis, *The Evolution of Modesty; The Phenomena of Sexual Periodicity; Auto-Eroticism*, 3rd ed., vol. 1 of *Studies in the Psychology of Sex* (Philadelphia: F. A. Davis, 1901), 64.

50. Ellis, *Evolution of Modesty*, 36–41; see also Ruth Bernard Yeazell, *Fictions of Modesty: Women and Courtship in the English Novel* (Chicago: University of Chicago Press, 1991), 229–34.

51. Cott, "Passionlessness," 233.

52. Acton quoted in Faramerz Dabhoiwala, *The Origins of Sex: A History of the First Sexual Revolution* (Oxford: Oxford University Press, 2012), 141.

53. Bland, *Banishing the Beast*, 54.

54. Mary Poovey, *Uneven Developments: The Ideological Work of Gender in Mid-Victorian England* (Chicago: University of Chicago Press, 1988), 34.

55. Wollstonecraft, *Vindication*, 207–18.

56. Cott, "Passionlessness," 223.

57. Jean-Jacques Rousseau, *Emile; or, On Education*, trans. Allan Bloom (New York: Basic Books, 1979), 361.

58. Geoffrey Chaucer, *The Wife of Bath's Prologue and Tale*, in *The Norton Anthology of English Literature*, 8th ed., vol. 1, ed. Stephen Greenblatt and M. H. Abrams (New York: W. W. Norton, 2006), 256–75.

59. Laqueur, *Making Sex*, 152.

60. Gordon Rattray Taylor, *The Angel Makers: A Study in the Psychological Origins of Historical Change, 1750–1850* (New York: E. P. Dutton, 1974), xii, 111–29. See also Bridget Hill, *Eighteenth-Century Women: An Anthology* (London: Allen and Unwin, 1987), 24: "For a man to be called a drooping plant would be a terrible insult—to say so to a woman would actually make her smile. She has so little physicality that the

ideal young lady has almost no appetite. In a certain seminary, reports Thomas Beddoes, forty girls were fed for two days on a single leg of mutton."

61. Richard Dyer, *White* (New York: Routledge, 1997), 14.

62. Dyer, *White*, 17.

63. But compare Trinh T. Minh-ha's statement that white, as the universal and "neutral" term, designates or assumes that "white human" means "male" human. Trinh T. Minh-ha, *Woman/Native/Other: Writing Postcoloniality and Feminism* (Indianapolis: Indiana University Press, 1989), 66–67. On white racism and literature, see Walter Benn Michaels, "The Souls of White Folk," in Scarry, *Literature and the Body*, 185–209. On race and gender in Elizabethan and Stuart culture, see Kim F. Hall, *Things of Darkness: Economics of Race and Gender in Early Modern England* (Ithaca, NY: Cornell University Press, 1995). On purity in colonialist imaginaries, see Ann Laura Stoler, *Race and the Education of Desire: Foucault's "History of Sexuality" and the Colonial Order of Things* (Durham, NC: Duke University Press, 1995).

64. How European rulers in the colonies used gender and racialized notions of "healthy sexuality" to breed (and police) "bourgeois bodies" is the theme of Ann Stoler's important *Race and the Education of Desire*: Proper sex was white sex, and neither working-class men and women nor colonial subjects could live up to the model of bourgeois restraint and "civility" (128).

65. Dyer, *White*, 26.

66. On the polluting effects of all sex, not just interracial sex, see Douglas, *Purity and Danger*, 152–59.

67. Dyer, *White*, 70–76.

68. See Elizabeth Abbott, *A History of Celibacy: From Athena to Elizabeth I, Leonardo da Vinci, Florence Nightingale, Gandhi and Cher* (New York: Scribners, 1999), 394–430.

Chapter Eight

Epigraph: Susan Brownmiller in conversation on the *Phil Donahue Show*, July 18, 1979, cited by Judith R. Walkowitz, "Male Vice and Female Virtue: Feminism and the Politics of Prostitution in Nineteenth-Century Britain," in *Desire: The Politics of Sexuality*, ed. Ann Snitow, Christine Stansell, and Sharon Thompson (London: Virago, 1984), 43–61.

1. The English feminist, actor, and playwright Cicely Hamilton (1872–1952) wrote in 1909 that "marriage was a trade" and women had no other. Denied all other means of support, they were obliged to submerge their humanity into this artificial "nature," unless they recognized that celibacy (feared and despised by men) actually offered them a palatable alternative. Cicely Hamilton, *Marriage as a Trade* (London: Moffat, Yard, 1909), 52.

2. Hermann Melville's *The Paradise of Bachelors and the Tartarus of Maids* leaves no doubt about the social difference. But independent women like Margaret Fuller and Susan B. Anthony believed celibacy was important for their careers as reformers, and Cicely Hamilton (in *Marriage as a Trade*) praises it. See also Kahan, *Celibacies*.

3. See Harol, *Enlightened Virginity*, 47–57.

4. Barbara Taylor's *Eve and the New Jerusalem*, is the definitive and brilliant study; see B. Taylor, *Eve and the New Jerusalem*, esp. 24–82.

5. Adrienne Rich, "Compulsory Heterosexuality and Lesbian Existence," in Snitow, Stansell, and Thompson, *Desire*, 212–41.

6. Bland, *Banishing the Beast*, 161–82.

7. Virginia Woolf, *Three Guineas*, 122–26.

8. Quoted in Bland, *Banishing the Beast*, 166–67.

9. Kahan, *Celibacies*, 142–53. Against the "terrorism" of the sexuality imperative, no one is more eloquent than Stephen Heath, *The Sexual Fix* (London: Macmillan, 1982).

10. See Heath's discomfort with the objections he wants to make to pornography, given that "the challenge for a left practice ... is to speak and act in relation to all this without falling into the terms of the right-wing opposition movements." Heath, *Sexual Fix*, 164.

11. See also Walkowitz, "Male Vice and Female Virtue," and, on the larger history of the rift over desire and sexual explicitness in the feminist movement, Lisa Duggan and Nan D. Hunter, *Sex Wars: Sexual Dissent and Political Culture*, 2nd ed. (New York: Routledge, 2006).

12. Hunt, *Governing Morals*, 140.

13. Kahan, *Celibacies*, 13, 23–26, 45–52.

14. K. Kelly, *Performing Virginity*, 63–70.

15. That the life and works of the holy in late antiquity and early Christianity were expected to be "histrionic" is something Peter Brown is very good at demonstrating. Why should the holy man or woman seem like the rest of us? Their "dissociation" from social and familial solidarity is a sign of significance rather than commonplace alienation or madness. Holiness is something you can display; it is nothing if not spectacular. See Peter Brown, *Society and the Holy in Late Antiquity* (Berkeley: University of California Press, 1982), 131–46.

16. Yeazell, *Fictions of Modesty*, 33–80.

17. See, among a number of excellent feminist studies of the "cult of true womanhood," Poovey, *Uneven Developments*; Nancy Cott, *The Bonds of Womanhood: "Woman's Sphere" in New England, 1780–1835* (New Haven, CT: Yale University Press, 1977); Nancy Cott, "Passionlessness," 219–36; Armstrong, *Desire and Domestic Fiction*; Barbara Welter, *Dimity Convictions: The American Woman in the Nineteenth Century* (Athens: Ohio University Press, 1976); Carroll Smith-Rosenberg, *Disorderly Conduct: Visions of Gender in Victorian America* (New York: Oxford University Press, 1986).

18. Tom Perotta, *The Abstinence Teacher* (New York: St. Martin's, 2007), 18–21.

19. C. Gardner, *Making Chastity Sexy*, 46–51. "The new sexy abstinence message is not about the absence of sex; it is about waiting for great sex in marriage."

20. See Adam Sonfield and Rachel Benson Gold, "States' Implementation of the Section 510 Abstinence Education Program, FY 1999," *Family Planning Perspectives* 33, no. 4 (August 2001): 166–70.

21. Clover, *Men, Women, and Chain Saws*, 39–40. See also Pete Falconer, "Fresh Meat? Dissecting the Horror Movie Virgin," in *Virgin Territory: Representing Sexual Inexperience in Film*, ed. Tamar Jeffers McDonald (Detroit: Wayne State University Press, 2010), 123–37.

22. Bernau, *Virgins*, xi–xii, 168–85.

23. Rousseau, *Emile*, 349.

24. See Hanne Blank, *Virgin: The Untouched History* (New York: Bloomsbury, 2007), 192–216.

25. See Casey Ryan Kelly, *Abstinence Cinema: Virginity and the Rhetoric of Sexual Purity in Contemporary Film* (New Brunswick, NJ: Rutgers University Press, 2016), 24–53.

26. Shadell and Lauren, "Is T. I. the Worst Dad Ever!?" November 12, 2019, *Paging the Simpsons*, podcast, Stitcher audio, 1:13:34, https://www.stitcher.com/podcast/paging-the-simpsons/e/65220764?autoplay=true.

27. Lauren Steussey, "Celebs Trash T. I. for Having Daughter Deyjah Harris' Hymen Checked," *New York Post*, November 7, 2019, https://nypost.com/2019/11/07/celebs-trash-t-i-for-having-daughter-deyjah-harris-hymen-checked/.

28. World Health Organization, "United Nations Agencies Call for Ban on Virginity Testing," news release, October 17, 2018, https://www.who.int/news-room/detail/17-10-2018-united-nations-agencies-call-for-ban-on-virginity-testing.

29. Gunter quoted in Lauren Steussey and Nadjine DeNinno, "Horrified Fans React to T. I. Having His Daughter's Hymen Checked," *New York Post*, November 6, 2019, https://nypost.com/2019/11/06/horrified-fans-react-to-t-i-having-his-daughters-hymen-checked-for-virginity/.

30. Jill Filipovic, "TI's Hymen Checks Are Horrific; So Is the Entire Concept of Female Virginity," Opinion: Gender, *Guardian*, November 8, 2019, https://www.theguardian.com/commentisfree/2019/nov/08/ti-hymen-virginity-daughter.

31. Carolyn Burke, introduction to the Mina Loy chapter in *The Gender of Modernism: A Critical Anthology*, ed. Bonnie Kime Scott (Bloomington, IN: Indiana University Press, 2000), 230–36, at 233.

32. I quote from Mina Loy, *The Lost Lunar Baedeker*, ed. Roger L. Conover (New York: Farrar, Straus and Giroux, 1996), 153–56.

33. All poems cited from Loy, *Last Lunar Baedeker*: "The Black Virginity," 42–43; "Virgins Plus Curtains Minus Dots," 21–24; "Three Moments in Paris," 15–16.

34. Mina Loy, "Feminist Manifesto," in Loy, *Lost Lunar Baedeker*, 153.

35. Nietzsche, *Human, All-Too-Human*, §141–44, italics in original.

36. Nietzsche, *Genealogy of Morals*, Essay III, §28, 162–63.

37. Kirsten Hastrup, "The Semantics of Biology: Virginity," in *Defining Females: The Nature of Women in Society*, ed. Shirley Ardener (Oxford: Berg, 1993), 34–50, at 41.

38. Stanley Cavell, "Being Odd, Getting Even (Descartes, Emerson, Poe)," in *In Quest of the Ordinary: Lines of Skepticism and Romanticism* (Chicago: University of Chicago Press, 1988), 105–30, at 129–30.

39. Nietzsche, *Genealogy of Morals*, Essay III, §10, p. 116.

40. Nietzsche, *Genealogy of Morals*, Essay III, §7, p. 107.

41. This is the hope of his *Pursuits of Happiness*.

42. Cavell, *Contesting Tears*, 7.

43. I am paraphrasing Cavell's introduction to his *Contesting Tears*, 3–10.

44. Davida Pines's *The Marriage Paradox* (2006) is subtitled *Modernist Novels and The Cultural Imperative to Marry*.

45. Kirsten Hastrup, "The Sexual Boundary: Purity, Heterosexuality and Virginity," *Journal of the Anthropological Society of Oxford* 5, no. 3 (1974): 137–47, at 146.

46. Douglas develops these ideas throughout *Purity and Danger*, with a helpful introduction to the way social and sexual boundaries are mutually constitutive on pp. 3–4.

47. Jia Tolentino and Amia Srinivasan are two feminist writers trying to say something thoughtful about what the Incel subculture means for contemporary sexuality.

See Jia Tolentino, "The Rage of the Incels," *New Yorker*, May 15, 2018, https://www.newyorker.com/culture/cultural-comment/the-rage-of-the-incels; Amia Srinivasan, "Does Anyone Have the Right to Sex?" *London Review of Books* 40, no. 6 (March 22, 2018). As the philosopher Srinivasan argues, "sex positive" feminism avoided the moral difficulties of desire. Srinivasan wonders whether a political movement advocating the "right to desire" and the ultimacy of personal preference has left the field of sexual ethics with nothing more powerful as a principle than "consent." How we have sex is a political question, she writes, and one only inadequately addressed by well-intentioned sex education and antiharassment programs. (The one sponsored at my institution explains to students that if someone offers you tea and you don't want it, you should not be bullied into drinking the tea. It doesn't seem a useful analogy.) But a political critique of desire, which includes for Srinivasan the acknowledgment that "no one has a right to be desired but also that who is desired and who isn't is a political question" will involve the need to revalue our desire, to distinguish between what is oppressive and what isn't, or isn't at this moment, since patterns of sexual desire are not the sort of things that stay fixed, or are removed from social pressure, fashion, anxiety, and a will to improvement.

48. Tolentino, "Rage of the Incels."

49. The words of Pozdnyshev in Leo Tolstoy, *The Kreutzer Sonata and Other Stories*, trans. David McDuff and Paul Foote (London: Penguin, 2008), 124.

50. Tolstoy, *Kreutzer Sonata*, 120.

51. Tolstoy, *Kreutzer Sonata*, 120–22, 125–27.

52. Tolstoy, *Kreutzer Sonata*, 126.

53. See Lev Tolstoy, *The Kreutzer Sonata Variations: Lev Tolstoy's Novell and Counterstories by Sofiya Tolstoya and Lev Lyovich Tolstoy*, ed. and trans. Michael R. Katz (New Haven, CT: Yale University Press, 2014).

54. *Catechism of the Catholic Church*, 2nd ed., revised in accordance with the official Latin text promulgated by Pope John Paul II (New York: Doubleday, 1995), 451–52.

Acknowledgments

Thanks to my strong-minded and discerning readers, who saved me from any number of authorial crimes: Cinzia Arruzza, Nick During, Ross Poole, and Francesca Wade. Thanks also to my talented research assistants: Hannes Charen, Katie Kelley, Olivia Rees-Taussig, and Zach Slanger. For their enthusiasm, curiosity, support, and interest, I want to thank a number of people: Christina Alvarez, Vivien Ashley and Richard Gott, Robin Blackburn and Margrit Fauland-Blackburn, Chiara Bottici, Hannes (again), Jean Cohen, Jeff Cohn and Brenda Kelly Kramer, Lyn Cole, Alice Crary, Pip Cummings, Penny Deutscher, Helen Klisser During, Bernie Flynn and Judith Walz, Judith Friedlander, Eric Godoy, Alex Hawkins, Regan Heiserman, Kathy Higgins, Patricia Hofbauer, Gregg Horowitz and Ellen Levy, Josh Karant, Rachel Klein and Lyle Rexer, Jenny Lloyd, Tom McCarthy and Eva Stenram, the late Doris McIlwain, Rachel Moore, Aet Nyman, Johanna Oksala, Brigitta Olubas, Olivia (again), Alison Ross, Jill Schoolman, Anna Schriefl, Lynne Segal, Mick Taussig, Katie Terezakis, Lisa Trahair, Eva von Redecker, Liz Watts, Jameson Webster. For help and forbearance, thanks to my colleagues Sameetah Agha, Cisco Bradley, Josiah Brownell, Caitlin Cahill, Macarena Gómez-Barris, Ann Holder, May Joseph, Ira Livingstone, Luka Lucic, Katarina Posch, Uzma Rizvi, Ethan Spigland, Jen Telesca, Zhivka Valiavicharska, Suzanne Verderber, Chris Vitale, and Carl Zimring.

At the University of Chicago Press, thanks to Elizabeth Branch Dyson, Kyle Wagner, Dylan Montanari, Christine Schwab, Lori Meek Schuldt, and Adrienne Meyers.

Debts that cannot be repaid, to those I hold most dear: Cinzia Arruzza, Richard Cohn, Simon Critchley, Nick During, Alex Poole, Ross Poole.

This book is dedicated to two people I miss very much: my mother, Carol Cohn, and my friend Aly Sujo.

Index